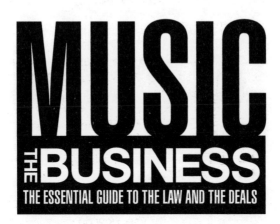

MUSIC
THE BUSINESS
THE ESSENTIAL GUIDE TO THE LAW AND THE DEALS

MUSIC

THE BUSINESS

THE ESSENTIAL GUIDE TO THE LAW AND THE DEALS

FULLY REVISED AND UPDATED 4TH EDITION

ANN HARRISON

This edition first published in Great Britain in 2008 by
Virgin Books Ltd
Thames Wharf Studios
Rainville Road
London
W6 9HA

First Virgin paperback edition published in Great Britain in 2000 by Virgin Publishing Ltd

The Random House Group Limited supports The Forest Stewardship Council [FSC], the leading international forest certification organisation. All our titles that are printed on Greenpeace approved FSC certified paper carry the FSC logo.
Our paper procurement policy can be found at www.rbooks.co.uk/environment

Mixed Sources
Product group from well-managed forests and other controlled sources
www.fsc.org Cert no. TT-COC-2139
© 1996 Forest Stewardship Council
FSC

Typeset by Phoenix Photosetting, Chatham, Kent
Printed and bound in the UK by CPI Mackays, Chatham ME5 8TD

Contents

Acknowledgements

Thanks to Rico Callejo and 'The Reporter' for the majority of my information on the law and cases; to Ben Challis for the general music law updates and to Rachel Ryding for her invaluable assistance in researching background material and updating the names and addresses section. Finally, to my husband, David Hitchcock, and my mother, Sarah Mary Harrison, for their continuing support.

Preface

qualified as a solicitor in 1983 and began working for a firm that did general work but also had a good reputation as entertainment lawyers. At first I just did general commercial litigation but found that I was naturally attracted to the entertainment cases. Somehow they seemed more 'sexy'.

When I moved to another firm to get more experience of the entertainment business I made a big mistake. The firm I joined was good at entertainment work, but in fact wanted someone to clear people off a large holiday camp in the North of England. I spent most of the next two years running 180 separate property cases with no connection to the entertainment business at all.

Luckily for me I'd kept in touch with a former flatmate who had become a very successful music lawyer at Harbottle & Lewis. He spent some time trying to persuade me to do the same work that he did. I thought my future lay in sorting out disputes in court and wasn't convinced. Then the law firm I was working for closed and that decided it. Luckily, the job at Harbottle & Lewis was still open and I joined the music group in March 1988.

At first I was convinced that this had been the second big mistake I had made in my career. My litigation training made it almost impossible for me to appear friendly towards lawyers on the other side, signing letters 'Kind regards' when often I could cheerfully have strangled them. I did get over that and stayed for about fifteen years, becoming a partner and head of the music group.

In May 2003 I left that firm to set up my own legal consultancy business, Harrisons Entertainment Law Limited. Yes the acronym does mean that I am truly a lawyer from HELL. I wanted to have the freedom to continue to represent artists and songwriters, managers and small record labels and publishers. I like working for the creative end of the business and now have the freedom to do so on my own terms. I've been lucky over the last 25 years to work with some of the leading players in the business. My clients come from every part of the music spectrum from hip hop and electronica music via classical, rock, indie and chart-topping 'pop' acts.

In writing this book I hope I will be able to convey some of the excitement of the music business to you. I have used 'he' throughout. This is not intended as a slur on female artists or on the many excellent women working at all levels in the music business. Indeed, how could it be when they were so kind as to give me an Accolade award at the Women of the Year awards ceremony a few years ago, something I will always cherish. Recognition by your peers and clients is just the best.

Ann Harrison
2 January 2008

Introduction

When I started work in the music business I had very little idea how it worked. Record and publishing companies were a mystery to me. It felt a little like trying to do a very hard jigsaw puzzle without the benefit of a picture on the lid of the box. I looked for books that might help me but there weren't many around. Those that were, were mostly out of date or applied to the USA and not to the UK music business. I had to learn from my colleagues as I went along. I was lucky in that they were very knowledgeable and very generous with their time.

Now there are many more sources of information available on the UK music business and there are several good full- and part-time media and law courses available to give you a head start. But we still lacked an easy-to-read guide to how the business works from a legal viewpoint – one that explains what a publisher does and what copyright is. Many of the books on the business are written from the US perspective. I wanted to write one based on the UK music industry which could be read as a road map through the industry. Where I've used technical expressions I have tried to give a non-technical explanation alongside. For the legally minded among you the detail is in the footnotes. This book is not, however, intended to be a substitute for legal textbooks on copyright, other intellectual property rights or contract. There are many good examples of these sorts of books around.

The music business is a dynamic one and each new edition involves a re-working of most of the chapters. In particular anything to do with new media is difficult to keep up-to-date. The chapter on New Media has been completely rewritten under the new title of Online Sales and Distribution as have the chapters on Touring, Getting a Record Made and Branding and Sponsorship. Video is now a dying format and references to it have been replaced with DVD as a revenue source.

Wherever possible I have tried to illustrate points with practical examples. I have to add a health warning that the examples produced and the guidelines given are mine alone and others may not agree or may have had different experiences

We've all been fascinated by newspaper reports of this or that artist in court over disputes with their ex-managers, record companies or even other members of the band. Are these reports accurate? Do these cases have any long-term effect? Do they matter? The facts of some of the more important cases have been highlighted, what was decided and the effects of these decisions on the music business. I've included several new cases in this edition, particularly in the chapters on band agreements, session musicians, piracy, plagiarism and publishing

What I've tried to do is to let you in to some of the things I have learned over the last 24 years in the music business. There is, however, no substitute for legal advice on the particular facts of your case. Chapter 1 deals with choosing your advisers. Please read it. Good advisers will help to save you from what can be expensive mistakes. Most artists only have one chance of a successful career in this business – make sure you don't lose it through poor advice.

Chapter 1
Getting Started

INTRODUCTION

How do you get into the music business as a performing artist or songwriter? How do you get your foot in the door and how and when do you start gathering your team of advisers around you?

Maybe you want to be a manager or set up your own record label or publishing company. This book is all about understanding the music business, the deals and how you get yourself started.

CREATING A BUZZ

How do you get your work noticed? The idea is to create a 'buzz' by whatever means you can. We'll see later that lawyers and accountants can help you to get noticed but you also need to work out your own plan and make it unique to you.

You can play as many gigs as you can and hope to be recognised by a scout on the lookout for a record or music publishing company or you can make a demo of your performances or songs and send it to an A&R person and hope. However, more and more companies, particularly the bigger ones, the 'majors', are refusing to accept unsolicited demos. They are following their US colleagues in this respect and many now only accept demos from a tried and tested or well-known source. Others are streamlining their submissions policy and asking for MP3s rather than CDs through the post.

There's no guarantee of success. No one is 'owed' a living in this business. You have to earn it often through sheer hard slog.

Many try and improve their chances by coming up with a previously untried marketing ploy. We all remember the famous online concerts given by Sandi Thom from her basement in Tooting. Sure got her noticed didn't it? Occasionally you still hear of artists pitching up at record companies with their guitar and doing an impromptu audition at which they are 'discovered' but the chances are very slim. These days you'd be lucky to get past the security guards.

You can also shamelessly exploit any and all contacts you have with anyone who has even the remotest connection with the music business. You can pester these hapless souls to 'get their mate to the next gig' or to listen to your demo or visit your MySpace page. This can improve your chances of at least getting your work listened to, but still isn't any guarantee it will lead to a record or publishing deal.

The live side of the industry is important and increasingly so in the last few years as traditional record sales have declined. Record and publishing companies send scouts out to find undiscovered talent playing in out-of-the-way pubs. If you happen to be based outside the M25 your chances of being spotted are slimmer than if you are in London. However, there are other areas of the country that get the attention of scouts – Sheffield, Liverpool, Manchester, Birmingham, Bristol, South Wales and Glasgow among them. Sometimes you get an ambitious scout who goes and checks out what is happening in a part of the country not on the traditional circuit. When this happens you can get a rash of signings from that area. Who knows, your area could be next.

A&R people live a precarious existence. They are only as good as their last successful signing. So they tend to like to have their hunches about an artist confirmed by someone else whose opinion they respect. This could be someone in their own company but, somewhat surprisingly, they will often talk to A&R people from rival companies. You would think that if they found someone they thought was good they would keep it to themselves until the deal was done. Some do, but many seem to need to be convinced that they have got it right even though this might push up the cost of the deal if the rival company also gets in the running to sign the same artist. For the artist this is a dream come true. He can choose the company that works best for him, and his lawyer will negotiate between the companies to get a better deal. This is what we call using your bargaining power. The more bargaining power you have the better your overall deal is likely to be. In the last couple of years the trend has been for several successful artists to make their mark elsewhere before becoming big with a major record company. Keane were signed to BMG Music Publishing for about three years before they got a record company interested in their brand of music. The Kaiser Chiefs with B-Unique and Domino Records with Franz Ferdinand are other good examples of independent labels punching above their weight. More and more it seems that the A&R people at major record companies want actual evidence of an artist's ability to complete recording an album and promote it before they come on board. This can be a depressing thought for a band just starting out, but it could also be seen as an opportunity to create and develop your own style on a smaller independent label first. Indeed one of the biggest growth areas of the business is that of independent labels making their own story and either feeding artists in to the bigger labels or releasing records themselves before the acts are picked up by the bigger labels. An example of an artist who made it big independently before being picked up by a major is Sounds Under Radio who was the only unsigned artist on the *Spider-Man 3* film soundtrack and went on to sign a multi-album deal with Epic Records.

THE BAND NAME

The name a band chooses is a vital part of its identity, its brand. It's a very difficult thing to get right and it's quite common for bands to go through various name changes before they settle on one they're happy with. It should be memorable, because if you combine a good name with a clever logo then you are already halfway to having the basis of a good advertising campaign. However you decide to market yourself, a distinctive name makes it that much easier. If it's a name that you can do some wordplay with, so much the better.

Finding a good name is easier said than done. I'm sure you've all sat around at some time in the pub after a beer or three and tried to come up with good band names. Despite all my advice on branding, I suspect that most bands choose their name for much more down-to-earth reasons, like it sounds cool, or it is the only one they can think of that is not naff and that no one else has already nabbed. Raiding books, old films and song titles are other good sources, for example, All About Eve, His Latest Flame and Janus Stark (from a comic). History is also a fertile source, Franz Ferdinand being a good example.

You might decide on a name not knowing that anyone else has already claimed it. You may then invest a lot of time and maybe some money in starting to develop a reputation in that name. You're not going to be very happy if you then find out that someone else has the same name. So how do you check if someone else is already using a band name?

There are some easy and cheap means of doing this. First, go to the nearest large record store and ask to borrow their catalogue listing all available records. Have a look if the name you want to use appears – the lists are usually alphabetical by artist name so that's not as horrible a task as it might seem.

If you've access to the Internet you can widen your search. Using a good search engine check to see if the name you've chosen appears. You could just do a UK search but if you plan to sell records overseas (and you do, don't you?) then you should do a worldwide search. You could apply to register a domain name and see if anyone has claimed any of the main top-line domain categories for that name. If it is available do register it quickly.

There are band registers online, including one called bandname.com, which claims to be the biggest online band names registry. You could consider registering with them or searching first for an existing band name. It is not, however, free and so you may want to consider other free online searches first. Bear in mind though that just because a band is listed on a band register database doesn't mean that they will automatically succeed in stopping you from using the same name. You have to also look at whether they have an existing name or reputation, whether they have registered a trademark or a domain name, and whether they had a reputation in the same area of the business as you.

If you choose a name and another artist objects to you continuing to use it because it is the same as one they have been using for a while, they may sue you. This could be for a breach of their trademark (see Chapter 8) or, if they haven't registered a trademark, they would have to argue that they had a reputation in the same area of music, in the same country as you and that you were creating confusion in the mind of the public and trading on their reputation. This is called 'passing off' (see Chapter 8).[1] If they can establish these things (and that is not always easy to do) and they can also show that they are losing or are likely to lose out financially as a result, then they can ask the court to order you to stop using the name and also to award them damages against you. They would have to establish a number of things, including an existing reputation. Just because a band has done a gig or two under the same name as you doesn't necessarily mean that they have a reputation or that they can satisfy the other tests of 'passing off'. You may have the greater reputation or the greater bargaining power or the other group may have split up. If you've already got a record deal or are about to release a single or album under that name you may be able to persuade them that they are in fact trading on your reputation and that they should stop using the name. A word of warning though, if you have a US label or intend to license recordings for sale in the US it is quite likely that the US company will be unhappy at the existence of another artist with the same or a very similar name. They may well put considerable pressure on you either to change the name or to do a deal whereby you can definitely get the rights to use that name from the other artist. US labels tend to be risk adverse and a potential threat to stop their sales will have them running scared.

---

1 For a more academic overview of branding, see 'Copinger and Skone-James on Copyright', 15th edition. Sweet & Maxwell, 2005.

If you do find another band with the same name then you could do a deal with them to buy the right to use the name from them. You pay them a small amount (or a big amount if you really want the name) and they stop using it, allowing you to carry on. If you're going to do these sorts of deals you should also make sure that you get from them any domain name that they have registered in the band name and, if they have a trademark, an agreement to assign the registration to you.

The law can be somewhat confusing on this question of band names as shown by two band name cases. The first involves the members of Liberty, the band formed from the runners-up in the television programme *Popstars* and the second a Scottish rock group and a pop boy band both called Blue. The decisions in the two cases could not have been more different.

The Liberty X Case[2]

V2 Music, the record company, had an exclusive recording contract with the members of Liberty and was preparing to release and promote their first album. The claimants were a funk band formed in the late 1980s who also went by the name Liberty. This band had had a lot of publicity and played a number of live concerts in the period up to 1996 but never got a record contract. Their three independent releases made between 1992 and 1995 sold only a few thousand copies. The public interest in them had become virtually nonexistent by the mid-1990s, although they kept going in the business, where they were known and respected, and appeared as session musicians on other people's work.

The question was whether they had sufficient residual goodwill left in 2001 to be entitled to be protected against passing off.

The pop group Liberty argued that even if there was residual goodwill their activities could not be seen to interfere with the old Liberty as they were in different areas of music.

The court found that the amount of residual goodwill had to be more than trivial which was a question of fact. The judge found that while the case was 'very close to the borderline' there was a small residual goodwill that deserved protection. He granted an injunction against the new Liberty band's continued use of the name. The band renamed itself Liberty X and went on to commercial success.

The Blue Case

In complete contrast, in June 2003 a case brought by the original band Blue – a Scottish rock group – came before the courts. Their last hit was in 1977 when a single by them reached number eighteen in the charts. They did have a long career spanning sixteen singles and seven albums. They had a fan base and nowadays sold records mostly be mail order or over the Internet. The new Blue was a boy band formed in 2000 who had had 3 number 1 singles. The old Blue sued new Blue and its record company EMI/Virgin for substantial damages for passing off arguing that there was confusion over the name leading to damage to their reputation and recording career. The case came before Judge Laddie, who is known for his forthright approach. He made it very clear at the beginning of the case that he found these claims somewhat dubious. He is quoted as saying, 'Are you seriously saying that fans of one group would mistake one for the other.' The judge also commented on the difference in their appearance saying that 'one is aged like you and me, the other is a boy band'. These

---

2 *Keith Floyd Sutherland v. V2 Music and others* Chancery Division (2002).

are comments that could just as easily have been made in the Liberty case but different times, different outcomes. In this case the early indication of the judge's view led to the two sides having discussions outside the court which led to an out-of-court settlement. Both bands were to be permitted to continue to use the same name. Old Blue was ordered to pay the costs of new Blue who agreed not to enforce this for so long as old Blue didn't try to apply to register a trademark or otherwise try to regularise ownership of the name.

TRADE MARK SEARCH

You can run a trade mark search to see if there is someone else with the same or a very similar name in the classes of goods or services that you would be interested in (for example, Class 9 for records). In the US the record company often makes it a condition of the record deal that they run a trade mark search and charge you for it by adding the cost on to your account. If the search reveals another band or artist with the same name, the record company will usually insist on you changing your name before they will sign the contract.

SHOWCASING YOUR TALENT

Let's assume you've got a name, can legitimately use it and are getting some interest from the business. Record companies have had their fingers burned by signing artists for large sums of money that they haven't seen perform and then discovering that they can't play or sing at all. This was a particular problem at the height of the dance music boom when behind the scenes producers were making the music and using front people to perform them on stage – often not live but mimed to backing tapes. So most record companies will insist on seeing you play live. If you are already playing the club circuit they may just turn up to a gig. If you aren't then they may pay for the hire of a venue or ask you to arrange one. This is called a showcase. The venue will either be a club or a rehearsal studio. These showcases may be open to the public but more often they will be by invitation only. It might pay for you to get at least some of your mates/fans invited so there are a few friendly faces there as an industry showcase can be a daunting affair.

You could hire a venue yourself and send invitations out to all the record companies. However, just because you've invited them doesn't mean they'll come. Don't be at all surprised if they say they're coming and then don't show up. It's a very fickle business. They probably got a better offer on the day. The more of a 'buzz' there is about you the more likely it is that they will turn up, as they won't want to miss out on what could be 'the next big thing'.

I once asked the MD of a major record company why he was paying for an artist to do a showcase which would be open to the public when he knew that the artist would then be seen by the A&R people from rival record companies. His answer was quite revealing. He said that he knew how far he was prepared to go on the deal and so was not worried that it would be hyped up. He felt that if this artist really wanted to be with his record company he wouldn't be influenced by the interest from other companies. Confidence indeed. In fact the artist did sign to his company and remained on the label for a number of albums. In these days of independent labels or production companies working with artists it is likely that they will set up the showcases and either invite a broad selection of bigger labels along or only those with whom they have a special relationship, maybe ones for whom they already act as a talent out-source.

PRESENTING YOURSELF WELL

Here are some tips that may help you showcase your talents successfully. First, do your homework. Read the music press. Find out the current 'happening' venues, the places that regularly get written up in the music press. Pester that venue to give you a spot, even if it's the opening spot, and get all your mates to come along so that it looks like you've already got a loyal following. Before you get to that stage you may need to start out in the clubs outside the main circuit and work your way in.

You should also find out what nights the venue features your kind of music. If you play radio-friendly, commercial pop you don't want to get a gig on a heavy metal night.

Make sure the songs you play (your set) are a good cross-section of what you do. What goes down well with your mates in the local may not work for a more urban audience (but you'll want to play one or two of the firm favourites to give you a confidence boost).

Be professional. Rehearse, rehearse, rehearse. Think about your image and style. Don't send mixed messages. Think about your relationship with the audience. If yours is the 'say nothing, the music will speak for itself' style, that's fine – but make sure you're sending that message clearly to your audience. We all like a 'personality'. If your band has got one make sure you use him or her to their best advantage.

Always tell your audience who you are at the beginning and end of your set. You'd think this was obvious but you'd be surprised how many gigs I've been to where it's been impossible to tell who the artist is unless you've seen them before. The line-up of the bands on the night can change and no gig ever starts at the time it's supposed to, so you can't even make an intelligent guess. Make life easier for us – tell us clearly who you are, this is not the time for a shoe-gazing mumble.

Try and get your local press behind you. I know of one Nottingham band that did this very successfully. They made a fan of the arts reporter on the local newspaper and kept him up to date on what they were up to and when they were playing. This made sure they got good reviews. A scout read one of these and went to the next gig, which was on the outer-London circuit. The band took 'rent-a-crowd' with them and were spotted by an A&R man tipped off by the scout. A record deal followed. The local reporter was the first one they told – after their mum, of course. In an innovative marketing spin of the kind I was advocating earlier, The Other used SMS to let fans know of their next gig relying on word of mouth and multiple texts to ensure a good turn-out at their 'secret' gigs and attention from the press for their innovative technique. It's a wonder that they didn't go further and sign up a sponsorship deal with a telecoms company for a cut of the SMS charges.

SHORT CUTS

It's a long haul and it needs determination and dedication to plug away on the gig circuit like this. Are there any short cuts? Yes, there are some. There are 'battle of the bands'-type competitions, and if you get through to the final three or even win then that will give you valuable exposure and should ensure a number of follow-up gigs in the local area and some useful publicity. They don't often lead directly to deals although, if you win, you may get free studio time to make a demo (see below). One band of under 18 year olds called The Flaming Monkeys won the *Kerrang!* unsigned bands award at the Vodafone Awards in 2007 and used that as a spring board to a spot at Glastonbury and (hopefully) to a record deal. Glastonbury now has an Emerging Performers Competition for bands to play on its main stage. Indeed the under 18s market is a booming one with venues turning over their clubs to promoters of special gigs aimed at the younger audience and obviously without the booze.

Then of course there are online band competitions – such as those promoted by the web-based slicethepie.com. For more on these social networking sites and different use of technology see Chapter 7.

There are also 'open mike' evenings at clubs, when anyone can turn up and ask to play one or two numbers. Tony Moore's unsigned acts nights at The Bedford pub in Balham, South London are a regular stopping off spot for scouts as is 014 in Baron's Court, West London and clubs in Soho such as Punk or pubs like The Betsy Trottwood. Tony Moore also opened an additional live acoustic venue, The Regal Room in December 2006, based at The Distillers in Fulham Palace Road, London.

Music industry organisations such as the Performing Rights Society Limited (PRS) or its US equivalents, The American Society of Composers and Publishers (ASCAP), or Broadcast Music, Inc. (BMI), occasionally arrange nights at a Central London venue to showcase two or three acts who are either unsigned or have signed a record deal but not a publishing deal (or vice versa). ASCAP sends out a CD containing a track by each of the acts it's promoting. These are popular with A&R people because someone has already filtered out a lot of the rubbish for them. See Useful Addresses for contact details.

There is also an annual UK music industry convention called 'In the City'. Attached to it is a series of showcases for unsigned acts at venues in the city where the conference is being held. Its regular home is Manchester but it does move around. The death of one of its founders, Tony Wilson, in 2007 did not stop his partner Yvette Livesey from continuing the tradition a few months later and it looks to continue for the foreseeable future. It's quite expensive to register for the conference but it's often possible to get into the bar of the main conference hotel where the executives meet to relax. You could get lucky and meet one or two A&R people and get your demo to them. Remember, however, that they get given many CDs, often late at night and possibly after several pints of beer, and they will probably need to be reminded who you are in a follow-up call a few days later. If you're chosen for one of the unsigned showcases, it should guarantee that at least one A&R person will be at your gig. In past years Suede, Oasis and The Darkness have all played 'In the City Unsigned' and more recent successes include The Automatic and Muse.

THE DEMO RECORDING

For most people making progress in the music business means having a demo recording of your work. This is your calling card, your way of introducing a stranger to your work. It should be recorded to the best standard you can afford.

STUDIO DEALS

What if you haven't any money? How do you afford to make a recording? One way is to beg 'down-time' from your local recording studio. This is time when the studio is not being hired out commercially. It may be at really unsociable hours such as 2 a.m. to 8 a.m. But who needs sleep you've got a record deal to get?

The studio may give you the time cheaply or even free, but they are more likely to let you have the time in return for promises of what they will get when you get your first deal. The studio owner may want some of the income (the royalty) you earn from the sale of your records. This is sometimes called an override royalty. This is fair if you get a deal using recordings made at the studio, but take care that the studio is not asking for too much. A 1–1.5% override royalty is usually enough. By that I mean that if you are offered an 18% royalty you have to give 1–1.5% to the studio owner, leaving you with 16.5–17%. Some studios try to get royalties on your second and third album too. They argue that you wouldn't have got your chance to record at all without their generosity. This is true, but there comes a time when your success has nothing to do with that original generosity. One album is plenty in most cases or if it goes beyond that then the royalty percentage should reduce to say 0.5–0.75%.

The studio may also want a guarantee that you use their facilities when you make your album. Or the studio owner may want to produce your first commercial album. You should be careful about agreeing to these sorts of conditions. Record companies don't like package deals on studio and producer. They like to have some say on these things themselves. If the producer is a proven talent they may be less concerned but you should try and build in flexibility.

The demo should feature a good cross-section of your work. Most people think that it should contain no more than three or four different pieces, with your best one first, your second-best one last and contrasting style pieces in the middle, but be careful of sending a confusing message by mixing too many different styles on one CD. The opening number should have immediate impact in case the listener fast-forwards it before you've got into your stride. Many A&R people listen to demo CDs in their car or MP3s on their MP3 player. If you don't grab their attention they'll move on to the next track or CD. If you are sending a CD then the case and the CD itself should both contain details of who you are, the names of the pieces, who wrote them and, most importantly, a contact number, otherwise when, inevitably, the case gets separated from the CD, there is no way of telling who the band are and how to get hold of them. This is harder to do with an MP3 so it is important that the file name is distinctive and that the metatags on the recording itself identify the artist and the name of the track. If you can include an email or webpage contact address so much the better. Make yourself as easy as possible to find.

FINDER'S AGREEMENT

These go in and out of popularity. At the moment they seem to have been overtaken by the production deal but they are still used where someone just wants to find a deal and not be further involved at any level. A studio owner, producer or an established writer that you may be working with might like what they hear but may not have the resources or the inclination to sign you up to a record deal themselves. They may also not wish to become involved in your career longer-term as a manager but might spot an opportunity to use their contacts to further your and their own prospects. Such people might offer to find a deal for you and if you agree in principle they may then want you to sign a finder's agreement.

This is usually a short document where you appoint them for a period of time to get you a record or publishing deal. The period varies from six months up to eighteen months and may be non-exclusive, in which case the period is of less concern, or exclusive, in which case you might want to keep the period quite short. On an exclusive deal you pass through any interest you get to the finder who is in overall charge. If it's non-exclusive you and others can go on looking for a deal but you need to have a mechanism for how to tell who actually made the successful introduction. This is why most finders favour an exclusive arrangement.

If the finder gets a deal within the agreed time span then that usually ends the ongoing relationship between you and the finder, unless, as sometimes happens, it changes into a different type of deal such as that of artist/manager/artist/producer or co-writer.

The fee that the finder gets varies. It may be a percentage of what you get on signing the deal, a percentage of all monies paid you in the first contract period of the deal or a share of these monies and of future royalties. The percentage is usually somewhere between 5% and 10%. Sometimes the finder argues for a percentage of monies beyond the initial contract period. This is less usual and I would want to see strong grounds to justify that and even then might well argue for the percentage to be reduced to say 2.5–5%.

DEMO DEAL

If an A&R man gets to hear of your music through the demo or indeed in a live gig he will undoubtedly want to hear some more.

If this is not a situation where there is an existing production company with access to studio facilities he may pay for some studio time for you to record more material or to try out different versions of what you've already recorded on your demo. In that case he may offer you a demo deal.

The deal will usually guarantee you a certain amount of time in a professional or in-house recording studio. Many record and publishing companies have their own studio facilities, which they may offer to make available. Perhaps you shouldn't look a gift horse in the mouth, but if the studio doesn't have the equipment you need to show yourself off to best advantage you should say so, and either ask for that equipment to be hired in or ask to go into a commercial studio. Cheeky, yes, but you can do it politely – it's your chance, so don't blow it.

The record or publishing company will expect to own the copyright in what you record (see Chapter 3). The company will want to own the right to control what happens to the recording. A record company will not usually expect to own rights in the song but a music publisher might. Try and take advice before you agree to give away rights in the song. At the very least they shouldn't own the song unless they offer you a proper publishing deal (see Chapter 4). The company offering you the deal will also own the physical recording or 'master'. This is fine as long as they don't stop you recording the same song for someone else if they don't offer you a deal. They should also agree that they won't do anything with the master without first getting your permission. This is important. When you finally sign your record deal you will be asked to confirm that no one else has the right to release recordings of your performances. The record company will not find it funny if a rival company releases the very track that they had planned as your first single. The company who paid for the demo will usually agree that you can play it to other companies if they decide not to offer you a deal within a reasonable period of time.

The record or publishing company will normally want some exclusivity in return for the studio time they are giving you. They may want you to agree not to make demos for anyone else or not to negotiate with another company for a period of time.

They may be slightly more flexible and want the right of first negotiation or refusal. This means that they will want either to have the first chance to try to negotiate a deal with you or they will want to have the right to say yes or no first before you sign to another company. This is a difficult call. You will no doubt be excited and perhaps desperate not to risk losing the deal but, before agreeing to exclusivity or these negotiating options, you need to be sure that the exclusive time period is not too long. If they tie you up for months you may miss your moment. If they have first negotiating or rejection rights then they should tell you as soon as possible where you stand. If they're not interested then you need to move on as quickly as possible.

Bear in mind, though, that the record company has to go through a number of stages before they can make a decision. They have to listen to the recording, probably then discuss it at an A&R meeting and then maybe also with their immediate bosses or even overseas colleagues. All this takes time and they may not want to risk losing you to a rival company. So you need to get a balance between the needs of the two sides.

Don't be surprised or depressed if, after you make the demo, the company decides not to offer you a deal. I know several artists who got demo time from two or three record companies and ended up with an excellent set of demos that they took to another company who then signed them up. What you don't want to happen is that people feel that you've been around for a while and are sounding a bit stale. This is a difficult balance to strike.

On a more positive note, the first company may love what you've recorded. The demos may confirm the A&R man's faith in your abilities and he may be ready to do a deal with you. You've passed go and, once you've read the rest of this chapter on getting yourself some good advisers, you should go straight to Chapter 3 (What Is A Good Record Deal?).

GETTING HELP AND PUTTING TOGETHER YOUR TEAM

All of this may seem a bit daunting. Don't worry about negotiating or signing a studio or demo deal. There are people that you can turn to for help. You should be looking to put your team of advisers in place as soon as you start to get a bit of a 'buzz' about you so that you are ready to move quickly.

THE LAWYER
A good lawyer with experience of the business can be of enormous help to you. So where do you find one and what can they do for you?

Finding a lawyer
General
You can ask the Law Society for their suggestions (see the Useful Addresses section for details). They have entertainment firms on their referral lists but make no judgement on the quality of the advice.

Many law firms have their own websites, which will tell you a bit about the firm and its areas of expertise. It will usually contain an email address, so you could try sending them a message asking for further information.

Some websites contain details of the last big deals the firm did and, where their clients allow them to, list the names of some of their clients. It is not necessarily a bad thing if there aren't many clients mentioned. Professional rules mean we have to keep client information confidential and not even say that someone is a client without the client's permission or unless it is public knowledge. If a client is kind enough to give me a credit on their album artwork, I take it that he's happy for people to know I'm his lawyer, but if in doubt I have to ask.

Other sources could be the Musicians' Union and the Music Managers Forum. The PRS runs a legal referral scheme where firms of music lawyers agree to give preliminary advice free or at a reduced rate. See Useful Addresses.

Directories

Not all law firms have websites, so you could also look in the two main books listing UK legal firms – Chambers and Legal 500 (See Useful Addresses). The general guides can be found in most of the larger public libraries and are both available online. Both have a similar approach, breaking down the lists into areas of the country and particular specialisations. Most UK music lawyers are based in London, but there are one or two in places like Manchester, Liverpool and Glasgow. Chambers writes short pieces on those it thinks are the leading players in a particular field and now also boasts a USA guide. Legal 500 operates on a league principle. When it interviews lawyers it notes which names are mentioned most frequently by others in the business and grades the firms accordingly. It also does some checking with individual clients.

In addition to these general legal guides the *Music Week Directory* also lists UK law firms and is a good first stop for an overview of lawyers who claim to have expertise in the music business. *Music Week* is the leading trade journal for the music industry in the UK. You need to take out a subscription to get the directory and online access but you may find it in bigger reference libraries or a contact in the business might lend you a copy. As with the more general guides an entry in the directory is not any guarantee that they are any good.

Managers and Accountants

If you already have a manager or an accountant they may be able to recommend a lawyer to you. You should check if your manager has the same lawyer. Most managers realise that for some things (for example, negotiating the management contract) you have to have a separate lawyer from your manager. There is a conflict in the interests of the two of you that means you must be separately advised. Where there is no conflict of interest there is usually nothing wrong in you and your manager having the same lawyer. You may, however, still feel more comfortable having your own lawyer on board.

Other bands

Other bands or contacts in the business may be able to recommend someone to you. This may be their own lawyer or someone they have heard others say is good. We lawyers love personal recommendations as a source of new work. It means we must be doing something right.

How do you go about choosing and employing a lawyer?

Occasionally lawyers are in the public eye because of a particularly high-profile piece of work they have done and everyone wants to have them as their lawyer. You must, however, try to find out whether the lawyer is experienced and not a one-hit wonder. How do you do that? Ideally you should have two or three names on your list, possibly gathered from a variety of sources. You should call them, tell them you are looking for a lawyer and ask to meet with them. Be wary of lawyers who promise the earth. We don't have all the answers. Before you meet up with the lawyers have some questions ready for them. Ask how long they've been doing this and who their main clients are. As we saw, they may be a bit coy about this because of their duty to keep clients and their business confidential. Ask them how their firm is structured. Will they be doing the work for you or will it be handed over to a more junior person? Can you call up the lawyer you are meeting at any time to discuss your case or are you expected to work with the junior person?

You should also ask the lawyers the all-important question of what they charge, when they expect to send you a bill and when they expect it to be paid. Will they accept payment in instalments and, if so, do they charge interest on the balance like you would on a credit card bill that you were paying off monthly? Can you pay by credit card? Beware of a lawyer who is reluctant to discuss his costs. If he tells you what he charges by the hour you may need to sit down. But quoting hourly rates doesn't really help you to compare two firms, as one lawyer may work faster than the other. A better way to do it is to ask them to give you a ballpark figure for what it usually costs for them to do a record or publishing deal. If you ask each lawyer the same question you'll have a better basis for a comparison. Don't necessarily go for the lowest price. It may be that the deal gets done faster but it's a short-term view. Where the lawyer really comes into his own is when something goes wrong in six months' or a year's time. Then the thoroughness with which he has done his job in protecting your interests really gets put to the test. Some lawyers will agree to do a piece of work for a fixed price. Since setting up my own business I often work in that way as it gives the client certainty but as with any job of work if it turns out to be far more complicated than it appeared at first I reserve the right to come back and revisit that fixed fee.

The lawyer you finally choose should send you a letter setting out the basis on which he is going to work for you, including details of what he expects to charge and who you should complain to if you have a problem. Your lawyer is a fundamental part of your team. Take your time in choosing one and don't be afraid to say if you're not happy with a piece of work, including voting with your feet and changing lawyers if it doesn't work out. Although you may want to give the lawyer the chance to explain his position before you leave. As a last resort you can sue but this is all very negative. In the majority of cases there isn't a problem that can't be sorted out with a phone call.

Conflicts of interest

There are firms of lawyers that work mostly for record and publishing companies and others that work for what we call the 'talent' (the creative end of the business). It is important to know this. If the record label interested in you uses the same firm for their own legal advice there will be a conflict of interest which will make it difficult for that lawyer to work for you if you're ever in a dispute with the record company. Some say it's possible to build Chinese Walls (artificial barriers where, in theory, one lawyer within a firm knows nothing about what another is doing, so can't be influenced in any negotiation). When things are going well this can work, provided everyone knows it is happening. When things aren't going so well will you feel confident that your lawyer is looking after your interests?

Beauty parades

When you go to meet lawyers it's only fair that you tell them that you're seeing lawyers from other firms. Lawyers call these meetings 'beauty parades' when we set out to impress you. There's nothing worse than spending an hour giving advice to someone you think has already chosen you as their lawyer only to be told as they walk out of the door, 'Thanks for that, I'll get back to you when I have seen the other firms on my list.'

If you're asked what other firms you've seen you don't have to say, but if you do it helps that lawyer, who then knows who he is in competition with and can adjust his 'sales pitch' accordingly.

When you've decided who you want to work with, you should tell the others who've given up an hour or more of their valuable time that they are out of luck. You never know, you may want to change lawyers at some point and there's no harm in keeping things civil.

What does your lawyer do for you?

A trite answer may be to say whatever you instruct him to do (provided it is legal). We do work 'on instructions' from you, but that's really not a true picture of all that we can do for you. We're there to advise you, to help you decide what the best deal is for you. We give you the benefit of our experience of similar situations. We know who's doing what deals and how much would be a good deal.

If you want, we can help you to target companies that our experience tells us should be interested in your type of music. This can help you to be more focused. This doesn't mean to say that we act as A&R people, although I have come across one or two lawyers who do think they are and indeed there are some law firms that employ young lawyers as quasi scouts looking for up and coming artists who might be future clients. The type of music you're into shouldn't influence your lawyer, who should be able to represent you whatever style of music you make, provided it's not so far out of his area of expertise that he doesn't have the necessary experience or commercial knowledge of whether the deal is good, bad or indifferent.

There's also a growing band of lawyers who, following the American trend, are acting as quasi-managers, only taking on clients who they think they can get a deal for. Managers seem a little uncomfortable about this, as it blurs the edges between their respective roles. It also means that the lawyer is making a judgement call, and those who really need advice may be losing out. With this breed of lawyer you need to be very clear what they are expecting to charge you. Is it their normal rate or is there a premium for this service? Are they charging a percentage of the deal they get for you? If so does that mean that they only focus on getting the most money and to hell with the small print?

Our role can be as wide or as narrow as you want it to be. If you are already clued-up on the type of deal you want, or have a manager who is, then you won't need that sort of advice. If you're quite happy about negotiating a deal direct with the record or publishing company, then you bring your lawyer in later when the commercial terms are agreed and you need to get the legal contract in place. On the other hand, if you are new to the business and aren't confident enough to negotiate commercial terms, you'll want to involve your lawyer at a much earlier stage.

I work differently with different types of clients. If it's a new artist who either doesn't have a manager or has a manager who isn't very experienced I run with things right from the beginning when a record company says it wants to do a deal. I contact the record company, get their deal proposal and, after talking to the client, I go back to the record company with any counter-proposals, continuing this process until the deal is in its final form. I then get the draft contract, check it, make any necessary changes, and negotiate those with the company until the contract is ready for me to recommend to the client for signature.

With other clients there may be an experienced manager on board who knows exactly what his bargaining power is and what sort of deal he would ideally like to end up with. My role at the beginning is more that of an adviser or sounding board. The manager will usually make sure I get a copy of the proposal and any counter-proposals, but won't want to involve me directly in the negotiations. He may telephone from time to time to ask if I think company X can do better than what they are offering. I'll tell him what I think based on other deals I have done with that company. I keep the names of the clients confidential, but I can say whether I know they can do better on a particular point or not. Once this type of client is happy with the commercial terms I'm then brought in to do the negotiation of the contract itself.

You should establish with your lawyer what kind of relationship you want to have. This may well change from deal to deal as you grow in experience.

I like to take an interest in my clients' work. I'm delighted to be sent a copy of the new album or single. It helps to cement the relationship between us. I also like to go and see my clients play live. I have to admit, though, that when I'm in the middle of a very long week at work and a client rings up and says, ' Hi, I'm on stage tonight at the Laughing Cow at 10.30 p.m.' (which means 11 p.m. at the earliest) then my wish to support the client is tested to the full.

What you don't want to happen is for your advisers to embarrass you. And yes, it does happen. I can still remember a gig a few years ago when four members of a top entertainment accountancy firm were standing proudly in the front row wearing the band's T-shirt over their work suits.

New breed of lawyers

There is a new breed of lawyers in the UK, of which I am now one. These are lawyers, usually qualified solicitors or barristers who, for one business reason or another, have decided not to practise as solicitors and be regulated by the Law Society. Instead, they practise as legal or business affairs consultants. In practice you will probably not notice any difference. In theory, because they are not bound by the Law Society's rules they can be more flexible in how they get paid for their work, for example, working on a percentage of your advances or royalties. Most however, including myself, stick to the rules we have operated for much of our working lives as solicitors even whilst not calling ourselves that. It does mean that we are more restricted in that we cannot do contentious work involving representing you in court. However, most legal consultants have arrangements in place to refer such work to lawyers who do contentious work and as it is a specialist field even if you were using a solicitor they would probably also refer you to a colleague if it became litigious. Of course, because we are not regulated by the Law Society you couldn't complain to the Society about us. But we are still open to being sued by you if we screw up and most of us carry professional indemnity insurance like solicitors as we are all human.

When should you get a lawyer?

There are a number of different views on this. Some say that there's no need to get a lawyer until you've a contract in front of you. I think you should get a lawyer earlier than this. I think that the whole process of getting a deal is so much of a lottery that anything you can do to reduce the odds must be worth doing. Most of us are happy to give initial advice and guidance for free, or only charge you when your first deal is in place. Just be careful and check this before going ahead.

Your lawyer can also help you to find a good accountant.

ACCOUNTANTS

This leads me neatly on to discuss how you find a good accountant and what they can do for you. How do you find one?

The Institutes

The Institutes of Chartered Accountants in England & Wales, Scotland or Northern Ireland and the Association of Chartered and Certified Accountants can recommend firms to you (see Useful Addresses). It's important that the accountant is qualified, preferably a Chartered or Certified accountant. Anyone can set up in business giving financial advice, so you should check that they're properly regulated. You shouldn't allow them to keep your money in an account to which they can have access without your knowledge. If they are to have signing rights on cheques make sure there are sufficient controls in place.

Directories

There isn't any general guide similar to the legal directories. The accountancy profession is broken down into the big international firms like Ernst & Young and Deloitte, medium-sized national firms with international networks like BDO Stoy Hayward, and smaller local firms.

The *Music Week Directory* has a section on accountants. The directory is not a recommendation that they're any good, but it is a good starting point.

AMIA

You could always try the Association of Music Industry Accountants (see Useful Addresses). They will be happy to recommend accountants from within their own membership and, as their name suggests, they are all associated with the music business.

Music Managers Forum

The MMF can give you recommendations for accountants as well as for lawyers. They have firms of accountants who are corporate members (see Useful Addresses) as well as individual accountants who provide business or quasi-management services.

Lawyers

Your lawyer should have had dealings with a number of accountants and should be able to recommend two or three to you that they know have experience in the music business.

Other sources of information

Your A&R or other record or publishing company contacts or friends in the music business may be able to suggest some names. It's always good to get a recommendation from someone who rates a particular accountant highly.

How to choose an accountant

As I suggested when choosing your lawyer, you should see more than one accountant. You should ask them the type of work they can do for you. Some are strong on tour accounting or in auditing (inspecting) the books and records of companies. They may also do general bookkeeping and tax advice, but they may not, so ask.

If you expect to do a lot of touring, it's worth having an accountant who's experienced in putting together tour accounts and is familiar with tour budgets and all the necessary arrangements to deal with VAT on overseas tours and taxes on overseas income (see Chapter 10).

It's less important that your accountant's offices are in the same city as the record and publishing companies. They don't have to be in London. The main thing is that they are familiar with the music business and how it works. They must know the sources of income and how and when it's paid. They need to know how to read and understand a royalty statement. These things are often, literally, written in code. You need to know what country A is and what the code for CD sales is. Your local family accountant can, of course, do the basic accounting work as well as the next man, but this probably isn't enough once you start getting deals. Just as you need a lawyer with specialised music business knowledge, so you need the same expertise from your accountant if he's to be able to look after your interests properly. The basic accountancy and tax rules do, of course, apply to artists and songwriters, but there are a number of specialised rules and regulations aimed at them. Your accountant must be up to date on these rules.

Some accountants don't claim to be experts in tax planning or advice and, if that is an area that you need to have covered, you would be best advised to go to an accountant that can provide that and then get a specialist accountant in to do the tour accounting or auditing.

As your accountant will have intimate knowledge of your finances and may have some control over your bank account, it is vitally important that you trust them, that they have a good reputation and that there are suitable checks and balances in place to protect you and your money.

Business Managers

There is another breed of accountant that could provide the sort of services you are looking for, and that is a business manager. This is a term that has come across from the US, where they are quite common. In the US they generally act as the business and financial adviser alongside a personal manager who looks after the day-to-day and creative aspects of the artist's career (see Chapter 2). In the UK the term means something slightly different. They provide day-to-day business advice and bookkeeping services. They'll do your VAT and tax returns for you. They can provide business plans and advice and some also do tour accounts. Most don't provide international tax planning or audits. Their argument is that this makes them more cost effective as you are not paying for a full tax planning and audit service when you don't need it. This means they can charge less than the bigger firms of accountants do. When specialist tax or international advice is required, they have relationships with more than one of the bigger accountancy firms and other financial advisers and can refer you to the right company for you, to get the advice you need when you need it.

How do they charge?

Accountants usually charge fees rather than commission. They may quote you a rate per annum for advising you. Some of the bigger accountancy firms run special schemes where the first year's work for you is done at a special, discounted rate. You don't have to stay with them after the first year. If you are tempted by these schemes you should ask what exactly is covered by the discount rate. It's likely that you won't get the same service as the full-price one. You should also ask what the non-discounted rate would be after the first year so that you can decide whether you think you'd be able to stay with them afterwards or will have to start the search for a new accountant, which could be disruptive.

You should ask them what their experience is and who will be doing the work. Often you find that the person who sees you and does the hard sell is the partner or even the marketing person. Someone quite different and possibly much less experienced may be doing the work. This sort of thing is more likely to happen in the bigger firms, particularly those that are offering a discount rate. You can be reasonably sure that it will not be a partner that will be doing the cut-price work.

What does an accountant do?

Accountants can do a number of things for you. They do the accounts books for you, advise and help you to complete your tax return. They register you for VAT, if necessary, and can do your quarterly VAT returns. Depending on your accountant, they may also do your tour accounts and help prepare a tour budget. Your accountant will advise you on whether you should be a sole trader, in partnership or a limited company or limited liability partnership (see Chapter 11). He can prepare partnership or company accounts. Some accountants can also act as the auditor of your company books; many can also act as the company secretary and can arrange for the company's registered office to be at their offices.

Your accountant can act as your financial adviser, telling you where the best place to invest your money is. Because this area is very closely regulated, not all accountants are authorised to provide financial services advice. You should ask if your accountant is. If he isn't you will need a separate financial adviser.

Your accountant can be your tax adviser and help plan with you things such as whether you could consider putting your income in an offshore tax haven or, indeed, if you could, or should, become a tax exile or non-domiciled. There are signs that the Government is tightening up on the tax benefits of being non-domiciled so this may not be an attractive option for much longer. Another reason why it's important your accountant is up to speed in this area.

Can your accountant help you get a record deal?

Yes, he can. You can use accountants in the same way as lawyers. Use their contacts and pick their brains for information on companies and A&R people. Some accountants also send out selected demo tapes on behalf of artists and songwriters.

If your accountant does find you a deal then he shouldn't charge you a commission for doing so. He should just charge for any accountancy advice that he gives you on that deal. If your accountant offers to get you a deal, ask him on what basis he is doing it before you give him the go-ahead.

The accountant should be able to work as part of the team with you, your manager and your lawyer. It's important that you keep your accountant in the loop about the deal so that he can advise how it can be structured as tax-effectively as possible before you sign anything.

All accountants should give you a letter of engagement, setting out the basis on which they will work for you and how they will charge. They should give you the name of someone in their firm that you can complain to if you've a problem with your accountant. If the complaint is about fees you can ask for a breakdown of the bill. The professional body that your accountant belongs to is the first port of call for complaints about your accountant. If they don't deal with the complaint to your satisfaction you can take it to court. This is looking at the negative side and most relationships proceed smoothly.

An accountant can have conflicts of interest just as your lawyer can. If your accountants act for one of the major record or publishing companies, and you then want to do a deal with that company, the conflict may or may not arise at that stage. However, if later on you aren't sure whether the company is accounting to you properly and you want to send someone in to look at (audit) the books, then your accountant will have a conflict of interest and you will probably have to take that work elsewhere. There are, in fact, specialist firms of accountants who only do audits. Sometimes it's best to use their specialised knowledge even if there isn't a conflict of interest with your own accountant.

So now you've got your lawyer and your accountant lined up. You have two members of your team, getting a manager could be the critical third stage. I'll deal with this in the next chapter.

CONCLUSIONS

- If you hope to get noticed through doing live work, do your homework first. Investigate your venues and rehearse thoroughly. Tailor your material to your audience and tell your audience who you are.

- Consider short cuts like industry-organised showcases, open mike evenings or music conventions as well as competitions.

- Make sure your demo is the best quality that you can afford and that it has a good cross-section of your work. Put your name and contact number on the CD as well as the packaging or make sure they have your email on any MP3 submission.

- If you do a deal with a studio for studio time, make sure it's for no more than 1–1.5% and don't agree they can be the producer of your first album unless there are excellent reasons to do so.

- If you do a demo deal, keep the exclusive period as short as possible and make sure that no one can do anything with the recordings without your agreement.

- If you do a finders deal keep the percentages to 5–10% and for as short a period as you reasonably can get away with.

- When picking a lawyer or accountant, arrange to see two or three different firms and ask them for estimates of their charges for a particular piece of work. Find out their expertise and, if possible, who their clients are.

- When you appoint a lawyer or accountant, get written confirmation from them of their charges.

- Your accountant and lawyer are vital members of your team – take your time to choose the right ones.

Chapter 2
Management Deals

INTRODUCTION

In this chapter I'm going to look at how to find a good manager, what to expect from a manager, and what you have to think about when entering into a management contract. I'm going to look at it from the artist's point of view, but when we get to the part on contracts I'm also going to put the manager's side of the argument. The section on what to expect from a manager should also be useful to managers. It'll give them an idea of what might be expected from them.

It gives me a real buzz to team up the right manager with the right artist; it's like watching a well-oiled machine going into action. It's also great to work with a good artist/manager team, as everyone's pulling in the same direction. A good example of this in action recently has been the relationship between Danny D and Tim Blackhurst as managers of the writing/production team of Norwegian writers 'Stargate'. They won 'Song of the Year' and 'Songwriter of the Year' awards from ASCAP in 2007 and at the ceremony credited their managers with having the faith to encourage them to take their skills to America. That leap of faith and the skill with which they then exploited the new market place was a direct cause of their subsequent success. What was slightly unusual was that the writers acknowledged this openly. Much more common is an artist who once they are successful begins to resent the monies being paid to the manager and forgets their origins and the crucial role played by the manager at the beginning.

HOW TO FIND A MANAGER

DIRECTORIES

One of the main music business directories in the UK is the *Music Week Directory*. It lists managers and the acts they manage. The Music Managers Forum also issues a directory of its managers and who they manage, which can be an excellent starting point for finding a manager who looks after artists who are similar to you or who share a particular musical genre.

The drawback with all directories is that they don't give you any clues as to whether the managers listed are any good. The information you get from them needs to be backed up from other sources.

MUSIC MANAGERS FORUM

One such source is the Music Managers Forum (MMF).[1] The MMF doesn't act as a dating agency for setting managers up with artists. It does, however, publish a directory of its members and is helpful in putting you in contact with individual managers.

---

1 The MMF was formed in the mid-1990s by a group of like-minded managers who felt that they could achieve more both for their artists and for themselves if they grouped together. They act as a lobbying group on behalf of their members in relation to national and international issues facing the music industry. The MMF has also established links with managers in other parts of the world. For contact details see Useful Addresses.

Membership of the MMF is not a recommendation that a manager is any good but, if a manager is a member, it shows that he is interested in talking to other managers and in keeping up to date with what is going on in the outside world that can affect the music business and their or your livelihood. The MMF also runs training courses for wannabe managers, mostly in London and Manchester, but occasionally regional courses in conjunction with other organisations such as the Welsh Music Foundation and usually at quite reasonable rates.

It can be lonely out there so, if you are a manager yourself looking for like-minded individuals, the MMF has Associate Membership at a reduced rate for new managers of as yet unsigned artists and there is also a category for self-managed artists.

RECOMMENDATIONS

You may by now have quite a lot of information about various managers, but you still may not know if they're any good or even if they're looking for new artists to manage. What you need are personal recommendations (references, if you like) from people who have worked with a particular manager or know him by reputation. Where do you get these? You can ask around among other bands to see if they have any good or bad experiences of particular managers. Bad reports can be as useful to you as good ones. At the end of the day you'll have to make up your own mind whether to trust a particular manager, but if people who know him keep saying bad things about him, you can't say you weren't warned.

LAWYERS AND ACCOUNTANTS

If you've already found yourself a lawyer or accountant then they should be able to tell you what sort of reputation a particular manager has. They are also good sources of information and can put you in contact with managers that you may not have discovered on your own. They may know that a particular manager is looking for more acts to manage or, conversely, is too busy to devote the necessary time to a new artist.

As with all major decisions you shouldn't rush into anything. In particular, if a lawyer or accountant has recommended someone, you should try and find out what the relationship is between him or her and that manager. If, for example, they get most of their work from that manager, how independent are they and is there any conflict of interest? They can't advise you independently if the rest of the time they are advising the manager. But just because a lawyer recommends a manager that they regularly work with doesn't mean that there is necessarily a conflict of interest. You just have to be clear who is looking after your interests.

SURGERIES

The Performing Right Society Limited (PRS) and the songwriter's body, The Academy, hold occasional 'surgeries'. These are meetings where music business professionals such as lawyers, managers and A&R people discuss particular topics and answer your questions. They are sociable events, often held in a pub or club, and are a good place to meet other songwriters and music business people. Details of their meetings are given in the PRS Newsletter or direct from the PRS. ASCAP (one of the equivalent societies in the US) also holds informal evening sessions when writers get together.

A&R CONTACTS

Record or publishing company scouts or A&R people can be an excellent source of information on managers and whether a particular manager is looking for new artists to manage. They can put you in contact with managers. In fact, they may insist on you getting a manager before they are prepared to discuss a possible deal with you, because they're happier dealing with a middleman (and preferably someone with a track record).

MANAGERS

There is always the possibility that a manager will approach you direct. They may have heard about you from an A&R man, a lawyer or accountant, or they may have seen you play live. It's not unheard of for a manager to come up to you after a gig to say that he wants to manage you. A word of warning – just because a manager approaches you doesn't mean they're any good, nor does it mean that you've to leap at the chance of being managed by anyone regardless of who they are. You still have to do your homework and make as sure as you can that this is the right manager for you.

You should always ask for a trial period to make sure that the relationship is working. It takes time to build up the necessary trust between you. The manager should agree to that, but he will be looking for commitment from you before he spends any significant amounts of his own time or money on you. He'll certainly be looking for you to confirm that you want him to manage you before he approaches record and publishing companies on your behalf. If he's prepared to commit time and spend money on you then it's reasonable to expect some commitment from you in return. Sometimes managers ask you to sign a short agreement to cover their expenses and any deals they may get for you during the short trial period. As with any legal agreement, if in doubt – get it checked out by a lawyer.

Having discussed how to find managers we should now look at one or two of the principles behind the artist/manager relationship. Many of these principles have been developed and applied to management contracts through a series of cases involving some of the leading players of the time.

THE PRINCIPLES

The first thing you have to understand is that it's a relationship based on trust. If the trust is lost then there's little hope for the relationship. The contract won't hold you together if the trust isn't there. All that a management contract will then do is tell you what your rights are and what happens if you part company.

This loss of trust has led to many disputes between managers and artists over the years. Some end up in court, many more settle before they get that far – even at the doors of the court. Most people don't want to air their dirty linen in public. It's not a pretty sight when you're sitting in court and the reporters are all lined up on the benches behind you ready to take down every sordid detail. One time I was in court and found myself sitting next to a journalist from one of the tabloid newspapers. He was obviously bored with the lack of juicy scandal and kept popping in and out of court. In one of the gaps in the proceedings I asked him if he'd been going out for a cigarette. 'Nah, love,' came the reply, 'I'm checking with my bookie who won the last two races at Sandown Park.' He then asked me if I fancied a bet on the outcome of the trial and could I tell him what he'd missed while he was outside on the phone. British journalism at its finest.

Anyway, the cases described below did get to court. The judgements in these cases helped to establish what lies behind the relationship in legal terms, what duties the manager has towards an artist, and what is acceptable in a management contract.

Gilbert O'Sullivan Case[2]

Gilbert O'Sullivan signed a management contract with Management Agency and Music Limited (MAM) in 1970. He was young and unknown at the time and had no business experience (this theme comes up time and time again in music disputes). MAM and the man behind it, Gordon Mills, already had an international reputation. Mills managed the superstars Tom Jones and Engelbert Humperdinck. Through MAM Mills also had interests in a number of other music companies.

O'Sullivan trusted his manager completely and, at Mills' suggestion, he also signed recording and publishing contracts with those related music companies.

O'Sullivan didn't have any independent legal advice on these contracts. He wasn't told that it would be a good idea for him to get such advice. It seems that he trusted Gordon Mills to such an extent that it didn't cross his mind to get a second opinion. If his manager told him to do something, then he did it.

The agreements tied O'Sullivan to Mills and to his companies completely, and the terms were far worse than if O'Sullivan had done the deals with independent companies and if he had taken independent advice.

O'Sullivan's debut single on MAM was the very successful 'Nothing Rhymed'. Early UK successes were followed by a Top 10 hit in the US with 'Alone Again (Naturally)'. In 1972 he had two No. 1 singles in the UK with 'Clair' and 'Get Down'. His second album reached No. 1 in the UK and he had a number of further hits.

By 1976 O'Sullivan's relationship with Mills had broken down; he'd lost his trust in him. This might have been because, for all these hits, he didn't seem to be making much money. He sued Mills, arguing that the various contracts should be treated as if they'd never happened (that they were void), because Mills had used his position of trust with O'Sullivan to wrongly influence him to sign them. He also argued that the terms of the contracts were so unreasonable that they unfairly restricted his ability to earn a living. These concepts of undue influence and unreasonable restraint of trade come up often in music contract disputes.

The court decided that Mills did owe a duty to O'Sullivan. This is called a fiduciary duty – a duty to act in good faith. Mills had a duty to put O'Sullivan's interests first. The court also decided that the contracts were void and could not be enforced. If O'Sullivan chose to ignore them, Mills couldn't do anything about it. The court tried to put O'Sullivan back in the position he would have been in had the contracts not been signed. It ordered all copyrights that had been transferred (assigned) by O'Sullivan to be returned to him as well as all master recordings of his performances.

This was a dramatic decision and it caused uproar in the music business. Record and publishing companies were afraid that, if this decision were allowed to stand, there would be a rush of other artists making the same claims and trying to get their rights back. They knew that many of the contracts around at the time were no better than those that O'Sullivan had signed. They were really worried that all the deals they had done for the records or songs

---

2 *O'Sullivan v. Management Agency and Music Limited* [1985] QBD 428.

would be void and unenforceable. It's no exaggeration to say that the whole basis of the music business, and the financial security of many companies, was at risk.

The Appeal

Unsurprisingly, Mills and his associated companies wanted to have this dangerous precedent overturned. They appealed against the decision that the companies owed any duty to O'Sullivan. They argued that the record and publishing companies had not used any influence over O'Sullivan. They also argued that the contracts should be declared void able and not void from the outset. If the Court of Appeal agreed with them, the contracts would be valid but could be set aside later if they were found to have been signed through undue influence or to be in unreasonable restraint of trade. Because the companies had already acted as if the contracts were valid, they argued it would be impossible to return everyone to the position they would have been in had the contracts not existed. They said that the copyrights and master recordings shouldn't be returned to O'Sullivan, but that he should be compensated by payment of damages.

In a very important decision for the music business, the Court of Appeal decided that the associated companies did owe a fiduciary duty to O'Sullivan, because Mills was effectively in control of those companies and was acting in the course of his employment by these companies when he used his undue influence over O'Sullivan. The court also confirmed that it was possible to set these contracts aside, even if the parties couldn't be put in exactly the same position they would have been in had the contracts not been signed. The court thought that this could be done if it was possible to reach a 'practically just' result for O'Sullivan.

So far so good for O'Sullivan, you might think. His lawyers must have thought they were home and dry, but there was a sting in the tail. The Court of Appeal decided that a 'practically just' solution would be for the copyright in the songs and master recordings already in existence to remain with the publishing and record companies, subject to suitable compensation for O'Sullivan. They also said that the contracts were void able rather than void, that they were an unreasonable restraint of his trade and that O'Sullivan was freed from them but only for the future. What he'd written and recorded before stayed with the record and publishing companies.

The music business breathed a collective sigh of relief. The refusal of the Court of Appeal to order the return of the copyrights has made it very difficult, if not impossible, to successfully argue for a return of copyrights in cases of undue influence or unreasonable restraint of trade.

Joan Armatrading[3]

At about the same time, another important case was reaching the courts. It involved Joan Armatrading.

Joan Armatrading is a singer-songwriter who is still recording and performing today. The case was about an agreement that Armatrading signed when she was young and relatively inexperienced and before she became famous. There's that theme again.

Stone was a partner in the Copeland Sherry Agency, which had signed a management agreement with Armatrading in March 1973. This was shortly after she released her debut

---

3 Armatrading v. Stone and Another (1985), unreported.

album *Whatever's For Us*, which was produced by Gus Dudgeon, who also worked with Elton John. Copeland is Miles Copeland, who managed The Police and Sting for some time. Stone advised Armatrading on business matters. She took charge of most creative issues herself. It seems she was confident enough to select the studios and producers she wanted to work with without needing advice from her managers, but didn't have a clue when it came to the business end of things.

In 1975 Armatrading released her second album *Back To The Night*. It didn't reach the charts. She then began work on an album that turned out to be the first to bring her properly to the public's attention.

In February 1976, as the term of the original management contract was about to run out, she signed a new contract under which Stone was to manage her on his own. He may have been worried she would go off to another manager when the original contract ran out and just as her career was starting to take off. Although he denied that in his evidence, the album that she released in 1976, *Joan Armatrading*, went into the Top 20 in the UK and one of the singles released off it became her most famous and successful song. It was called 'Love And Affection' and it reached the Top 10.

Things continued to go well for her at first and in 1980 she released her most successful album to date, *Me Myself I*, which also contained the hit single 'All The Way From America'. Shortly after that she seems to have become disillusioned with Stone and commenced proceedings for the management contract to be declared void on the grounds that Stone had used undue influence to get her to sign the contract and that the terms were unreasonable and a restraint of her trade.

It became clear from the evidence given in the case that the lawyer who drew up the contract had been introduced to Armatrading by Stone and had done some work for her. Coincidentally, I worked with that same firm of lawyers for a couple of years. The contract was done before my time there, but the court case was going on when I was there and I know it caused a lot of strain on everyone concerned. When preparing the management contract, it seems the lawyer acted on the instructions of Stone and not Armatrading. In particular, Stone asked for two specific things to be added to the draft contract. The lawyer billed Stone for the work and it's clear from the description on the bill that he thought he was acting as Stone's lawyer.

At a meeting on 4 February 1976 at the lawyers' offices, Armatrading received a copy of the draft contract to take away with her. She returned the next day to sign it. She didn't ask for any changes to be made to it.

Stone claimed that the lawyer acted as lawyer for both of them. When he gave evidence the lawyer said that he thought he was just acting as lawyer to Stone. A very confusing state of affairs. Stone and Armatrading were both present at the meeting with the lawyer on 4 February when the contract was discussed. That must have been very awkward. If a manager turns up at a meeting I'm due to have with an artist to discuss a management contract, I insist on him staying outside while I take the meeting. I can't be open with the artist about what I think about the contract or the manager if the manager is in the same room. The same would apply the other way around.

The contract was strongly biased in Stone's favour. It was for five years and during that time Armatrading was exclusively tied to Stone as her manager. The contract didn't say that Stone had to do very much at all for her. He could manage other artists. He was to be paid a management commission of 20% (which, as we will see, is quite common) but 25% on any new recording or publishing deals she signed (which is not). He got 20% commission on touring whether or not the tour made a profit. The court thought this was particularly harsh, as was the fact that Stone's right to commission was open-ended. For example, if Armatrading signed a new record deal in year three of the five-year management term, Stone would be entitled to 25% commission. He might stop being her manager two years later, but he'd still go on earning at 25%. If Armatrading got herself a new manager and he negotiated some improvements to the recording contract in return for, say, a two-year extension on the record deal, then Stone and not the new manager would get commission at 25% on the extended term. Not much of an incentive for the new manager (or expensive for Armatrading if she had to pay out two lots of commission to the original and the new manager).

When he gave evidence, Stone agreed that he knew that he had a duty to act in Armatrading's best interests and that she had trust and confidence in him. This fiduciary duty already existed when the 1976 management contract was being discussed. Stone knew that his interests under this contract were not the same as Armatrading's and yet he still seemed to think that the same lawyer could act for both of them.

Stone admitted that it was very likely that Armatrading didn't realise she should have separate legal advice. Even though he accepted his fiduciary duties existed, he didn't seem to accept the idea of a conflict of interest and couldn't seem to see that if something in the management contract was in his interests it would not necessarily be in Armatrading's best interests. This doesn't mean that a manager can't look out for his own interests just that it's up to him to make sure that the artist has separate advice and is able to come to an informed decision.

The court found Stone's evidence very contradictory. It decided that Armatrading relied heavily on Stone in business matters. She trusted him and he'd told her that he would look after her. The court thought it was clear that he had influence over her. She didn't look at the detail of the contract. She relied on Stone, who told her that it was a standard and fair contract, even though he had asked for two specific changes to be made to the draft.

The court decided that the contract should be set aside by reason of undue influence by Stone. The terms of the contract were said to be unreasonable ('unduly onerous and unconscionable' in the words of the judgement). The contract was void able and not void from the outset. On this point they came to the same conclusion as in the O'Sullivan case.

The fact that Armatrading didn't have separate legal advice was seen as very important. On its own this wouldn't have been enough to set aside the contract. For example, if the contract had been a perfectly reasonable one, so that any lawyer who advised on it would say it was all right to sign it, then the absence of that advice wouldn't have been fatal. The absence of separate legal advice coupled with the particularly harsh terms of the contract was enough to convince the court to set it aside. The court found that, although she had some experience of the music business, because she concentrated on the creative side it was important that she be given a proper understanding of the business side of the contract. She hadn't understood the implications of the open-ended commission clause and hadn't been able to form an independent view after full, free and informed thought. She had signed the contract relying on her manager's claim that it was fine. He had failed in his fiduciary duty to her. She was freed from the contract and went on to record several more successful albums.

Although this case wasn't reported in the Law Reports, it had a very significant and practical effect on management contracts. We lawyers still use it as a yardstick to measure the reasonableness of management contract terms. It's also quoted as an authority for saying that artist and manager should have separate lawyers when discussing the management contract and whenever their interests are not the same.

After this case it became usual to add a clause to management contracts saying that the artist has been advised to take independent legal advice. I don't think this goes far enough. Just advising someone they should get advice and then not making sure that they do is not good enough. I think that the manager should insist on the artist having separate legal advice from a lawyer who understands the music business, and should make sure he understands what he's being asked to sign.

The Armatrading case also cast doubt on whether a five-year contract term was reasonable. After the case, some managers decided to go for a shorter term or otherwise tried to make their contracts more reasonable. No manager wants to risk having an artist walk away from a management contract at the height of his or her success. However, as we shall see below, the trend these days is back to longer minimum management terms.

The judge was also quite critical of the 25% commission rate on new record and publishing deals (25% rates are now rare, but do still occasionally occur). He was even more concerned about the fact that Stone took commission on touring money even if the tour made a loss. Music business lawyers reacted to these criticisms by introducing new protections for artists in this area.

Elton John[4]

Another case on management contracts that was reported in the tabloids as well as the Law Reports involved Elton John.

Elton John signed a series of publishing, management and recording contracts starting in 1967, when he was still under age and unknown. Although these themes come up quite often in these cases, each case played its own part in developing how the business operates and how contracts have to be adapted to deal with criticisms made by the judges.

Elton John and his lyricist, Bernie Taupin were originally taken on as in-house writers for James's new publishing company, DJM. It's said they were on wages of £10 per week. It took quite a while for them to be commercially successful. The first successful album was produced by Gus Dudgeon and was called *Elton John*. The 1972 album contained the now-classic work 'Your Song'. Seven consecutive No. 1 albums followed in the next seven years.

Although Elton was making a lot of very successful records, he didn't seem to be seeing much of the proceeds. For example, the publishing set-up consisted of a number of inter-related companies, each taking its own slice of the income, so that a very small amount was left for Elton. What he did get he had to pay management commission on.

He sued to try and recover his copyrights and damages for back royalties. He relied on the tried and true arguments that he had signed the contracts under undue influence and that they were an unreasonable restraint of his trade.

He hadn't taken separate legal advice before signing any of the contracts. He'd placed trust and confidence in James. The contracts weren't as beneficial for him as they could have been had they been with independent companies. The publishers could take rights in his songs and not have to do anything with them. They could be shut away in a drawer and never seen again and Elton couldn't do anything about it. He was also signed up exclusively, so he couldn't take his songs to another music publisher.

---

4 *John v. James* (1991) FSR 397.

The court decided that in these circumstances it was to be assumed that there was undue influence at work and that it was up to the manager to show that he didn't use his influence in the wrong way. The court found that James had failed in his fiduciary duties to Elton. It felt that James couldn't be acting in the best interest of Elton if James's publishing and recording companies were also entering into contracts with him. How could James be advising Elton as his manager while he also had an interest in making as much money as possible for his record and publishing companies out of those contracts?

Once again, the decision in this case had a knock-on effect on the music business. It was fully reported in the Law Reports, so had authority and it confirmed the existence of the fiduciary duty owed not only by the manager, but also any companies under his control. It also brought home the importance of separate legal advice.

The other important thing it changed was what happens where your manager also has a record or publishing contract that he wants you to sign up to. If your manager also has an interest in a record or publishing company, the management contract will now usually ask the artists to confirm that he won't consider it a failure of the manager's fiduciary duty to him if he signs up to the record or publishing company on the manager's advice. I don't think this would be enough to get the manager off the hook if he did, in fact, break his duty to the artist especially if the artist hadn't had separate legal advice. There's also usually a clause that says the manager can't take a double hit on the income from the record or publishing deals. For example, if the artist releases a record on the manager's record label, the manager should get his money from the record label's profits on the record sales. He shouldn't also take a management commission on the artist's record royalties. As we shall see below this blurring of the edges between the roles of managers is becoming a key issue and a potential future problem area.

WHAT TO LOOK FOR IN A MANAGER

This all depends on what you expect your manager to do for you. You may only need a manager to advise you on business matters. You may want that but are also looking for creative advice, comment and guidance. Some artists already have a clear idea of what they are doing creatively and have a good business sense and grasp of contracts. They don't want an all-round manager and may only be looking for a good organiser. We saw in the Armatrading case (above) that Stone only looked after Armatrading's business interests. She looked after the creative side herself. This tends to only apply to more established artists. Those who are new to the business tend to look for all the help they can get from a manager.

You may be looking for a svengali, someone who will come up with the cast-iron plan for world domination in three years. Such managers do exist, for example, people like Tom Watkins, who has successfully managed acts like The Pet Shop Boys and Bros to considerable success and Nigel Martin-Smith who masterminded the early days of Take That and Jonathan Shalit an early manager of Charlotte Church and now behind several successful R'n'B acts. Then there are managers like Simon Fuller, whose marketing background meant that he could see the worldwide possibilities of an act like The Spice Girls and S Club 7 and more recently the first album by Amy Winehouse and the career of Will Young.

When you expect a manager to devise an all-encompassing game plan and then to implement it, you can't expect to get away with no effort on your part. You and your manager will have to put enormous amounts of time and energy into making the plan work and both of you must completely buy into the whole idea behind it. There is, of course, also the type of artist who's been formed for a particular purpose, such as TV-based acts like S Club, or those who have won reality TV competitions such as *The X Factor*. Provided the artist fits in with this game plan then all is well. It's only when the artist, or one or more members of the group, starts to rebel or baulk at the situation that problems occur. Bands that have come together for the purpose of a TV show struggle when it comes to the cut and thrust of the music industry and it is rare for them to have a career beyond the album that comes out quickly when they win the competition. Interestingly, most of the successful artists from these shows have been solo stars like Lemar, Kelly Clarkson and more recently, Leona Lewis.

IS IT ESSENTIAL TO HAVE AN EXPERIENCED MANAGER?

Someone who hasn't managed anyone before can make a good manager if they have the flair for it. They may have been a musician themselves, a tour manager, a producer or may have worked in-house at a record or publishing company. Those with a marketing background can be very useful in developing a strategy to get you noticed. These people will have seen how the music business works and can bring valuable experience to the job of manager. However, their skills are not necessarily those that make a good manager, so be careful. On the other hand, a manager may be experienced and still not right for you because his experience is in a different arena (for instance, as a tour manager) rather than skilled in managing an artist's career. So take your time before making up your mind.

QUALITIES TO LOOK FOR IN A MANAGER

The manager has to be a diplomat, motivator, salesman and strategic planner – and has to have the patience of a saint.

Record and publishing companies like to have managers around to act as middlemen so they don't have to have unpleasant conversations with you. They'd like you to choose someone who's already successfully steered an artist through getting a deal, getting a record made and who's already done the whole touring and promotion side of things. This doesn't mean to say that they won't work with an inexperienced manager, just that they would prefer one who was not. They would also like you to be managed by someone they already know, someone they know they can work with. This doesn't necessarily mean that that manager will be in their pocket. It could mean that they have a healthy respect for him for being tough but fair, someone that gets the job done, but if you are being pushed by your record company towards a particular manager, take the time to stop and ask why and to do some research of your own before meekly accepting their choice. There is a growing trend amongst major labels to seek to reduce their risks by only working with artists who have a manager on board that they like or with whom they have an existing relationship. This can work well but you need to be sure the manager has the necessary degree of independence.

WHAT DOES A MANAGER DO FOR YOU?

PERSONAL MANAGERS

A personal manager looks after your day-to-day needs. This usually includes some advice on the creative side of things. The personal manager also acts as go-between with the record and publishing companies and the outside world. This might involve working with you on creative issues such as the choice of songs. A personal manager is also usually someone who organises your life and tries to make everything run smoothly. They put into action plans others have come up with. They don't necessarily get involved in day-to-day business decisions or strategic plans.

BUSINESS MANAGERS

A business manager doesn't usually involve himself in the day-to-day business of running your life. It's the job of the business manager to work out where you should be in terms of business planning and to help you put the plan into action. He will liaise with the record and publishing company, but usually more at the level of negotiating deals, changes to the contracts, setting video and recording budgets and getting tour support when it's needed.

It's much more common in the US to have a separate business and personal manager. There the business manager is often an accountant or financial adviser. The idea of these roles being filled by different people hasn't yet become popular in the UK. What tends to happen here is that one person will do both jobs, sometimes with the assistance of a personal assistant (see below) or you have co-managers with complementary skills.

If you do have separate business and personal managers, you need to be sure that you're not paying too much by having two people on board instead of one.

Don't assume that because you have a business manager you can do away with the need for an accountant. You will need one to oversee your tax and possibly VAT returns and someone to prepare company or partnership accounts. Bear this in mind when you agree what to pay your business manager. If you're paying your business manager 20% of your income, your personal manager another 10% and then paying an accountant, that's not a great bargain.

The manager is there to advise you, to guide you through your career in the music business. A successful career as a performer or composer can lead into other areas such as films, television, writing or modelling. One of the many things you have to consider in choosing your manager is whether the manager can also look after these other areas of your life.

The manager should spend a reasonable amount of time on your affairs and your career. He should help you to get a record and/or publishing deal, live appearances, sponsorship and merchandising deals.

The manager should advise you whether or not you should take up a particular offer. It may not fit in with the game plan that you and the manager have worked out. Putting together that game plan is a very important job for your manager. You and he need to be on the same wavelength on it.

PERSONAL ASSISTANTS

As you become more successful, so the manager may employ someone to act as your personal assistant (PA). If the PA is working full-time for you, the manager will expect you to pay their wages. If they work some of the time for you and the rest on general work for the manager or for other acts that he manages, then the cost is likely to be shared between you. If the PA works most of the time for the manager and only occasionally runs errands for you, then you would expect the manager to bear all the cost.

FIDUCIARY DUTIES AND PROBLEMS WITH BANDS

As we saw in the section on the cases (above), the manager has to always act in your best interests. He has a fiduciary duty to you, which means that he has to always act with the utmost good faith towards you.

This duty can cause problems when dealing with a band. Something that may be good for the band as a whole may not be good for one of the band members. There's a very narrow line that the manager has to tread. Sometimes you may feel that the manager has stepped the wrong side of that line.

This issue was one of several behind a dispute between Nigel Martin-Smith and Robbie Williams.[5]

The Robbie Williams management case

I have to declare an interest here, as this was a case I inherited when I became Robbie's lawyer a few years ago. Martin-Smith was the manager of Take That from the early days to the height of their success. Take That was made up of five members, including Robbie. He became fed up at the direction his life was taking and was thinking about leaving the band. His version of events is that he was prepared to see his commitments to a major tour through to the end before leaving the band. He says that, on advice from Martin-Smith, the band sacked him. The other members and Martin-Smith say he walked out.

When Martin-Smith later sued Robbie for unpaid commission (Robbie had refused to pay him), one of the arguments that Robbie used was that Martin-Smith had failed in his fiduciary duty to Robbie and was not acting in his best interests in advising the band to sack him.

Martin-Smith acknowledged that it was very difficult in such circumstances to advise a band when he also had a duty to each of them as individuals. He admitted that he had had discussions with the other band members about Robbie and how disillusioned he was, but he said he also tried to advise Robbie on what was best for him. He said that he had acted in the best interests of the band as a whole, while trying to balance this against the interests of the individual members. He denied that he'd advised the band to sack Robbie.

The judge accepted his evidence that he had acted in good faith and was not in breach of his fiduciary duty to Robbie. The judge acknowledged the difficulties that a manager faces in such circumstances, but decided that in this case Martin-Smith had stayed the right side of the line.

If you're in any doubts as to the good faith of your manager, you should seek independent advice, if only to be aware of your legal position.

NEW BUSINESS MODELS

There is a growing trend for managers to also take a financial interest and possibly ownership of rights in some other capacity. For example, a manager may say that he also wishes to act as your record label or your publisher. These are big issues and are driven by the fact that as manager he doesn't have any ownership of rights and can only take a financial cut on catalogue sales of records or songs for so long as his management contract allows. Some managers now feel that is not enough. They say it is taking longer

---

5 *Martin-Smith v. Williams* (1997), unreported.

to get an artist a deal and each album is taking longer to make and the promotion associated with it is even longer. On a basic three or even five year management term the manager may, at best, only get paid on songs and recordings on a couple of albums. Some managers want more. They are also aware of the personal nature of management contracts and that their artist may leave so they seek to gain some future security through ownership of recordings or of rights in your songs. Whilst the commercial reasoning behind these actions is easy to see it doesn't necessarily mean it's a good thing. The skills that a manager brings to bear may not be the same ones that are needed to successfully release and sell records or promote uses of songs. If the manager has to bring in others to fill some of his skills gaps or to fill these roles overseas then the artist./songwriter may lose out financially and/or have to wait longer to be paid.

There is also the big problem of potential conflicts of interest. As a manager he has to put your interests ahead of his own. What would happen if he felt, as your publisher, that it would be best for you to put one of your songs in an advert for a particular brand of lager as it would earn a lot of money but you feel that this would jeopardise your image as an artist popular with the 12–15 year age group. Who would fight your corner? Finally, there is also the issue of the manager having more than one source of income i.e. he has his management commission on your earnings but also his profits as your record label or publisher. It is very important that the management contract doesn't allow the manager to take commission on any source of income that he has other interest in e.g. record sales or income from songs.

Seal v. Wardlow[6]

A recent case on this point is that of *Seal* v. *Wardlow*. John Wardlow began working with Seal who was then an unknown artist in 1987. Mr Wardlow provided studio time, instruments and musicians free of charge. Over the next two years he helped Seal to record some demos and in time his role grew into that of a manager. He had very little experience of management but that in itself is no bar to being a good manager in this industry. The efforts of Mr Wardlow did not at this time result in any deal from a record label or publisher and in 1988 Mr Wardlow went into business as a music publisher himself as part owner of the company Beethoven Street Music. That company entered into a publishing agreement with Seal to publish his songs. Seal had legal advice before signing that deal. The following year Seal collaborated with Adamski and they had a number one hit single with 'Killer'. In 1990 Seal signed a record deal with ZTT Records and a couple of months later finally signed a written management agreement with Mr Wardlow. That deal allowed for Mr Wardlow to receive commission at 20% on Seal's income including publishing monies. As we will see below as Mr Wardlow also benefited as publisher it is usually unacceptable for him to also then take commission on the publishing money paid to the writer. In this case this so-called 'double-dipping' went on for some time. By 1995 Seal felt he had outgrown Wardlow's capabilities as a manager and ended the management agreement. Seal continued with more experienced US management and a settlement agreement was entered into between him and Wardlow in 1995. He continued to pay Mr Wardlow in accordance with that settlement through to 2000 when he stopped. Mr Wardlow sued for what he said was properly due to him. Seal was trying to get out of his agreement to pay on the basis amongst other things that

---

6 *John Wardlow v. Henry Olusegun Adeola Samuel* [2006] EWHC 1492 (QB) 22 June 2006.

Mr Wardlow had used undue influence when in 1988 he had gone behind Seal's lawyers back direct to Seal to persuade him to enter into the publishing agreement and accept the double-dipping. The judge said that Wardlow had not convinced him that he had not used undue influence in relation to that agreement. But the judge thought it was academic as the settlement that they had entered into in 1995 put in place new arrangements, was not a variation of the original agreement and superseded it. The settlement had not been entered into using undue influence; Seal has independent advice and the help of his more experienced new manager. It was a settlement by which Mr Wardlow gave up rights to income from future albums and the settlement was meant to draw a line under these issues.

Seal did not accept the decision and appealed to the Court of Appeal. In February 2007 the Court of Appeal upheld the earlier decision of Mr J Gray and went slightly further to say that it did not matter if the settlement was a variation of the original agreement or a new set of arrangements; it was intended to replace the earlier agreement and was not entered into through undue influence. The Court of Appeal judges felt that by 1995 Mr Wardlow could not have been in a position of trust and confidence with Seal to exercise undue influence; by that time he was no longer the manager.

Some commentators have suggested that this case now takes over from the *Armstrong* v. *Stone* case (above) as the definitive view on undue influence in management cases. In fact the two continue to exist side by side as the judge in this later case found that there was a clear distinction between the two cases on their facts and on what was in the two management contracts so a direct comparison could not be made.

Some managers are better than others at walking the delicate tight-rope here. For example, the 19 Entertainment Group, (formerly owned by Simon Fuller and sold in March 2005 to a US investor on condition that Fuller remains on board and which he is apparently now in the process of buying back), has management contracts with artists but often also acts as record label and music publisher and sometimes as a merchandising/sponsorship company. But the management contract is then only for the remaining activities e.g. live work and there is therefore no conflict of interest or double-dip of the money. In theory the artist can bring in other managers to look after recording, songwriting, merchandising activities etc., in practice few artists do so.

There are other managers who are not so fastidious in keeping the lines clearly drawn as the Seal case shows.

It is a fact of the current business that such arrangements exist and you may well be offered such a deal and may have no alternative than to accept it if you want to work with a particular manager. Many of these arrangements work very well but before you go into them take legal advice and be aware of potential pitfalls.

WHAT IS IN A MANAGEMENT CONTRACT?

Once you've found yourself a manager you think you can trust and who will do a good job for you, you need to think about putting a contract together between you.

What you want out of this contract will be different depending on whether you are an artist or a manager. In what follows I'm going to look at things from the artist's viewpoint, but in my time as a music lawyer I've acted for both artists and managers and so I'll try to present both sides of the argument.

INDEPENDENT LEGAL ADVICE

As we've already seen, when negotiating a management contract the artist must have separate legal advice. The manager may decide not to take legal advice at all but this is rare. He may be experienced enough to feel comfortable with the deal he's prepared to do and doesn't need advice. If he's experienced with management contracts this isn't really a problem. If the artist decides that he doesn't want legal advice, then this is a problem for the manager. The manager should insist on you getting separate advice from someone who is familiar with the music business and with management contracts.

What if you haven't got the money to pay for a lawyer? The Musicians' Union (MU) has a limited free legal advice service for its members, but you can't expect it to be as detailed as if you were paying proper rates for it and it may take some time for you to get the advice (contact details are in Useful Addresses). The Music Managers Forum has forms of management contracts they recommend to their members, and which are drafted from the manager's perspective and so may need adjusting if you are looking at it from the artist's viewpoint.

Some managers will lend you the money to take independent legal advice, because it's in the manager's interests to make sure you're properly advised. If the manager does lend you money to get a lawyer, he will usually put a limit on how much he'll contribute. You'll either have to get the lawyer to agree to do the work for that much or you'll have to put some in as well. The manager will get his contribution back out of your first earnings. Your lawyer may agree to accept payment by instalments if you ask and if he thinks he'll get more work from you in the future.

TERRITORY

The first thing you have to decide is what countries the contract will cover. We call this the territory of the deal.

The manager will probably want to manage you for the world. This isn't just so that he can get as much commission as possible, although that is a factor. He may want to keep overall control of the game plan, which he won't be able to do very easily if he only manages you for part of the world.

You may be fine about this because you're confident that he can look after your interests around the world. But you must bear in mind that the way the music business operates, in the US in particular, is very different from the UK. Does the manager have an office in the States? Does he have an associate there? Or will he be spending half his time on planes crossing the Atlantic? If he is, who's going to end up paying for that? Sometimes it'll be the record company, sometimes it'll be part of a tour budget, but sometimes it'll be you.

If you don't think that the manager can successfully look after your interests worldwide, you could insist that he only manage you for part of the world, for example, the world outside North America.

Even if you aren't sure he's up to being a worldwide manager you could initially give him the benefit of the doubt. You could make it a worldwide deal to start with and, if he's not up to it, you could insist that he appoint a co-manager, probably for the US but possibly for other parts of the world, like Japan, to look after your interests there. This is a very personal thing and both you and your manager should agree the identity of this person.

The co-manager is usually paid out of the commission you pay to the manager. Apart from the co-manager's expenses, you shouldn't end up paying out more in total commission just because there's a co-manager on board.

There are several ways that the manager and co-manager can split the commission between them. They could just take the total worldwide commission and split it down the middle. They could each just take commission on the income earned by you in their particular areas of the world. For example, the co-manager could take commission on the income you earn in North America and your original manager on the rest of the world income. The manager could decide not to share his commission but to put the co-manager on a retainer or pay him a fee. It's a complex subject and the manager should take legal advice on it.

ACTIVITIES COVERED

The next thing to think about is whether the contract will cover everything you do in the entertainment business or just your activities in the music business. You might start out as a songwriter or performer and later move into acting or writing books. The manager may be perfectly capable of managing you for all those activities, or he may be an expert at the music business and know nothing about the business of writing books or acting. If you're not convinced he can look after your interests across the whole of the entertainment industry you should limit it to the music business only. The manager may be unhappy about this. He may think that it will be his management skills that will help turn you into a success in the music business which will in turn open doors to acting or writing books. He may feel that he should share in your income from those other activities. On the other hand, you may be concerned that he's not up to representing your interests and may want a specialised acting or literary agent involved.

Many managers will agree to compromise and say they have no objection to you bringing in specialised acting or literary agents if you are acting in roles or writing books that have nothing to do with you being a successful musician or songwriter first. If the acting role or book is directly connected to the fact that you are an artist, they will want to share that income and manage those projects. For example, if you are asked to write a behind-the-scenes look at your time out on the road with the band, the manager will expect to take commission on your income from that book. If, however, you are asked to write a book on climbing in the Himalayas that clearly has nothing to do with your fame as a successful musician or songwriter, the manager may agree not to take commission on that income.

By the time you get a manager you may already have established yourself in another part of the entertainment business. For example, you may already be a successful TV actor or model. The manager may agree not to manage those areas of activity. He may also agree not to manage or take commission on work that comes from a particular contact or source of work, such as a recording studio, that was in place before he came along. If, however, you ask him to manage projects that come from that source, perhaps by chasing them for payment for you, then it's only reasonable that the manager should be allowed to take commission on that work.

EXCLUSIVITY

Once you've decided what activities he's going to manage and in what parts of the world, the manager will expect to be your only manager for those activities and those areas. He will want to be your exclusive manager. You will not be able to manage yourself or to ask someone else to manage a particular project unless he agrees. This is not only reasonable it's practical. You can't go around accepting work without referring it to your manager as it might clash with something he is putting together for you.

KEY-MAN PROVISIONS

What happens if your manager manages other acts or is part of a management company that manages a number of people? How can you make sure he'll be there for you when you need advice? How do you make sure you aren't fobbed off on to someone else because your manager is busy with the others he manages? Well, first of all you make sure that your management contract says that he has to spend a reasonable amount of time on a regular basis on managing you.

You could possibly go further and insist on what we call a 'key-man' clause being put into the contract. I believe this term comes from insurance policies that are taken out on the life of key individuals in an organisation, which pay out if the key-man dies or is unable to work. You name the manager as a key-man and say that if he's not available to you as and when you need him, you can bring the contract to an end.

Your manager may be very flattered at being named as a key-man, but he or his bosses may feel that it's a bit harsh to allow you to end the contract so abruptly. He may want to say that you can only terminate the contract if he has regularly not been available to you or has been unavailable to you for over, say, six weeks at a time. You have to be sensible about this. If you're buried in a residential studio in the depths of the country, writing or rehearsing material for your next album, it may not be reasonable to expect your manager to be there all the time. If you're in the middle of a major renegotiation of your record contract, however, you can reasonably expect him to be around.

These key-man clauses are also sometimes put into record or publishing contracts, but the companies hate them because they give the artist and the key-man a huge amount of power. If they sack the key-man you can end the contract. Unconfirmed rumour has it that the band Oasis had a key-man clause in their record contract with Creation Records. When Sony first looked to buy the remaining shares in Creation that they didn't already own, they are said to have had to rethink things because Oasis could have walked out of their contracts at the height of their success if the key-man at Creation Records, Alan McGee, was no longer in control at the label. So it seems they had to do a deal with either Oasis at Creation or Alan McGee or with both. It is becoming increasingly difficult to get such provisions as the industry becomes more uncertain as to its future profitability and instances like this don't help.

HOW LONG SHOULD THE CONTRACT RUN?

The contract could be open-ended and carry on until one side or the other decides it's over. This is a very confident position for the manager to take as in theory the artist could dump him just as things are starting to come good and few are this brave.

It could be for a fixed period of, say, one or two years and then, if everything is going well, could continue until one party wanted to end the relationship.

More usually it's for a fixed period of three to five years and at the end of that time the contract is renegotiated or it just ends.

Until the early 1980s, terms of five years or longer were common, but the Armatrading case cast some doubt on that. This is not the case in the US, where terms of five years or longer are still common and given that artists seem to take longer to record and promote each album terms of five years are becoming very common In the UK too.

I can usually be persuaded to agree to a three-year term with the manager having an option to extend it for one or two years. The right to exercise that option should be linked to the manager achieving something for the artist – what I call hurdles.

HURDLES

A hurdle could be that the artist has to have a record or publishing deal or have earned a minimum amount of money within the first three years, although it's difficult to say what the right minimum level of income is.

It's also possible to put hurdles in at an earlier stage of the contract. You could have a get-out if the manager hasn't got you a decent record or publishing deal in the first twelve to eighteen months. Or if he got you a deal in that time and it's come to an end and he hasn't got you another one within, say, six to nine months.

ALBUM CYCLES

This is a US concept, but has gained ground among a number of UK lawyers, where the length of the contract is linked to an album cycle. An album cycle starts with the writing of the songs to be recorded on an album, and runs through the recording of the album and all the promotion that then goes on after its release. The cycle ends with the last piece of promotional work for that album.

My problem with it is that it's very difficult to say how long it will last. You don't know at the beginning how long it will take to write, record and promote an album. I'm uncomfortable with agreeing to two- or three-album-cycle deals, which could easily run for five years or longer. If you're offered this type of deal, I advise you to put a time backstop on it, for example, two album cycles or three years, whichever comes first.

ENDING THE TERM EARLY

Sometimes an artist or a manager wish to part company whilst the term of the contract still has some time to run. If it's all amicable then that's one thing and an agreement on the manager's share, if any, of future income earned by the artist can be reached and put in writing as you would in say an amicable divorce.

If, however, one party wants to go (usually the artist) and the other (usually the manager) doesn't agree or think there are any grounds for an early termination, then the matter is more complicated. In such cases if a settlement can't be reached by negotiation the matter ends up in court. A recent case on this involved Australian singer, Holly Valance.

Holly Valance case

In November, 2003 the case brought by Holly Valance's former manager, Scott Michaelson, came to court. Michaelson was arguing that Valance had wrongly terminated the management contract with him in January 2002 just as her career was taking off. Valance argued that she was in the right in terminating the contract because Michaelson was ill-equipped to manage her burgeoning music career. Like her, Michaelson was a former actor

> in the *Neighbours* television soap. The court sided with Michaelson and found that the contract was unfairly terminated. Michaelson was claiming £160,000 in lost income plus a 20% cut of income from sales of her second album and exemplary damages.

Sometimes you get a settlement which one party then becomes discontented with as in the Seal case above. That old adage of 'where there's a hit there's a writ' certainly seems to hold true.

THE MANAGER'S ROLE

I've already explained a little of what you can expect the manager to do for you. What you can't do, though, is list every single thing that you expect a manager to do. Murphy's Law says that it will be the very thing that isn't listed that causes the problem. There are still some contracts around that try to list things the manager is expected to do: for example, the manager will advise on clothes, image, voice training etc. I think these have an old-fashioned feel about them. I end up imagining what the reaction would be if the Scissor Sisters' or Magic Numbers' manager tried to advise them on their stage image. My management contracts just say that the manager will do all he reasonably can to further the artist's career and to do all the things expected of a manager in the entertainment or music business.

WHAT IS THE MANAGER PAID?
Some would say too much, but if you ever saw a manager working round the clock, seven days a week to make an artist successful, with not even a thank you from him, you'd say it wasn't enough. It is a measure of the fact that many managers are branching into publishing or setting up as production companies that they are unable to make a good living from an averagely successful artist once they've paid the staff, overheads and taxes.

The average rate of commission for a manager is 20%. If you're very successful the 20% could be negotiated down to 10–15%. Some record-producer managers only charge 15% because, arguably, there is less management of projects or a career than there is with performing artists. Very few managers try for a 25% rate though there are some circumstances in which it could be justified. The manager may have invested a lot of his own money in making an artist successful and may want to get that back in commission as soon as possible. He may agree to reduce his commission down to 20% when the artist becomes successful and he's got his investment back.

PERCENTAGE OF WHAT?
A percentage of your gross income but net of some expenses is the simple answer. For example, if you were paid a £100,000 personal advance on signing a record deal, the manager on a commission of 20% would take £20,000.

What if you have to use some of that money to record your album or pay a producer? What happens if you are advanced money by your record company (which they get back or recoup from your royalties) to make a video or to underwrite losses on a tour? Is it fair that the manager takes 20% off the top? The answer is no, it's not. There are a number of exceptions. It's not usual for the manager to take commission on monies advanced to you as recording costs, video costs, and payments to record producers or mixers, sums used to underwrite tour losses and sometimes monies advanced to you to buy equipment.

Example: The record company sets a budget of £200,000 for you to make an album, £50,000 to make a video and £100,000 for you to live on for the next year. The manager usually won't take commission on the £200,000 or the £50,000, but will take commission on the £100,000, i.e. £20,000.

Depending on the manager and the contract, he may say that if you decide to use £20,000 of your £100,000 to buy some equipment, then that's your choice and he's still going to take commission on the full £100,000. Or he might treat the £20,000 spent on equipment as an exception and take his commission on the balance of £80,000.

Commission on earnings from live work can be a problem. The manager usually has to work very hard putting together and running a successful tour. He may feel that he should take his 20% off the top from the income that comes in from that tour. What if the expenses of putting on the tour are so high that the tour makes little or no profit? For example, you take £50,000 in ticket sales and the expenses are £40,000. If the manager took his 20% off the £50,000 (i.e. £10,000) there'd be £40,000 profit left, which would be wiped out by the expenses. As an artist performing every night of the tour you may start to resent the manager making £10,000 when you are getting nothing. As we saw in the Armatrading case, the judge was very critical that Stone took 20% of gross income on touring regardless of whether the tour made a profit.

What tends to happen is that the manager takes his commission on net income on live work after some or all of the expenses are taken off. There are various formulas to arrive at a fair compromise, your lawyer will advise.

Trent Reznor Management Dispute

In June 2007 a US court awarded Trent Reznor of 'Nine Inch Nails' approx. $2.9million in his claim against his former manager John Malm. He brought the case back in 2004 alleging that Malm had mismanaged his finances and in effect defrauded the band out of money by tricking them into signing a contract that gave Malm the rights to 20% of the band's gross income as opposed to the net income. The manager claimed to have not taken advantage of this and that he had not actually collected the additional money. He also pointed out (presumably as evidence of his bona fides) that he had worked for no money for many years. The court nevertheless found that he had taken funds that he was not entitled to and awarded the damages to Mr Reznor.

This case shows the difficulties managers get into when they step outside the established norms.

POST-TERM COMMISSION

This means how long after the end of the management contract the manager continues to get paid commission. It has two sides to it. Firstly, should the manager take commission on albums made or songs written after the end of the management term? Secondly, for how long should he earn commission on albums made or songs written while he was the manager?

WHAT IS COMMISSIONABLE?

Until the early 1980s it was quite usual to see management contracts that allowed a manager to go on earning on things the artist did long after he'd stopped being the manager. If he negotiated a five-album record deal while he was the manager and he stopped being the manager after two albums, he'd still take commission on the remaining three albums because that contract was done while he was the manager. Some contracts also allowed him to continue to take commission after he stopped being manager if someone else negotiated an extension of or substitution for that original contract. Again, because he had done the original work. This led to some very unfair situations. The new manager had no incentive to improve upon deals because it was the former manager who got the commission. Artists found it difficult to get new managers and were forced to stay with the original manager or the artist ended up paying out two lots of commission. This situation was strongly criticised in the Armatrading case and led directly to a change in the way UK managers operated and it is this aspect that the judge distinguished in the Seal case in saying that the facts of the two cases were not the same. Managers now accept that they only get commission on work done, recordings made and songs written while they are the manager.

How long should the manager continue to receive commission?

After it was established that managers should only take commission on what was recorded or written while they were the manager, the question then came up of how long they should go on earning commission on those recordings and songs.

Some managers, notably Sanctuary and other 'old-school' managers, still take the view that they should go on earning commission as long as the artist goes on earning income from a particular song or recording. It remains to be seen whether Sanctuary will continue to take this stance now that it is owned by the Universal Music Group. I can see the logic in this but again it can lead to some unfairness. A manager might have only been around for one album's worth of recordings. It may be a second manager that makes the artist successful. Fans of successful artists want to own all the artists' back catalogue of records and so buy the first album, or a track from the first album may go on a Greatest Hits album. The first manager has done nothing to help ongoing sales of that first album. Should he get full commission on it? Most managers accept that after a period of time their influence cannot be affecting continuing sales of early records, so they agree to a reduction in their commission rate. Most also agree that it should stop altogether after a given period. For example, the first manager could agree that his commission on the first album drops to 10% after five years after the end of the management term and stops altogether after ten years. This means the artist can give the second manager an incentive by giving him 10% of the income on the first album after five years and 20% after ten years. Or the artist could keep the saving himself and give nothing to the second manager.

These periods of time are negotiable. Some music lawyers insist that the commission stop after two or three years. In my view this is far too short for a manager to be properly compensated for the work he has done. It may, however, be acceptable if the artist is established and successful and has greater bargaining power than the manager.

WHAT HAPPENS IF THERE'S NO WRITTEN CONTRACT?

A few managers prefer to work without any written contract. They say they'd rather work on a good-faith basis, trusting you to do the right thing by them. This is a comparatively rare situation but it is also possible for a manager to work for a trial period and then not carry on. Sometimes the manager just can't get the artist to commit to a contract and carries on reluctantly without one. Even where there is no written deal you still have to deal with what the manager gets paid for the work he did. It is, of course, perfectly possible for there to be a verbal contract in place. The difficulty with verbal contracts is that it's very hard to prove what exactly was agreed.

If it's not possible to show that there was any sort of agreement, the manager has to rely on what would be a fair price for the work he has done (a quantum merit claim). If you and the manager can't agree this and there is a court case, the judge will take expert evidence of what's usual in the music business and will make an order of what he thinks the manager should be paid. The court will order payment for the work already done, but it's rare for them to order payments going forward. For example, if the manager got a record deal for you then the court might order that he's paid a percentage of the money payable on signing that deal; but rarely does it order that the manager is paid a share of ongoing royalties. So the manager wouldn't usually get post-term commission. For these reasons it's usually more important for the manager to have a written contract to protect his commission on future royalty income than it is for the artist. However, both sides may want the certainty of knowing where they stand and want to reach some form of agreement.

WHO COLLECTS THE MONEY?

It's very important to know who's looking after the money. The manager may be unhappy at the thought of you looking after the money just **because** you're an artist. Artists are notoriously bad at hanging on to money (they say). 'They can't even keep the money back to pay the VAT or the taxman; how can I trust them to keep enough back to pay me?'

On the other hand, you may be very responsible with your money. You may not want your manager controlling your money, but also may not want to have the bother of looking after it yourself.

A compromise would be for you to appoint an accountant (see Chapter 1). The money is paid into a bank account in your name that the accountant looks after. The manager sends in an invoice for his commission and expenses. The accountant checks the sums are right and writes out a cheque for you to sign. The accountant may also deal with the VAT and he'll almost certainly advise keeping some money back for tax. What happens with the rest of the money depends on what you've told him to do. He could pay it into another account for you or leave some in the bank account to meet expenses.

EXPENSES

On top of his commission, the manager is entitled to be repaid his expenses. That doesn't mean everything he spends. The costs of running his business, his office, staff, computers etc. are all paid for by him. These are called office overheads. If he pays for a taxi to pick you up from the recording studio or for a courier to deliver your demo recording to an interested A&R man, then he will probably reclaim that money from you.

He should keep receipts and bills and have them available for you or your accountant to check. He should also agree that he won't run up expensive items in expenses without checking with you first. I wouldn't expect him to buy a plane ticket to New York without checking that you're all right with him spending your money in that way. On the other hand, it's not practical for him to have to come running to you for every small item of expenses, in which case you might agree a float account. This is a special account with a fixed sum of money, say £500, in it. The manager is authorised to draw money out of that account for expenses and the account is then topped back up to £500 on a regular basis, like a float in a till of a pub or shop.

TAX
You are responsible for your own tax and National Insurance and for paying your VAT. Don't expect the manager to do it for you. As we saw in Chapter 1, your accountant is a very important part of your team. Your accountant may keep the books, do the VAT returns and prepare the tax return for you. This doesn't mean you can sit back and do nothing. You have to tell your accountant what has come in and give him receipts for anything he might be able to reclaim or recharge. Your accountant will also advise what you can expect to have to pay in tax and ways in which you can, legitimately, pay as little tax as possible. But remember, there are, they say, only two certainties in this world – death and taxes.

SIGNING AGREEMENTS
It's practical to allow the manager to sign one-off short-term contracts in the artist's name. For example, when you do an appearance on *Later with Jools Holland* or *The Jonathan Ross Show*, the television company needs the artist to sign a short release or consent form before he can appear and get paid. If you are busy rehearsing, it's all right for the manager to sign that form for you.

What isn't acceptable is for the manager to sign a long-term contract, or indeed anything more than a one-off. It's dangerous for the artist – who won't know what's in it or what's been agreed. It's also dangerous for the manager. You may not object at the time, but when you find something in the contract that's not to your liking you can be sure you'll blame the manager for not telling you.

CONCLUSIONS

- Different lawyers must advise the artist and the manager on the management contract.

- Treat with caution any management contract capable of running for longer than five years.

- 20% is the average management commission for artist managers.

- Commission is on gross income net only of certain exceptions which should be set out in the contract.

- Commission on 'live' work should be after deduction of some or all of the expenses.

- The management deal doesn't need to be for the whole world.

- Make sure it is clear who is handling the money.

- Only the artist should be able to sign potentially long-term contracts.

Chapter 3
What Is A Good Record Deal?

INTRODUCTION

E verybody's idea of what's a good deal is different. For some it's a question of how much money is on offer. For others it's how much commitment there is from the record company. Some artists are more interested in how much control they have over what sort of record they make. We call this creative control.

I'm going to look at these different ideas of what's a good deal. I'm going to do it from the artists' point of view because that's what I know best. But, because I've negotiated so many record deals over the years, I've heard all the arguments from the record companies, so I'll try and put their side too.

There's more than one type of record deal. I'm going to look at four basic types of deal – the licence, the development deal, the exclusive recording contract and the production deal. As we will see it's this last type which is gaining ground fast in the music industry at the moment.

To understand record deals properly you also need to know some law, so I'm going to look at the basic performer's rights, at copyright and at what rights a record company needs in order to exploit recordings.

Incidentally, in the music business we use the word 'exploit' a lot. Some people don't like this word because they associate it with exploitation in the bad sense – misuse of the weak and that sort of thing. When we use it in the context of music business contracts we generally mean 'to use', 'to sell' or 'to make money from' recordings or songs. It's a positive use of the word not a negative one.

You won't be surprised to learn that there have been some celebrated cases over the years to do with recording contracts. I'm going to look at four in this chapter to see what the problem was, what the court decided and what the music business learned from them. I will be concentrating on different models for recording deals involving the company that is releasing the records sharing in the artist's other income streams. This trend was begun by the Robbie Williams/EMI deal in 2002 but has been taken further by Madonna's new deal with Live Nation.

NEW BUSINESS MODELS

Consolidation and change amongst the major record labels continues. Sony and BMG merged their record operations at the beginning of 2005 but that merger was later challenged by European independent label pressure group Impala, which resulted in the decision to allow the merger being reinvestigated by the European Commission. Impala argued that the Commission's original decision to allow the merger did not look sufficiently closely at the effect on the monopoly position in the market place if the catalogues and power of two major labels were merged. The decision to re-open the review led to considerable uncertainly in the two companies concerned and some commentators believe it also led to unwillingness to consummate the long mooted merger between Warners and EMI on the basis that this merger would also be closely scrutinised in Europe. In autumn 2007 the European Commission completed its reinvestigation and once again gave the merger the go-ahead, thereby reducing the number of major record labels to four: Sony/BMG; EMI Group; Warner Group and Universal. As a knock-on effect of these mergers, BMG had to divest itself of its publishing division, which was bought by Universal. That also caused complaints of a monopoly position arising in Universal but the Commission has given its go-ahead to that take-over. Universal Music Group has been on a bit of a buying spree recently buying up the rump of the Sanctuary Group, supposedly to concentrate on its special projects catalogue and on the management activities of the Sanctuary Group. It also acquired independent V2. In the meantime EMI has been bought by a consortium of venture capitalists largely from outside the industry and headed up by Guy Hands. Mr Hands took over the reins in mid-2007 and most of the old level of senior management has gone, including the Chairman Eric Nicoli. Mr Hands is now learning all about the company he has bought and rumours abound that one way he intends to increase the value for his investors is to securitise (a kind of mortgage) the income earned by the music publishing business or even to sell off that part of the business. And it's not only the majors who have been doing deals; Beggars Banquet has bought up the independent label Rough Trade – the home of The White Stripes.

All these labels are focusing on fewer acts and even then it is estimated that only 5% of their signings are successful, which is a pretty poor strike rate. So they are trying to improve the odds, by taking fewer risks and focusing on tried and tested teams of people. The upshot of this is a safer signing policy with more focus on the sure-fire bigger sellers. This makes it more difficult for the more innovative acts to get signed to big deals with the full-blown international support of a major label. Indeed, even those who do get signed to majors will rarely get a cast-iron guarantee that they will get releases outside their home market. Job insecurity in a rapidly shifting market place has also led to 'safe' signings. No one wants to stick his or her neck out and be associated with a 'duff' artist when it comes to the annual job appraisal.

As a direct consequence of this, there has been a growth in the number of independent labels such as Beggars Banquet, B-Unique and Domino, although many of these have financial support from bigger companies either through distribution deals, international licensing deals or actual assistance with overhead funding and provision of a signing fund. There has also been a proliferation of small studio-based production companies whose aim is to develop an artist to the stage where he becomes of interest to the bigger labels who can inject investment to take the artist to the next level whether that be moving from recording an EP to a full album or in marketing or releasing the album overseas. A good example of an artist that came through from the ground level is the 2007 Mercury Prize nominee Fionn Regan. Fionn financed the recording of the Mercury nominated album *The End of History* himself. He then did a licensing deal with independent label, Bella Union and with Damien Rice's label in Ireland. The album was released to critical acclaim if not huge initial sales. This led to interest in the album from US label, Lost Highway, a sub-label of Universal, and ultimately to a world deal with that label.

The idea behind these smaller labels is to act as a nursery or feeder for bigger labels. These independents find the new talent early, sign them up on modest deals, make some recordings either to master or demo quality, depending on the game plan and then hope to attract the attention of the bigger labels whether in the UK or in overseas markets. Often these independent labels have arrangements of a more or less formal nature with bigger labels to act as scouts for them. For the majors some of the risk has been taken away and for the smaller label they get to retain some ownership of copyright and to build their companies on the back of support for marketing and distribution from the bigger company. It is also often the case now that record producers are acting as talent scouts and in the role of developing an artist, building on song-writing skills, rehearsing the artist and making master recordings with them. Their aim is to use their connections to sell the artist on to a label who, they hope, will use them to produce the first album by the artist. The development role used to be one undertaken by the record label but the cutbacks and conservatism, which is pervading the industry, has led to producers and studio owners having to take the initiative. There is more on this subject later in this chapter.

THE HYPE OF THE MILLION POUND RECORD SIGNING

We have all read in the press about new, unknown acts being signed supposedly to million-pound deals. Can you believe what you read? Well, I guess in one or two cases it could be true, but it's pretty unlikely if it's a completely unknown artist. Also have you noticed how it's always a million pound deal not 1.2 million or one and a half million?

What is much more likely is that the deal has been hyped up in the press to make it seem bigger than it is. If you add up all the money that the record company could spend on making an album you could get to a million pounds. That would include the recording costs, the cost of making one or two videos, marketing and touring costs. The artist might only see a fraction of that money himself.

When the record company is making up its mind about what to offer you, it will look at a number of things. First, and most importantly, how much it wants to sign you to the company. If they desperately want you, they'll pay over the odds to get the deal done. If you've got more than one company fighting over you then you've much greater bargaining power. Your manager and lawyer can play one company off against the other and get you a better deal. There is less of that going on at the moment than previously what with the overall uncertainty in the business, the drop in the profits and sales and the reduction in the number of major labels from five down to four but you do still get major companies trying to outbid each other.

If the record company is doing it scientifically they'll use various formulas to work out what's a reasonable deal to offer you. There are computer models that they can use. They look at the type of act you are, at how much they think it's going to cost to record the album and to make videos. They also look at other commitments, possibly to touring. They put these estimates into the model and it tells them how many records you'd have to sell before they break even. If they think that's an unrealistic number they may scale down the offer. This is the theory anyway. I suspect that while they do this number crunching they then go with their hunches anyway as to how well they think you're going to do. There are also other factors at play such as whether it is a good deal to sign in order to get a good slice of the market (so-called 'market share') in a forthcoming quarter so as to look good for the shareholders. Sometimes a deal is done for strategic reasons in order for a particular label or label head to set out their stall as being an important player or wanting to attract a particular type of artist. There are some who believe that Live Nation did the deal with Madonna in order to send the message to other artists of a similar stature that this was a potential new home for them. For more on the Madonna deal see the chapter on Touring below.

We saw in Chapter 1 some of the ways in which you can get a 'buzz' going for you. The 'hotter' you are, the more the record company is likely to pay or the better overall deal you'll be offered. The better your lawyer is, the less likely it is that the record company will get away with paying below the odds – a very good reason to get a good lawyer on your side.

Your manager should sit down with you and discuss what's important to you. Are you only interested in big-money advances, or would you prefer to go for a smaller advance in return for creative control or more commitment from the record company? Once he knows what you want, your manager can make his 'pitch' to the record company along those lines.

It should be a balanced contract, where the record company can reasonably protect its investment, but also one where you get some commitment from the company and the chance to earn a decent living from the deal.

THE LEGAL PRINCIPLES

Before I look in more detail at these questions of money, commitment and creative control, I need to run through with you one of the guiding legal principles in deciding what's a good record deal.

RESTRAINT OF TRADE

We have already seen in the cases of *O'Sullivan* v. *MAM*, *Armatrading* v. *Stone* and *John* v. *James* that the courts can be highly critical of clauses in contracts that are unfair on the artist.

In deciding whether a contract is fair, the court looks at a number of things. It looks at the bargaining power of the artist and the company. It will also look at whether the artist had independent specialist advice before he signed the contract, and at how experienced the artist was in the music business at the time the contract was signed. It does this against the background of what was the norm for these contracts at the time.

Another guiding principle behind the court's decisions is that of restraint of trade. The basic principle behind the doctrine is that, where someone has to provide services or be exclusively employed and the contract contains restrictions on what someone can and cannot do, that contract is automatically a restriction on the ability to earn a living, or trade. Because it's an exclusive arrangement, the person concerned can't earn money in any other way than through that contract.

In the UK it was decided long ago that these contracts were contrary to public policy. A person should be free to earn his living wherever he can. That said, the courts recognised that there would be circumstances where it was commercially necessary to have restrictions in contracts. They decided that such restrictions would be allowed if they were reasonably necessary to protect the legitimate business interests of the person imposing the restrictions. If the restrictions were unreasonable they couldn't be enforced – the contract would be unenforceable.

Because it was so important to the music business, the case of *Macaulay* v. *Schroeder*[1] went all the way to the House of Lords before it was finally clear that the doctrine did apply to recording and publishing agreements.

Macaulay v. *Schroeder*

Macaulay was a young and unknown songwriter who entered into a music publishing agreement with Schroeder Music Publishing Ltd. It was an exclusive agreement for his services for five years. The contract was in a standard form used by the music publisher. Macaulay's copyrights in the songs he wrote were assigned for the life of copyright throughout the world. The contract specifically prevented him from working as a songwriter for any other music publishers during this five-year period. There's nothing wrong in signing someone up to an exclusive deal, but because it restricts that person's ability to go and work for anyone else, we have to look at whether as a whole such a contract is fair, at whether the restrictions still allow him to earn a reasonable living. The House of Lords looked at the specific terms of the agreement to see if, taken as a whole, they were reasonable. It found, in fact, that they were unduly restrictive and an unreasonable restraint of trade. Macaulay didn't have a reasonable chance to earn a decent living from his trade of song writing.

In contrast, the George Michael case described below is an example of an exclusive contract that was found to contain reasonable restrictions.

CREATIVE CONTROL VERSUS LARGE ADVANCES

Earlier in this chapter I spoke of getting the right balance in the contract terms. Behind that statement lies this principle that any restrictions in an exclusive services contract should be fair and only go so far as to protect the record company's interest and not unreasonably restrict an artist's ability to earn a living. So let's look at some of these terms.

DO YOU GO FOR THE MONEY OR TRY TO PROTECT THE INTEGRITY OF YOUR ART?

Of course it's important for you to be able to eat, to have somewhere to live, and transport to get you to and from gigs, rehearsals and the recording studio, but it may not just be a question of money. For many artists, creative control of their work is at least as important. Being able to make a record with minimal interference from the record company is crucial to some artists.

If creative control is the most important thing for you, then getting that control would mean you had a 'good' deal, even if there was less money on the table as a result. Some record companies are more flexible than others on questions of creative control. If this is an important issue for you, you need to look at this at the point when various record companies are still courting you. You should ask each of them what their attitude is to this issue. What is their track record? If you can, you should talk to other artists signed to the record company to find out their experiences. You should also ask if the record company is prepared to guarantee creative control in the record contract. Sometimes they'll say it but won't put it in the contract so you can't rely on it.

---

1 *Macaulay v. Schroeder Music Publishing Co. Limited* (1974) 1WLR 1308, HL.

Your wish to have creative control must be balanced against putting so many restrictions on what the record company can do that they can't sell your records properly. They may in such circumstances choose to use another artist's recordings – one who isn't so particular about creative control. For example, a proposal comes in from an advertising company to put one of two tracks into a major new jeans campaign. Artist A has full creative control in his contract and is known to be completely against the idea of his work being used in ads. Artist B, on the other hand, has an eye to the integrity of his work but realises that a campaign like this, if done properly, can really help him break into the big-time. Artist B says yes and the record company puts their track forward not Artist A's.

You may be very interested in getting as much commitment as possible from a record company. If so, then you'll concentrate on getting a commitment from them to a specific figure in marketing 'spend' or to underwrite tour losses up to a fixed amount. The record company may be reluctant to go this far. They'd be in difficulties under the contract if, for example, there weren't enough suitable tour dates or they were unable to find the money to pay for the full marketing spend. It used to be the case that artists were concerned that there'd be a commitment to make at least one promotional video per single release, or to get a commitment to the release of a minimum number of singles. Now with the increase in popularity of single track downloads release of singles is rarely the issue. The problem is how to make sure that you make money from some source whether that's actual record sales or as a taster to drive the fans to buy the album, a ticket to your live show and a T-shirt at the show. Because of the continuing importance of radio play in promoting a new release (and to some extent in getting the artist to perform the single on TV or radio shows like those hosted by Jonathan Ross, Paul O'Grady or Russell Brand), A&R people are very interested in hearing tracks that they know will get radio play to promote the artist. There is a strong belief amongst labels that in order to get commercial success in terms of number of sales you need to get radio exposure, preferably 'A' or 'B' list at Radio 1 or 2. To some extent, therefore, marketing is driving creativity and artists that are not necessarily radio friendly have to look for other ways to attract the attention of the public.

The attitude to videos is also changing. The decline in music programmes on television which are likely to show a promotional video has led to a down-sizing in the number of and spend on promotional videos. Now it's much more likely to be a 'behind the scenes' long form DVD on the making of the album or out on the road with the artist. It's expensive to make videos and record companies may not want to commit to making one that only gets played once or twice. That said there has been a growing interest in the availability of visual images in recent years to feed the demand for DVD and online content, so you may find it isn't necessary to insist on a commitment to make videos because it will happen in practice.

Whatever the issue may be and no matter what big statements and promises they make when they want you, if it's not specifically in the contract you won't have a chance of making them keep their promises if they go back on what they said or if the person who said it is no longer with the company.

Whatever your particular needs (and it may be a mixture of all of these things), if you get a reasonable number of them in your record contract you'll have what is a good deal for you.

This whole issue of creative control versus money has caused a lot of problems over the years. It's one of the reasons why Prince became 'Symbol' became The Artist Formerly Known As Prince, then The Artist, before finally reverting to Prince for a sell-out 21-date concert series at the new live venue, O2, in the former Millennium Dome in Docklands. He may have believed that by changing his name he could use a loophole to get out of his record contract. He was probably also hoping that it would show his record company, Warner Bros., the strength of his feeling over the type of records he wanted to make. He was in the news again in 2007 when it was announced that he had done a ground-breaking deal with newspaper publishers of the *Mail on Sunday* to offer the whole album 'free' with the newspaper ahead of traditional retail distribution. It is said he received $500,000 for the deal. Plans for a traditional physical CD release were cancelled. Unsurprisingly, many more copies of the newspaper were bought than on a normal Sunday and Prince got exceptional publicity out of this marketing coup. More people bought tickets to see him live than might otherwise have done so and he presumably got a good financial return firstly from the price he got off the *Mail on Sunday* and secondly in his increased share of ticket sales and extra merchandising sales. There is a growth in the use of cover mounts to market artists. The practice was decried by record companies and artists because it seemed to be a way of getting a large one-off payment for the record company in the licence deal with the newspaper without having to share that necessarily with the artist (depending on the deal). It was also felt to be devaluing the artist's work. Now we are seeing this practice evolve into one where perhaps ahead of an artist's new album release they may bring that artist back into the public eye by a cover mount DVD or album of some of their old material or previously unavailable film footage of a tour. Sometimes it works, other times it doesn't. The record company behind Ray Davies' latest release thought to do this by releasing a cover mount album of versions of his old material but it didn't have the hoped for boost in first week sales of the new album.

Disputes as to issues like this or as to how an artist is presented creatively, as well of course as to whether the artist is getting paid a fair price take place on a daily basis between record company and artist or manager. It is part of the daily cut and thrust between them. I regularly have to arbitrate or advise on issues like who has final say on choice of single, or the look of the artwork for the new album because artist and label have different views. Another area of common dispute is what happens when a label decides after hearing the finished album that they don't want to release it. This is part of my daily working life but most of these disputes don't get to court. One that did was the acrimonious case between George Michael and his record company, Sony Records.

The George Michael Case

To understand the case[2] and the decision you need to know a bit about the background.

As we all know, George Michael was part of the very successful pop duo Wham! along with Andrew Ridgeley. The first exclusive record deal that George and Andrew signed was with the record company Innervision, owned by Mark Dean, in 1982. As is often the case, they were young, unknown and inexperienced. The record deal was for up to ten albums, which was a lot even in those days. They were exclusively tied to the company until they'd

2 *Panayiotou v. Sony Music Entertainment (UK) Limited* (1994) EMLR 220.

delivered all the albums that Innervision wanted from them. Applying the doctrine of restraint of trade, the restrictions in the contract were immediately contrary to public policy and were unenforceable unless they were reasonable.

Innervision was a small record company. It had a deal with Sony whereby Sony provided funding and facilities for the manufacture, sale and marketing of Innervision's records. The Innervision contract with George and Andrew, therefore, also included Sony's standard business terms. If the Innervision contract was criticised as being unenforceable and an unreasonable restraint of trade, this could also have been an indirect criticism of Sony's terms of business.

At first things went well, and their second release, 'Young Guns', was a UK Top 10 hit in 1982. This was followed by 'Bad Boys', 'Club Tropicana' and the chart-topping album *Fantastic*. By 1983, however, the relationship between Wham! and Innervision had broken down. They sued the company to get out of the contract, arguing that it was an unreasonable restraint of trade. The case was settled before it got to court. It was part of the settlement that George and Andrew signed an exclusive recording contract direct with Sony label Epic Records. Again, that contract contained Sony's business terms, but an experienced music business lawyer negotiated it on George and Andrew's behalf.

Once again things went well at first. Their first single on Epic – 'Wake Me Up Before You Go Go' – went to No. 1 in the UK and was followed by four further No. 1s in quick succession.

In 1986, George and Andrew parted company. George embarked on a solo career with Sony. And it was a very successful one, although not until 1988 with the release of 'I Want Your Sex', which was a deliberate move to break with the playboy Wham! image. His first solo album, *Faith*, was a huge success, selling over 10 million copies. On the back of that success, George renegotiated his contract with Sony again with the help of that experienced music business lawyer.

In return for a substantial sum of money, George agreed to record three solo albums in the first contract period and gave Sony options for up to five more albums. *Faith* counted as the first of the three albums and he went on to record and release a second hugely successful album, *Listen Without Prejudice (Vol. 2)*, which also sold millions. His star was also rising in the US, where he had a No. 1 with 'Praying For Time' off that album.

Not surprisingly, Sony wanted George to continue in the same style with his third solo album. By this time, George wanted to move away from the out-and-out commercial pop style of records. He wanted to be regarded as a serious artist.

Because the contract ran until he had delivered up to six more albums, or for a maximum period of fifteen years, George couldn't record for anyone else. Sony also had the final say on whether an album by him met the necessary artistic and commercial criteria. They could go on rejecting more serious material from him, so a deadlock existed.

George sued, arguing that the record contract was an unreasonable restriction on his ability to earn a living, and as such was an unenforceable contract.

He refused to record for Sony and instead did a number of projects with other artists that were within the terms of his contract, just. For example, he did guest spots on other people's albums. He also concentrated on live work.

The case finally came to court in 1994. The decision to throw out George's case was made on somewhat surprising grounds. The judge ruled that, in order to decide if the 1988 renegotiation of the contract was an unreasonable restraint of trade, he would also have to consider the earlier 1984 contract. He decided that he could not reopen a review of the 1984 contract because it had been entered into as a result of a settlement of a dispute. It's contrary to public policy to reopen something that was agreed by the parties as being a final settlement of a dispute.

It wasn't difficult to imagine that George would appeal. Perhaps the judge realised this because, even though he had decided that he could not look at the 1988 contract, he went on to say what his conclusions would have been if he had done so.

The contract was an exclusive worldwide deal. It was for potentially a very long time and Sony had the absolute right to reject recordings and a limited obligation in the contract to do much with any recordings that it did accept. Obviously, Sony argued that the contract represented only the contractual obligations that it had and that, in fact, it would have done far more to help sell as many records as possible. In deciding whether the contract was unfair and unenforceable as being an unreasonable restraint of trade, the judge looked at the relative bargaining power of the two sides. By 1988 George Michael was a very successful and powerful artist and well able to stand up to Sony. He had had the benefit of advice from his long-standing lawyer, who was very experienced in music business contracts. Finally, the judge looked at what George would get out of the contract. Financially, he stood to get a great deal.

Balancing out all these factors, the judge decided that the benefits George got out of the contract meant that the restrictions in it were reasonable to protect Sony's investment and its legitimate business interests.

Sony, of course, was delighted, but it was nevertheless seen by most of the 'talent' in the business as a blow for creative freedom.

While the case was going on it was much easier to get improvements in record contracts, particularly those parts of the contracts that George was specifically attacking. For example, on CD sales, Sony was only paying 75–80% of the royalty at the time. While the case was going on Sony was much more inclined to agree a 100% royalty rate. As soon as Sony won the case it was business as usual. George, as expected, appealed. The thought of prolonged, expensive litigation with an artist who clearly wasn't going to record for Sony, and who could see his own recording career stalling with all the delays, led to a settlement before the appeal was heard. George was released from the contract and signed to Virgin/Dreamworks in return for a payment back to Sony. As part of the settlement, he later recorded some new tracks or new versions of old tracks for a Greatest Hits album that was released on Sony.

Aston Barrett v. Universal Island Records and others

In a dispute over monies due the bass player for 'Bob Marley and the Wailers, Aston Barrett sued Island Records and the Marley family on behalf of himself and his brother, Carlton (who was the drummer with the band and was murdered in 1985). Aston argued that he had not received the money they were due after Marley's death in 1981. Aston and Carlton had played on a number of Marley albums. They had had their own successful act The Upsetters and joined Marley after Peter Tosh and Bunny Livingstone left. Their claim for royalties arose out of a contract made in 1974. Ashton was also suing separately for his proper share of song-writing royalties on songs he co-wrote with Marley. Originally Marley and the two Barrett brothers had shared royalties equally. It was alleged that under a new agreement made in 1976 Marley took 50% and the Barrett brothers shared the remaining 50% between them. In 1994 Aston took part in a settlement where it was said he agreed to forego any right to future royalties in return for a share of a $500,000 settlement paid by Island Records. At the trial Marley's widow and the founder of Island Records both played down the role played by the Barrett brothers and said that the 1994 settlement represented a fair share to them for what they had done. The judge accepted that and refused Aston's claim. He also did not accept his claim that he had co-written several of the songs. Aston was something of a serial litigator having sued three or four times before. The judge ruled that he would not be allowed to start any more litigation unless allowed to do so by a court.

TYPES OF DEAL

What types of deal may be on offer, what basic rights does a performing artist have, what is copyright and what rights does the record company need in order to release records?

Although there are many variations, some of which will be looked at below, there are two basic types of record deal – the licence and the exclusive long-term recording contract. Variations include the production deal, which contains elements of the latter two types, the partnership or joint venture between record label and artist, and the so-called 360 degree model which embraces not only recordings but also other areas such as publishing, live and endorsements under the one umbrella deal. The latter are currently 'flavour of the month' with the Madonna deal being the most highly publicised. More on these below. Let's look first at the basic types.

LICENCE DEALS

Legal Principles
Licensor is the technical term for a person or company who owns rights, which it is licensing to someone else. **Licensee** is the person or company to whom the rights are licensed.

A **licence** is an agreement to allow the Licensee to do certain things with the rights that the Licensor has to a particular product – a recording, a song and so on. A licence can be for as long as the life of copyright (see below) but is usually for a shorter period. The Licensor continues to own the rights but gives someone else permission to use some or all of those rights.

In contrast an **assignment** is an outright transfer of ownership of rights by an owner to someone else. It's usually for the life of copyright, although sometimes the rights are returned (reassigned) to the owner sooner than that. The assignment can be of some or all rights and can have conditions attached. The **assignor** is the owner of the rights being assigned. The assignor no longer owns the rights once they have been assigned. The **assignee** is the person or company to whom the rights are assigned.

You will often see in agreements a reference to rights being granted for the **life of copyright**. This is now the same period throughout the EU. For literary and musical works (e.g. songs) it's seventy years from the end of the year in which the author dies. For sound recordings and performer's rights it's fifty years from the end of the year in which the recording was released or the performance was made.[3] The situation is different in the US where in many cases the sound recording copyright can run for up to 99 years.

---

3 Section 16(2) CDPA.

There was considerable political lobbying going on with the UK Government and to some extent in Europe, whereby interested parties tried to further extend the life of copyright. A detailed report was prepared by Mr Gowers, which was published in 2007. It declined to recommend any extension and only offered up a small amount of comfort for the music industry e.g. an increase in the budget for Trading Standards to assist them in their anti-piracy efforts. The political battle has now moved to Europe. Part of the reason for the fuss is that many recordings including those by artists such as Elvis Presley and Cliff Richard are coming out of copyright and as such any future uses of those recordings will not be subject to the payment of record royalties to the artists or to their record label. Representative bodies for the lesser performers were also seeking parity with their song-writing colleagues by getting an extension to seventy years. For the moment this plan has failed and re-issue labels are already cashing in with early 1950s recordings which are already out of copyright. The record company who owned the original recordings will find that its market is no longer protected. Some argue that this is a good thing as fifty years is long enough to have achieved a reasonable return on the investment in making and promoting the records and it is right that they are then made freely available. However, there are also others who believe that the loss of revenue from these recordings will result in yet another nail in the coffin of the record industry and mean less investment in new artists. There are some practical difficulties in the way of companies seeking to take advantage of this, for example, in getting hold of original recordings or good quality copies of the same. The artwork or sleeve notes and the songs may still be in copyright so use of the artwork or changes to the original songs will not be possible without consent. But if the re-issue label is willing to invest in some new artwork and will pay the mechanical royalties to the owners of any songs that are still in copyright (see publishing chapter) then the re-issue label is still making a good profit by not having to pay for the recording nor the artist for the performances or the record label for the right to license those recordings. The record companies are running scared – hence the rush of re-releases of Beatles box sets and wholesale re-releases of the Elvis singles in order to cash in on what may be their last chance before their market is undermined as copyright ends. This is also why they are doing new versions such as remixes or mashups of the Elvis songs so that they can claim a new copyright in the new version and hang on to rights in that for another fifty years.

The **author** is the first owner of the copyright.[4] The CDPA 1988 says that in the case of sound recordings it's the producer. This could be confusing, and for a time record producers were claiming they were the copyright owners. The position is in fact the same as before the 1988 Act. The copyright owner of a sound recording is the person 'who made the arrangements for the recording to be made'. This is generally taken to mean the person who paid for the recording to be made. With the changing role of managers and producers in making independent recordings there will be issues about whether the artist, the manager, the producer or even the studio owns the copyright. I am already dealing with situations of multiple ownership of copyright with the attendant problems of trying to decide mechanisms for what is to happen to the copyrights when it comes to commercial exploitation. The artist may need to rely more than ever on their performance rights to ensure a measure of control and also through song-writing where they are writers of the songs being recorded.

4 Sections 17-27 CDPA.

Copyright is the right that an author has to prevent anyone else doing certain things with his work without his permission. It underlines all creative aspects of the music industry so it is important to try and get to grips with it. The basic rights of copyright are the right to copy the work; the right to issue copies of the work to the public; the right to rent or lend out copies of the work to the public; the right to perform, show or play the work in public; the right to broadcast the work or include it in a cable programme; the right to make an adaptation of the work and the right to do any of these acts in relation to that adaptation.[5] Before anyone can do any of these things with a copyright work, they have to get the permission of the owner of the copyright. This may be the author as first owner or he may have assigned his rights to someone else or given someone else an exclusive licence to deal with the copyright instead of him. There was some doubt until 2001 as to whether the copyright laws of the EU extended to digital, online or Internet-based uses of the copyright. A 2001 European Directive confirmed that copyright did indeed extend to such new media. The Directive was implemented into UK law late in 2003. The UK Government took the view that the existing UK law already covered many of the key aspects of the Directive so the changes to UK law were more to clarify than to extend the law. The definition of what constituted communicating and making available a copyright work to the public was clarified as including Internet, cable and satellite broadcasts, including on-demand services. The law was confirmed as applying to authors, record labels, film producers, broadcasters and performers. There was much debate about the exemptions to the basic rule requiring the copyright owners' permission to reproduce the whole or part of a copyright work. These are the so-called fair dealing exemptions where, for example, an excerpt from a recording or part of a video could be reproduced for purposes of a critical review or commentary. It was felt that there was greater scope for abuse of this exemption in the widespread and fast moving online world. In the end the exemptions were not extended and quoting of a 'reasonable amount' will still be permitted. We will see in Chapter 7 an aspect of this debate in connection with social networking sites like YouTube or MySpace. Are they allowed to rely on these fair-dealing exemptions to put up copyright works on these sites without consent of the owner?

As I mentioned above with the growing complexity of record deals and multiple potential copyright owners the issue of performing rights will become more important. **Performing rights** are the rights performers have to prevent someone else from doing certain things with their performances, or with recordings of their performances, without their permission. The basic performing rights are in some respects similar to the rights of copyright. They are the right to prevent someone making a recording of a live performance; the right to prevent the making of a broadcast or its inclusion live in a cable service programme. It is also a performer's right to prevent someone from making a recording of his performance directly from a broadcast or cable programme. The performer's permission has to be obtained to do any of the above. Recordings of performances for personal use are allowed. The performer also has the right to refuse to let someone make a copy of a recording; to issue a copy of a recording to the public; to rent or lend copies of the recording to the public; to play a recorded performance in public; or to include it in a broadcast or cable programme service. As we've seen above

---

5 Directive 2001/29/EC.

the performer's rights also extend to online methods of making their work available to the public. The performer should make sure he only grants his performing rights when he is reasonably sure that the agreement gives him either control or sufficient financial reward for losing control.

Licence versus assignment

When deciding on whether to license or assign rights it is important to make a distinction between a licence and an assignment. When an owner grants a licence, he keeps the underlying copyright. He only gives the licensee permission to do certain things with the copyright for a period of time (the licence term). In contrast when rights are assigned then ownership and control of the copyright has passed from the owner to the assignee.

It is clear from the Gilbert O'Sullivan case that, even where the court finds that a contract is unenforceable, it won't usually order the return of copyrights or other rights that have been assigned. If it's a licence then the underlying copyright has not been assigned; there is nothing that needs to be returned to the original owner because it never left him. If O'Sullivan had licensed his rights rather than assigned them he wouldn't have had such a problem. The licence would have come to an end because MAM were in breach of its terms and he would still have had his copyright in his songs and masters. So from the point of view of an artist, a licence should always be preferable to an assignment, all other things being equal.

There are two problems with this. The first is that the record company will in many cases be the one who made the arrangements for the recording to be made (i.e. paid for it) and so will be the first owner of copyright. The artist may have his performing rights, but will probably not own the copyright in the sound recording. The second is that record companies don't want to do licence deals if they can take an assignment of rights instead. They have investments to protect. It can take up to a million pounds or more for a major record company to launch a new act. They will want to own the copyright outright. They don't want to lose their rights when a licence ends, because these rights represent assets of the company and have money value to the company. The longer they have them and the more secure the ownership is the more value they have.

The more successful an artist is, the more chance he has of being the owner of the copyright in the sound recording and in a position to license it to the record company. In production or partnership deals or joint ventures it is more likely that the artist and label will jointly own the copyright and may well be in a position to keep that copyright and license it on rather than assigning these rights away. The argument would be that the bigger label had not taken the commercial risk in investing in the making of the recordings so should not take ownership either at all or unless the money paid is significant.

Exclusive and non-exclusive deals

You might licence rights in a recording that you own to a record company for inclusion on a particular compilation only and probably on a non-exclusive basis. You might want to put the recording out yourself or license it to another company for a different compilation. You couldn't do that if you'd given the first record company an exclusive licence. The same principle applies to the grant of the right to put a recording in a film or advert.

On the other hand, you may be an artist or a small label that has recorded a track or an album yourself and own the copyright in it. You may not have the financial resources to do anything with that recording. Perhaps you can't afford to press up copies of it to sell or you can't promote it properly. You might go to another record company for those resources. If they agree, the licence is likely to be an exclusive one to protect their investment.

The licence term
How long should the licence last? If it's non-exclusive it doesn't matter as much. An exclusive licence could be as long as the life of copyright or as short as a year. Three- to five-year licence terms are common. The licensee wants to have long enough to get a reasonable return on his investment, but if it is a short licence term the licensor will get the rights back sooner and may be able to re-license them to someone else (perhaps with a new mix) or release them himself. Most licence deals I'm doing at the moment are for five years or longer with European and US companies often wanting seven to ten years. As usual it's down to knowing and using your bargaining power.

Territory
It could be a worldwide licence or it could be limited to particular countries. If, for example, you've already licensed the rights exclusively to a company in the US, you can only then grant other licences in the same recordings for the rest of the world outside the US.

A distinction used to be made between the UK and other European counties, but one of the consequences of closer European integration has meant that Europe-wide deals, including the UK, are now more common than UK-only deals.

There are people who specialise in trying to get you licence deals for particular countries. They usually take a commission (called a finder's fee) of 2–5% of the advances or royalties. Sometimes they also take a finder's fee off the licensee for bringing the recording to them and so are rewarded by both sides. Nice work if you can get it.

The main problem with individual-country deals is keeping on top of a number of different licensees. Record releases and marketing campaigns have to be co-ordinated and there isn't just one company to chase for payment of royalties. The main advantage is that there is the chance to license the recording to the company that most wants it in each country. You may also be in the fortunate position of ending up with more in total advances from individual-country deals than you'd get from one multi-territory deal, and may also receive more than you need in contributions to make videos or do remixes.

Options
When you're doing a non-exclusive licence of a single track for a compilation, you don't usually give the licensee any options to any further recordings you may make. It's usually a one-off.

If it's an exclusive licence for something other than just on a compilation, the licensee may be keen to get follow-up products. The licensee may be encouraged to invest more in promoting the first track or album if he knows he's going to get the follow-up.

When doing your exclusive licence deal, you can agree up-front the basis on which you are going to give them any follow-up product or you can leave it to be agreed at the time they exercise the option. This can be to the owner's advantage if the first track has been successful, as his bargaining power will be higher. It's not a very certain state of affairs though and often leads to problems, so I don't generally recommend it.

Another possibility would be to give the licensee an option, which gives him the opportunity to be the first to try and do a deal with you for the follow-up. For example, you might deliver a demo of the follow-up and give the licensee the exclusive right for a month to try and negotiate a deal with you. If no deal is done in that time you can take it into the market place. This is called a first negotiating right.

You could give the licensee a matching right. This is the right to match any offer for the follow-up that you get from someone else. You have to tell the licensee the details of the offer, and if the licensee matches or betters it within a given period of time then you must do the deal with him. This has to be handled very diplomatically if you are not to seriously upset the first record company making the offer that has been 'matched'.

Sometimes you do a combination of the two known as a 'first and last matching right' i.e. they get the first option to negotiate, if that fails you can go into the market place to seek a deal, if you get one you must first give the first company a chance to match it, if they do they get to do the deal. Again diplomacy is the order of the day.

EXCLUSIVE RECORDING CONTRACT
This type of deal may give you the greatest potential investment and commitment from a record company but in return, of course, the record company will expect to be able to protect its investment and is likely to seek greater financial and creative controls.

Development Deal
A variation on the exclusive recording deal is a development deal where the record label signs an artist up exclusively for a period of time during which they may record some demos or enough tracks for an EP. The artist is given a recording budget and the means to pay for a producer but not usually much by way of money to live on. It is not yet time to give up the day job. If things go well with the development stage then the record label usually has the option to decide to go on to make the rest of the album and probably then have options to more albums as in a normal record deal. If you get offered one of these deals you may be disappointed that it isn't a commitment to the whole deal. But it is a foot in the door and if you make the most of it you can use it as a stepping stone to your end goal. If they don't proceed with the deal you can ask for the demos back so you have at least got some well recorded material with which to continue your search for fame and fortune.

It will be up to your advisers to make sure that whatever contract you are offered is a fair one. It should also be in the record company's interest. If the contract is so unfair that it's an unreasonable restraint of trade it will be unenforceable and you can walk away from it. Most major record companies have now moderated their contracts to deal with this issue and, while individual cases will still arise of unenforceable contracts, you should never enter into a contract thinking you can tear it up if it no longer suits you. Quite apart from this being a very negative approach it is likely that you will not just be allowed to walk away and may get embroiled in a lengthy dispute or court case. Whilst this is going on it will be difficult for you to carry on with your career and could stall it permanently.

It's likely under an exclusive recording contract that the sound-recording copyright will be owned by the record company, and the contract will usually confirm this. The contract will also make sure that the record company will be able to exploit the performances by getting all necessary performers' consents. So it is important that the contract is also balanced by suitable controls over what the record company can do with the recordings and performances.

One thing you might not want them to do is to put your recording with an advert for a product that you don't approve of. I was once involved in a case where Sting was furious that a recording of his track 'Don't Stand So Close To Me' was used in an advert for deodorant. Tom Waits also took exception to a use of one of his songs in a Levi ad. Not everyone wants, or perhaps needs, to make money at any cost. In fact Tom Waits is something of a serial defender of his image and creative output. You would have thought by now that advertising companies thinking of using his work or that of a sound-alike would have learned that he does not take kindly to this but yet again this year he has had to take a company to court to protect his position.

Term of the contract
The contract will usually run for an initial period of one year. The record company will usually have a number of options to extend the contract term. In each contract period they'll expect the artist to record a minimum number of tracks. It could be single tracks or enough tracks to make up an album. The commitment is generally for an album unless it's a development deal when they might call for five or six tracks to start with and then decide whether to go for the balance of an album. Despite the fact that there has been a growth in downloads of single tracks with over 2 billion dollars of revenue generated for record companies in 2006 according to the IFPI the emphasis is still very much on the delivery of enough tracks to make an album. Indeed some artists/labels are refusing to allow their music to be available on the Apple websites because Apple will not commit to selling tracks as a bundled together album as opposed to unbundling the tracks for single track downloads. About forty years ago singles were the norm and albums consisted mostly of collections of previously successful singles. Whilst there is no sign at present that record labels are returning to these days the traditional seventy minute plus CD album consisting of singles/album tracks and tracks which quite frankly are 'fillers' may evolve into something new – maybe a hybrid of a singles and an album deal. Each contract period is usually extended by up to six months after the artist delivers the last of the recordings the record company wants. The more slowly these are recorded and delivered, or the longer it takes to release them, the longer each contract period will be. It is however generally accepted that there should be a maximum backstop for how long each period can be extended. Otherwise the fear is that the contracts will be unenforceable as they are too open-ended and potentially a restraint of trade Three or four year backstop dates are common.

Why is it only the record company that has options?
The record company will have invested a lot of money in making the records. It will probably also have made videos and may have supported the artist while he's been out touring. These costs are recoupable (i.e. the record company gets some or all of them back from royalty from sales of records) but, if they don't sell enough records, or the artist were to walk out of the contract before the record company had the chance to recoup their investment, then all these unrecouped costs would be down to the record company.

Then there are the promotional and marketing costs, which for a major release can run into hundreds of thousands of pounds, as well as the manufacturing and distribution costs. In most deals these costs are non-recoupable from the artist's royalties. If the artist could just up and walk away from the contract whenever he felt like it the record company wouldn't be able to protect its investment, its business interests. This is why the options are in their favour not the artist's.

Why can't you get your copyright back?

It is easy to understand why a record company justifies its ownership of copyright in the recording by the fact that it's invested a lot of money. What's less easy to understand is why the company won't transfer that copyright to the artist once they've recouped that investment. George Michael argued this point in his case with Sony, but the way the case went meant that there is no definitive decision on the point. Given the reluctance of the courts in cases like Gilbert O'Sullivan's to upset the economic order, it seems that the courts would be very unlikely to order a return of copyrights.

Record companies claim that the vast majority of artists don't recoup their investment. Recent statistics suggest that as many as 95% of all artists fail to achieve profitability. This is a depressing thought, and it is one of the reasons why the record industry is having such a massive rethink about how it makes money from artists who are successful. Falling CD sales because of the problems of free downloads means that unless they can either improve the number of successful artists or get more money for the number who are successful and preferably both then the doom mongers declare the end of the record industry is nigh. I speculate a little more about this in Chapter 7 but if anyone did have the magic answer then they would presumably already be applying it and making themselves a fortune. In the meantime the rest of us struggle on earning what we can and in my case facilitating the contracts that provide the financial support for artists to sell records. Those contracts are for the foreseeable future going to insist that the record companies hang on to the copyrights of the small minority of artists who are successful as without these assets their companies become almost worthless. Record companies also say that they have to spend a lot of money in researching and developing new talent. If they had to return the copyrights of successful artists they say they wouldn't be able to invest as much in new artists in the future and that the culture of the nation would suffer as a result. Well, I can think of a few bands that made barely a dent in the cultural richness of my life, can't you? But seriously though that is also not so true as it once was as more and more record companies are not developing artists but are waiting until they are presented to them almost fully formed with a body of songs, many of which will have been recorded and produced to a high standard and with an artist with professional managers or production companies in place. So this argument too is getting to look quite spurious. The reality is that you just aren't going to get those copyrights back unless you are a David Bowie or a Rolling Stone and even they would be less likely to achieve that if they tried it in the current climate.

How many options should the record company have for future albums?

Most major record companies in the UK want options on four or five further albums.[6] Independent record companies may accept less. That said, every now and again one or two unusual deals occur where record companies have been so keen to sign up particular

---

6 In the US options for six or seven further albums are commonplace.

artists that they have done non-exclusive, one-album deals, with no options. In some cases the deals are seen as purely short-term deals to improve the record company's share of the record sales in a particular quarter or before a company's financial year end. A good or improved slice of market share can significantly improve the company's share price and the A&R or label head's end-of-year bonus, but in other cases it's because the artist may not be perceived as having a five album career ahead of them. If this turns out to be wrong and they wish to renegotiate then the boot will be on the other foot.

The number of options, and therefore the overall length of the contract, is a key issue when considering if a contract is an unreasonable restraint of trade.

This issue was at the heart of a major court case between Holly Johnson of Frankie Goes To Hollywood and his record company ZTT.[7] (He also had a similar dispute with the sister publishing company, Perfect Songs, which I will deal with in Chapter 4 on publishing deals.)

ZTT v. *Holly Johnson*

Holly Johnson and the other members of Frankie Goes To Hollywood were unknown when they attracted the interest of the directors of ZTT, Jill Sinclair and her husband, the highly successful record producer, Trevor Horn. The band was broke and very keen to work with Mr Horn. They were told that ZTT would only do the record deal if they also signed an exclusive publishing deal with Perfect Songs. Now you might detect a whiff of undue influence here but, in fact, this point was not seriously argued in this case. The band signed up to both deals. Although they were inexperienced and had very little bargaining power, they were represented by a lawyer who was experienced in music business contracts.

Frankie Goes To Hollywood had two very successful singles with 'Relax' and 'Two Tribes', both of which attracted a great deal of controversy because of the subject matter in the case of the first and the video for the second. At one stage the tracks were Nos. 1 and 2 in the UK singles charts. The band's first album *Welcome To The Pleasure Dome* sold well and produced two more hit singles. They failed to make a success in the US and by 1986 the pressure was on them for the second album to be a success.

The band had a lot of trouble with the recording of this album, to be called *Liverpool*. Trevor Horn controlled the recording costs, he was the record producer and the recordings were being made in his studios. The costs were escalating alarmingly and the band was horrified by how much they would have to recoup. After a lot of problems the band split up but ZTT (and Perfect Songs) wanted to hang on to Holly Johnson. Johnson didn't want to continue with them and sued on the grounds that both the recording and publishing contracts were an unreasonable restraint of trade.

The term of the record contract was for an initial period of six months and was extendable by two option periods and up to five contract periods, all in favour of the record company. Each contract period was to be for a minimum of one year and extendable until 120 days after they fulfilled their minimum obligations to the record company (known as the Minimum Commitment). There was also no maximum extension of the contract period. It was open-ended and depended entirely on when the band fulfilled its Minimum Commitment.

The Minimum Commitment was one single in each of the initial period, first and second option periods and one album in each of the third through to seventh option contract

7 *Zang Tumb Tum Records Limited and Perfect Songs Limited v. Holly Johnson* [1983] EMLR 6.

periods. This is a very odd way of structuring a contract, but basically it meant that if the record company exercised every option the band had to record three singles and five albums.

The record company was free to bring the contract to an end at any time. The record company also had the right to reject recordings delivered to it by the band. As the term continued until after delivery of recordings that were satisfactory to the record company, this meant that the record company controlled how long the contract lasted. There are echoes of this in the George Michael case.

The court decided that the contract was one-sided and unfair and was an unreasonable restraint of trade and unenforceable. It thought that the potential term of the contract was far too long, as it could easily last eight or nine years. In that time the court felt that the band wouldn't have had the opportunity to earn a decent living from their work. The record company wasn't obliged to do very much with the recordings. There was no commitment to release them. The court freed Mr Johnson from the contracts and awarded him substantial compensation.

As a result of this case, UK record contracts now almost invariably contain a clause committing the record company to releasing records in at least the home country. If records are not released the contract usually gives the artist the right to end the contract and sometimes to get the recordings back, possibly in return for an override royalty. This is not always the case outside the UK and I recently had to fight for a release commitment in a US deal I was doing.

TWO-ALBUM FIRM DEALS

If you've enough bargaining power, it is possible to get a record company to commit in advance to a second album. These types of deal are called 'two-album firm' deals. They are not currently very common. Record companies are more likely to agree to these when they're in competition with another record company or perhaps where they are licensing in a finished album (so know what they are getting there) and are then more inclined to take the risk on committing to a second one but most record companies don't want to give this commitment. They want to see how the first album does before committing to a second. Some artists and managers favour them because they believe they provide commitment and certainty, which allows them to do some forward planning. Others feel they only work if things are going well. If things aren't going well, the record company will probably try and get out of it after the first album. If your only alternative is to sue the company for failing to honour their side of the bargain, you'll probably agree to accept the offer they make to end the contract, so the commitment may not mean much in the end. Sometimes the record label will give the commitment but will insert what is sometimes called a 'disaster clause' where if the first album does not sell over a given number of units the record company does not have to make the second album. To my mind this type of clause negates the whole point of seeking the certainty of a 'two-album firm' deal.

TERRITORY AND SPLIT-TERRITORY DEALS

Long-term exclusive record deals will usually be offered on a worldwide basis. This may be perfectly acceptable, particularly if the record company has a strong presence in most major markets of the world. However, because the US is a very different marketplace from that of the UK, an artist sometimes asks for what is known as a 'split-territory deal'.

This means that you do one deal with a record company for the world excluding the US and another deal with a different record company for the US. To make these types of deal work the artist and his manager have to juggle the demands of two record companies. Record companies don't like doing these sort of deals, because they say they need a worldwide market in which to recover their investment. They also say that their own companies are strong worldwide and should be given the chance.

Split-territory deals are therefore usually offered to artists with considerable bargaining power. Sometimes these deals are done because the record company has a strong reputation in one part of the world but not in another. A US branch of a UK record company may not have a track record in 'breaking' non-US artists in the US. However, it is doubtful that without some strong bargaining power behind you you will succeed in getting a split-territory deal even in this situation.

Smaller record companies may not have their own offices in all parts of the world. They may have a network of licensees in different countries. Those licensees might take all the records they produce. These are called catalogue licence deals. Alternatively, the UK company may look for different licensees for each artist. For example, the UK record company could do a deal with Atlantic Records in the US for all its acts or it could do a deal with Atlantic for its mainstream acts and with a smaller label for its indie acts. Whatever the situation, you need to know who the licensees are going to be. They need to be well-established, trustworthy companies that will do a reasonable job of selling your records in the country concerned. If a licence deal isn't in place in a particular country when you do your record deal, you should have the right to approve that part of the licence deal that affects you at the time the licence deal is done. I recently successfully argued for this right of approval when the label my client was signing to was in the process of renegotiating its international licensing set-up and so couldn't tell us who would be releasing the album overseas.

Smaller companies use overseas licence deals to help to fund their operation in the UK. For example, a company in Germany could pay an advance against the royalty it expects to pay on sales of records in Germany. It may also pay a contribution to the cost of doing a remix in return for the right to use the remix in Germany. If the artist does a promotional or concert tour in Germany, the German licensee may provide some financial back-up. If you have a small low-key deal in the UK with a label that can't afford to pay you very much up-front, you could ask that some of the advances paid by overseas licensees of your recordings should be paid through to you. For example, if the German licensee paid an advance against royalties of €100,000 you might get 25% (i.e. €25,000). This will help to make up for the low advances in the UK. This is something that should be negotiated at the time the original UK record deal is done.

NEW FORMS OF RECORD DEAL
360 deals
At the time of writing these are the 'flavour of the month' deals. They are not new – variations on them have been around for years. The Robbie Williams deal done in 2002 was a particularly striking example of one of these deals but only now, some six years later, are they starting to filter down into the mainstream. Very few artists have been able to attract deals with the big numbers involved in the Robbie deal and most of these deals are at a much lower level. The one that is causing considerable discussion at the moment

is the deal Madonna has struck with promoters Live Nation. This is dealt with in more detail in Chapter 10 dealing with touring.

So what are these deals? They have acquired the name 360 because they involve all important aspects of an artist's career. A record label may say to an artist – in effect – 'We cannot make enough money just from selling your records to justify the level of advances, royalties and recording costs you want us to pay. We cannot invest the kind of marketing budget this record needs because we can't make enough money from record sales alone. So if we are going to sign/extend your record deal we can only do so on the basis that we also get a share of the money you make from other activities.' These activities might be song-writing but more commonly it means they want a share of the money the artist makes from selling tickets to their live concerts and selling merchandise at those concerts. Sometimes it also extends to any sponsorship deals the artist may do for that concert tour. The reason the record labels have latched on to this is because at the moment the live industry is doing well in relative terms. Prices of tickets to live events continue to rise and with fans spending another £20 or more a head on merchandise once they get to the concert this is currently proving a very lucrative business for the artists. The record companies have convinced themselves on the rightness of their stance by the fact that they feel it is their work in promoting the album and the artist that is at least in part responsible for the artist being able to sell so many concert tickets and therefore they should share in that money.

These 360 deals can take a number of forms. The record company might just tack on to their already long recording contract clauses which give them a share of income from things like the artist's website, merchandising, sponsorship and ticket sales. The artist agrees to pay over a percentage of this income together with supporting statements which the label can check. The percentages are variable with figures around 10–20% being common but 50% not being unheard of. In these types of deals the record label doesn't interfere, but just selects a share of the money. In other cases the record label may insist that it controls things like the merchandising and sponsorship deals which the artist does. It is here that many artist advisers start to get more nervous as this gives the record company a great deal of control over the artist's wider career. The Madonna deal outlined in Chapter 10 goes still further as she has signed such a deal not with a traditional record label but with her live promoter who will in future be releasing her records.

One deal that I did in the last year was an innovative variation on this 360 model which involved the artist and the label setting up a partnership which would hold assets like recording, trademarks, videos, artwork, but which the artist ultimately owned. These assets were licensed to the partnership for a period of time before going back to the artist. The partnership embraced records and all other activities that the artist undertook in the entertainment industry excluding song writing as that deal had already been done. There was however no other reason why song writing could not form part of such an arrangement if all agreed. The partnership was initially funded by the record label 'partners' and it is a net profits deal. So far reasonably similar to other production deals with added income-producing areas. Where it got innovative was after the contract term ended. The artist would then be free to go off and sign to another company if he wished but for a period of time after that the artist would continue to pay a percentage of his profits from live work and other non-song writing activities back to the record label 'partners'. This deal is not for everyone but it has now been picked up by an influential US label and so we may see more of them in future.

Many managers are up in arms at the 360 model because they see it as the record label taking slices of income that traditionally they are not entitled to and arguably therefore reducing the monies that the artist receives and which are then commissionable by the managers. However, as I said above in relation to production deals, these deals are very common at the moment and it is rare these days for new start-up labels not to at least be advised to consider whether they should spread their risk by taking a share of other income. This must not however be confused with deals where the artist is signed exclusively for recording, song writing, merchandise and sponsorship to one or more companies controlled by the same people who may also manage the artist. These are variations on the production deals described below and should be very carefully handled as unless conflicts of interest are adequately addressed they are deals just waiting for an artist with a bit of money to challenge in the courts.

Production Deals

As I've already mentioned a type of recording deal that has grown significantly in importance over the last five years is the production deal. This is usually a form of an exclusive recording agreement for the world but where the record label is an offshoot business of a record producer or recording studio owner or a manager who has access to cheap recording facilities or a fan or a song writer who has decided to set up his own 'label' to record an artist he has found who he thinks is talented. These production companies may be partially funded by a bigger company and act as a talent outsource e.g. their studio rent and other office overheads may be wholly or partially met by the record label (Heavenly is one of these labels and is supported by EMI) or they may be self-financed. Sometimes the funding comes from venture capitalists that set up schemes to invest in artists and labels and in so doing exploit legitimate tax arrangements to maximise the investors' tax breaks. Companies such as Ingenious are heavily involved in this and amongst Ingenious's recent investments have been a label venture by IE the managers of Robbie Williams and the label appropriately named Independiente. Many more are self-financed or use what we call 'friends and family' funding – which as its name suggests means funding provided not by official financial institutions but by people known to the label owner. These production companies aim to exclusively sign up artists at an early stage in their careers before there is too much interest in the industry leading to a bidding frenzy. So the advances and recording budgets are likely to be low. The production company will expect to own the copyright for life of copyright and to have at least a couple of options to extend the contract beyond an initial period. The aim of these production companies is either to record up to say five tracks to good demo or master quality and use these to tempt a bigger company to come on board or the production company records and releases some tracks themselves in order to hopefully create a buzz and have the bigger company come along and either buy the contract off them or license the rights off them exclusively in return for an investment into marketing and promotion and reimbursement of recording costs. The production company will obviously also hope to make a profit on the deal

There is some debate amongst managers and their legal representatives as to whether these production deals are a good thing. I tend to take the pragmatic view that these structures are here to stay and if this is the only type of deal on offer you should think carefully before turning one down. There may seem to be a distinct advantage in signing direct to a bigger label, not through a small production label. On the other hand at least you are very important for the small production company who is likely to give you more attention and perhaps more creative control than you might expect from a bigger label with other artists to also deal with. The big potential downside is that many of these deals are on the basis that they share net profits with the production company and usually that will be a 50:50 equal split. Sometimes it is a little more in the artist's favour but in the early stages many are 50:50.

In an ordinary royalties deal only the recording, video costs and personal advances and possibly a percentage of independent promotion and tour support is recoupable from royalty earnings. With a net profits or net receipts deal all costs are recoupable.

With an ordinary royalties deal the record company recoups the recoupable sums just from sums earned in royalties. With a net profits or net receipts deal all costs are recouped from all income attributable to the recording i.e. including advances/fees paid by licensees, the record company's share of earnings etc.

So all the income generated by the recordings goes to recoup all the expenses and any profits or receipts left at the end are divided between record company and artist in the agreed proportions. The division is usually a minimum of 50:50 but can go considerably higher in the artist's favour with 75:25 splits being not unheard of.

At the outset, net profit or net receipts deals can work quite well for the record company, as that is when costs are high. The record company still bears the risk on costs initially, but it doesn't pay out anything to the artist until the deal goes into profit. Also, the record company gets to recoup costs it wouldn't normally be entitled to offset against you, such as manufacturing costs. You can still receive an advance to live on. Where these deals start to become less attractive to a record company and much more attractive to the artist is when the initial costs have been recouped and ongoing costs are going down. If the record continues to sell well and you're on 50% of more of profits, you're doing considerably better than you would be if you were on a straight royalty basis.

Such deals almost inevitably benefit the label in the early days because they do not have to pay the artist anything until the deal goes into profit. This means they have all their costs of recording, manufacturing and distributing the records repaid first as well as things like press and promotion costs. Only once all those costs have been recovered and the project goes into profit do profits start to get shared. If the artist has had an advance against his share of profits he will have to also repay that before he sees anything more. Once the costs have been recouped and start to tail off then if the records continue to sell the label in theory should be making larger profits. These profits are then shared with the artist who stands to do much better out of it than he would if he were on a royalty from a bigger label. So if costs are kept under control and the record sells both sides stand to do very well.

Where the scales tend to tip away from the artist is if the production company sells on the contract to a bigger label. The production company may then recover some or all of the costs it has paid out for recording and so is doing quite well but may not yet be in profit so perhaps the artist may not have seen any more money at this point. The bigger label is not likely to do a net profits deal. They are much more likely to pay a royalty to the production company – let's say 22% of the dealer price of the records. That then is the 'net income' that comes into the production company for sales of these records. That 22% is then what the production company shares with the artist. If it splits it 50:50 the artist is, if you like, on the equivalent of a 11% royalty deal. Now that doesn't sound so good does it? So it is often the case that the lawyer for the artist will ask for an increase in the share payable to the artist to say 70% if a deal like this is put in place to give the artist a better 'royalty equivalent' deal. Even though it may seem that the artist has not done as well here as he would have with the bigger label that bigger label was not showing any interest at the time the artist signed; the production company invested in the future of the artist and maybe helped nurture their creativity – so is it wrong to say they shouldn't get a fair reward for that investment? You decide.

OTHER ASPECTS OF RECORDING CONTRACTS

Now that I've looked at the main types of deal and some of the things that distinguish them, I want to look at some aspects of contracts that are common to all types.

DELIVERY REQUIREMENTS – MINIMUM COMMITMENT
Each type of record contract has a minimum that is required from the artist. Licence deals can be for single tracks or albums. Development deals may start out as being for four or five tracks and then develop into a commitment to record albums. Exclusive album deals can either be for a single track or an album initially, usually with options to acquire further product. Production deals will be either for four or five tracks with options on further recordings or an album commitment with options. One of the artist's obligations is to deliver the required minimum number of recordings.

This obligation may be simply to deliver the masters of these recordings to the record company. More often, however, the commitment is not fulfilled until the record company has agreed that the recordings meet the required standards. As we saw in the *George Michael* and *Holly Johnson* cases, if these standards are not met the company can reject the recordings and make the artist re-record them until they are satisfied. It's important that these standards are realistic and that they're set out in the contract. They could be technical requirements or commercial ones or a combination of both. What you should try and avoid is a subjective standard. This is someone else's view of whether the recordings meet the required standard or whether the recording is commercially satisfactory. What a record company executive thinks is commercially acceptable may not be anything like your own views on the subject. It's best if you can try and set an objective standard, a standard against which the quality of your recording can be measured. For example, measuring it against a recording of the artist's that the record company has previously accepted as being satisfactory.

It's also usual to try and put a time limit on when the record company has to give an answer as to whether a recording is satisfactory. It must be a realistic time period, as the company may have to go through various stages and processes before it can give an answer. The A&R man will have to listen to it and probably play it to his colleagues at the weekly A&R meeting. He may talk to record producers to get their view of the recording. He'll probably talk to the artist's manager for his views. He may have a hunch that the record could be improved if one or more tracks are remixed by someone other than the record producer or original mixer. Depending on the contract, he may have to get the artist's permission before he does that. The contract with the record producer may mean that he has to give him the first chance to remix the track in question. Now obviously it's unlikely that the A&R man will be hearing the recordings for the very first time. He is likely to have been involved in the process to a greater or lesser extent at an earlier stage but nevertheless this approvals process takes time.

Once the record company is happy with the standard of the recordings it may say that the recordings have been accepted and that the Minimum Commitment has been fulfilled, but most companies want more information from you before they do that.

Acceptance or fulfilment of Minimum Commitment usually means that the record company has to start planning the release and maybe has to pay a further instalment of the artist advance. The record contract may set a last date by which the record must be released. The record company won't want that time to start running until they're in a position to start the processes for a release. This means that they usually require you to hand over a number of other things before delivery is said to have taken place and before they accept the recordings. This could be artwork for the packaging of the records, details of who performed on the masters, and confirmation that those performers have given their performer's consents. If there are samples of anyone else's recordings or songs in the masters, the record company will want to know that you have permission from the copyright owners of those recordings or songs to use the samples (see Chapter 13). If permission to use the samples hasn't been agreed then the record company can't put the recordings out without being in breach of copyright. With a production deal it is likely that the delivery of the five or more tracks will start the time running for when the production company has to get a bigger company on board, release the records themselves, or release you from the contract. So they are going to be pretty sure they have all they need before they officially 'accept' the recordings.

Because it's important to know when a recording has been accepted, I often ask the record company to agree that the recordings are said (deemed) to be accepted if the record company has not said that they aren't within four to six weeks of delivery of the masters, artwork etc. to them. Depending on how long they think it will take for them to go through the acceptance process, they may agree to this or they may not. With a production deal you are more likely to be closely involved in the whole process with the label and you choosing songs, producer, remixer etc. together. There is less likely to be a very formal procedure for notification of delivery and acceptance in such cases but they will still want to know they have all the parts they require to get a release and the artist will still want to know that he has done all that is required of him for the moment.

ADVANCES

For many artists this is one of the most important issues. Remember that these monies will have to be recouped out of the royalties earned from sales or other uses of the recordings. Unlike a loan, however, advances aren't usually repayable if the record company doesn't sell enough of the records. That's the record company's risk. If, however, the artist takes their money and then doesn't deliver any recordings, the record company may try and come after you to get the advance back. If it's all gone, they **may** not bother to sue because it would cost them more in legal fees than they would get back. I wouldn't like to rely on them not suing though.

What's a good advance on an exclusive recording agreement?

A good advance is one that meets your needs. You may only care about getting as much money as possible and aren't concerned if you never sell enough records to recoup. There are a lot of cynical managers with that view in the business – take the money and run. In that case you'll just be looking for the most money you can get up-front. It's a short-term view because the greater the record company's investment in advances, the more pressure there is going to be on you to perform and the more likely it is that the record company will want to dictate to you. If you go for a more reasonable advance payable in reasonable instalments, the record company may put you under less pressure to deliver. You should also recoup the advances sooner out of your royalties. Because so few artists recoup advances and costs, this will put you in a strong bargaining position with the record company. I have, however, recently heard a very successful and influential music manager take completely the opposite position. His view is that an artist who has proved that he can sell records if the record company does its job properly can get more commitment out of a record company by being unrecouped, as this will encourage the company to work harder. This could well be the case with certain labels or individuals, but I'm not convinced that this applies to everyone, particularly in the current climate when so few artists are getting beyond their first album. One of the reasons the contract does not go further is because overall it is just too expensive. A prudent manager would consider renegotiating if the label was otherwise a good bet to stay with. If however the A&R or MD who signed the act is no longer there then you may be better off cutting your losses, walking away from the debt and trying to start again.

Whatever the position on recoupment, a good advance is going to be one that allows the artist to live and have a roof over his head for at least a year (preferably eighteen months) while the recordings are being made and then promoted. It's a good idea for the artist or his manager to do an outline budget of what he may need.

If a manager is only interested in getting as much of the advance as possible as early as possible as an artist I would be suspicious. Is he only concerned about his commission? Is he only in it for the short term? Doesn't he expect to be around when the record is finished or when it's time for the option to be exercised? Whose interests is he looking after – the artist's or his own? It may be a perfectly legitimate approach, but don't accept it without question. If he's pushing for a very short deal with most of the money up-front, is it an agreed approach of 'take the money and run' or doesn't he have faith that you can cut it beyond one album? You may accept a lower advance in return for other things such as greater creative control. It's possible to get both, but usually only when you have a lot of bargaining power. If you go for a lower advance you should also be able to argue for a higher royalty and this argument also holds good in production deals but do not expect the production company to necessarily move beyond a 50:50 deal in the early stages.

Min-max formula

The level of advances payable could be calculated according to a formula (called a 'min-max formula'). Under this formula a minimum advance is payable to the artist and a limit is also set on the maximum the company will pay. The actual amount is calculated as a percentage of the royalties the artist earns. The formula usually applies from the second contract period or album onwards. This method of calculating option period advances is often favoured by production companies as it allows them to reward sales success.

At the beginning of the second contract period, the record company looks at how much the artist has earned from sales of the recordings he made in the first contract period. It then takes a percentage of that and, if the amount then arrived at is more than the minimum and less than the maximum, then that is the advance payable for that period. For example, in the twelve months following the release of the first album the artist may have earned £100,000 in royalties. The formula for calculating the advance for the second contract period is linked to 66% of those earnings; 66% of £100,000 is £66,666. The minimum advance payable in the next contract period is, say, £50,000. This is above that. The maximum advance payable is, say, £100,000, but it's not got to that point so the advance payable is £66,666.

This formula can work and many record companies favour them because they give them a degree of certainty for budgeting purposes and a payment linked to success. The artist needs to make sure that the minimums are enough to meet his minimum living requirements. In the example I gave above, could he live on £50,000 for a year or longer in the second contract period?

The maximums are usually double the minimum, but may be more in later contract periods. Is the maximum a reasonable advance if the artist is doing very well? To be honest, I don't worry about the maximums as much as the minimums. If you're hitting the maximums it's because the artist is doing well and the record company is more likely to want to keep him happy by renegotiating these figures upwards.

Payment terms

Advances are normally paid in instalments, usually one on signing the deal, another when the artist starts recording the Minimum Commitment for that contract period, and the final instalment either on delivery of the completed recordings to the record company or on commercial release of the recordings. With a production deal the later instalments may be linked to the production company getting a bigger company on board. As the release could be some months after delivery, the artist will want the final instalment to be paid on delivery. The record company may want to protect itself by only paying the last instalment when the record is released, when there is a reasonable prospect of record sales reducing its financial exposure. However, a lot can happen between delivery of the finished masters and their release. A client of mine once delivered finished masters to the record company and they were accepted. A few months later, and before the last date on which the record company had to release the recordings, the company closed down and the copyright in the client's recordings was transferred to another record company. That record company then hesitated for a few months more about whether or not they were going to release the album. In the end the artist's manager asked me to send the record company a formal notice under the terms of the record contract requiring the record company to release the album and pay the final instalment due under the deal. When the record company got the notice it rang me up and said that it had decided that it didn't want to release the album. It offered to give my client the copyright in the album back in return for an override royalty until such time as it had recovered the recording costs that had been spent on the album. The client and his manager decided to take this offer, but more than seven months had passed since the recordings were delivered and the artist didn't get the advance due on release of the album. From the artist's perspective therefore it would have been better to have payment linked to delivery of recordings not their release.

Costs-inclusive advances

The advances I have been describing so far are called personal advances. They go towards the artist's personal needs. The costs of making the recording are separate recoupable amounts (see Chapter 5). The record company may offer an advance, which includes the costs of making the recordings. These costs-inclusive deals are often called 'recording-fund deals'. Both artist and the record company have to be quite careful that the amounts advanced under a recording-fund deal are at the right level. The artist has to be sure that he can make the album he wants to make with the available funds and still have something over to live on. Often, costs-inclusive deals work out at less money than one for a personal advance plus recording costs, unless the artist can record very cheaply. The record company has to know it's not being too generous but also that the artist won't run out of money before the recording is finished. If he does, the record company inevitably ends up paying out more money if it wants to get the recording finished. Recording-fund deals can work for established artists, for those with their own recording facilities or more mature artists who can be relied on to make the recording without spending all the money on themselves. I have recently successfully negotiated just such a deal with a company in the EMI Group. The artist had a track record of making records and the manager was very experienced and respected by the record company. It's worked out well for the artist, as much of the recording was done in a home studio.

RECORD BUDGETS

If a record company is not offering a recording-fund deal you'll need to have some idea of how much it's going to cost to make the recordings. You need to know that the record company is committed to spending that amount of money. If you're doing a licence deal you'll usually have already finished making recordings, and so the issue is whether they will compensate you for the costs you've incurred. So you need to know what you've spent.

The budget must take into account how much it will cost to rehearse the material, to do any necessary pre-production (preparation for recording and programming), to record the material in the studio, to have it produced, mixed and edited. Some record companies include the cost of cutting or digitally mastering the recording in the budget. This can add thousands to the deal so, if the budget is tight, try and get them to pay for that separately. You also have to bear in mind the cost of hiring in specialist equipment and engaging the services of additional musicians and vocalists. The budget also usually includes what are called per diems, an expression meaning a daily expenses payment to cover food and drink and sometimes also transport to and from the studio.

The record company may commit to a guaranteed minimum spend on recording costs in the contract, but most are reluctant to do that. This is either because they're afraid they may get it wrong, or because setting a minimum figure means you tend to spend that amount of money whether it's necessary or not. On the other hand, you'll want to know the record company is committed to a particular level of spend so that you know that you can make the kind of record you want. Both sides have to be realistic. It's no good a record company thinking you can make an album for five pence, but neither is it any good you thinking the record company will let you have a blank cheque. This is where a decent recording budget is invaluable.

Recording costs are usually fully recoupable. There are, however, some elements of the recording cost budget that may be wholly or partially non-recoupable. A classic example is the costs of remixing. Mixing costs are very expensive. If you're on a tight budget these costs can take a lot out of the total. The record company may want to commission a remix that you don't think is necessary. Who is to pay for this and are the costs to be recoupable? Some record companies will agree that the first mix comes out of the recording budget as does any remix that you want to do, but if the record company wants to do additional remixes they pay that on top of the recording budget. So, you know what to do – make sure it's the record company that asks for the remix, not you.

ROYALTIES

This could be the subject of a whole book in itself. No two companies calculate royalties in exactly the same way. This is an area where there is really no escaping the need for experience and legal advice.

Record company executives usually have guidelines as to what is or is not allowed. Certain top artists may have been given 'favoured nations' terms. This means that they have the best deal that the record company can offer on that particular point. If any other artist is offered better terms by that record company, the artist with the 'favoured nations' provision must also be given these better terms. As this has potentially huge financial implications for the record company, an executive crosses these boundaries at his peril. It may be impossible to do so and will definitely require agreement from someone high up the corporate ladder.

Retail versus dealer price

You need to know what price basis the record company is using to account to you. An 18% royalty on the retail price of a CD would be good, but 18% on the dealer price of the CD would be just average.

Until about ten years ago, the majority of UK record companies calculated their royalties as a percentage of the retail price of the record in question. However, the retail price is not within the record company's control and varies considerably. Most UK companies have, therefore, moved over to using the dealer price of the record as the basis of calculation. Outside the UK and in particular in countries like Japan and the United States, they have very different methods of arriving at a dealer or 'wholesale' price basis. In order to make a proper comparison, you should ask the record company to give you the actual figures they are talking about so you can do what is sometimes known as a 'pennies' calculation. This means that you can calculate roughly what you'll get from each record sold. This calculation is essential when you're trying to compare offers from more than one record company. It's also important for a record company executive trying to make a deal to know how much he will have to pay in record royalties per record sold. He or his finance officer will need to calculate how many records will need to be sold before the advance they offer will be recouped. It has to make some kind of commercial sense even if the A&R man is so determined to do the deal that he wants to pay over the odds. At least he'll know what he has to aim at in terms of record sales.

What percentage of sales?

Is the royalty calculated on all records sold or a lesser percentage? Many record companies build in a 'free goods' allowance of up to 15% of total sales on which they do not pay a royalty.

Packaging and other deductions

The most common deductions are packaging deductions, sometimes also referred to as container charges. This is a charge supposedly to cover the cost of making the cases or other packaging in which the record is sold. In reality, the actual cost is usually far less than the average packaging deduction and is a way by which the record company artificially reduces the royalty paid to you. These deductions must be taken into account in order to compare offers from different companies. An average packaging deduction for CDs is 20%, although many companies charge 25%. More and more companies – including EMI and BMG before it was merged with Sony – dispensed with packaging deductions altogether as part of a drive for simpler contracts and greater transparency. Whilst I am all for that the problem is that, because not all labels have adopted this approach, many are still making a packaging deduction and therefore comparing like with like is very difficult. A royalty rate offered by a company which does not deduct a packaging allowance may seem low and uncompetitive until you take this into account.

Other traps for the unwary are the reductions that some record companies apply to certain types of records. For instance, sales by mail order, through record clubs or at budget prices will be at a lower royalty rate. The principle behind all these deductions is that, where the record company gets less than the full price for a sale, it will reduce the amount payable to the artist on that sale. A record sold as a budget record will usually attract a 50% reduction in the royalty rate. A 50% reduction also applies to records advertised on television, sold by mail order or through record clubs. The reduction in the royalty for mail-order sales is important when you think that many companies will now offer mail-order sales over the Internet. If this becomes the established method of selling records then we ought to look again at whether or not a 50% reduction is appropriate.

A detailed exploration of all the royalty reductions is beyond the scope of this book. Your lawyer and accountant will be familiar with these. Most UK record companies usually apply the principles behind the reductions in a similar way, but the details will differ a great deal.

What's a good royalty?

As a very general guideline, a basic royalty of more than 18% of the dealer price calculated on 100% of records sold with no reduction for CDs and a packaging deduction of no more than 20% would be acceptable. It's unusual to see royalty rates of more than 24% of the dealer price for new signings to exclusive record deals. However, royalties on licence deals could well exceed 24% on the above basis, because the record company is getting a finished recording and can assess the commercial potential upfront. The record company also hasn't taken any risk on the recording costs. On non-exclusive licence deals between record companies, for example for a compilation, the royalty may well be more than 24% of the dealer price with no packaging deductions, because they recognise the deduction for what it is.

RELEASE COMMITMENTS

Obviously, once the album has been delivered and accepted it would be good to have some kind of assurance that it's going to see the light of day and not just sit on the shelf. You need a commitment from the record company to release the record in at least the home market and preferably also the main overseas markets. The release should usually take place within four to six months of delivery of the masters. If it doesn't, the usual remedy is to serve a notice telling the record company that if it doesn't release the record within another two to three months then the artist has the right to end the contract and not have to deliver any more masters. Even better would be a commitment from them to return the unreleased masters to the artist (perhaps in return for an override royalty until the recording costs have been recouped).

Some record companies don't want to do this, because they would rather negotiate such things at the time. They may also want to hold on to the masters in case another company has better luck in making you successful. They then have back catalogue material they try to release to cash in on this success. I think this is pretty daft because, although the tried and true fans will buy all records, there's no artist to promote the record so it's unlikely to go very far. Sometimes they hold on to the unreleased masters in order to try and sell it to the artist's new record company at a later date and this strategy is often successful.

Overseas, if the record isn't released within four to six months of the UK release (depending on the contract – it might be longer if it's a small label) you can serve another notice of thirty to sixty days; if there hasn't been a release the artist may have the chance to find a licensee and make the record label then license it to that company to release. They're unlikely to automatically give the masters back, as they know it's difficult to make their overseas companies or licensees release recordings. It's mad though if you think about it – why bother to do a worldwide deal if you can't even guarantee that your sister companies overseas will even release the records in their territory? It's all part of that argument, 'We have to do this because for the few that are international artists we would look stupid and get fired if we didn't have world rights.'

ACCOUNTING

The artist should get paid at least twice a year, possibly four times with smaller companies doing their own distribution. The accounts statements will be sent out sixty to ninety days after the accounting date. If all advances are recouped (oh happy day!) the statement will have a cheque with it – yippee! If you aren't certain what the statement says, check it with your accountant. If he doesn't think it's right you should challenge it, but don't leave it too long as you probably can't object after a period of time, say one to three years. You have the right to audit (inspect) the books at least once a year. Send accountants in to audit if you've had a successful period or at the end of a deal that has gone well.

WHAT HAPPENS IN A PRODUCTION DEAL WHEN A BIGGER COMPANY COMES ALONG?

Well, first the production company either sells or licenses on the rights it has in its deal with the artist and the rights it has in any recordings it has already made, to the bigger label. This is either an outright sale where the production company steps out of the picture on an active level and passively continues to earn its income from future sales or it remains as an active middleman. The decision is usually made between the bigger company and the production company but as we will see below the artist may have an indirect say. If the production company stays in the picture the bigger company does a contract with the production company and not direct with the artist. It pays the production company an advance, maybe reimbursement of specific costs such as recording costs already incurred and a percentage of future royalties. Out of these monies the production company pays what is due to the artist under its separate contract with the artist.

If the production company drops out of the picture the bigger label does the deal direct with the artist and a separate deal with the production company for its share of future earnings. In the latter case the artist is free to negotiate new terms. In the former case where the production company stays in the middle the artist is generally stuck with the original production deal he did so it is important that that contract anticipates that this is going to happen and ensures the artist gets a fair share going forward. This may involve a bigger percentage of the profits going forward and/or a slice of the advances paid by the bigger company.

There is also a small window of opportunity for the artist to attempt a renegotiation of his deal. The bigger company will usually want the artist to confirm that it won't lose out if the artist and the production company fall out at a later stage; or if the production company goes bust or doesn't want to continue with the artist whilst the bigger company does. This document, called an inducement letter, allows the artist a little bargaining power as it is important to the bigger company that it is signed. Therefore the artist has an opportunity to try and improve his terms a little bit.

CONCLUSIONS

- There are four main types of record deal – licences, development deals, production deals and exclusive recording agreements.

- With each type of contract you need to work out how much exclusivity you're going to give and what territory the contract is to cover.

- Advances against royalties can include recording costs or these can be dealt with separately. Recording and personal advance budgets are useful in setting the level of the deal.

- Royalties can be calculated on the retail or the dealer price of the record. It's important to establish which, as it makes a great deal of difference to the deal.

- Some record labels no longer deduct the cost of packaging. It is important to know this as it can explain what may otherwise seem a poor royalty.

- Record contracts often contain reductions in royalties on certain types of sale or method of distribution.

- Net profits deals work for the record company at the beginning but the scales can tip in favour of the artist after the initial costs have been recouped.

- New types of recording deals based on the artist sharing income from his other activities (360 models) are emerging which may work for you either once you are a successful artist or as alternatives.

Chapter 4
What Is A Good Publishing Deal?

INTRODUCTION

In this chapter I'm going to look at what rights a songwriter has and what he can expect from the various types of publishing deals. I'm going to ask whether you need to do a publishing deal at all. If so, whether, ideally, it should be before or after you've done your record deal. Just as we have seen with recording deals there have also been changes in how publishing is viewed by the smaller operators and there has been a move amongst managers and smaller record labels to also take an interest in publishing rights. I will explore how they do this and whether or not I think this is a good idea.

Before I go into any detail about the contract, I need to look at how you find a music publisher, what a music publisher actually does, and what rights a songwriter has. You will not be surprised by now to learn that the doctrine of restraint of trade comes up here too. Since the last edition of this book there have been a number of significant cases to do with publishing rights possibly reflecting the greater interest in songwriting as a source of income. As well as looking at some restraint of trade cases these new cases will be dealt with in full below.

HOW TO FIND A MUSIC PUBLISHER

Music publishers employ A&R people and scouts in the same way as record companies do. They're on the lookout for talented songwriters who either perform in a band or as a solo artist, or who mostly write songs for other people. Hopeful songwriters send demos to publishing companies in the same way as record companies.

You can find lists of UK music publishers in the *Music Week Directory* (see Useful Addresses). All the major record companies also have well-established music publishing companies within their group of companies. For example, there is an EMI Records and EMI Music Publishing. There has been a spate of mergers in the major music publishers in the last few years and threats of significant changes with others. Universal Music Publishing has acquired BMG Music Publishing in a move which was initially scrutinised by the European Commission but which was subsequently cleared on the condition that Rondor UK, Zomba UK, 19 Songs and BBC Music were sold off. When Guy Hands' private equity group Terra Firma bought EMI for £2.4billion in 2007 there was rampant speculation that the deal would be funded at least in part by the sale or securitisation (mortgaging) of the EMI publishing catalogue. So far this has not happened and the focus seems to have moved away from this as a source of revenue but it must remain a significant possibility. There is also talk that if Warners and EMI were to ever conclude their long on-off, love-hate courtship that this too might result in the sale of certain assets such as the Warner Chappell publishing catalogue either to raise funds or to reduce the likelihood of the merger being rejected on monopoly grounds. So we are now down to four major music publishers: Warner Chappell, Universal, Sony and EMI. There are also independent music publishers that aren't associated with record companies, for example

PeerMusic or Bucks Music Group, as well as administrators such as Kobalt and Bug Music amongst others. Your lawyer, accountant and manager can all refer you to publishers they think will be suitable for your style of songwriting.

WHAT DOES A PUBLISHER DO?

Have you ever wondered why we call them publishers? As far as I can work out, it comes from the early days of the music business when music was published in the form of sheet music in the same way as a book is published. Nowadays, of course, sheet music forms only a small part of the income that a songwriter and a publisher can make. These days the largest share of income comes from the use of songs on sound recordings (mechanicals) or with TV, film or other moving images (synchronisation). As digital distribution of music develops, the rights in a song may well be far more valuable than a physical sound recording like a CD as we will see in Chapter 7 on digital media.

Publishers have traditionally had three main roles. Firstly, they issue licences to people who want to use music. Secondly, they actively look for ways to use music – for example, putting it in an advert or on a film soundtrack. Thirdly, they collect the income from those licences and uses. The first of these roles is often done in conjunction with the collection societies (see Chapter 15), including now the area of online uses where, after initially feeling their way, the societies have now begun to establish links with international societies and to have mandates from their members to grant commercial licences for online uses. Their position has been strengthened legally by the bringing into UK law late in 2003 of the EU Directive which confirmed the extension of rights of copyright owners and performers to online, digital uses which has removed the previous uncertainty.

Some publishers are better than others in finding uses for music and collecting the money earned. Obviously, a songwriter has to be satisfied that they can do a reasonable job of collecting in the money. Whether he also needs them to be good at finding uses for his songs will depend on the type of songwriter he is (although most songwriters probably wouldn't turn down additional ways of making money).

So that people know who to approach when they want to ask to use a song, and in order to track the money and collect it properly, the publisher has to register the songs with all the main collection societies around the world. Sometimes this just requires that the songwriter fills in a form and files it with the society. Sometimes they also have to send in a recording and a written copy of the words and music, called a lead sheet.

If the music publisher is one of the bigger publishers, it will have its own companies in each of the major countries in the world. One or two of the independent publishers, most notably PeerMusic, also have their own companies worldwide too. Most of the independent and smaller publishers don't have the resources to set up overseas companies. They appoint local publishers in the country concerned to look after their interests there. This is called sub-publishing.

The traditional roles of the publisher are however changing as they too look for different ways of making money in a difficult market place. If one of their traditional main sources of income has been mechanical royalties on record sales and if, as is the case, CD sales are declining then their income is also dropping so they have to supplement it in other ways as well as becoming better at collecting it and more efficient in running their companies. Publishers will also now do some of the things that were originally only done by record companies. They will provide studio time for an artist or songwriter to record demos. In order to get interest from record companies to sign singer–songwriters, some publishers act almost like record companies, putting records out in limited editions as a way to attract record company interest. There are even some that will provide financial support for you when you're out on the road promoting your records, or extra funds for promotion or press coverage. These costs and payments are usually recoupable from your publishing income as and when it comes through. The main reason they do these things is in order to give you a bit of a boost, a head start, or to top up funding that may or may not be provided by your record company. EMI was one of the first publishers to look at licensing song lyrics for inclusion on merchandise like mugs and T-shirts. EMI has also developed an arm of its UK company which is involved in the management of songwriters – many of whom are producers and not necessarily performers. These artists do not have to be signed to EMI for publishing. With the decline in mechanical income licensing songs for use in ads and films has become more important and many publishers are strengthening their synchronisation departments.

WHAT ARE MUSIC PUBLISHING RIGHTS?

Before you can have any rights in a literary or musical work[1] (i.e. in lyrics or music) you have to establish that the words and music are original and that they have been recorded in some way. This could be sheet music, with the words and music written down, or a demo of someone singing the words and music.[2]

HOW DO YOU PROVE THAT YOU HAVE COPYRIGHT IN A WORK?
There are a number of recognised ways of doing this.

You could put the sheet music or demo recording in a safe deposit box marked with your name and the date on which you wrote it and get a receipt.

You could send it to your lawyer and ask him to write back to confirm when he received it from you. Some lawyers aren't happy about doing this. They don't want trouble later if they lose the CD in among the one hundred and one others in their office. Also, they can't really confirm something that they have no direct knowledge of. They don't know who wrote it or when. They can only say that you sent a tape to them on a particular day.

The most popular way is to put the lyric sheet and recording in an envelope addressed to yourself that you then post to yourself by recorded mail (so you have a receipt). When it arrives you keep it unopened in a safe place. The postmark and the fact that it's still sealed means that you have proof that that recording/lyric/sheet must have existed some time before the postmark date. So, if someone later copies the song illegally, there is evidence that your version was written before theirs.

WHO OWNS THESE RIGHTS?
The first owner of the copyright in a musical or literary work is the person who is the 'author' or creator of an original work and records it in a tangible form.[3]

1 Section 3(1) CDPA.
2 Section 3(2) CDPA.
3 Section 9(1) CDPA.

There can be more than one writer or composer.[4] These are called co-writers. One person might write the words and the other the music, or the co-writers might all work on both elements.

Famous examples of successful co-writing partnerships are Elton John and Bernie Taupin, Andrew Lloyd Webber and Tim Rice and, more recently, Robbie Williams and Guy Chambers. It's perfectly possible for two separate publishers to control parts of the same song.

Where there are co-writers the song is jointly owned, and it's very important to record who owns what part of the music or lyrics. When you finish a new song and give it to your publisher, they fill in a form on your behalf called a Joint Registration Form. This is the form needed to record the details about the song, which is then sent to the collecting societies, MCPS and PRS (the Mechanical Copyright Protection Society Limited/the Performing Rights Society Limited). The form contains the title of the song, who wrote it, what shares of it they wrote and if there are any restrictions on what can be done with it. If you don't have a publisher and you're a member of PRS or MCPS or both, you should complete and file that form yourself.

Most publishing agreements will say that all songs are assumed to be written in equal shares by all co-writers unless the publisher is told something different when the work is completed and details given to them for registration. The whole question of who wrote what can be the cause of major arguments between co-writers, who are often members of the same band or the producer of the album. This can be the case even where not all members of a band contribute to the writing. Those members that do write resent those that don't. These issues ought to be sorted out at an early stage before it becomes a real issue (see Chapter 11).

You won't be surprised to learn that disputes over ownership are commonplace. A well-publicised 1999 case over songwriting shares involved members of Spandau Ballet.[5]

Spandau Ballet case

Spandau Ballet' was formed in 1979 and made up of the two Kemp brothers, Martin and Gary, together with Tony Hadley, John Keeble and Steve Norman. They were part of the New Romantic movement and, after turning down a record deal with Island Records, they set up their own label that they eventually licensed to Chrysalis Records. Their first single, 'To Cut A Long Story Short', went Top 5 in the UK. They released a couple more singles before having a Top 3 hit with 'Chant Number'. They released six albums plus a Greatest Hits compilation. The last album, *Heart Like A Sky*, was released in 1989. Ten years later they were in court arguing over song royalties. Martin Kemp was not involved in this case.

Everyone agreed that Gary Kemp had written the lyrics to all the songs. The dispute was over who composed the music. Gary Kemp's company received all the publishing income from the songs. He volunteered to give half of this money to the other band members, but stopped this arrangement in 1987. The other band members sued, saying that there was a legally binding agreement to continue to pay this money. They also argued that, if there was not a binding agreement, they were entitled to the money anyway because

4 Section 10(1) CDPA.
5 *Hadley and Others v. Kemp and Another* (1999) Chancery Division.

they were co-writers of the songs and therefore co-owners of the copyright. They said they'd contributed enough to the music to make them co-writers. The judge decided that there was no binding legal agreement. Gary Kemp was sole writer of all the music save for a song called 'Glow'. The judge also confirmed that to be a co-owner you have to have contributed to the song's creation, not just to its interpretation. So if a drummer just adds a short drum loop that doesn't make any material difference to the song, that won't qualify for a claim that he has co-written that song. A bassist who takes the melody line and just converts it into a part that is suitable for his instrument will also probably not have claim to being a co-writer.

More recently there are threats of a court case against James Blunt by record producer Lukas Barton who claims to have co-written a number of songs by Blunt which feature on his album *Back to Bedlam*, which has so far sold over 14 million copies worldwide. Blunt denies Barton was a co-writer and says that he wrote all the songs in dispute himself, either whilst he was serving in Kosovo or before that at his parents' home. It is not certain that this case will come to court; it is possible it will settle beforehand.

Mark Taylor v. Rive Droit Music Limited

One case that did make it to court was a claim by Mark Taylor, co-writer of Cher's hit record 'Believe' against music publishers Rive Droit Music Limited (RDM).[6] Many of the problems that surround this case turn on bad drafting of a publishing agreement and a dispute as to who owned two songs which Mark Taylor co-wrote and which were recorded by the artist Enrique Iglesias.

In 1995 Mark Taylor entered into two agreements with RDM, the second of which was a written publishing agreement which was renewed twice, the second time in 1998. At the end of November 2000 Mr Taylor stopped working for RDM and joined a rival set-up Brian Rawling Productions Limited (BRP). Brian Rawling had originally been recruited by RDM to bring together a stable of songwriters. Songs written by these songwriters would be pitched to other record labels and artists. The idea was that RDM would produce the subsequent recordings of those songs and receive both a production fee and royalties from sales of the records and a share of the songwriting royalties.

Mr Taylor collaborated with Paul Barry (another songwriter signed to RDM) and together they wrote a number of songs including 'Believe' which made their name. Mr Taylor entered into the third publishing agreement with RDM in about December 1998.

Two years later in early December 2000 Mr Taylor and Mr Barry went to America and worked on songs which were to be recorded by Enrique Iglesias. On 6 December Mr Taylor decided to end the production arrangements with RDM with effect from 1 December 2000 and sent the owner of the company a fax to that effect. Over the course of December 2000 all of the producers and most of the administrative staff left RDM for BRP.

In April 2000 Mr Taylor sought a declaration from the court that his 1998 publishing agreement had expired on 30 November 2000 and that he was due royalties. RDM disputed this interpretation of the contract and said that the term of it was three years not two. Presumably on the basis that they may have been found to be wrong on this they tried to argue that they had the rights in the two Iglesias songs which Mr Taylor was arguing were

---

6 *Mark Taylor v. Rive Droite Music Limited* November 2005 (unreported).

written after the end of the 1998 publishing agreement because he had in fact not created new works but adapted parts of songs written by Mr Barry (who was presumably still under contract). RDM alleged this amounted to an infringement of their copyrights and asked the court to award them damages.

At the first hearing the judge found that it had been a two year contract and that Mr Taylor was under no obligation to deliver to RDM any song written in whole or in part after 1 December 2000. However, Mr Taylor did not have it all his own way because the judge also found that some of the two Iglesias songs had in fact been in existence on 1 December 2000 and the copyright in those parts belonged to RDM. Taylor felt that RDM didn't acquire the copyright until he had delivered a completed song. So both parties appealed to the Court of Appeal which finally gave judgment on the case in November 2005. Well you do know that saying 'Where there's a hit there's a writ'. It might have been coined for just such a case as this.

There were considerable difficulties in deciding what the publishing contract on 1998 actually meant. The Term appeared to be for two years but then in another clause this was contradicted by a reference to three twelve-month periods not two. Eventually the judges agreed that it was two years not three and that the earlier clause which defined the Term was stronger than the later, contradictory one. The court also decided that the relevant point for determining the ownership of the copyright was when copyright subsisted and when it was intended that that copyright could transfer to another. The judges accepted this was not always easy to determine but in this case decided that copyright vested in RDM at the moment there was a complete work. Now this could have implications for drafting of publishing agreements in future as many publishers take the view that even if a song is a work in progress they still own rights in it. There were also echoes of our old friend the doctrine of restraint of trade in that if they were to decide that this meaning of composition included ALL of the writer's output then that could be seen as a restraint of his trade.

As a post script to this case, in late 2007 Rive Droit Music Limited went into administration. Whilst the arguments surrounding these cases may suggest they turn on their own facts there are clearly lessons to be learned: be clear in your drafting, and make sure all rights of session musicians and band members are clearly set out. This point will emerge again in a later chapter when we look at the rights of session musicians but before we leave this area let's look at a recent case (currently under appeal) which seems to throw some doubt on what rights the original composer of a song has when part of that song is then replayed by a member of the band.

Matthew Fisher v. *Gary Brooker – The 'Whiter Shade of Pale' Case*[7]

This was a case decided some forty years after the song was originally written and recorded and turned into a massive hit by the band Procul Harum. Mr Fisher was the band's ex-organist and he argued that he was entitled to a share in the musical copyright (not the lyrics). The band's pianist Gary Brooker argued that Mr Fisher's organ solo was essentially the same as the original piano composition. The judge preferred Mr Fisher's version of events and ordered that Mr Fisher was entitled to claim a 40% share in the music. It is sometimes difficult to follow a judge's logic as in this case, having decided that Mr Fisher

---

7 *Matthew Fisher v. Gary Brooker* [2006] EWHC 3239 (Ch) 20 December 2006.

had made a significant contribution to the original musical work so as to make him a co-author with Mr Brooker he decided that that contribution was not as 'substantial' as Mr Brooker's contribution so awarded him a 40% not 50% share. The judge also ordered that Mr Fisher was not entitled to any royalties for the time before he brought the case. The song was originally released as a single on 12 May 1967 and was a huge hit, going on to sell over 6 million copies worldwide. Around the time of the release the two authors Mr Brooker and a Mr Reid assigned their copyright in the words and music to Essex Music Limited, those rights are now owned by the successor to Essex Music Limited, Onward Music Limited. When the song was being written the two were forming a band which Mr Fisher joined as Hammond organist. In rehearsals Mr Brooker and Mr Fisher improvised their respective piano and organ parts over the original chord sequence that Mr Brooker had composed. It is this improvised organ accompaniment that formed the basis of Mr Fisher's claim for a declaration that he owned 50% of the copyright in the music.

In a further twist in law the furthest back Mr Fisher could go in his claim for back royalties would be six years from the date of his claim. However, the judge decided that ignorance of his rights to claim was no defence to the fact that Mr Fisher had sat back for over forty years and allowed the collection societies and publishers to collect the money and distribute it on the basis of a 50:50 split between Mr Brooker and Mr Reid. The judge therefore only allowed Mr Fisher damages in unpaid royalties from the date of his claim saying that if he allowed the collection societies to collect and pay out despite his view that he was entitled to a share then he must have in effect granted a free licence for all this time to use his share of the song. As it was a licence he was entitled to end it and is deemed to have done so by bringing this claim. The music publishers who stand to lose their publisher's share of the 40% interest in the music now attributed to Mr Fisher are appealing the decision.

The lesson to be learned from this case is to make it quite clear at the time what claims any interested parties may have in the work. If at the time it was first written Mr Fisher had signed an acknowledgement that he had no rights in the composition then this claim would never have arisen.

DURATION OF COPYRIGHT

The copyright in a musical or literary work lasts for seventy years from the end of the calendar year in which the author dies.[8] If a song has been co-written, the rights last until seventy years from the end of the calendar year in which the last surviving co-writer dies.[9] This was not always so and this extension to seventy years is a relatively recent one. When dealing with older compositions it is essential to also look at the laws which pertained at the time and what effect subsequent laws have had on the position.

Solomon Linda's case

The family of South African composer Solomon Linda brought a case alleging infringement of copyright on the basis that copyright in a song had reverted to Mr Linda under British Commonwealth laws of copyright 25 years after the death of the author. The

8 Section 12(2) CDPA.
9 Section 12(8) CDPA.

song in question is best known to us at 'The Lion Sleeps Tonight' but which was originally written by Linda with the title 'Mbube' (meaning 'Lion' in Zulu) in 1939. It was a hit but as Linda and his wife had sold their rights in the song to a local company they never properly benefited from the song's success. Mr Linda died in poverty in 1962. The song 'Mbube' was adapted and covered by American folk legend Pete Seeger who translated the lyrics and renamed the song 'Wimoweh'. It sold over 4 million records in different versions and was covered over 150 times. In the 1960s another writer, George Davis Weiss, added new lyrics and called the new version 'The Lion Sleeps Tonight' and it is this version that was subsequently licensed to Disney for inclusion in the box office smash film *The Lion King*. Linda's widow received only 3/24ths of the income. Lawyers for the family argued that the rights in the original song, on which these later versions were based, had reverted to Mr Solomon Linda and thence to his family and were able to bring the company who had licensed the song to Disney, Abilene Music, to the negotiating table and agreed a settlement which remains secret but at least part of which now allowed Mrs Linda to receive 100% of the composer's share of the performance income. The settlement is also thought to include a back payment of royalties and future royalties as an 'equitable share' of the version 'The Lion Sleeps Tonight'.

As more works come out of copyright and into the public domain (and therefore can be freely used without payment of royalties) questions will inevitably arise as to whether a work is out of copyright. It has long been thought in the classical recording world that an editor of a work to be performed by musicians which was out of copyright didn't acquire any new copyright in what he edited.

Hyperion Records v. Dr Lionel Sawkins[10]

This view was challenged by Dr Sawkins. He has spent time and effort editing three performing editions of works by the court composer to Louis XIV and Louis XV, Richard de Lalande. Clearly de Lalande's original works were out of copyright but was the effort, skill and time which Dr Sawkins spent in making three modern performing editions of his work give him any new rights as 'original musical works'. Dr Sawkins thought it did but classical label, Hyperion Records, disagreed and made sound recordings of Dr Sawkins' editions in 2002 without acknowledging him as having any rights of authorship and without paying him any royalties. Dr Sawkins sued. He was successful in the first instance. The judge agreed that the Hyperion's recordings infringed his rights in the performing editions originated by Dr Sawkins and also found that his moral rights had been infringed because he was not identified as the author of those editions. The court ordered an inquiry into the amount of damages which should be paid to Dr Sawkins. Hyperion appealed on the basis that these editions were neither original nor musical with the meaning of the 1988 Copyright Act. In this case the Appeal Court judges also considered that just because Dr Sawkins sought to get as close to the original as possible and had no intention of adding any new music he could still claim to have created an new original copyright in edition. He did edit, transcribe them into modern notation, make them playable, correct errors and omissions and include a figured base. Hyperion also tried to argue that creating an edition to be played did not amount in itself to the creation of a new musical work. They also said

10 *Hyperion Records Limited v. Dr L Sawkins* 19 May 2005 (unreported).

that to allow Dr Sawkins to claim a new copyright would have the effect of greatly extending copyright and that this was contrary to public policy in making ancient music available to modern listeners. It is this latter point which seems to have been the basis for the opprobrium that was heaped on Dr Sawkins from many quarters of the classical music world, who clearly thought his action was 'not on'. There is however also the fact that Hyperion had a vested commercial interest in arguing against Dr Sawkins claim as it may open the flood gates to other editors doing the same thing resulting in Hyperion having to pay composer royalties that they had not budgeted for. The classical world feared that a consequence of this action might be that fewer classical recordings might get made. The Appeal Court judges rejected Hyperion's argument that what Dr Sawkins had done could not be a new musical work as he had added no new music just corrected errors and omissions. The judges thought this the wrong approach as a musical work was not just notes but the overall structure of the musical compositions, including how the notes were to be played. They dismissed Hyperion's appeal. Overall this is a case which turns on what is mere copying and what is the application of sufficient original skill and labour to create a new copyright. It is both a qualitative and a quantitative test.

WHAT RIGHTS COME WITH OWNERSHIP OF COPYRIGHT?

The copyright owner of a literary or musical work (i.e. a song) has rights very similar to the recording copyright rights we looked at in the last chapter. The main ones are the right to authorise the reproduction of a musical or literary work with or without visual images (mechanical and synchronisation rights);[11] the right to authorise distribution of the work;[12] the right to rent or lend the work to members of the public;[13] the right to authorise public performance of the work or its making available to the public[14] and the right to make an adaptation of the work or to do any of the above in relation to an adaptation.[15] As the copyright owner, you can allow or prevent someone from doing all or any of these things either throughout the world or in a particular country. When you do a publishing deal you are giving someone else the right to deal with some or all of these matters on your behalf. The publisher might do this itself throughout the world or may subcontract the rights to a sub-publisher.

WHERE DOES THE MONEY COME FROM?

MECHANICAL LICENCES AND ROYALTIES

Originally, when a recording was reproduced it was literally done mechanically, using mechanical piano-rolls. So the licence to reproduce the song on a sound recording is called a mechanical licence. It remains the biggest source of income for most songwriters. For example, if a record company wants to record a performance of a song, it has to ask permission from the author or the publisher or the person who administers the song. This may seem a bit strange where you've written a song that your band wants to record. It seems odd to have to ask permission from someone else to record your

---

11 Section 16(1) (a) and section 17 CDPA.
12 Section 16(1) (b) and section 18 CDPA as amended.
13 Section 16(1) (c) and (d) and sections 19 and 20 CDPA as amended.
14 Section 16(1) (e) and section 21 CDPA as amended.
15 Section 21 CDPA as amended.

band performing it. But remember that different people are going to control the rights in the sound recording and the rights in the song. They are separate copyrights and the same people will probably not control both. The record company has to pay a licence fee to the owner of the rights in the song. The fee for this, the mechanical royalty, is either fixed by negotiation between representatives of the record and publishing companies in the country concerned or set by law or legal tribunal.

The present licensing system in the UK was the result of a referral to the Copyright Tribunal in 1992. The record and publishing companies couldn't agree on what was a proper licence fee. The 1988 Copyright Designs and Patents Act states that the solution in such situations is to refer the dispute to the Copyright Tribunal. The scheme approved by the Copyright Tribunal is operated by the MCPS on behalf of most of the music publishers in the UK. The current licence fee is 8.5% of the dealer price of the record. The MCPS can only licence the mechanical reproduction of a song if it's a straight 'cover', i.e. a faithful reproduction of the original by someone other than the original performers. If it's not a faithful reproduction then the MCPS does not have the authority to issue a licence and permission has to be asked from the writers or their publishers.

Until recently, mechanical reproduction took the form of physical product such as a vinyl record, a cassette tape or a CD, with new formats such as DAT, DCC and Mini-disc added from time to time. With the coming of the digital era of music being delivered by means other than physical reproduction the law has had to adapt to deal with this new means of distribution. The download of a computer file containing music on to an MP3 or similar player or a computer hard disc is treated as a reproduction akin to a physical reproduction such as a CD and this is now accepted in the EU and confirmed in UK legislation by the 2003 amendment to the Act.[16]

Since 2002 MCPS/PRS have issued blanket licences to use music online and to download music off the Internet and, through its reciprocal arrangements, offered these worldwide. There is now a whole range of licences available for other uses such as CD-ROMs, music in toys and in computer games and most recently for DVDs and digital radio stations. However, they failed to reach a negotiated settlement with some record companies and significantly with some Internet service providers like Yahoo and the matter had to be referred to the Copyright Tribunal in a long and very expensive hearing. The outcome is discussed in more detail in the chapter on Collection Societies but suffice it to say that it was not that far removed from the rate applicable to physical reproduction which makes some of us at least wonder what all the fuss was about. The Tribunal's decision did at least end the uncertainty over whether or not you could get a blanket licence for downloads of music.

CONTROLLED COMPOSITIONS

Although in this book I'm mostly dealing with UK copyright and licensing schemes, the situation in North America is important as it can have a huge impact on publishing income coming from the United States (and to a lesser extent, Canada, as it is a much smaller marketplace).

In the UK we have a licensing scheme and a fixed rate that has to be paid for a licence. In the US the law also sets a fixed rate (currently 9.1 cents a track) for the right

---

16 The Copyright and Related Rights Regulation 2003.

to reproduce a song on a record, but in the US the record industry has more bargaining power than the music publishers. It lobbied the legislators and got a clause included in the law that allows a different rate to be set by agreement. Well, surprise, surprise, the record companies have insisted on a different rate. And is it higher? What do you think? The almost universal position in the US is that the record companies will only pay 75% of the fixed rate. This is referred to as a 'controlled compositions' or 'reduced mechanical royalty' clause. They are called 'controlled compositions' because the compositions and what happens to them are under the control of the writer or his publishers. Obviously, you can only agree to a reduced rate if you're the owner or controller of the song. Most US record deals start from the standpoint that you will agree to this 75% rate. This means that you're losing a quarter of your US publishing income from the reproduction of your songs on records. The pressure will be on to accept this and if you really want to do the US deal then there may be little you or your advisers can do about it. However, if you already have a publishing deal, you probably won't be allowed to accept this reduction without your publisher's agreement. You can use this to get your publisher to fight on your and its behalf to get improvements on this rate. If you've a lot of bargaining power you can get a 100% rate. If you've medium bargaining power you can get them to agree to increase the 75% rate to 85% and then to 100% based on sales of a given number of records. Sometimes they will not budge at all and in most cases you have to give in or not do the deal.

Most US record companies try to further reduce their liability to pay full mechanical royalties by limiting the number of tracks on a record that they will pay royalties on. This is usually no more than ten or eleven. If you have twelve tracks on your album you won't get a mechanical royalty in the US on at least one or two of those tracks with such a limitation in place. Perhaps yet another reason for aiming to keep the number of tracks on your record within the ten or eleven track limit.

These controlled compositions clauses cause problems in every record deal negotiation. There are some improvements that your lawyer can try to get for you, but this is usually one of the most keenly fought clauses in the whole recording contract. A lot of money is potentially at stake for both sides.

SYNCHRONISATION LICENCES AND ROYALTIES
If you're a songwriter who writes mostly music for films, adverts or computer games, then your main source of income may not be mechanical royalties but fees from the issue of licences to use your music with visual images. This licence is called a synchronisation licence, because it gives the right to synchronise music with visual images. The publisher also licenses and collects income from these licences. The fee for this use is called the synchronisation fee. The growth in DVD sales (now tailing off again) also saw a big growth in this as a source of income. MCPS has authorised a DVD rate on a sliding scale up to 8.5% ppd depending on the amount of music in the DVD. There is some evidence that synchronisation income is becoming more important as a source of revenue with the decline in mechanical royalties on declining album and single sales but at the moment mechanical royalties remains the main source of income for most songwriters.

We can all think of artists who have broken into the big time via an advert or indeed where a flagging career has been boosted by a track used in a particularly good ad campaign or in a film. The Fine Young Cannibals track 'She Drives Me Crazy' regularly appears in car adverts. Devo re-recorded their biggest hit 'Whip It Up Good' as 'Swiff It Up Good' for a TV ad for the floor cleaner Swiffer and seminal punk band Violent Femmes track 'Blister In The Sun' was used in an ad campaign for Wendy's hamburgers. Now you might argue that some of these uses did the original artists no favours at all in the credibility stakes but for the right music an advertising company will pay a lot of money – £70–100,000 or more as a synchronisation fee for the right work isn't unheard of. I should just say, though, before you all rush to get your music into adverts or films, that many advertising companies pay a lot less than this. Many also commission writers to write songs that sound like, but aren't, famous songs or which are in the then current music style. Some songwriters make a career of writing jingles for adverts or in composing sound-alike songs. For some this is their main source of income. Others do it as a way to fund them writing their masterwork – that film soundtrack or concerto they otherwise wouldn't have the money to do.

In some countries there's a fixed rate for synchronisation licences. In most cases, though, it has to be fixed on a case-by-case basis. So this again is an area where your publisher or lawyer can get a good deal for you.

If you want to put one of your songs in a promotional video for one of your singles your publisher will probably give you a free synchronisation licence. If there is any chance that it will earn income commercially then they will want a separate fee for the commercial use. They will definitely want a separate licence fee for a DVD.

If there is a synchronisation fee payable, it is usual that the writer's share of the income goes towards recouping any advances which have already been paid to the writer. The publishers will keep their publisher's share of the income. For example, if the writer is on a 75:25 split of royalties in his favour, the publisher would keep 25% of the fee for itself and use the remaining 75% to help recoup the advances. Different scenarios to this are also possible in individual circumstances where some of the publisher's share also goes to recoupment of advances or some of the writer's share is paid through to the writer, but in the current fairly difficult economic climate it does not happen often.

A situation may arise where a writer is commissioned to write some music or a song for a specific project like a film soundtrack. Publishing contracts will often say that, even though they may have an exclusive arrangement with the writer, he can do these deals and keep the commission fee, provided the synchronisation fee (which is also required) is paid through to them. Now, it doesn't take much intelligence to work out that, as a songwriter, you may want to increase the commission fee and decrease the synchronisation fee. Publishers are obviously wise to this and may try and direct some of this money to recoupment.

PERFORMING RIGHTS

We have looked so far at two main sources of publishing income – the mechanical licence and the synchronisation licence. The third significant source of income is the right to publicly perform a song. Public performance doesn't just mean live concerts – it includes the playing of music in shops, restaurants and clubs, in fact anywhere that music is played in public.

Most songwriters who have had some success become members of the PRS or one of its overseas affiliates. The PRS is the only UK performing right society for the administration of the right to perform a work in public, and it is responsible for the collection of income generated by the public performance of the music. The income comes largely from licences taken out by broadcasters, shops, pubs and so on. When you become a member of the PRS the rules say that you have to assign your performing rights in your songs to the PRS. If you send your membership the performing rights are returned to you or as you direct. The performing rights controlled by the PRS are the right to publicly perform a work, the right to broadcast it and to make it available to the public, and the right to authorise others to do any or all of the above. The PRS monitors use of music on TV and radio programmes by means of cue sheets. These are lists of music played on each programme, which the station producers complete after each show. The PRS has a random sampling policy for live shows. They couldn't possibly cover all live gigs, but do monitor the main venues and a selection of the smaller ones and they keep the type of venues monitored under review.

So that there doesn't have to be a separate licence every time a song is played in public, the PRS has entered into licences with most of the broadcasters. They have done the same with major places of entertainment like clubs and restaurant chains. These are called 'blanket licences' because they cover all songs controlled by the PRS. If you've a blanket licence you don't have to worry about whether you can play a particular song provided you've paid the annual licence fee negotiated with the PRS. So every time your song is played on television, radio, cable or satellite you'll receive (eventually) some income from that use of your song. Gradually blanket licences are also becoming available for a variety of uses of music on websites where the PRS now licences use of extracts, Internet radio, podcasts and a variety of other online uses. Their website is very useful in giving you to the right licence for what you want to do and in many cases the application form can be downloaded. It is however still too early to say how effective they are going to be in collecting in this new source of revenue which explains why in many cases the licences require an upfront advance payment. If you plan to use music in a way which is not covered by one of the current licences you can apply to their commercial committee with details of your proposal and ask them to propose an appropriate rate which in many cases is open to some negotiation particularly whilst you are establishing the commercial violability of your scheme.

Through the cue sheets and samplings and the data they collect from online uses the PRS gets a good idea of what music has been performed and calculates the amount due under the various blanket licences. The share due to the songwriter members of PRS is paid out at regular intervals (four times a year) after the PRS has deducted its fee for doing the administration. The PRS rules require that at least six-twelfths (i.e. 50%) of the performing income is paid to the songwriter direct. This money does not therefore go through the publisher's hands to be used to recoup any advances but comes direct to the writer. This can be a valuable source of income for an impoverished songwriter who is unrecouped and can't expect any royalties or further advances from his publisher for some time. The other 50% can be paid to a publisher nominated by the writer as having the right to publish his songs. This 'publisher's share' can be divided between the songwriter and the publisher. If they do share any of it with the songwriter, that share usually goes first towards recouping any outstanding advances. If there isn't a publisher the songwriter can collect 100% of the income himself but may have difficulties in collecting or administering it and may need to get an administrator on board to help. The PRS's role is not a proactive one. It does not actively seek ways in which to exploit the performing rights in your songs but is there to make sure that public places playing records do so under a proper licence scheme so that there is a chance of earning some money from this use of music. The PRS acts as a sort of clearing house collecting in this money and paying it out to its members, both songwriters and publishers. The publishers are happy to allow the PRS to do this job for them, provided, that is, that they don't charge too much – there are periodical renegotiations of the collection fee.

PRINT
Although not as relevant these days, the publisher also has the right to issue licences for a song to be reproduced in printed form as sheet music. In relatively few cases do they do this themselves now; usually it's third party specialist print companies who do it under licence. The exceptions tend to be classical music publishers. Whilst print income from sales of sheet music isn't a large source of income for a popular-music songwriter, for classical composers it can be a very lucrative source of income. Included in this print category is the hire-out charge the publisher makes to orchestras wishing to have access to the 'parts' of the work, i.e. the sections written for the different instruments in the orchestra – £30–40,000 fees for the hire out of parts for a large orchestral or operatic piece aren't unheard of. This of course helps to shed a little more light on the Hyperion case above as if the publisher had to pay royalties to the editors of the scores that generate this income then that would significantly eat into their profit.

As publishers look for new ways to make money from the songs they control we may find that this print music royalty or other miscellaneous royalties payable to the songwriters increase importance. I am thinking here of plans to license lyrics for merchandise. The publisher would presumably charge the merchandiser either a flat fee or a royalty per unit sold and the songwriter ought to be entitled to a share of such income.

RECORD DEAL BEFORE PUBLISHING?

It used to be invariably the case that you did your record deal first and got a publishing deal later. Nowadays the publisher fills many of the same roles as a record company in finding the right co-writers and producers, and even recording and releasing limited edition single records. The decision therefore becomes much more of a personal one. For some, it's important that they have got a deal, *any* deal. So if the publishers come courting first they will do the publishing deal first. Others stick to the tried and true method of getting a record deal first and then hoping that that deal and the success of their first release will push the bidding up for their publishing rights. This can be a dangerous game as, if the first release doesn't prove to be a success, the publishing offers may dry up. You may be a songwriter who wants to hang on to your publishing rights for as long as you can, in which case you're going to be concerned to get a record deal that will give you enough by way of personal advances to live on for a reasonable period of time without having to go looking for money from a publisher.

If a songwriter doesn't need to do a publishing deal in order to get some money or other form of 'leg-up' he can become self-published. This way he fully controls the copyright in his songs and how they are used. How do you do this? Usually by becoming a member of the various collecting societies like MCPS and PRS. The collection societies fulfil a lot of the administrative functions of a publisher, but a self-published songwriter still has to do a lot of work himself. The collection societies don't always notify all foreign societies of their interest in a particular song or chase up individual payments. The songwriter will have to track down where the music is being used and check if the song is registered locally and if the right amount of money has been paid.

Most creative people aren't known for being organised enough or inclined to do this, nor will they necessarily have the resources. This is one of the reasons that most new songwriters look for some form of support from a publishing company. If you're a more established songwriter, you may be more comfortable with this kind of arrangement or will appoint someone to administer it for you.

TYPES OF PUBLISHING DEAL

If being self-published isn't an option then there are three basic types of music publishing agreement that can provide outside support: the administration deal, the sub-publishing deal and the fully exclusive songwriting deal. Within the category of exclusive songwriting deals there is a sub-category where rights are just assigned in a single song. This is called the single song assignment.

THE ADMINISTRATION DEAL

Administration deals are popular with songwriters who have a small but potentially lucrative catalogue or collection of songs. It may not be worthwhile for them to join the collection societies and be self-published. They may not have the necessary time, energy or organisational abilities to go tracking down the income. They may prefer to employ someone to do it for them.

These types of deal also appeal to established songwriters. They may not need a publisher to try to exploit their songs. They may be disillusioned with exclusive publishing deals or want to own their copyrights. They may not need up-front advances against income and may relish the increased control that they would have if there were no publisher breathing down their neck. The same comments I made in Chapter 3 still apply to these assignments as they do with sound recordings.

The administrator doesn't usually take an assignment of any interest in the copyright, but is granted a licence for a period of time. If an administrator asks to take an assignment of rights outright, I would need to be convinced that there was a very good business reason to do it. If you assign your rights you aren't in a position of control and there isn't very much of a difference between this and exclusive publishing deals, except you're likely to see only small or no up-front advances. So what's the advantage? At least if it's for a licence term then you retain control of the underlying copyright. A licence term can vary greatly from one year upwards but with a three- to five-year licence term common. Many are for much longer. I have concluded ones that were for the life of copyright. Even with such a long term the client was still comfortable to do it, because the deal overall worked for him and at least if it was a licence and things went wrong he wouldn't have to worry about getting his copyrights back, as he'd held on to ownership of them.

As the name suggests, the administrator administers the songs for the owner of the copyright. The administrator registers the songs with the various collection societies and licences others to use the songs. They also deal with the collection of the income from these licences and prepare accounts showing how much has been earned. The terms of the contract dictate whether the administrator has complete freedom to issue whatever licences he thinks right for the songs, or whether he must first consult with the songwriter. It may say that commonplace licences, such as the right for the writer to record his own songs, can be issued without asking him first, but if someone wants to use a song in an advert or a film the songwriter has to first give permission. Don't put too many restrictions on what licences the administrator can grant if you want to maximise what can be earned from the songs. By all means put a stop to something that is a real issue, for example if the songwriter is a vegan he may quite rightly not want his work used in adverts for beefburgers, but think carefully before you block all uses of the songs in adverts, because you are cutting off a potentially very valuable source of income.

The administrator could be an individual, perhaps an ex-musician or songwriter himself, or it could be a company that specialises just in administration. Most but not all music publishers who sign up songwriters to exclusive deals will also do administration deals in the right circumstances.

The administrator will usually charge 10–15% of the gross income as his fee. You wouldn't usually expect an administrator to pay any advances. Payment will only be made when the administrator has collected in some money. It's therefore very important to know how often the administrator will account. They should pay at least every three months. It's also important to check out their reputation for efficient collection of money, particularly outside the UK. The administrator may be very good in the UK, but overseas he may not have the necessary resources or contacts. In which case, it's likely that all he will do is to collect what comes through collection societies overseas that are affiliated to the MCPS and PRS. If this is the case then you have to ask yourself whether it's worth it, because you can get this income yourself through direct membership of MCPS and PRS. You ought to be getting some kind of added value by having the administrator on board. It may be as little as taking the load off you, but it wouldn't be unreasonable to ask the administrator to try and track down unpaid licence fees or royalties on your behalf, and if he has a worldwide deal with you he shouldn't just limit his activities to the UK.

A songwriter will often do an administration deal when he isn't too concerned about getting other uses for his songs. If you know people will either not want to put your songs in a film or advert, or if they do you're so well known you don't have to sell yourself and they will come to you, then you won't worry about someone going out and actively looking for these extra uses. Administrators will look after the administration side but won't normally be out there pitching your songs to advertising agencies or film companies. However, even those who have old catalogues of songs which are more or less dormant can still be tempted by promises of a bit of an extra push on their songs and a bit of extra cash.

THE SUB-PUBLISHING DEAL

The sub-publishing deal is a mixture of an administration deal and an exclusive publishing agreement. The owner of the copyrights sub-licenses some or all of these rights to a publisher. The original owner usually keeps the copyright, so it's normally a licence rather than an assignment of rights. These types of deal come up in two very different circumstances.

Established songwriters or songwriters who want to own or control their copyrights may want something more than a pure administration deal. If so, a sub-publishing deal may suit. They may not need an advance or may be prepared to do without an advance in return for keeping control of the copyrights. That isn't to say that a sub-publisher won't pay any advance at all. They may pay modest sums in advances, but they may not be as big as you'd get under an exclusive publishing deal. Why? Because the sub-publisher doesn't get as much ownership or control from a sub-publishing deal as he would from an exclusive songwriting deal.

If a songwriter needs someone to go and search out deals for him then he won't get that from an administrator, so a sub-publishing deal may work for him. Under a sub-publishing deal the songwriter gets someone actively looking for other ways of earning money from his songs.

In some cases the publisher will want an assignment of the copyright.[17] As you know, my advice is to avoid this if you can but, if you don't have much choice, then try and get them to agree that this is only for a limited period of time. This period is called 'the Rights Period' or 'the Retention Period'. The shorter you can make it, the better in terms of control of the copyrights. Bear in mind, though, that the shorter the period of time that the sub-publisher controls the copyrights, the fewer opportunities he has to make money from the songs and this may be reflected in the type of deal he offers. If you do get a publisher to agree a licence term then this could be as short as a year, but is more likely to be for at least three years and in some cases much longer.

The sub-publishing deal also appeals to smaller publishers, ones that don't have their own established systems overseas. Instead of the cost of setting up their own companies in each of the main overseas countries, such publishers do sub-publishing deals in those countries. They keep the rights they have, but grant the overseas publisher the right to use some or all of those rights in their country for a period of time.

Whichever type of deal we are talking about, the sub-publisher needs to have the right to register the songs, to license some or all of the main publishing rights such as mechanical and synchronisation rights, and to collect in the income.

The sub-publishing contract will set out the extent to which the songwriter or small publisher has the right to grant licences to exploit the publishing rights. Don't be surprised if the sub-publisher presses for overall control and only wants to have to get approval on certain very specific matters. You may have approval over alterations to the songs or over the grant of licences to include them in adverts for products that you may disapprove of. If you tie the sub-publisher's hands too much then they can't easily get further uses for the songs. You're employing a sub-publisher and paying them a large fee to be pro-active on your behalf, so you need to balance the need for creative control against commercial realities.

How much you have to pay a sub-publisher will depend on a number of factors such as your bargaining power, how much the sub-publisher wants to control your catalogue of songs (whether for market share or income or to have the kudos of having you on their books), and how much you are expecting them to do. I recently had a bidding war going

---

17 Often this is in order to get 'market share', which is the measure of how many copyrights a publisher controls either in terms of numbers or, more often, in terms of how much income they generate. Market share is watched by the money markets and the analysts and is also keenly contested by the publishers themselves as a measure of how well they are doing.

on for an old catalogue of songs because they were very iconic and 'of their period' and it happened that this was a period that is popular at the moment for films and ads and so the publishers involved in the bidding war could easily see how there was a lot of money to be earned from licensing these songs. The fee is likely to be more than you would pay under an administration deal but probably a little less than under a fully exclusive songwriting agreement. A sub-publishing fee of 15% of the gross income received is common. If you expect a big advance then that may increase to 20% to compensate for the additional risk the sub-publisher is taking. The sub-publisher has paid out some money to you on the strength of what it knows about you and your potential. If you don't live up to that then that's the sub-publisher's risk. The contract very rarely allows the sub-publisher to demand that money back.

What does a sub-publisher do?

A sub-publisher should provide the same basic services as under an administration deal, including registering the songs, granting licences, collecting income and accounting on a regular basis.

Some larger publishers can account and pay you what you're due in the same accounting period that they receive the monies from overseas. For example, the sub-publisher grants a mechanical licence to reproduce your song on a record in the US. The record sales take place in the period between March and June 2007. The US record company will probably pay the mechanical royalty in the next three months, so it will be in the sub-publishers account by the end of September 2007. The deal with the sub-publisher says that it accounts in September for income received in the period up to the end of June. On the scenario I have given, the income won't have come in until after the end of June. If the deal were that you got paid in the same accounting period, you would get it in September. If it's not then you'll get it at the next accounting date, which would normally be March 2008. This is a six-month delay which, when you're first expecting your money from overseas, can seem a very long time to wait. If prompt payment and cash flow are important to you, and let's face it, they are to most of us, then you need to check this out carefully. Needless to say, the sub-publisher is usually the one earning interest on the money sitting in their bank account for six months and not you.

In addition to the basic administration services, the sub-publisher should give you more for the extra money it's getting. This could just be payment of an advance, but the sub-publisher should also be more proactive, going out and looking for other uses for the songs, suggesting co-writers, finding film projects or adverts and so on.

A smaller publishing company appointing a sub-publisher overseas would expect them to act as if they were a branch of their company overseas.

If you are a songwriter with your own publishing company you may not notice any difference between what a sub-publisher does and what you'd expect from an exclusive publishing agreement. The sub-publisher will usually expect exclusive rights to sub-publish your songs and will charge a similar fee to an exclusive publisher. The crucial difference is that you retain the copyright in your songs and have more control.

THE SINGLE SONG ASSIGNMENT

The single song assignment is a bit of a halfway house. It's not an exclusive publishing agreement. The songwriter is free to publish individual songs himself or through a variety of different publishers. Unlike under a sub-publishing agreement, he assigns the rights in a song to a publisher; he doesn't license them. The assignment could be for the life of copyright or it could be for a shorter Rights or Retention Period. There may be an advance, but it's likely to be small. The publisher is likely to get a fee of about 20–25% of the gross income received.

Deals such as these would be attractive to a songwriter who only writes a small number of songs on an irregular basis, or who wants to keep his options open. The publisher still gets the rights it needs in the particular song and market share in that song. Because the publisher controls the copyright in the song, it's in its interests to get as many other uses for the work as possible. The publisher will also carry out all the usual administrative functions and should account regularly. The same comments that I made above about accounting delays apply here. The song assignment will decide how much control the songwriter has over how the song is used. Because it's a one-off, he may not have as much control as with an exclusive deal for all his songs, but if he has enough bargaining power he should certainly be able to prevent major changes to the words or music and some control over the use of the song in films or adverts.

EXCLUSIVE PUBLISHING AGREEMENT

If none of the above options appeal or are on offer then there is the exclusive publishing agreement. For most songwriters this is important at some stage in their careers. Getting an established publisher behind them means that they've arrived, that someone else has faith in their work and is prepared to put money and commitment behind that conviction. In many cases a publisher is instrumental in getting record company interest. There are stories of music publishers of songwriters who are now household names who spent months knocking on record company doors trying to convince them of the strength of the songs. Sometimes it's just a case of waiting until your time has come whilst honing your craft in the meantime. It can be good to have a music publisher supporting you during this time in the wilderness.

RESTRAINT OF TRADE

As we saw in Chapter 3, whenever there is an exclusive arrangement containing restrictions on what you can and can't do, there is an assumption that it is in restraint of trade. We also saw that the leading case in this area, *Schroeder* v. *Macaulay*,[18] had decided that this doctrine also applied to exclusive record and publishing contracts. We know that the contract was found to be an unreasonable restraint of trade and, as such, unenforceable, but so far I have not gone into any details as to what in the contract was found to be unreasonable. It was a publishing contract so it is better dealt with here.

Maucalay v. *Schroeder*

The particular parts of the contract that led the court to decide that it was unenforceable were that it was an exclusive arrangement – it required absolute commitment from Macaulay, but there was no corresponding commitment on the part of the publishers to do anything with the songs. They could accept them and tuck the copies away in a drawer or

18 *Macaulay v. A. Schroeder Music Publishing Co. Limited* [1974] 1 WLR 1308.

put them on a shelf and forget about them. The term was for five years, but Schroeder could extend it for a further five years if more than £5,000 worth of royalties had been earned in the first five years. This was not a lot of money even then. Macaulay had had to assign the copyright for the life of copyright. Even though in those days this was fifty years after the end of the year in which he died not seventy years, it was still a long period of time to have a publisher controlling the copyright in his songs exclusively without having any obligation to do anything with them. The advance that he received was very low. It was £50 with further payments of £50 as each earlier advance was recouped. This was almost like putting him on a wage, but with no guarantee of when he would receive his next pay cheque. The court felt that, taken as a whole, the contract was an unreasonable restraint of trade.

As a result of this and later cases there was a change in UK music publishing contracts. The length of the term is now limited and there is a maximum backstop – usually no more than three years per contract period. There is also usually a requirement that the publisher has to do something with the songs. For example, the contract will often say that if the publisher has not granted a mechanical or synchronisation licence for a song, or no sheet music has been printed of it or it has not been performed in public within, say, a year or two of the song being delivered or the end of the contract term, then the songwriter has the right to ask the publisher to do something with it. If nothing happens within another three to six months then the songwriter can usually get the copyright in the song back. I have recently completed a deal where a songwriter got rights back after a wait of two years from his first publisher and used that as the basis of a catalogue of material to offer to his new publisher.

WHAT IS IN A TYPICAL PUBLISHING CONTRACT?

Exclusivity
If you sign an exclusive publishing deal, you are usually agreeing that the publisher will own and control all your output as a songwriter during the term of that contract. In return for that exclusivity you can expect a commitment from the publishing company to do something with your songs. You can also usually expect that your publisher will be reasonably proactive on your behalf.

Even though it's an exclusive deal, you can sometimes have exceptions to this. As I explained above, the exclusivity may not apply where you're commissioned to write a song or some music specifically for a film. The film company will usually want to own the copyright in that piece of music or song. Your exclusive publisher may agree that these commissioned works are excluded from your publishing deal. This could be agreed at the time the contract is done as a blanket exception or your publisher could agree to consider specific requests on a case-by-case basis.

If you are regularly commissioned to write music for films, your publisher isn't going to want to automatically exclude all these from your agreement. By not automatically agreeing that the film company can own the copyright, your publisher may gain some bargaining power with the film company to get a better deal. As the terms of the contract should say that you benefit one way or another from income from these deals, it should be in your interests for the publisher to argue on your behalf.

Occasionally a publisher will agree that the songs you write for a particular project are excluded from the deal. For example, you might write some songs for a largely uncommercial project that the publisher isn't interested in. In a recent deal I did the songwriter did a bit of 'bread and butter' work writing for a library music company and it was agreed that these songs, which earned very little money, could be excluded. If you've a lot of bargaining power, you could insist that songs you write for a particular commercial project are excluded from the deal but this is pretty rare. Just bear in mind that the more songs you keep back from your publisher, the more it is likely to reduce the size of the deal on offer.

Rights granted

The publisher will expect to have assigned to it the copyright in all your songs already in existence that no one else has the right to publish. The assignment is usually of all rights in those works, subject to the performing rights that you may have already assigned to the PRS.

If you have done a publishing deal before then another company may still have the right to act as publisher of those songs. If the Rights or Retention Period of that earlier deal runs out while your new publishing deal is still running, the new publisher will expect to get the right to publish those songs too. If you don't think they should then you need to argue for this at the time the new publishing deal is done.

It's possible to grant a publisher some but not all of the rights of a copyright owner. I have tried in the past to hold back rights to exploit music online from a few publishers, but it's true to say that they felt very uncomfortable about it and, now that there's a licence scheme for downloads in place and an emerging online marketplace as a legitimate source of income, publishers are now unlikely to agree to exclude online rights. In other deals I've done I've given a publisher the right to issue mechanical licences but not synchronisation licences. Obviously you can do this if you've the necessary bargaining power, but there's no point in doing it unless you can do something with the rights you've kept back. Remember also that the more rights you hold back the more likely it is that you'll get a less attractive deal from the publishing company.

Territory

The rights that you assign could be for a particular country or worldwide. We saw in Chapter 3 that it was reasonably common to have one deal for the US and another deal for the rest of the world. Split-territory deals aren't at all common in exclusive publishing contracts. Depending on who the publisher is and what its overseas set-up is like it may have sub-publishing deals in some countries. As a songwriter you should find out what the situation is overseas. You need to know that the sub-publishers are good, efficient companies and that there won't be any accounting delays.

Rights Period

You could assign rights for the life of copyright or for a shorter Rights or Retention Period, which runs from the end of the term of the publishing contract. This period can vary considerably from anything as short as two to three years to more than twenty years. For the last three or four years the average deal on offer from the major publishers has been twelve to fifteen years.

The Rights Period often gets shorter when there is a more positive economic climate and if there is a lot of competition to sign good songwriters. Ten years ago I could get Retention Periods from some of the major music publishers as short as five years. This was when there were lots of good songwriters and a lot of money around. Publishers were going for short-term market share and weren't as concerned about hanging on to copyrights for any length of time. Many of the copyrights were for dance music songs and I guess they gambled that most of these would have a short lifespan. Now there's less money around, songwriters are expected to prove their worth over a longer period of time and it's difficult to get Rights Periods of less than ten years unless you've got a lot of bargaining power. There are, however, always the one-off crazy deals for one album or song at ludicrously high levels, but these are usually for short-term market share to boost a publisher's standing in a particular quarter, possibly to impress their shareholders or other investors.

Term

The term of a UK music-publishing contract is usually shorter than that of a record contract. It's quite common to find a music-publishing contract with an initial period of one year and then options in the music publisher's favour for a further two or three option periods. Each contract period is usually for a minimum of twelve months, but can be longer depending on how long it takes you to fulfil the minimum requirements that a publisher has for each contract period. For similar reasons to those given for record contracts, the options are in the publisher's favour not the songwriter. The publisher has too much invested to allow the songwriter to just walk out the door when he wants to.

Rolling contracts

Some publishers use a different basis for the term of the publishing contract. Instead of a term made up of a number of optional contract periods, the publisher fixes the term up-front and says it will run for, say, three or five years with no options. That fixed period may be extended until you have fulfilled a minimum requirement. Sometimes, but not often, there is no minimum requirement; the publisher just publishes anything you do in the fixed term. This is a big risk for the publisher to take. You could take the advance payable on signing the deal and then not write another thing. To offer this kind of deal, the publisher has to know you well and be convinced that you are going to continue to write good songs. For a songwriter this isn't only a great show of faith from the publisher, it's also a relief. You don't have to worry about fulfilling a minimum requirement or delivering songs to order.

With a rolling term you get an advance when you sign the deal and this is recouped from your earnings. When the initial advance has been wholly or partly recouped you are paid a further advance. This is called a rolling advance. The publisher won't usually pay you an advance in the last twelve to eighteen months of the fixed term because it won't have enough time to recoup it before the deal runs out. When working out how recouped you are, to see if you should get a further advance, you should try to get the publisher to take into account income that's been earned from your songs but hasn't yet come through to its or your account in the UK. This is called 'pipeline income'.

Minimum Commitment

There are a number of different types of Minimum Commitment. The simplest is where you're just required to write a minimum number of songs. If you co-write, your share of all the co-written works must add up to an equivalent number of whole songs. For example, if the Minimum Commitment is to write five new songs and you always only write the lyrics, so only control at best 50% of each song, then you'll have to write ten half-songs to add up to the five whole ones. This type of commitment works best for a pure songwriter who writes for others and doesn't perform and record his own material.

There may be an additional requirement that, in order to count towards the Minimum Commitment, the song must be exploited in some way, for instance commercially released as an A-side of a single or as an album track. This puts a greater burden on you if you're a pure songwriter who can't easily control whether anyone else will want to record your songs. The publisher usually insists on this when it wants to be certain there will be some form of exploitation (and hopefully some income) before it commits to any more advances or decides whether to exercise an option to extend the term.

There may be a requirement that you have to write a minimum number of the songs on an album. That percentage varies depending on the songwriter and the style of music. For a band, the requirement is usually that you have to write at least 80% of the songs on your own album. There is also usually a requirement that that album has to be commercially released. This sort of arrangement works better for a songwriter who also performs and records his own material.

A much less common commitment is one that you get when you have a songwriter who records some of his own material, writes to commissions from others, or writes for a number of different styles of music, for example, film, TV, classical and popular. The Minimum Commitment could be a number of 'points', with a different value being given to each type of usage, genre, format and so on. For example, two points for a ballet commission, five for a track on a popular-music album, with, say, thirty points in total required per contract period. The publisher is only likely to agree to this sort of commitment where you're already established in a number of these areas and they are not common.

Advances

It's usual under an exclusive publishing agreement for the publisher to pay advances. As we saw with record contracts, this is a pre-payment of your share of the gross income from the use of your songs. It's not a loan and isn't repayable to the publishing company if you never earn enough from the songs it controls to cover the amount of the advance then you usually don't have to pay it back, but if you take the money and run, never delivering a single song, your publisher may get a bit upset and may sue for return of their money on the basis that you've failed to fulfil your side of the bargain.

What size of advance can you expect? This will change with circumstances. Your bargaining power, the number of co-writers there are, how much is your own material and how much is sampled from others will all help to determine the figure. It will also depend on how much the publisher thinks it's likely to earn from your songs on average. If the record deal has already been done, the publisher may take its lead from what it knows of the level of that deal. If that was a particularly 'hot' deal the publisher will know that it probably has to increase the overall terms of its offer. There are also financial models that help a publisher to decide how much they can realistically risk. Some publishers rely on these models, while others work on more of a gut instinct or a combination of the two. You also have to factor in market forces. If the publisher really wants to sign you up, whether to increase the profile of the company, for market share or just because the A&R man wants it, then that publisher will pay whatever it takes.

The higher the advance, the more the publisher will expect from you in return and the larger percentage of the income that the publisher will keep as their fee. The publisher will be more reluctant to give you a higher than average royalty if they've had to pay out a high advance − £75,000 for a writer for 80% or more of the songs on an album isn't unreasonable from a major publisher. Much higher figures can be expected if there is 'hype' or if you have a proven track record. If the publisher knows that there is already some income out there from your catalogue waiting to be collected, or that you have a song on the next album to be released by a chart-topping act, they're more likely to risk paying higher advances. A recent deal doubled in value when in the course of the negotiation it was confirmed that one of the songs was to be covered by a top artist and included on her next album which was expected to sell in the millions. A smaller publishing company cannot usually hope to compete just on money and if you are considering a deal with a smaller publisher you have to weigh up things like the greater degree of control versus advances.

The publishing deal is likely to recoup a lot faster than the record deal because, with a publishing deal, you only have to recoup the personal advances and maybe some money in demo costs − there aren't the additional recoupable expenses like recording costs, video costs and tour support. Also, the publisher pays through to you a much larger percentage of the income earned for the use of your songs than most record companies do with the income from sales of your records.

Royalties

The publishing advance is recouped from your royalty earnings after first deducting the publisher's fee. For an exclusive publishing deal this will usually be about 20–25% of the gross income.

Royalties can be calculated in one of two ways, either 'at source' or on 'receipts'. 'At source' means that there have been no deductions made by anyone (after the collection societies, the VAT man and payments to any arranger or translator) from the gross income earned from your songs. This is an 'at source' means of calculation. In a 'receipts' deal in addition to these deductions the publisher's sub-publisher's overseas have to be paid and these fees are deducted from the gross before the income is paid through to you.

Let me give you an example. Ten thousand euros are earned in France in mechanical income from use of your songs on a record after paying the collection society and the tax. If you are on a 'source' deal then, as far as you're concerned, nothing else gets deducted from that 10,000 by the sub-publisher in France before it's paid through to your publisher in the UK. The UK publisher would then deduct this fee of say 2,500 euros from the 10,000 euros and pay through 7,500 euros (or the sterling equivalent) to you. If you are on a 'receipts' deal then the sub-publisher in France would first take their 'cut' of, say, 15% (1,500 euros) leaving 8,500 euros to be sent through to your publisher in the UK. They then take their 25% of that 8,500 euros, leaving you with just 6,300 euros.

As a songwriter you should try and get an 'at source' deal, but your publisher may not have any choice. The deals done with their sub-publishers may mean they have to do deals on a 'receipts' basis in order to make any money out of use of your songs overseas.

If you're offered a 'receipts' deal, the very least you should do is to try and limit the amount the sub-publishers can take off the 'gross' income. For example, you might want to say in the contract that the sub-publishers can't deduct any more than 15–20%. We saw in the *Elton John* v. *Dick James* case that the sub-publishers were spread all over the world and many were associated with Dick James and his UK companies. There was no limit on what these sub-publishers could take off the top as their cut. As Elton was on a 'receipts' deal he could have, and did in some cases, find himself in a situation where the sub-publisher took 50% or more, leaving small amounts to come into the UK, where a further percentage fee was deducted by Dick James – leaving very little over for Elton. Putting a 'cap' on the deductions would have gone some way to reduce these problems.

Synchronisation and Cover Royalties

Sometimes the publisher justifies taking a larger piece of the pie by saying that, in order to do certain work for you, it needs the incentive of getting more of a fee. Part of me says that getting 20–25% of your income should be enough for most purposes. The reality is that the business has accepted that publishers will get a larger fee for these types of work and it's hard to buck against the trend unless you have a great deal of bargaining power. What areas am I talking about? The two usual areas where the publisher takes a larger fee are synchronisation licences and covers.

They usually look to get about another 5–10% for obtaining synchronisation licences for your songs, so if you were paying your publisher a fee on mechanical royalties of 25%, you would see that increase to 30–35% for synchronisation royalties.

If you find that the publisher won't move on this point, the best thing is to make sure that they don't get this increased percentage on projects that you or someone other than the publisher introduces. For example, if one of your mates from drama school brings a film project to you, you wouldn't expect the publisher to take a bigger fee because it didn't go out and find that work.

The same sort of rules should apply to a cover. A cover is a recording of a song done by someone other than the songwriter. So, for example, if a track were first recorded by U2 and is later recorded by Sinead O'Connor, Sinead's version would be the cover. Once again, the publisher will probably want an increased fee for finding other artists keen to cover your works. The answer is to make sure that something doesn't count as a cover unless the publisher has actually done something positive to get it. For example, if you bumped into an artist at an awards show and he was raving about what he thought he could do with your song, if he then goes on to cover that song, it hasn't happened because of anything the publisher has done. The publisher should not get an increased fee for that cover.

You have to be particularly careful where you're a songwriter who doesn't perform his own songs. Otherwise, you'll find that you're paying the higher fee for most of what you're doing, because the recording will always be by someone other than the person who wrote it, i.e. you, and everything will be a cover. In these cases I always push for all recordings to be treated in the same way and not as covers. The publishers are sometimes reluctant to do this, saying that getting anyone to record a song requires effort and that it's harder if the songwriter isn't the performing artist. You have to stand your ground on this. If you're a songwriter you'll be paying a publisher to find ways to use your songs. You shouldn't expect them to increase their fee just because you aren't going to record your own songs.

Performing income

The PRS rules require that at least six-twelfths (50%) of the performing income has to go to the writer/composer. This is called 'the writer's share'. The other six-twelfths is called 'the publisher's share'. Depending on the deal you have, the publisher will either say that they intend to keep the whole of the publisher's share or they will agree to share some of it with you. You get to keep the writer's share and don't have to put it towards recoupment of your advances. Your share of the publisher's share will go towards recoupment of any unrecouped advance.

When you're dealing with contracts for the use of music in a film or TV programme, it's still common for the publisher to insist on keeping the entire 'publisher's share' and not putting any of it towards recoupment. TV and film publishing deals have lagged behind popular-music deals, where it's usual for the publisher to share up to 50% of the publisher's share with the songwriter.

Accounting

The publishing company will usually account to you every six months. You'll be sent a statement of what use has been made of your songs in the previous six months and how much income has been received. It should show the percentage that your publisher has kept as their fee and the amount that has been credited to your account. Your share of income will go first to recoup advances. After that your publisher should send a cheque with the statement for the royalties due to you. Even if the account isn't recouped, you or your representatives should check these accounting statements to see if they seem right and that the correct fee has been deducted. If, for example, you know that your music was used in an advert in the last six months but there is no mention of income from this in the statement, you should ask your publisher to explain. It also pays for you to audit the books of the publishing company from time to time. You don't want to be doing this every five minutes, but you may want to run a check after you've had a particularly successful time. You'll probably also want to think about doing an audit when the deal comes to an end, as that is going to be your last practical chance to check up on your publisher. Because it can be very expensive to carry out an audit (£10,000 plus isn't unusual), you only want to do it when you think there is a reasonable chance of getting something back from it. If the audit shows up serious errors in your favour, you should expect them to reimburse you the main costs of doing the audit as well as paying you whatever sums the audit has shown are due to you.

You shouldn't delay in raising any concerns you might have about an accounting statement, as the publishing contract will probably put a time limit on you doing so. Usually, if a statement hasn't been challenged for three years, sometimes less, then it's said to have been accepted and no objection can be raised to it after that time.

WHAT CAN YOU EXPECT FROM A PUBLISHER UNDER AN EXCLUSIVE PUBLISHING AGREEMENT?

We've already seen that there is a presumption that an exclusive songwriting agreement is in restraint of trade and it's up to the publisher to show that the contract, taken as a whole, is reasonable to protect its interests and fair to the songwriter. As we saw in the *Macaulay* v. *Schroeder* case, a publishing contract should require the publisher to do something with your songs that it controls, and if the publisher doesn't manage to do so within a reasonable period of time you should be able to get those songs back. The publisher has to ensure that it does what it can to get the songs used, to maximise the income from all uses and to make sure the songs are properly registered, and income properly collected and accounted through to the writer.

Your publisher should also take steps to protect your songs from unauthorised uses. Sampling of songs is rife and it's up to the publisher either to prevent such uses by court action or, if you and your publisher are prepared to allow the sample use, to ensure a proper amount is paid in compensation (see Chapter 13).

Open-ended contracts are likely to be seen as unfairly restrictive, as we see in the case of Holly Johnson *and* Perfect Songs.[19]

Frankie Goes To Hollywood

This case came to court at the same time as the related case involving Johnson's record contract. Both the record and publishing companies were trying to get an injunction to bind Holly Johnson to the contracts, even though the band he was a member of, Frankie Goes To Hollywood, had disbanded. Holly Johnson argued that both agreements were unenforceable as being an unreasonable restraint of his trade.

When the court looked at the publishing contract, it found that it was potentially a very long contract and that it was exclusive but there had not been equal bargaining power when it was entered into. It found that the restrictions in the contract were not reasonable and declared that the publishing agreement was unenforceable. The judge was concerned that Holly Johnson and his fellow band members had not had any choice in whether they did the publishing deal. It was offered as a package with the record deal. There was also no obligation on the publisher to do anything with the songs. There was no re-assignment of the rights in the songs if the publisher failed to exploit them in any way. The judge also thought that it was unfair that Perfect Songs had full control over what happened to the songs once they were delivered. The songwriters had little or no creative control. The judge considered what financial benefits the songwriters got out of the deal and found that the 35% fee retained by the publisher was too much.

Stone Roses publishing dispute

Another case that has had an effect on the form of publishing contracts is the Stone Roses publishing dispute.[20]

The Stone Roses were a Manchester band that had a hit with an album called *The Stone Roses*, released in 1989. They were signed to the Silvertone label, part of the Zomba Group. The members of the Stone Roses were also offered a package deal. They couldn't do the record deal without also signing the publishing deal. As we saw in the case of *Armatrading* v. *Stone*, it's very important that the songwriter gets independent advice from his own lawyer, someone who is familiar with the music business and its contracts. In this case, the songwriters had their own lawyer but he was not experienced in music contracts and made hardly any changes to the terms of the contract from the initial draft that the publishing company's lawyer gave to him. There was no equality of bargaining power. The agreement was an exclusive one and the rights were assigned for the life of copyright. There

19 *Perfect Songs Limited* v. *Johnson and Others* [1993] E.M.L.R 61.
20 *Zomba* v. *Mountfield and Others* [1993] E.M.L.R 152.

108

was a limited obligation on the publisher to do something with the songs under its control. After five years the Stone Roses could ask for the rights back in any of their songs that hadn't been exploited. The first contract period was linked to that of the record deal. The court found that the first contract period of the record deal was capable of being extended indefinitely. As the two were linked, this meant that the publishing agreement was similarly open-ended and, as such, unreasonable. The court also found that the advances were not reasonable and objected to the lack of artistic or creative control by the songwriters. Because Zomba had obtained an injunction preventing the band from recording for anyone else, they couldn't bring out any more records until this case had been decided. When it was they signed a big deal with US label Geffen. The band went on to release another album called, appropriately enough, *The Second Coming*, but split up shortly afterwards.

As a result of this and similar cases it's now common to have clauses in UK publishing agreements making it clear that the publisher has to do something with the rights it has. Also that the songwriter should have some say on what happens to the songs once they're delivered. It's usual to say that no major changes to the music or any change to the lyrics can be made without the songwriter's approval. The criticism of the 65:35 split has led to the average publishing royalty rising to at least 70% in the songwriter's favour and in many cases to 75% with the publisher keeping no more than 25–30% but this is by no means universal and 65:35 deals are still being done with 50:50 deals in the TV and film industry still being common.

MORAL RIGHTS AND CREATIVE CONTROL

A songwriter may have strong views on what he wants or doesn't want to happen to his songs. For example, a songwriter may believe passionately that no one should be allowed to alter the words or music without his approval. This doesn't usually extend to straight translations. Those are taken to be a logical part of the exploitation process. But if, in the translation, the translator wanted to give the lyrics a different meaning and the songwriter objected to this, he should be entitled to prevent this happening. Obviously, I'm not talking about minor changes, but major ones that change the meaning significantly. This contractual control overlaps with a songwriter's moral rights. Moral rights are described in more detail in Chapter 12. Where you're able to retain your moral rights then you should do so. The reality is that, because our copyright laws acknowledge these rights but allow you to waive them, all publishers have put clauses in their contracts requiring you to waive these rights. What lawyers now do is to put contract clauses in to give you the same or similar rights to what you would have got from using your moral rights. So you might ask why we bother with this farce. Why don't we acknowledge that the songwriter has certain rights to object to what is morally being done to his songs? Well, the essential difference is that the moral rights usually go a bit wider than what you get under your contract and a moral right is capable of being enforced by you even if your publishing company doesn't want to take any action.

Other creative controls may involve the songwriter reserving a song for himself or his band to record and stopping another artist applying for and getting a mechanical licence to record that song first. The publisher will usually agree not to issue a first mechanical licence to another artist where the songwriter wants to reserve it, but will usually require that there is a time limit of, say, six months on this. If it hasn't been recorded in that time then the restriction can be lifted.

Finally, of course, the songwriter will want to ensure he is properly credited.

WHAT TYPE OF DEAL SHOULD YOU DO?

How do you decide which deal is best for you? To some extent this may be out of your control. You may not be offered anything other than an exclusive publishing agreement. You may not be able to afford to keep control of your copyrights. You may be able to afford to do so but haven't got the organisational talents necessary to make sure that your works are properly protected and the income collected. In these cases the exclusive songwriter agreement is for you. But if you aren't bothered about getting an advance and you do want to control your copyrights, you may want to go for either a sub-publishing or an administration deal, depending on how much activity you require from your publisher.

NEW BUSINESS MODELS

As we saw in relation to management deals in Chapter 2, some managers now insist on taking an interest in your publishing as well. There are also many more package deals involving a production company acquiring rights in your recordings as well as your songs. You also have to consider the issue of a potential conflict of interest between his role as your manager and as your publisher. Try to make sure that the set-up is a proper, arm's length one; that the manager/publisher/production company has thought about how he is going to administer the rights he is getting, and make sure that the manager does not take management commission on your publishing royalties for so long as he is also acting as your publisher of those songs. And of course there are the 360 deals where not only publishing and record rights are involved but also live and merchandising rights. Look back at the last chapter for the reservations I have expressed about these deals.

CONCLUSIONS

- Decide what type of deal would ideally suit you.

- Decide if you need an advance and, if so, how big an advance – this will help you decide whether to go for a sub-publishing or an administration deal.

- You should try and do deals where your share of the income is calculated 'at source' – but if you have to have a 'receipts' deal then make sure you put a limit on what the overseas sub-publishers can deduct in their fees.

- If you're receiving 75% or more of the gross fees you're doing well.

- Look at the Minimum Commitment. Is it realistic? Can you achieve it within a reasonable period of time?

- If you're a songwriter who doesn't also record his own works, try not to agree to a contractual commitment that means your songs have to be exploited in some way, as this will be outside your control.

- If you're a songwriter who doesn't record his own songs, hold out for no reduction in the amount of royalty you receive on 'covers'.

- Make sure there's no delay in you receiving your money from overseas.

Chapter 5
Getting A Record Made

INTRODUCTION

Just to make things a little clearer in this chapter I'm going to assume that you've signed a record deal and that the money for making your record will come from the record company, either as a separate recording budget fund or as an all-inclusive advance. At the end of the chapter I'm going to look at other ways of making a record, for example, where you're funding the making of the record yourself.

PRODUCTION DEALS VERSUS DIRECT SIGNINGS

Before I go into the process of getting a record made, I need to look at two different ways of structuring a record deal. This has an impact on how the recording process is organised. We covered both types of signings in Chapter 3 – the direct signing or a signing to a bigger company through a production company. Now we're going to take a closer look at the production deal and compare the pros and cons of this versus a straight signing.

PRODUCTION DEALS

Don't confuse production with the process of producing a record by a record producer which I'll deal with below. As we've seen a production deal is one where someone (whether it's an individual, a partnership or a company) acts as a middleman between the record company and the artist. This middleman is the production company.

Sometimes a smaller label or someone who doesn't want a full-time role as a manager finds a talented artist. They may not have the necessary funds to make the record or, even if they can afford to make it, may not have the necessary clout to get decent manufacturing, distribution, marketing or promotion. The label or individual could sign up the artist and then look for a company with more resources to fund the recording and all aspects of putting out the record. In effect, they are selling on the rights they have to the artist's services, either by a licence of rights or an assignment of them.

The contract between the production company and the artist is called a production deal.

WHAT IS A PRODUCTION DEAL?

The contract may look very similar to a record deal, more details of which are in Chapter 3. The production company could sign the artist up to record an album with options to make further albums. The number of options may be less than in a straight record deal, perhaps two or three options instead of four or five. The money available will often be less than with an exclusive record deal with an established larger record company and, in some ways, may resemble a development deal. The deal may be a 'net receipts' deal as opposed to one where the artist is paid a royalty on record sales. It will also probably say somewhere in the contract that the intention is to try to get another company involved with greater resources.

It's a little difficult to agree up-front what sort of deal will be done with the bigger company. If I'm acting for the artist I usually try to ensure he gets the chance to be involved in the negotiations with the third party whenever that arises. After all, the bigger company needs to know the artist is on side, so should want to co-operate. If the bigger record company is going to pay advances to the production company, the artist will want to know that he'll get a decent share of them. Also, if the artist is on a 'net receipts' deal, he will need to know that the royalty being paid is high enough when it's split between him and the production company. For example, if the artist is on a 50:50 net receipts deal and the royalty is 18% then he'll be on a 9% royalty, as will the production company. Maybe the artist's percentage should be higher – 65% or 75% instead of 50:50. If you're the production company you should work out what's a good deal for you and should be looking at getting a clear profit equal to a 3–4% royalty. Obviously each negotiation is different so these percentages are guidelines only.

WHAT'S IN IT FOR THE OTHER RECORD COMPANY?
The bigger company has the advantage of having someone else find and develop a new artist. By the time the project is brought to them they can hear what it's going to sound like. Some of the risk has been taken away. If they're licensing a finished record from a production company, they know exactly what they are getting. There's also a middleman to deal with the artist – who becomes someone else's problem. One downside for the bigger company is lack of control. They need to be confident that the production company can deliver the goods, so they are more likely to trust someone who already has a track record.

WHAT'S IN IT FOR THE PRODUCTION COMPANY?
The production company has a much closer involvement with the artist. It has the thrill of discovering an artist early and of developing them. It gets another company to take the risk on manufacture, distribution and marketing costs, but at that stage it loses control. If the bigger company then fails in what it has to do, all the production company's work will have been wasted. For the production company it's essential they choose a bigger company with a good marketing department and that they try and get a clause in the contract with the bigger company which allows them to insist on outside press and marketing people being brought in if necessary. If it works, the production company get their costs and expenses repaid, the financial risk on the manufacture, distribution and marketing taken off their hands, and a decent royalty into the bargain.

WHAT'S IN IT FOR THE ARTIST?
If a production company is interested in an artist then it's a step up the ladder. If they know what they're doing, there will be a second chance later of getting a bigger company involved. There should also be greater artistic and creative freedom, unless the production team are control freaks. The downside for the artist is that, if he doesn't get the deal right, he could end up sharing a larger than necessary piece of the pie with the production company. He is also a further stage removed from the record company that's promoting the record, so it's that much harder to get his views heard and therefore it's important that there are plenty of creative controls in the contract which flow through to the bigger deal.

FINDING A STUDIO

Whether you're signed direct or via a production company, one thing you'll have to do is to find a suitable recording studio. It could be as simple as the studio in your back bedroom or as complex as a full-blown commercial studio. Before you decide on a studio you should look at several – at the ambience as well as whether it has the necessary equipment. If equipment has to be hired in, it will add to the recording costs. You should listen to material produced in the studios and, if you can, talk to other artists who have used them. You should also talk to any in-house engineer or producer. How enthusiastic are they about the place and how it's run? If you have a record producer in mind or a favourite engineer, ask them what they think of the various studios on your shortlist.

You also need to think about where it is. Is it easy to get equipment in or out? Is it secure? You'll have seen stories in the press of recordings being 'leaked' from the studio and appearing on the Internet. Record companies are doing what they can to tighten security but do check if the studio keeps recordings safe and secure, and who is responsible for this. Can leaks be traced? Also, provided you can keep it safe yourself consider making a backup copy of the final versions of the recordings and keeping it somewhere safe away from the studio. This might prove invaluable if there are problems of security or if the studio proves difficult in releasing the final recordings. I have known studios hold artists to ransom asking for a bigger fee in return for release of the master recordings. Most do not descend to this level but disputes can arise over what is properly due and the studio may legitimately have a lien or hold over the recordings until this is resolved.

A studio can either be one that you go to day to day or a residential one where you stay in accommodation at or near the studio. Your own personal arrangements might decide which is better for you. Some bands respond best when they're immersed in the project in a residential studio. For others, the idea of spending 24 hours a day, 7 days a week with the other band members is their idea of hell.

STUDIO PACKAGE DEALS
The recording studio may block out a period of time and the studio is yours for the whole of that time. These arrangements are sometimes called 'lockout' deals. Other deals are for a fixed eight- or ten-hour day. If you overrun, you may either find that the studio has been hired out to someone else or that there are heavy financial penalties. Some studios will give you discounts on their usual rate if you record at times when the studio wouldn't normally be in use, for example, in the early hours of the morning. This is called 'down time'. It's fine if you're on a very tight budget or if you just want to record some demo tracks. But if you're planning to use down time to record your whole album, you're putting very great limitations on yourself. It's mentally and physically tough recording an album without adding to this by having to record it all at two in the morning.

Some studios will offer a package deal that includes mixing and mastering of the finished recordings. There are two things to bear in mind here. First, the studio must have the technical capabilities to do a good job and secondly, the price offered should represent good value.

Your A&R man or production company representative is going to be an important source of information on where you choose to record. These people also have a vital role to play in giving you feedback on how the recording is going. It's far too easy to lock yourself away in a studio and become isolated from reality. You'll need feedback and constructive criticism. The A&R man won't be sitting at your shoulder all the way through the recordings, but he will want to visit the studio regularly during the recording process. Don't surround yourself with yes men – you'll need people who can be objective and whose opinion and judgement you respect.

Once you've chosen your studio you need to haggle on a price – or your manager, production company or A&R man will do it for you. Before you book the time, make sure that any people you want to help with the recording, like a producer, engineer or session musicians, are available. If you really want to work with a particular person then you may have to adjust your recording schedule to work around their availability. If they live outside the UK they may need a permit to work in this country. This can take time and has to be factored into the recording timetable. If you want to record overseas you may need visas or work permits so allow time for those to be put in place too.

Another key factor in the choice of the studio is whether you can afford it. Studio costs and fees to a producer usually make up most of the recording costs. You'll have to recoup these, so it's important that you keep an eye on them.

It is becoming quite common for a record producer to offer an all-in rate for his services which includes studio costs. This of course assumes the producer either has his own studio or open access to one. With these deals in particular you need to be sure that the studio is up to the job in hand.

THE RECORDING BUDGET

When you or your manager were pitching for your record deal you may well have done a 'back of an envelope' calculation of how much it would cost you to record. Now you're going to have to do a much more detailed budget. You and your manager are going to have to work out how long you think you're going to take to record the album, how many days of studio time and what that will cost at the studio of your choice. You need to know how much your producer of choice will charge, how long a mixer will take to mix it and what he's likely to charge. If there are session vocalists or musicians who will need to be there for all or part of the time, you need to know how much they will charge per day or session. There are minimum rates set by bodies like the Musicians' Union and Equity (see Chapter 17), but good people will want more than the minimum rate. If special equipment is required, you need to work out how much this will cost to hire and whether it's more cost-effective to buy it. It may be a piece of equipment that you'll need to have later when you're out on the road promoting the album. You may have an equipment budget as part of your deal or the cost may be built into the recording budget. Another possibility is that you'll have to buy the equipment out of your personal advance.

Don't forget rehearsal time. You don't want to spend expensive studio time rehearsing the songs until you're ready to record them. Do this before you set foot in the studio. Whether you do this in a professional rehearsal room or in a room over the local chip shop will depend on your budget.

Once you've thought of everything you should add at least 10% to it. This is called a contingency. It's to cover extra costs when you spend another day in the studio or on mixing or when you have to hire in equipment because yours or the studios isn't up to the job.

If you have a recording fund deal, your total budget should not exceed about 60% of the total advance to give you enough to live on. If you have a deal where you have an advance plus a recording budget, you'll have to keep within the maximum set by the record company and you'll have to take your finished outline budget to them for approval. Bear in mind that most record contracts say that if you overrun the agreed budget without first getting clearance from the record company, you'll be liable for the extra expense. It will be deducted from your royalties and possibly also from any further advances due to you under the deal.

MASTERING AND DIGITISATION COSTS

These are a grey area. Mastering costs are the costs that are involved in getting the final mixed recordings into a state ready to be made into records. Where those records are to be made available as digital downloads then the masters have to be digitised. I'll deal with the process in a little more detail below. The record contract will say whether these costs are to be included in the recording budget or not. Mastering can cost several thousand pounds, so it's important to know this when setting your financial budget. The situation with recharge of digitisation costs is in a state of flux. Some companies treat these as part of the costs of online distribution akin to the transport costs they incur for physical distribution. Others pass on the costs as a recoupable amount.

THE PRODUCER

The role of the producer has been described as getting the dynamics and emotion of the music on tape. The producer makes your material come alive. It's possible for you to produce yourself and many successful artists do. By the same token most artists, particularly when they are starting out, might find it difficult to get the necessary distance in order to hear how the music will sound to an outsider. The producer can be your external critic. You're going to be working closely together, so it's helpful if you have similar musical tastes and influences. You have to like working with them, respect them and have a common vision of how the music should sound.

Your A&R man can be very helpful in pointing you in the direction of possible producers. They can do a lot of the filtering process. They may play your demo to a series of different producers to see who's interested. They may invite producers to come to your gigs to get a feel for how you sound. Some vocalists need a little help in the studio in keeping in tune. A good producer will realise that when he hears you play live. Increasingly the producer is through necessity taking on the role of a finder and developer of talent, sometimes as a formal production company but sometimes just by default as part of his role as record producer.

WHAT DOES A PRODUCER GET PAID?
Fee or advance

A producer will usually expect to be paid a fee per track that they produce. This could be a pure fee, which isn't recouped. It could be an advance against the producer's royalty, or it could be part non-recoupable fees and part advances. Good producers can charge £5,000 plus per track and many of those will expect some of it to be a non-recoupable fee. Whether they get that will depend on the negotiation. If it's being recorded in the producer's studio he may include recording costs in the fee so the total may be nearer £10,000 than £5,000.

Royalty

The producers may just work for a fee, but they will often expect to receive a royalty calculated in the same way as the artist's record royalty is calculated. A good producer may insist on a royalty of 4% of the dealer price or 3% of the retail price. They may ask for increases in the royalty if sales exceed a given amount. Producers who work with very commercial acts see themselves very much as key parts of the team and charge royalties accordingly. Some producers charge over 5–6% of the dealer price and the rates will definitely be higher if the advance is low.

RECOUPMENT OF COSTS

Another big bone of contention is whether the producer receives the royalty as soon as he has recouped any advance he has received, or if he has to also wait until his royalty, together with the artist's royalty, has also recouped the recording costs on the tracks he has produced. If he agrees to the latter, the producer may say that once that's achieved, his royalty is calculated as if he had been paid from record one after recouping his advance. Let me give you an example:

A producer is to be paid a 3% royalty and has received a £30,000 advance. The recording costs on the tracks he worked on came to £200,000. The artist's royalty together with the producer's 3% is 12%. Say each record sold makes the artist £1.25. He'd have to sell £230,000 ÷ £1.25 = 184,000 copies of the record in order to recoup the advances. Say the producer's 3% royalty earns him 31p. To recoup his £30,000 advance he'd have to sell £30,000 ÷ £0.31 = 96,774 copies. If he's on a deal where he's paid retrospectively he would then get paid on the number of copies sold between 184,000 and 96,774 copies, i.e. 87,226 x £0.31 = another £27,040. If the artist sells 96,775 copies, the producer recoups his advance and receives the extra £27,040 but if the artist doesn't sell more than 184,000 copies he doesn't recoup the recording costs and the producer gets no more royalties. So the producer is taking a risk, but if it pays off he gets a windfall.

The producer is almost invariably expected to have to wait until all recording costs have been recouped and often it's only with great reluctance that record companies accept that this should then be retroactive. Where the producer doesn't have to wait until any recording costs have been recouped and is paid his royalty as soon as he has recouped his advance, this can be a problem for the artist. He can only really do it if his record company agrees to advance him the money to pay the producer. The artist is unlikely to be recouped as he will have all the recording costs, video costs and so on to recoup first. This pushes the artist further into debt, but he will often agree to this if it's the only way he's going to be able to do the deal and get that particular producer.

WHO DOES THE CONTRACT?

In the UK it's usually the record or production company that will do the deal with the producer, will issue the contract and negotiate its terms. In the record contract it should say whether or not the record company has to get the artist's approval of the commercial terms. At the very least the artist should have approval of the royalty, because it will usually come out of his royalty, and of the advance, which will usually be a recoupable recording cost.

In the US the artist issues the contract and negotiates the deal with the producer – or his lawyer does. The contract isn't with the record company, but between artist and producer. If the artist doesn't pay, the producer can only sue the artist, who may not have the money. In the UK the contract is between the record company and the producer, so if anything goes wrong the record producer can sue the record company not the artist. This puts the producer in a more secure position. The US record company will usually do the royalty calculation and, if asked, will pay royalties direct to the producer as a favour not as a legal obligation.

REMIX ROYALTY REDUCTION

The royalty to the producer almost invariably comes out of the artist's royalty, so it's in the artist's interests to keep the royalty at a reasonable level. If the record is to be mixed or remixed then a good record mixer will also want to be paid a royalty. You could try and get the record producer to agree that, if the mixer is paid a royalty, the producer's royalty is reduced by the same amount. Some producers will agree to this. Others are adamant that if they've done a good job of production there shouldn't be any reduction in their royalty just because the record company or artist decides to bring in another person to mix the records. If this becomes a real sticking point, it's sometimes possible to get the record company to contribute to the royalty for the mixer, perhaps by paying another 0.5%. Producers who do agree to a reduction will usually limit it to no more than half the total producer royalty or 1%.

CREDITS

The producer will usually want to receive a credit on the packaging of the record and in marketing material.

Sometimes a 'name' producer will insist on having the right to remove his name from the packaging if his work is remixed and he doesn't like or wish to be associated with the end result.

There isn't any one way that I have come across to credit the producer in online uses. It is of course possible to embed information in the data for the recording when it is digitised. You see this when you download music to your MP3 player (totally legally of course) and the software you use to do this 'reads' the metadata to identify artist and track. However, it still hasn't become commonplace to demand this or any other form of credit for downloads

STANDARD OF WORK

Whether it's the artist or his record company that's doing the contract, they'll want to know that the producer's work will be of a high standard. There will probably be instalment payments to the producer so that he isn't paid in full until recordings of the required standard have been delivered. So what is that standard? Well, just as we saw with record contracts, it's usually a question of whether the producer has to deliver technically satisfactory recordings or whether they have to be commercially acceptable. The latter is, of course, a very subjective test and the producer may well argue that he has no say in what the artist chooses to record, so it's not his fault if the finished recording isn't commercial. A common compromise is to say that it must be a first-class technical production and of at least the same high standards as the producer's previous productions.

RIGHTS

The producer usually assigns any and all copyright he has in the sound recordings he produces to the artist (US deals) or to the record or production company (UK deals). The recordings may have been made in a studio owned by the producer. In that case there is a possibility that the producer made the arrangements for the recording to be made. If so, the producer could claim to be the first owner of copyright.[1] The record company will therefore want to make sure that it takes an assignment of any copyright the producer may have.

In the US they deal with it slightly differently. There the contracts will say that, for the purposes of copyright, the producer is employed by the artist. Under US copyright laws the artist owns the copyright in anything a producer creates where he is employed by the artist. This is called a 'work for hire'. US record companies often adopt the same approach which you have to watch out for if you are in fact doing a licence not an assignment of copyright. You will want to get rid of these 'for hire' clauses in a licence deal.

The producer may perform on the recordings. He may play an instrument or programme a keyboard. He may therefore have the same rights as any other performer.[2] The record company will therefore want to know that he has given all the necessary consents to his performances being used. The fee or advances that the producer is paid will usually include any fees for his performances.

If the producer has made any original creative contribution to the writing or composing of the music or the words then he may have rights as a co-author of that song.[3] If the artist and producer agree on what each has contributed this isn't usually a problem. The artist will want to know that a mechanical licence will be available on standard industry terms so that the producer's share of that song can be included on the recording. If the artist has agreed to reduced mechanical royalties in the US and Canada (the so-called Controlled Compositions clauses as explained in Chapter 4) then the artist should make sure the producer accepts the same reductions. He may, however, refuse to do this and there is no requirement that he do so. If the producer co-writes a number of the songs on the album, this could affect the artist's ability to fulfil the Minimum Commitment requirements that he may have in his publishing deal. This must also be taken into account when agreeing what share is allocated to the producer. If a producer co-writes the songs, he will have moral rights in his work. He may also have moral rights as a performer. The contract will usually require him to waive those moral rights (for more on moral rights, see Chapter 12). If he hasn't co-written any of the songs or isn't claiming any publishing rights, the contract will usually require him to confirm this on a warranty.

1 Section 9(2) (aa) CDPA and Chapter 3.
2 See section 191A ff CDPA for performers' rights and Chapter 3 for more details on what these rights are.
3 See section 9(2) (3) CDPA on authorship of words and music and section 10 on co-authorship.

PRODUCER'S DUTIES

In addition to making sure that the production is of the required standard, it's also the job of the producer to try to keep the recording costs within the budget and to let the artist/record company know if it's likely to run over budget. The contract may make the producer responsible for any overrun on the budget that is his fault.

The producer is responsible for getting all session musicians to complete the necessary forms, buying out their rights and getting all the necessary performers' consents. He has to deliver these signed forms to the record company with details of who did what on each recording. He also has to keep all recordings safe and deliver them up to the record company when asked to do so. It is usual to make one or more backups. The delivery up includes all outtakes, i.e. recordings that didn't end up in the final mix on the record.

One case in which these 'outtakes' then found their way onto a commercially released record involved Bruce Springsteen.[4]

The Springsteen Case

> Bruce Springsteen had had agreements early in his career with a record company called Flute. Those agreements had been declared to be void from the outset in a previous court case. As we saw in other cases such as *Elton John* v. *Reed*, this was unusual. Most courts won't declare agreements to be void (i.e. as if they'd never been entered into) but voidable (i.e. could be set aside as to future rights). Because the recording and publishing agreements were said to be void, Springsteen argued that he was the owner of the copyright in all previous recordings, including any outtakes or other unreleased material. He couldn't produce any evidence in court to back up his claim that all copyrights had been reassigned to him, but the court accepted that he was the owner of the sound recording copyright and therefore could control what happened with them. The court decided he was within his rights to claim that CDs containing outtakes of his recordings released by Flute were an infringement of his rights.

While a record company is unlikely to risk upsetting an artist by releasing records containing outtakes while he is still under contract to them, they may not have any such qualms after the end of the contract. The producer will have handed those outtakes over to the record company, so the artist's agreement with the record company should cover what can or can't be done with those outtakes.

MIXING

This is the stage between production (i.e. the recording and capturing of the essence of the song) and mastering (when the recording is made ready for duplication).

The mixer selects from all the various recordings he has of a song those that will be mixed together to make up the final version. He also chooses which aspects to emphasise, for example a guitar part or a vocal might be brought into more prominence.

The producer might do the mix and, as he's been close to the recording process throughout, you'd think he would be best placed for the job. He may be, but very

---

4 *Springsteen* v. *Flute International Limited and Others* [1998] Chancery Division.

particular talents are required for mixing and sometimes a fresh 'ear' can hear things that the producer and the artist can't.

There are also mixers who take the finished, fully mixed recording and play around with it – maybe changing the rhythm or bringing in elements either sampled from the recordings themselves or from elsewhere. These are called remixers and the resulting recordings are called remixes. When samples are being introduced, the artist (in the US) or the record company (in the UK) has to make sure that all necessary rights have been cleared and that the mixer has permission to include them (see Chapter 13). Remixes are often done to create a different sound for radio or to play in the clubs.

MIX CONTRACTS

The contracts for mixers and remixers are very similar to (and follow the same format as) producer contracts.

Fees and advances

A mixer or remixer may only receive a non-recoupable, one-off fee for his work. This can be as much as £10,000-plus for one track to be remixed by a big name.

Increasingly mixers demand an advance, which as with producer deals is sometimes partly non-recoupable, and partly on account of royalties. The same comments apply here as with producer deals above.

Royalties

If a mixer has enough bargaining power, he can ask for and get a royalty of 1% or more. This is usually calculated in the same way as the artist's royalty. As we saw with producer deals, the artist has to work out if there is enough left for him after producers and mixers have received royalties, whether the producer will take a reduced royalty, and whether a royalty has to be paid to a mixer or if he will take a fee instead.

The same issues apply to mixer deals: who does the contract, whether the mixer gets his royalty only after all mix costs have been recouped, and what standard of work is expected of him.

Rights

As with producer deals, the record company will usually require the mixer to assign any sound recording copyright to the record company. When dance remixes were at their peak remixers argued for the right to retain a separate sound recording copyright in their mix. It's possible, if they have added enough original elements or have re-recorded the track as part of the remix process, to create a separate sound recording copyright. I think if I was the artist I would be nervous about some mixers owning a version of my track, and I'd want to have restrictions on what they could do with it. If they wanted to just put it on one of their own record compilations that might be all right. If I were the record company who had paid for the remixes, I'd want to own them and perhaps license rights back to the mixers for that compilation.

Mixers don't usually contribute to the creative writing of the song. Some remixers may claim that they have added enough original elements to create a new work. This may be true, depending on what they have done, but more likely they will be said to have made a new arrangement of it and can receive performance income on that version. This eats into the writer's performing income and most publishers will expect it to come out of the writer's share. The remix contract could ask the mixer to confirm he has no interest in the underlying song at all or, as we saw with producer contracts, if he is a co-author that licences to use the remixer's part of the song will be granted without difficulties on usual industry terms.

MASTERING

This is part of the post-production process when the recordings have been produced and mixed to everyone's satisfaction.

The next stage before the recording goes to be manufactured into records is mastering. It straddles recording and manufacturing. It's not just a mechanical process of ensuring all the right digital notes are in the right places. It's the means to give it a final 'tweaking' before the record is released. A person skilled in mastering can make the sound punchier, warmer, deeper or louder. He can bring out details not already obvious. Mastering is a separate process from the mix and needs a different set of ears. Some bands swear by a particular person mastering their records in much the same way as film directors have their favourite editors.

The mastering process helps the recording sound great no matter what medium it's manufactured in and whatever hardware it's played on. I'm sure you can think of albums that sound fantastic played over headphones on your CD Walkman but awful on the car CD player. This could be a problem of the mix, but it's just as likely that someone didn't get the mastering process right.

When mastering a recording, equalising and compression of the sounds gives a consistency from track to track. Have you ever found yourself constantly having to adjust the volume between tracks on a compilation? It's either earth-shatteringly loud or so quiet you're straining to hear the words. That's an example of bad mastering. Radio really brings out the difference, as the radio process itself compresses the material. If a recording hasn't been properly mastered it can sound thin and weak.

Purists also believe that the compression involved in creating an MP3 loses a great deal of the original, in particular the top and/or bottom registers. The average listener will not know what he is missing and most people's home hi-fi equipment is not of studio quality so no one is any the wiser.

When you've spent a small fortune on making a recording, you shouldn't spoil it for a few thousand pounds in mastering costs.

The person doing the mastering is engaged to do the job by the record or production company. He either provides the mastering suite and equipment or the company hires or pays for one. He is paid a fee for his work. The record company usually pays it and, depending on the contract, will either treat it as a recoupable recording cost or as a non-recoupable manufacturing cost. Some, but not all, artists credit the person who did the mastering, although the actual studios used are often referred to on the packaging.

DELIVERY REQUIREMENTS

There are a number of things that have to be delivered to the record company before the artist can be said to have completed his side of the recording process.

As well as the finished, fully mixed and edited recordings, he will also have to deliver up all outtakes and all copies of the recordings. He may also have to deliver finished recordings of additional tracks to act as B-sides or second tracks on singles, and will definitely have to deliver up all signed session forms and clearances for any samples that have been used in the recording.

The artist will have to deliver a list of all the tracks on the record in the order in which they appear (called a track-listing). He'll probably also have to provide 'label copy', that is all the information that has to appear on the label and packaging of the record. This includes things like who performed on each track, who wrote each track and who publishes those writers. If there is an agreement to give credits to producers and mixers or a name check to the studio, then those details will have to be given to the record company. This is also when the artist gets to say thanks to particular people who have been helpful or supportive.

The contract will be very specific about what has to be delivered and to whom. It will also be quite technical about the form in which the recordings are to be delivered. It's very important that the artist does deliver all that is required of him. If he doesn't, then he'll find that all sorts of things don't happen. He won't get the instalment of advances due on delivery, the manufacturing process won't start nor will time start running for when the record company has to release the record.

The artist should try to get written confirmation from the record company confirming that everything has been delivered from the person identified in the contract as the person to whom delivery has to be made, for instance, the senior vice-president of A&R.

ARTWORK

One key item that usually has to be delivered is the artwork for the cover of the album. Without the artwork the record can't be released in its physical form and rather naff generic 'covers' have to be used for digital downloads, so it may be reasonable to assume (depending on the contract and individual circumstances) that delivery has not taken place until the record company has the finished artwork. The record company usually wants the artwork delivered in a specific format, which these days is usually online, probably with a hard copy to follow up.

Some talented bands do the artwork themselves. Some leave it to the record company's art department. Most hire someone else to do a design to their brief or specification.

If the record company is doing it, the artist should try and make sure he has final approval. If someone else is being brought in, make sure they have a good, professional reputation for their work. The artist should look at covers he admires and who designed them. It's wise to interview a few designers and ask to see examples of their work. Remember that if a potential customer doesn't know who you are, they may be attracted to pick up your CD over all the others by the striking artwork on the cover. You could use art students or friends to do it on the cheap, but then you could end up spending a lot of time supervising the work and would have been better off using a professional in the first place.

The artist's logo should be on the artwork as well as the label or production company logo and name. This is all part of making the package look inviting and identifiably part of your image. Striking artwork and logos repeated on the website and in any other marketing and promotional material not only make the association easier but also help to brand the artist and to make his work stand out from the crowd. Sometimes artwork is used as a marketing tool in itself either by design or by accident. Take the artwork for the last Beck album. It was released with a variety of different stickers that the buyer could use to customise his own copy. The company in charge of the Charts decided that there were too many versions to count for the album charts and debarred the release. This potential disaster was turned into a classic example of 'marketing' spin to raise awareness of the album in the press and amongst the public. Brilliant.

Once the artist has decided on a designer who he thinks can do a good job in the required time, terms need to be agreed. You need a contract setting out what they are going to do, by when and for how much. You may want to make payment in two instalments, one when they start work and the other when they deliver finished work that is satisfactory.

If photographs are to be used, the artist needs to agree who is going to be responsible for supplying those and at whose expense. The record company will usually organise and pay for a photo-shoot, but it may not necessarily be with the top-name photographer the artist would like to use.

Whether or not there are to be photographs, there needs to be an agreement with the designer or photographer that confirms that the commissioner is the owner of the copyright in the photographs and the copyright and any design rights in the artwork and graphics. There should be an assignment of any copyright or design rights they might have acquired. Ideally, there should be no restrictions on what the commissioner can do with those designs and photographs. However, designers and photographers are now wise to the fact that they can earn more money if you have to go back to them for permission to reuse their work. For example, they may now agree to license the artwork or photo for the album cover only. If the artist wants to use it on a poster, T-shirt or other merchandise, or as a backdrop on live stage shows, then he'll have to come back to the photographer or designer for further permission. If they give it – and they don't have to – then they will probably want another fee for it.

The cost of commissioning someone to create original artwork depends on who you use, but record companies don't usually want to pay more than about £2–3,000 for the basic design. They will go higher if it's a top designer or 'name'. The record company doesn't usually have any rights to use the artwork in any form of merchandise other than sales of the album, so they will only be interested in getting album cover rights. If the artist thinks he'll want it for other purposes, he'll probably have to pay for those himself. The cost of originating the artwork is usually non-recoupable and the record company will usually give the artist the right to use the artwork for other purposes, for example, for merchandising, if he pays to them 50% of the origination costs.

The value that attaches to a distinctive artwork design was highlighted by the application for an injunction made by Creation Records (Oasis' record label at the time) against the publishers of various newspapers, including the *Sun*.[5]

---

5 *Creation Records Limited v. News Group Limited* EMLR 444 1997 16.

The Oasis Case

Oasis was going to release another album in the autumn of 1997 and decided that the photograph of it should be taken at a country hotel. Noel Gallagher, the lead guitarist and deviser of the band's artwork, had a particular idea in mind, a kind of homage to The Beatles and their cover of the *Sergeant Pepper* album. The hotel swimming pool was drained and a number of different objects were delivered to the hotel, including a white Rolls-Royce. This was lowered into the pool at an angle and Noel Gallagher supervised how the other objects were to be placed. A professional photographer took a number of photos from various angles so that the band had a choice of different images in different lights. Oasis thought it was essential that the plans for the photography were kept secret, and only a few people were allowed in on it.

Inevitably, perhaps, word leaked out and a couple of newspaper photographers turned up including one freelancer attached to the *Sun*. One of the photos he took was published a few days later in the *Sun*. It was very similar to the one chosen for the album cover, but had been shot from a different angle. The *Sun* offered copies of the photo for sale to readers in a poster form. Although other newspapers also published photos it seems none were very clear and none were offering posters of them for sale.

Creation got an immediate injunction restraining the *Sun* from publishing any more photos or from offering copies for sale. The judge then had to decide if that injunction should continue.

Creation Records were arguing that the freelance photographer had infringed their copyright or had breached confidence.

The judge rejected the argument that the way the scene was put together attracted a copyright as a dramatic work. He also rejected the argument that the scene was a work of artistic craftsmanship, a sculpture or a collage (those lawyers were trying hard, weren't they!). A film set can sometimes be said to be a work of artistic craftsmanship, but the judge decided that this was just an assembly of disparate objects without the necessary element of craftsmanship.

Creation Records and Oasis might have been thought to be on stronger ground in arguing that there was copyright in it as an artistic work of collage – being a collection of unrelated items. Their barrister argued that it should be put in the same category as the infamous Carl André bricks displayed at the Tate Gallery or Gilbert and George's living sculptures. The judge declined to follow that line of argument, as the assembly of objects didn't have the same degree of permanence – it was going to be dismantled after a few hours. This is a very restricted view of what would be entitled to copyright protection.

The judge did find that there was copyright in the photograph, but the *Sun* didn't copy that original – the freelancer took his own photograph of the same scene. Which was why Creation Records was trying to establish some kind of copyright in the scene.

So, having failed on all their ingenious copyright arguments, the lawyers then argued that the freelance photographer had breached confidentiality. Here they had more luck. The judge decided that any reasonable person would have assumed that, in viewing the scene, they were getting confidential information and so the freelance photographer was obliged not to photograph the scene. The *Sun* had admitted their photographer had to get around a security cordon to get the film out, so they must have known it was intended to be confidential.

On balance, the judge decided Oasis/Creation Records had more to lose if the *Sun* were to continue to be allowed to sell posters and continued the injunction on the basis of breach of confidence. If he had not then potentially huge sales of posters and other merchandise by the band and their record label would have been lost.

Once the artwork is delivered the artist should then be in a position to press for a release date for the album. This will depend on a huge number of factors, some of which I'll deal with in the next chapter, but once a provisional date has been set then the manufacturing process can begin and the whole marketing department should start to swing into action.

If the artist or production company intends to release a record themselves then they will also attend to all the other formalities such as sample and session work clearances, obtaining barcodes, getting a mechanical licence and paying the licence fees. These are dealt with in more detail in Chapter 6.

CONCLUSIONS

• Choose your studios well. Decide if they'll be residential or not.

• Set a reasonable recording budget and stick to it.

• Get the best producer and mixer you can afford.

• Don't skimp on mastering costs, but keep an eye on remix costs, as these can get very high.

• Check you've complied with the delivery requirements in your contract.

• Try to get copyright ownership of the artwork.

Chapter 6
Manufacture, Distribution and Marketing

INTRODUCTION

U ntil about ten years ago there was no serious viable alternative to the tried and tested method of distribution. You finished your record, it was mastered and 'cut' – literally cut into the vinyl or digitally mastered, (i.e. put in digital form in a computer program from which digital records such as CDs and DATS could be made). The only discussion or change here was digital versus analogue manufacturing methods. Once you had your physical CD, tape, vinyl record or whatever, you packaged it up and it was distributed out to the record stores on the back of a van.

Over the last five years there has been a dramatic increase in the number of tracks that are being sold online as digital downloads, although illegal downloads remain a major problem and challenge (see Chapters 7 and 14). In 2004 the industry began to turn a corner commercially with the arrival of services such as iTunes and the iPod and new carriers such as mobile phones also helped to drive the legitimate side of use of music online. Most singles are now being offered as downloads, many off aggregator sites like iTunes or off individual artists' pages on social networking websites like MySpace. Indeed in 2007 I was involved in several releases that were digital only. Clients didn't want to go to the expense of pressing up physical copies of the single; they waited first to see how well the release went in publicity terms. Major record companies are either pulling out of distribution (EMI) or are combining their manufacturing operations either in one place in Europe or through deals with other companies. By pulling out of these two traditional means of earning profits the record companies may be saving millions of pounds but they are also focusing their money-making activities on the more risky aspects of the business, the marketing and promotion of artists and their records. So the stakes will be higher in future to get those expensive aspects right more often than they do at the moment. This of course feeds into the more cautious outlook referred to in Chapter 3 on record contracts and on the greater use of middleman production companies to filter out some of the artists less likely to succeed commercially.

MANUFACTURING

The compact disc is however still a significant carrier, even though year on year sales are declining by as much as 20%. The cassette tape has pretty much disappeared as a format just as the VHS tape has ceased to be a video format for new releases, and retailers like Curry's have announced they will no longer sell VHS tape players. The prediction of the death of vinyl was, however, premature. It survives (albeit in a niche market), beloved by DJs and specialist collectors. Sterling efforts were made to establish the Minidisc format. It was first launched in the early 1990s but singularly failed to impress. A potentially much more serious threat to the music business was thought to be the phenomenal increase in sales of recordable CDs (CDR). Originally intended as an alternative to the floppy disc, the CDR became the format of choice for 'burning' copies of whole albums or favourite compilations. But it was also a boon for the small producer, new artist or production company because with a little effort they were able to reproduce their own CD albums for sale at their gigs or for sending out to record companies, publishers and managers. Then just as we were getting used to this came the MP3 player and mobile phones which could store and play music. It then became so easy to copy and send copies over the Internet that the idea of an ordinary member of the public becoming a pirate became a reality. This ability was manipulated to the full by peer-to-peer websites such as Napster, MP3.com, Grokster, Kazaa etc. These issues are discussed in more detail in Chapters 7 and 14.

Most mainstream releases are made available in physical format as well as downloads and so let's have a look at the sort of legal agreements you will come across. If you've paid for the recording yourself or via a production company then you won't have a record company to organise the manufacturing for you. You're going to have to go to specialist CD manufacturers and shop around for a deal. Lists of manufacturers can be found in the *Music Week Directory*. Before you decide on a manufacturer, you'd be well advised to gather together as much information on what is available as you can. You also need to make your arrangements with manufacturers at least four months before you intend to release physical copies of your record, and even longer at popular times such as Christmas. This is to try and ensure that the manufacturing/pressing plant has capacity and won't squeeze your record out because a release by a big star is slotted in. Bear in mind in setting your timetable that it is usual to release records to radio stations (via pluggers if necessary – see below) at least a month before they are available in the shops.

You also need to ask what service each company provides. Is it a full-service company that will produce a production master from which to reproduce the CDs, or will you have to find a company to make a production master for you and deliver that together with film or discs for the artwork to the manufacturer? If so, would it be cheaper, easier and quicker if you looked for a full-service company? You'll need to check the small print very carefully. What hidden costs are there? Do they charge you to deliver the finished records to you?

What other services can they provide? Can they offer a distribution service or any marketing services like sales teams? If they do, is it better to use them for these services or to look for separate companies to do them?

Look at the quality of their work. Ask to see samples. Do they do everything in-house or is it farmed out? Who else do they work for?

Once you've narrowed down your choice you have to look at how quickly they can turn things around. They may have a minimum production run (say 5,000 copies). Is that all right for you or were you looking for a more modest 500 copies? To be honest, if you're going for a very short production run, possibly for promotional purposes, you might be better off burning the CDs and putting the finished product together yourself.

Once you've decided on your manufacturer you'll need to agree a price, the number of units to be produced and a time for delivery. You ought to try to keep some of their fee back until you see things are running according to plan, but if you're a small unknown company they're likely to want cash up-front. Even so, keep an eye on things. Check the quality of the sound and of the artwork. Is the running order correct without any gaps in the songs? Have all the names been spelled correctly and correct credits given? If anything is wrong pull them up on it immediately. Always check a sample of the finished product.

You also have to be sure that they can continue to manufacture repeat orders as your first batch, hopefully, sells out. You need to keep close contact between your distributor and your manufacturer so that you can put your repeat order in as soon as your distributor sees stocks are dwindling. This need for close co-operation is one of the reasons why some people prefer to keep production and distribution with the same company.

P&D DEALS

As you can probably guess, 'P' stands for production (i.e. manufacture) and 'D' for distribution. A P&D deal is one that combines both of these services in one contract with one company. Companies that offer P&D deals can often also offer marketing services like a telephone sales team (telesales), a strike force (a specialised team targeting record stores to take your records) or pluggers, who try to persuade radio stations to play your record. Whether you want these additional services will depend on your overall marketing plan and on the price and reliability of the service.

You should ask the same questions of P&D companies as you would of a manufacturer, but you'll also have to ask another series of questions about their distribution operation. Who do they supply records to? Is it just the small specialist stores or can they get into the major retail chain stores and vice versa?

MAJORS VERSUS INDIES

Until recently, all the major record companies had their own distribution facilities. Mergers in recent years have resulted in some of those facilities being combined to save costs by pooling operations. The independent sector is now dominated by Pinnacle and PIAS (formerly Vital). Clearly, the risks are outweighing the possible profits from this activity. Without an efficient distribution system, all your talents and efforts in making the record and the marketing people's work in getting you noticed will mean nothing if the distribution company doesn't have the records in the stores for the public to buy. In the last couple of years there has been a growth in the activities of aggregators like Nova, Pebble Beach and Remote Control amongst others. These companies have arrangements with a larger distributor to put through that distributor all of the aggregators output under all the labels it looks after. The aggregator then does individual deals with independent labels or artists to distribute their product and combines all of this with the one deal with the larger distributor. The trick with this type of deal is to ensure that the labels' accounts are kept separate and that profits from one label aren't used to subsidise another label's losses. Whatever the company you are using try and check their financial viability – if it's at all suspicious do not risk your stock and your income from sales. Even the bigger distributors are not immune from this but there are some things you can do in your contracts to protect against this – see below on retention of title.

All distributors have to also balance efficiency with a speedy response. If they can't meet demand quickly, your records won't be available, the customers won't be able to buy them and you won't get your chart position.

The major record companies tend to manufacture their records locally and then shop them to a centralised depot, usually somewhere in Europe, and from there to local distribution centres in different countries. It doesn't take much thought to see how savings could be made by pooling the local distribution centres.

As well as dealing with their own artists' records, some of the majors act as separate distribution companies for other companies' records.

If you aren't signed to a major or can't get a deal with a major distribution company, you may not have any alternative but to go to an independent distributor. The BPI has a useful guide to setting up your own record label and distribution on its website www.bpi.co.uk.

You also need to be aware that some smaller distributors are a bit like production companies and pass on the job of actual distribution to another company. You should ask if that's what your chosen distributor does; if it does you should try to find out how reliable and financially stable that other company is. As we'll see below, there are some things you can do to protect yourself by retaining ownership of the records until you've been paid.

CATALOGUE OR SINGLE ITEM DISTRIBUTION DEAL

Most of what follows in this section is geared towards physical distribution but for the last six months or so all new deals with Pinnacle have required that you also give them exclusive online distribution rights alongside the physical distribution. Existing clients are being sent variation agreements to extend their physical deals to online distribution as well. It is likely that all distribution deals will offer both physical and online distribution in future. This can be a problem if you have an existing arrangement with an online aggregator like The Orchard or online retail sales outlets like 7Digital or iTunes. If that arrangement is already in place then you will have to exclude the online rights from the deal. If it's non-exclusive there may be room for both. Even if you haven't already done a deal you should not just slavishly sign up to it without first thinking if the distributor has enough specialist knowledge to do a good job and get it out to all the decent online etailers. There are some signs that companies who have had a presence in physical distribution have a few teething problems with online releases and may need closer supervision than you would imagine. I have also had an example recently of a client who only wanted the distributor to release online and wanted to reserve all the physical releases because they did not want to jeopardise a possible future record deal for that record. These are all possibilities you have to consider.

So are you doing a deal for all the records you're likely to produce in the next year or so? These are called 'catalogue deals' and would be suitable for a small record label or production company. They would also work for a company that was going to license in rights to records by other artists, and also for an artist who has decided that he doesn't want or need the facilities of a record company and wants to distribute his own recordings. In recent months, some very successful artists have seriously considered bypassing record labels altogether and doing it all in-house. Simply Red announced they were doing so and more recently Radiohead looked like they were going down that road when they announced online sales of their new album at prices to be set by the customer. However, they have now also decided to use a traditional record label for first international and then physical distribution of this new album

If you aren't doing a catalogue deal, you could just give distribution rights to a single track to a distribution company. You might choose this route if you were just seeing this release as a stepping stone to getting a record company interested in you. Just bear in mind, though, that if the distributor is only dealing with one track for you, you'll not have much bargaining power and will have to push hard to ensure that you get any kind of priority.

EXCLUSIVE VERSUS NON-EXCLUSIVE

Catalogue distribution deals are likely to be exclusive, but there may be one or two exceptions to the exclusivity. For example, you could have the right to put tracks on compilations to be distributed by another distributor or a major record company. Or you could have the right to distribute small quantities of the records yourself to one or two specialist outlets or online although mainly distributors or physical records are concerned to ensure that the record is not made available online before physical copies are in the shops.

Term
This is really only relevant for exclusive catalogue deals.

The distributor deals with your entire product over a period of time. This could be open-ended, continuing until one or other of you gives notice, usually three months at least. Other possibilities are a fixed period of one year with the distributor having the option to extend the term for another year, or the term could be for one year with further one-year extensions unless you give notice before the end of that time that you don't want it to carry on. You have to be careful with this one because, unless you're good at remembering when to give notice or have an efficient reminder system, you might miss the relevant 'window' and find yourself locked in to another twelve months. Some distributors are now insisting on two years initially but that is negotiable.

If you think you might want to move your label and catalogue at some point to a bigger distributor or major, the more flexible the term is and the easier it is for you to get out of it will be important. It could also be very important if you aren't sure how good the distributor is. On the other hand, the distributor might have greater commitment to you and be more inclined to give you priority if they know you're going to be with them for a pre-determined minimum period of time.

Territory
The distribution deal could be a worldwide one, but is more likely to be for a limited number of countries, for example just for the UK or the UK and Europe. If you're a UK artist or label looking to distribute your records beyond Europe (for example to the US) then you're much more likely to do it through licensing the rights to another record company with its own distribution set-up (see Chapter 3). It is possible to have deals where you ship finished records to them and they distribute them, but this is less common. They are sometimes referred to as 'consignment' or 'sale and return' deals and Japanese labels are quite keen on them, as are some Canadian and US labels where it isn't worth them manufacturing copies locally and it is cheaper for them to do it on a sale or return basis.

There is a problem, though, with distribution deals for just one country, for example the UK, its imports or, more particularly, what is often referred to as parallel imports.

What are these? Let's take an example. You have the rights to distribute a particular track in the UK. Another record company has the rights to distribute the same record in France. If the record is released in France first, the French record company could export the records into the UK, where they might take some of your market from under you. You may think that wouldn't be allowed as they only have French distribution rights. Ah yes, that's right, but there is the principle of a common marketplace throughout the European Union (EU), which is meant to encourage the free movement of goods. So, within the EU, it's illegal for you to outlaw these imports. You can tell the UK distributor that he isn't to actively try and get orders from outside the UK, but it's very difficult to police it. How do you know who approached who?

It's easier, in theory, to prevent parallel imports coming in from outside the EU. For example, if you were giving one UK distributor European distribution rights and licensed the rights to a record company in the US for North America, your contract with the US record company could specify that they aren't allowed to ship records outside North America. The problem is that there are specialised exporting companies who also act as genuine domestic distributors. The US record label could legitimately sell records to such a company and then deny any knowledge or responsibility if that company then exports the records to the UK.

This is why there is a lot of pressure to ensure that a record is released simultaneously in as many countries as possible, or to ensure that there is something special about the release. For example, Japan, which has suffered badly from cheap imports, often insists that releases in Japan have extra 'bonus' tracks to make the records more attractive to the domestic market than the imports.

There is also pressure on price levels within the EU. The idea is that if the dealer prices are the same throughout the EU, there is less demand for imports brought in cheaper than the domestic product.

There are, of course, new issues to be addressed by distributors as a result of the possibility of buying records online. The Internet is a global marketplace and one challenge is to try to find new ways of dealing with the fact that it's one big territory. Suppose you had a distribution deal with one company in the UK and another with a company in the US. Your licence deal with each would have to say either that it was open house on export sales and both could offer records for sale on their websites, for purchase anywhere in the world, or you could limit the territory to the UK/US and put it in each licence that they aren't to solicit offers or to fulfil orders from the other's country. For example, your email address is UK registered and you go online to try to buy a CD of an album that you know has been released in the US but isn't yet on sale in the UK. If you went to a US website to try to buy the CD they should refuse to accept orders for distribution outside the US. This solution is potentially off-putting for the consumer, which is the last thing anyone wants. Obviously, if you'd done a worldwide distribution deal with one company then that wouldn't be necessary. It may be that any solution to this territorial issue will have to be addressed by one-stop deals or reciprocal agreements between distributors in different countries. They could, for example, agree to pay each other a percentage commission for sales generated in the other company's territory. So far we're seeing some attempts at reciprocal agreements for licensing via MCPS and PRS, but international co-operation between record companies or distributors is taking longer. The solutions being adopted seem to be practical – in the case of physical sales you have to provide a delivery address in the country concerned. Although of course in the spirit of true enterprise there are now companies who, for a fee, will give you a PO Box address in the country and forward the goods to you. Other solutions are technical in that you have to have an email address in the country concerned to purchase goods online in that country.

Record companies and music publishers are now investing large amounts into systems called rights management systems that will police where a file is being downloaded to ensure that payment is being made, and which would also enable them to track whether a distributor was breaking the terms of his distribution licence but, as we'll see in Chapter 7, these systems are taking time to deliver a fully workable solution.

Rights granted

If you're doing a P&D deal you'll be required to give the distributor the right to reproduce the sound recording and the right to distribute and sell those copies whether that is as physical copies or in the form of online downloads.

Price

The distributor will take a fee off the top of the price they get paid. So, for example, if the distributor gets paid £7.49 for each record sold, they take a percentage of that as their fee.

The percentage can vary a great deal depending on how many additional services they provide, for example, a telesales service or a strike force dedicated to pushing your records. It can be as high as 28–30% of the dealer price if you're unknown or only have one track to distribute. Deals of 15–18% or less are available to successful independent companies with a high turnover of successful product. Major record companies will usually pay distribution fees in single figures. Sometimes the percentage the distributor gets as a fee goes down as the turnover increases. An average amount for a distributor to charge would be 23–25% to independent record labels or artist production companies. For online distribution the opening price is around 20% but all things are usually negotiable with the right level of bargaining power.

The distributor will also usually have a discount policy. This is a sliding scale of discounts on the dealer price that have to be given to the various retail outlets. For example, major national chains like Woolworths or Virgin Megastores would be able to command a discount on the price because they order in bulk and are such important outlets for the music. Supermarket chains such as Tesco and Asda are also now in this category and, indeed, often undercut the high-street chains. You'll have little or no say on these discount rates, nor have a chance to change them. However, you should know what they are in order to check you're being paid properly. Discounts haven't really established themselves in the online world but as volume increases then they may well follow. What does appear online is the deduction of whatever charges are laid against the distributor. For example, a distributor may first offer the tracks to an aggregator who acts as a kind of clearing house and does a variety of deals with different etailers. These aggregators deduct a percentage from the gross revenue after the deduction of the etailer's mark-up. So it is starting to mirror the physical world – even down to 'packaging deductions' (see below).

Payment terms

The distributor will often pay half of what is due within 30–45 days of receiving the payment from the retailers and the balance within 60–80 days. So if they get paid for a record sold on 28 February, the label might get half of their money by the end of March and the rest by the middle of April. Make sure that for online sales all the necessary technical requirements of the online distributor are in place to ensure that you can track the number of sales and check whether you are getting paid correctly, not just for online sales but also the payment of mechanical royalties for reproduction of your songs in the online copy downloaded. As we will see in the chapter on Collection Societies, there are now licensing systems and rates set for most uses. The challenge now is to ensure that these rates are paid. So check who is responsible for ensuring mechanicals are paid – you or the distributor, or the etailer.

The distributor will probably keep back some of the money as a reserve against records that are returned. This of course only applies to physical sales as in theory at least the customer should not pay for a download which fails. Distributors usually have a fixed policy on this, but will sometimes negotiate the level of reserves. The reserve on singles is generally higher than for albums unless the album has been advertised on television. Retail stores may take copies of your record on a sale-or-return basis. So although the distributors have sent out, say, 1,000 copies, they don't know how many have actually been sold and won't include these copies as sales until they've been paid. They keep back a reserve against these returns and any other returns that appear to be sales (i.e. they've been shipped out but may be returned to the distributor for some legitimate reason such as being damaged or faulty). The distributor has to hold back money against such an eventuality.

The distributor won't usually take responsibility for bad debts. It also won't usually pay out before it gets paid, because that can lead to big problems. For example, you do a P&D deal with a local distributor who agrees to pay out on the number of records it actually sends out, less a reserve against returns. It ships out 1,000 copies of a record to the retail stores and pays you on 750 copies, keeping back a 25% reserve, before it has received payment of the 1,000 sales. Months later, the stores return not 250 but 500 copies; the distributor is then out of pocket by 250 copies and will look to you to pay it back. Even worse for you is the case where you do a deal with a local distributor who pays you on what they get paid. They do a deal with a bigger distribution company and ship records to that bigger company. The bigger company sells those records but, for whatever reason, fails to pay the smaller distributor, who can't then pay you (even though records have been sold) because they haven't been paid for them. Again though this problem should not arise with online sales because once the customer has paid and received his download there is a very limited opportunity for returns.

Retention of title

A way of protecting yourself when you're in a chain of deals like the one described above is to retain your title (your ownership) of the records until you've been paid. These sections of the contract have to be very carefully drafted in order to have a chance of working. Assuming the bigger distribution company has gone bust, the liquidator of that company will want to hold on to whatever stocks, i.e. records, that he can. He'll want to sell them to raise money for the creditors of the company, so he'll want to get around the retention of title if he can legitimately do so. Specialised legal advice is needed on this and again it should not be necessary with online sales. There the issue should be making sure that once the deal has ended they take down the copies off the Internet and do not continue to sell them.

Advances
Before I leave this section, I just want to touch on the question of advances. Will a distributor give you an advance? Well they might if you've got a good track record for finding hit records or have a catalogue that has a regular turnover. The advances for small independent labels or individual artists aren't likely to be high – possibly only a few thousand pounds. As with most advances, these sums aren't usually returnable if you don't sell enough records, but they are recoupable from monies you would otherwise receive from sales.

MARKETING

Once you've got a record mastered, copies manufactured and you've found a company to distribute it, another crucial step in the process is to let the public know about you and your record. The marketing process has many elements to it and it's an ongoing process. As soon as you've got something to sell – a record, live performance, merchandise – you need to let people know about it.

ARTWORK
Getting the right artwork for the record is crucial – it should form part of the whole campaign. It could be used as the backdrop to a stage show and on a poster campaign. It could appear on T-shirts and other merchandise. Make sure you own the copyright in the artwork and that there are no restrictions on what can be done with it. This still applies even though the artwork is much smaller being only for a CD booklet as opposed to 12" vinyl record. These days, however, the challenge for artists and graphic designers is a design that works well online and uses the interactive technology of the digital era and the global possibilities of the Internet to the fullest extent. There are also now ways to make simple versions of the artwork available as a download when you buy the record online so it is essential that you get the right from the designer of the artwork to use it in all these ways. Focus on standard packaging that contains the correct copyright notices and the all important barcode. PPL has a leaflet explaining the copyright notices and BPI produces a leaflet explaining how to get a barcode. For online sales make sure you have the correct metadata embedded in the digital copy and that all necessary technical requirements of the online distributor are in place to ensure sales are correctly tracked and fed back to you.

PHOTOGRAPHS AND BIOGRAPHIES
You're going to need to have some decent photographs. They'll be needed for information packs, for the press, for letting overseas licensees or associated companies abroad know what you look like. You'll also need to post photos or graphics up on your website or page on MySpace, Facebook etc. The costs the record company pays are not usually recoupable or repayable by you unless you want to use the photographs for

merchandising, for example on a T-shirt or poster, when they may expect you to repay half the costs.

If there's an exclusive record contract in place it will usually, but not always, give the artist approval over which photographs are used. It will also usually give the artist approval of the official biography. This is a bit like a life history. It also ensures that a consistent message or image is presented of the artist, which forms part of the brand, as we'll see in Chapter 8 on branding. Some record contracts now also require the artist to contribute to online diaries or blogs.

If you give the record company photographs or biographical details they will assume they are approved, so make sure you're happy with them.

IN-HOUSE OR EXTERNAL MARKETING

Most big record companies will have in-house marketing and press departments. These are staffed by dedicated marketing and press people, one or more of whom will be allocated to marketing your product. You need to be sure that these people understand the game plan and, preferably, that they love your music. At the very least they should like it, because otherwise they won't sound convincing when they try to sell you to the press, radio, TV and so on.

If the marketing is to be done in-house it will normally be paid for by the record company on a non-recoupable basis.

The position changes if it's a smaller company without its own in-house marketing departments or outside specialists have been brought in for particular aspects. The costs are then usually partly or wholly recoupable from the record income.

Whether it's being done in-house or with a number of outside specialists, the whole campaign has to be co-ordinated.

The sales force and any special strike force have to be primed with artwork, photographs, biographies and campaign details. Promotion packs have to be sent out to any exporters, to clubs, DJs and to some retail outlets. For bigger releases the record company may arrange for a private 'play through' of the new album to selected key retailers.

The fact that the record is being released has to be notified to the music press, to the chart compilers and to MCPS/PRS to get the relevant mechanical licence and details registered for when the record is performed publicly. Each release has to have its own catalogue number. I once acted for a label called Produce Records and their catalogue identity was MILK 1, 2, 3, etc. It is usual to prepare a summary of all the information known as 'presenters' or 'sales sheets' of about a page long consisting of the name of the artist, the title of the record and a picture of it, its catalogue number, barcode, dealer price and release date. You should then add details of how to order it and contact details plus some brief points on what the marketing campaign is.

The adverts for a co-ordinated advertising campaign will have to be designed and approved well in advance so that they're ready for distribution at the same time as the promotional packs, posters, promotional items and so on.

The strike or sales force goes into action several weeks before the release date, trying to get orders from the retail shops. These are called the 'pre-sales'. Everyone is interested in getting these figures, as they're a good indicator of how well a particular record is being received. It will help determine the chart position, it tells the marketing people how much more work they have to do, and pre-sales can give you some information to pass on to your manufacturer and distributor to help them assess how many copies of the record will be needed. The figures may also tell you in what areas of the country the record is selling best, so the distributor can know to make more copies available in those areas. There is also now a reason to collect 'pre-sales' for online sales as these help to determine a chart position in digital charts and greater exposure for the artist. A theme that I will return to in the next chapter is how you come up with a marketing plan which raises your music above the 'noise' of all the other competing releases that week. Why should a potential customer listen to and possibly buy your record over anyone else's? How do they even know you have a record released? You need to come up with a marketing plan or idea that makes your release stand out. This takes talent and you may need to bring in specialist marketing people. As with all experts that you engage, make sure it is clear in writing what you want them to do, how they will be paid and what constitutes a successful outcome.

TV ADVERTISING

If you are on a major record label (or perhaps an independent one owned by a millionaire!) then part of the marketing campaign might be to advertise the records on television. This is an expensive business. A basic television campaign in four ITV regions can easily cost £75,000. The record company is only going to want to spend this money if they think they will earn it back in extra record sales. To keep their risk to a minimum, the record company will try and recoup some or all of these costs, either as a further advance or by reducing the royalty payable to the artist. How this works is that the record company reduces by 50% the royalty they would otherwise have had to pay on sales of the records until they have recouped (from that reduced royalty) 50% or more of the costs of the TV ad campaign.

We lawyers try and get artists the right of approval over whether an advert is made but have to fight for this, as record companies know if you get the right of approval you'll only give your approval if you get a better deal on recoupment. Then they don't recoup so much of the cost. Otherwise we try to limit the ways in which your income is affected, either by restricting the reduction to sales in the country where the campaign is run, or limiting the time over which they can recoup the costs from reduced royalties, or both. Currently the trend is to just treat the cost of the campaign as a further recoupable advance which makes some of these restrictions redundant and the arguments then tend to centre on how much is recoupable.

Don't rule out the idea of a television campaign without carefully looking at the proposals. A good, targeted campaign could be what it takes to lift your record into the Top 20 albums chart, which could make all the difference. However, be aware of the cynical attempt to reduce royalties to you when your record has been particularly successful by rushing out a cheap TV campaign in the same accounting period as your album was released and achieved most of its sales. By doing this the record company can add a further advance to the bottom line or halve royalties on *all* sales in that accounting period even if they were before the ad campaign. Don't think this is fanciful. One of my colleagues found that a major record company was trying to do this with an artist who had had a very successful debut album. A TV campaign wasn't needed and the lawyer and manager had to fight hard to get a deal whereby the royalties were not artificially reduced. It is also true that record company executives might panic into doing a TV campaign when they fear that the sales are not at the level they expect. It is the job of a good manager to try and decide whether the fear is real and would be helped by a campaign. I know of one very experienced manager who had to persuade their artist's record label not to rush out a TV advert for an album at Christmas. They were afraid that they had over-supplied the stores and would get masses of returns in the New Year. The managers had to fight long and hard to stop this happening but they did have an ace up their sleeve – they 'knew' that the next single was a winner, stood their ground, were found right and the artist went on to have a very successful album. Guy Hands – of venture capitalist Terra Firma – has recently announced that he wants to ship fewer records so there are fewer returns and lower overheads. This is a fine principle – the problem is that it is not an exact science which can determine in advance precisely how many people will decide to go into their local record store one weekend and buy a particular record. If the demand is higher than anticipated then the stores will run out and the prospective purchaser – maybe an impulse buyer – will move on to his next purchase.

TV AND RADIO PLUGGERS
Even in these days of the Internet it's still important to the success of a record that it gets exposure on radio. Unless the record gets a decent number of radio plays, it's unlikely to enter the charts. Although it is becoming a little easier now that downloads count towards chart positions.

The people who decide what is played on Radio 1 or 2, XfM, Heart and other pivotal regional radio stations are very powerful, and some feel that the records chosen for the playlists are towards the commercial pop end of the market. There was a big problem a couple of years ago when 27-year-old artists were being thought of as too old! Now, however, Radio 2 has stepped into the gap, picked up many of the ex-Radio 1 DJs who had been influential opinion-formers and given them shows. Those who had grown up with these people gravitated to Radio 2, which has become much more the station of mainstream commercial releases by older artists as well as middle-of-the-road tracks by younger artists. Now, ironically, for many releases failure to get on the Radio 2 playlist is a kiss of death.

The TV and radio pluggers who have the tough job of trying to get records playlisted are either employed in-house by the record company or are from outside agencies that specialise in this work. Their costs are dealt with in similar ways to press agents (see below).

WHAT DO YOU PAY EXTERNAL MARKETING AND PRESS PEOPLE?
There are many different ways of paying for external marketing and press work.

Retainers
Press people and pluggers could be on retainers. These are regular, monthly payments that are made to keep them on board as the press agent, constantly having an eye on press opportunities. When you aren't actively doing any promotion, for instance when you're in the studio recording the next album, the level of retainer could be quite small. It would then increase when press/promotion activities rise around the time of the release of the record. However, as the economy slows down and competition among these

companies hots up, the number of people on retainers has declined and now many are only paid when they do some work.

Bonuses
If someone is on a retainer or a fixed fee they may be paid a bonus for achieving certain targets. For example, a press officer could get paid a bonus for every front page/cover he gets that features you.

A plugger might get a bonus if a record goes into the Top 10 or whatever.

Fixed fees
Marketing and press people could be on a fixed fee, possibly with bonuses linked to success.

Royalties
Press and pluggers could be on a retainer or a fixed fee with bonuses. Good pluggers and those in great demand (usually the same ones) can insist on 'points', i.e. a royalty (usually 0.5–1%) on each record sold. If you want the best you may have to pay this. It will either come out of the artist royalty or be paid by the record company, or a combination of the two.

Where do you find them?
The usual ways – word of mouth, those companies already on a retainer arrangement with your record company, those companies known to your manager as doing a good job in this area of music. The *Music Week Directory* carries a list of press and promotions companies, but it would be a good idea to get a recommendation from someone in the business before you choose one.

Do they want a contract?
If they're on a fixed fee they will probably just invoice you for the fee when the work is done. If you've agreed they'll undertake something out of the ordinary, or you're putting them on a retainer, you'll probably want a simple contract. If they're being paid a royalty you'll definitely need a contract setting out how that royalty will be calculated and when it will be paid. The simplest thing is to do this on the same basis as you get your royalties under your record deal.

EPQS

This is the name given to electronic press packages. That is pre-recorded interviews, photos and biographies, together with promotional clips of your latest single release, that are put together by your in-house or external press officer. These usually take the form of a DVD and they're sent out to reviewers, press reporters, DJs, radio station controllers and so on as an additional means of promotion. Some companies are now sending them out as file attachments to emails. Most new record contracts contain a clause that says that the record company can put one of these together and that the artist will co-operate with them. There seems to be no reason why you wouldn't want to agree to the compiling of an EPQ, but you might want some creative control and you'll need to agree whether some or all of the costs can be recouped.

VIDEOGRAMS

Promotional videos were a key part of the marketing process for most artists who were aiming for a commercial chart position. They are still important for the pop market and can be useful for putting something interesting on your MySpace page and on YouTube; however there are limited outlets for promotional videos other than music stations like MTV as well as all the cable and satellite channels.

However, they can be very expensive to make and there's no point in making one if your record doesn't get radio plays or TV airtime. It will be a waste of money and you'll end up paying for it in one way or another. It has to fit in with the overall marketing plan so don't overspend or make a video unnecessarily. If you can pull in some favours and get your mates who've studied film-making to make a cheap video for you – good enough for YouTube and maybe as a video mobile phone clip – then that may be worth doing but again only if it is part of a well thought out campaign.

The creative elements such as what the story is going to be (the storyboard), who's going to produce and direct it, and when and where it is to be shot will probably be agreed between artist and record company. Depending on the contract, the artist may have a final say on some of these things and the record company on others.

LONG-FORM DVDS

Unlike promo videos which are generally there to accompany a single release, a DVD may well be a full-length 60–90 minute production. Robbie Williams's *Live at Knebworth* was an early example of how to use the medium as a marketing tool for the artist but also as a commercial product in its own right. Yet when it was first issued the record label didn't get it and had to be persuaded that it would sell enough to recoup. It went on to sell over half a million copies and recoupment was not an issue. Kylie Minogue has released a DVD of her comeback 'Diamond' tour alongside her latest album *X*, and such releases can also help to keep the artist in the public eye in between album releases. For example, if no new album is expected for a year then it might be worth putting out a DVD of the last tour to keep fans interested. There is a separate DVD chart just like the Albums and Singles charts. The VHS video format has been killed off and you should not make videos in that format – DVD is now the format of choice. According to the major record companies trade body BPI, commercial videos had a retail value of £93.5 million in 2006 outstripping the retail value of digital downloads which stood at £70million. But like the CD market 2007 proved to be a difficult market for DVDs too, with prices of DVDs falling significantly but without the hoped for increase in sales. In the third quarter of 2007 the sector showed a 31% drop in sales over the corresponding period in 2006 according to the Official Chart Company statistics. Part of the problem seems to lie in customers being prepared to watch poorer quality video films online than good quality DVDs in their living rooms. Again, as bandwidth increases and download times for films reduces there are also going to be increasing pressures from piracy and illegal downloads. So in an attempt to capture some of this illegal market record companies are now offering video clips as downloads alongside or possible slightly ahead of an artist's album release. The idea is that if they can see a clip of the video or can download the video to go with the single then the customer may go out and buy the full-length DVD. Streaming of long-form DVDs on online TV stations is also being explored as a new outlet or revenue stream. Some also see a synergy between the fact that the new owners of EMI, Terra Firma, also have a stake in the chain of Odeon cinemas and speculate on DVDs in cinemas as another possible outlet.

RIGHTS

The record company will usually expect to own all rights in any audio-visual recordings of the artist's performances they have paid for.

If you have a lot of bargaining power, you can limit the rights you give them to audio-visual rights on recordings you make for them under the record deal. Most major record companies won't agree to this, as they want to know that if someone else makes a recording of your live set they can't then put it out as a competing record or DVD. You might have to agree that you won't do that with any recordings of your performances without their approval.

Some artists or DJs have people who film them going about their professional business, doing public appearances, backstage at gigs etc. and use some of that footage in a DVD. The trick here is to ensure they have the right to use the footage of other people who may get on the film like backstage crew or audience members but lawyers can advise how to do that.

The record company may have the exclusive right to make long-form DVDs, or they may have the first option to bid for the right to make one, or the right to match an offer that someone else may have made to make one.

The cost of making a long-form DVD is usually mutually agreed between the artist and the record company and a separate account is set up. You usually get to dictate, or at least approve, all the creative aspects of the long-form DVD.

ROYALTY

The royalty rate will be the same or slightly lower than that for records. There may be an advance payable for the long-form or the record company may have had to match any offer made by a third party. The advance and the costs should only be recoupable from the royalties on this long-form DVD. Income from records or any commercial use of promotional videos should not be used to recoup these costs.

CONCLUSIONS

• Decide on whether you need separate manufacturing and distribution deals.

• Check the returns and discounts policy of your distributor and for any hidden costs.

• Try to retain ownership of the records until you've been paid.

• Get the marketing campaign organised well in advance.

• Agree whether the press and plugging is to be done in-house or by outside agencies.

- If outsiders are doing press or promotion, try to get the record company to agree that only 50% of the cost is recoupable.

- Get approval of any photos and biographies.

- Gets approval, if you can, of any television advertising campaigns for the records – particularly if your royalty will be reduced.

Chapter 7
Online Sales and Distribution

INTRODUCTION

Digital technology is changing the face of the music industry on every level. This is not of course the first time that it has done so. The development of the CD 25 years ago used digital technology to create a whole new medium of music distribution free from the constraints of analogue media such as vinyl, which had severe limitations on the amount of music each record could store. CD sound quality was also 'cleaner' although not all agree that that was necessarily a good thing. So the current developments could be seen as the latest in a long line of changes wrought by technological advances.

However, this time the changes are more fundamental. Improvements in digital reproduction mean music is now available via an almost bewildering array of carriers – mobile phones, PDAs, memory sticks, MP3 players and of course streaming and downloading via the Internet. The availability of broadband in most homes and certainly all places of further education has made the distribution of music via the Internet fast and almost uncontrollable. I will review in this chapter and in the later one on piracy some of the issues that this has created.

OVERVIEW

The vastly expanded digital market has highlighted the flaws in the major record companies, whose monolithic structures were built around the distribution of physical copies of music, over which the record companies had a measure of control, and for which they could demand a high price. The CD did not render this model redundant, it just meant there was a whole new set of hardware they could develop and sell and the marketing men had a field day persuading us to buy again in CD form records we already owned on vinyl. Even the introduction of players which made music portable like the Sony Walkman did not alter the model fundamentally as it still required the distribution and sale of physical products.

It is a different story with digital distribution which takes the form of streamed digital radio or podcasts and downloads where there is no physical product at all and where the hardware development is not in the hands of the traditional developers like Sony and Phillips but with outsiders like Apple and distribution in the hands of Internet Service Providers (ISPs), and other providers of online services, like Google and Yahoo and mobile phone companies and it is marketed by third parties like MySpace and YouTube. The major record companies may also have lost the battle to try and control illegal copying through digital rights management (DRM) systems. Pricing too is no longer in the control of the record companies. Several monopoly enquires into the supposed high price of CDs may not have shown there was an abuse of a dominant market position by the major record labels, but the whole issue is redundant as the battle has moved to a different ground. The issue now is how you get people to pay for music at all when they can get it so easily for free. This battle is one that the record companies are losing hand over fist.

They are rapidly coming to the conclusion that they must change their business model or die. Let us hope they have not left it too late.

The winners in this new digital world are not the traditional players. Outsiders, telecoms companies and technology whizz kids, have spotted an opportunity. Being new to this industry they are not hampered by the old ways of the record labels, but can approach matters with a fresh perspective. I am thinking here of the social networking and gambling websites or the multiplicity of services which use music as added value to drive customers and advertisers/investors to their services. Music is just another commodity, it is not the reason for the existence of these services in the first place. The inroads that these new players are making into the music industry bring with them new challenges of how to make music pay and how to find the music you want to listen to, particularly that of new artists where the breadth of available music has never been greater.

Piracy or free availability of music is a major problem. As we will see in more detail in the later chapter on piracy, the organisations representing major record labels such as RIAA and the BPI continue to tackle Internet piracy head on as opposed to embracing the technology as opening up a massive potential market. I have always taken the view that criminalising ordinary people who download music for free is counter-productive. Tackle the large-scale pirates by all means, but otherwise I think it is far better to educate people as to the law on copyright, which to be fair lately the BPI has been doing, but also to use the new technology in a positive way to reach more fans. For example, older users of the Internet, the so-called 'silver surfers', have proved to be a lucrative source of online purchasers of music via websites like Amazon. Until recently they have been buying physical copies for mail order but with Amazon expanding into the download market who is to say that they won't also purchase downloads if the process is made straightforward enough? These buyers may not have gone into a high street record store as they can be quite intimidating places for the uninitiated and so could be seen as a potential whole new market.

The changes in how we receive music via the Internet and on mobile phones have also given the lawyers and legislators a number of knotty legal problems to resolve. As we will see below the law has finally caught up with the online world and recognised that copyright is capable of protection and should be given protection for online uses. The issue of piracy and illegal file sharing remains problematic, as does the whole question of the licensing of rights across countries given the global nature of the Internet. Much remains to be done to ensure cross border co-operation but the collection societies at least are taking steps in the right direction across Europe as we will see in the later chapter on collection societies.

A key indicator of the reality and the growing importance of the digital music business was the launch of the official UK Download Chart in September 2004 when, for the first time, download formats were acknowledged as a viable commercial format. This was followed by the incorporation of downloaded tracks into the Official Singles Chart on 17 April 2005. Mobile phone plays will also count for chart positions as soon as the technical difficulties are resolved. From 22 October 2007 sales of Digital Memory Devices (DMDs) count towards both the singles and albums charts. They have been eligible for the singles chart since September 2007. DMD formats include SD memory cards for mobile phones, USB flash devices as well as memory sticks, so greater marketing experimentation may follow. USB releases in 2007 included a single by Keane and limited releases by Kanye West and Amy Winehouse. USBs can take many forms and designs so the possibility of creative artwork, design and marketing is there for all to seize. EMI has announced it plans to release the entire Radiohead back catalogue on a limited edition USB stick in the shape of the band's 'Fanged Bear' logo. Artists like Arctic Monkeys, Leona Lewis and Koopa have all used Internet chart positions to boost their own profile.

Many new artists now only release singles online initially, moving to a physical release only if online sales warrant it. Distributors like Pinnacle have added online distribution to their standard distribution deals.

There has been considerable progress in the penetration of new technology with greater uptake of broadband; portable players such as iPods are now available at affordable prices; and mobile phones, including the new iPhone which can download both sound and video clips are within the price range of many more people. The growth of these new types of players and uses, in particular mobile ringtones, has led the major record companies to alter their contracts to give them rights to distribute music on these new platforms and they are establishing business models for being paid on these new uses as well as a royalties system for paying the artists and songwriters.

Dominic Pride writing in *Impact* magazine in 2007 claimed that there was a potential market of 3 billion mobile phone owners compared to 1 billion Internet users. He was advocating the growing importance of the song and claimed that as the song was no longer restricted by formats used by the record industry, this opened the way for new partnerships with songwriters and publishers working together to monetise the use of music. He mentioned one use in particular: mobile caller ring-back tones and the potential to tailor these to the market place or to personalise them to the individual customer. He emphasised the delivery of a service to the customer over mobile phones, Internet TV and broadband with music as a key constituent of the service. If he is right then in the future artists and songwriters might get paid for music not as an element on its own but as part of the fee charged for access to a service. This makes sense to me as a new business model and the basis of new partnerships with service providers, but accepting this view means acceptance of the fact that the record company is no longer in full control. This will come hard to those who make their money from that business or perhaps more importantly those who are answerable to the shareholders of those companies.

If the future is paying for access to a service rather than access to individual artist downloads then we need to consider if giving away music for free is a way of tempting consumers into this new world? Many artists believe strongly that their music should not be given away. Cover mount CDs are detested by many artists. Why would a consumer pay for a classic song when, if they wait, they will be able to get it for nothing with their Sunday newspaper? And yet, for every artist that takes this stance you will find others who embrace the idea of music for free. Artists like The Bees have been making acoustic podcasts of material available and Ocean Colour Scene gave away downloads of their last single free. There have been attempts like the Spiral Frog website to get consumers to accept that they can access music for free but have to first listen to a bunch of ads, but as a service it may be struggling.

At the opposite end of the spectrum from the music for free idea are those deals which make the most of the idea of added value by offering fans premium products like the CD with extra tracks, a free ticket to a show near the fan's home, lyrics and additional background to the songs and so on but all at a premium price. There is more on this in the marketing section below.

Of course, even if you accept the view of the growing importance of the song and partnerships between publishers and service providers such as mobile phone companies, there is still the fact that in many cases the song has to be recorded to a reasonable quality. Polyphonic ringtones and real tones are improving but not to the standard of a properly produced and mixed studio recording. It is possible that the mobile phone companies will commission their own recordings of music or expect the publishers to step up to the mark and pay for good quality recordings but that is not the traditional role of the publisher and it is unlikely that the owners of the publishing companies will sanction large expenditure on acquiring sound recording facilities. The more obvious route would be to use the systems already in place at the record companies or perhaps the newer, leaner production companies.

If the business model is to change to shares of revenue from access to services then the publishers will suffer a drop in mechanical royalties, but they hope that this will be balanced out by an increase in flat fee usages, performance and synchronisation royalties, and shares of income with new partners like the telecoms companies. It is also important that the industry is able to move fast and a one-stop shop across territories and between recordings and songs will be needed, and accurate payment tracking systems will need to be put in place.

The IFPI estimates that there are twenty illegal downloads for every legitimate one. John Kennedy, chair of the IFPI, called for a united approach across the industry to tackling the issue of greater co-operation from the ISPs over piracy and illegal downloading. He described the ISPs as the 'gatekeepers' and that their co-operation could make 'the single biggest difference' to the music industry. What the industry wants is for the ISPs to accept they have some responsibility for the content that is on the websites that they host. If the ISPs were to agree to share the data from websites believed to be involved in illegal downloading then stopping those pirates would become infinitely easier. Kennedy says a precedent has already been set when the ISPs responded to a call from the Government to put in filtering software to block access to child pornography websites. We will see more of this in the section on social network sites below.

There are some pundits who claim that the growth in the number of new potential partners means that the power has shifted towards the artist and away from the traditional record company. The example is quoted of Sir Paul McCartney leaving EMI after forty years and releasing his new album through Starbucks' label Hear Music. Other examples might be Madonna's deal with her promoters Live Nation or Radiohead going ahead with its own digital release of its latest album. However, things are never quite so simple. What all these artists have in common is that they are well established and have a large fan base. It would not be anything like as easy for a new, unknown artist to do the same thing. It is also true that whilst many of these well-known artists are using new and unusual partners they haven't completely abandoned the traditional routes either. McCartney's album was made available to traditional outlets through a distribution deal with Universal. Radiohead signed to XL for physical release of their album and The Eagles, who are quoted as one of the success stories of 2007, may be unsigned but they also used a major label (Universal again) to act as their distributor. There is a place for newer artists to do their own thing, but they need the means to attract attention to their music, which means a greater than ever emphasis on marketing.

This brings me neatly on to the last significant development I want to highlight in this overview and that is the phenomenal growth of social networking sites in particular MySpace, YouTube, FaceBook and Bebo. Alongside these pure networking sites are those which use music as the 'hook' to attract the consumer to some other aspect of their website such as the website slicethepie which uses the discovery and finding of unsigned artists and the purchase of contracts in the future success of these artists as a commodity to be traded online. Once again these are examples of how music is just one aspect of a bigger service. The challenge for the music industry with these sites is to see how the artists, songwriters and rights owners can benefit financially from this 'free' use of their music.

REPRODUCTION AND DISTRIBUTION

There have been some positive developments in the area or reproduction and distribution. Record companies have entered into licensing agreements with online music services, and are trying to establish systems which should facilitate tracking of uses, collection and accounting to the artists. Many record labels are now putting their entire catalogue online with Warner Music the latest to announce it is doing this in the US via the Amazon.com website. If record companies can make enough money from these new sources then in theory at least they should be able to continue to invest in new music.

Of course, online distribution threatens the bricks and mortar retailers as illustrated by number of artists issuing tracks only as downloads. Gorillaz' release of 'Feel Good Inc.' only as an Internet download was one of the first to get the high street retailers claiming foul as did more recently the release of Prince's new album as a cover mount on the *Sunday Mail* newspaper, for which he was said to have been paid £500,000. This particular marketing 'first' attracted a great deal of interest. It undoubtedly led to increased sales of the newspaper that week and also helped to market the fact that Prince was about to embark on a record breaking 21 day residency at the new O2 venue in East London (housed in the Millennium Dome). You might say that was his main aim, not record royalties or chart positions.

The retail music stores have suffered, not only because of the difficulties caused by illegal downloads, but also from enhanced competition on the high street and a slowdown in the economy. Some retailers, such as HMV, have experimented with in-store kiosks for burning custom-CDs and others have sought to improve the retail experience as well as providing music subscription and legal downloads through their own branded websites. However, flexibility was not enough for chains like Fopp, which went into administration in 2007. Virgin Retail also sold its music stores in 2007, which have been rebranded with the name Zavvi. This sale, together with Virgin effectively selling up its stake in the record label V2, now a label within the Universal Group, means that Richard Branson has ended his long love affair with the music business, at least for now. Interestingly the retailers association ERA is amongst those clamouring for DRM free music downloads as the retailers realise they have to compete with the illegal music download sites and adapt their own business practices to survive.

In an attempt at winning back some of their lost business the traditional distributors of physical product are now expanding their operations to encompass online download distribution, with Pinnacle being the latest to do so. The new Pinnacle contracts include online rights and Pinnacle, like most distributors, tries to get these exclusively where it can. If you already have deals with companies like The Orchard or iTunes then it will not be possible to do an exclusive deal with your distributor so you will have to negotiate changes. You may also want to maintain flexibility because if, for example, you do an online only distribution deal exclusively with one distributor and the tracks are then included on an album that you do an exclusive licence deal for or which forms the basis of the commitment under an exclusive recording contract for your band then you are going to be in trouble as you will have granted away the all important digital rights. So again you have to negotiate exclusions or compromises.

These new distribution deals seem to be taking the same form as for traditional physical distribution, with the distributor putting the record out through aggregators or direct to retailers online, collecting the income generated, and paying the rights owner after deducting its cut. The percentage the distributor keeps is open to negotiation and will often start at around 20%. Do remember that the traditional physical product distributors are relatively new to the world of online distribution. There may be teething problems. You may need to be more 'hands on' than you might expect. Make sure the tracks are correctly digitised and that the correct metadata is included with the online file to enable the downloads to be tracked and payment made. If at all possible do a trial run or a 'soft' release, where you let the track out a few days before the official release date or just through one or two key outlets to test all is well. I had one client who was releasing his latest track online in early November 2007. He had all his promotion lined up: a live date; some radio and some press ads and articles all directing the fans to buy the release through certain websites and services. The release date came and with it a host of complaints from the fans that they could not get the record or that the download had failed but the company had still taken their money. The release was a disaster and the artist had to make up a great deal of lost goodwill with his fans. The response of the distributor was a very nonchalant: 'Oh yes, we sometimes get teething problems but they sort themselves out in time. Complaints from fans help us find what's wrong.' Well needless to say we were not impressed with this line and the client will think twice about using that distributor again.

STREAMING AND ONLINE BROADCASTING

About ten years ago webcasting was seen as the future of pay-per-view television to enable all fans to access an artist's live concerts. But this means of distribution seems to have run out of steam due largely to problems of poor reception and instability in the technology: if too many people tried to watch at once it often crashed the system. However, streaming of music has been given a new boost by the idea of podcasting music i.e. making it available to your iPod or other similar portable music device at a time suitable to you. Radio led the way on this. There is also definitely a move towards you being able to view your favourite television programmes or listen to a radio show you've missed or want to listen to again at a time of your choice and some television programmes have started to make highlights programmes available again as a listen again service. Evidence of the fact that this is becoming an established form of broadcast is the establishment of a Podcasting Association and the granting of blanket licences for use of some music in podcasts (see the chapter on collection societies). At the moment most of these podcasts are free, so are essentially used as marketing tools, but I am sure that soon it will develop into a service that will try and generate revenue for the broadcaster concerned.

But it is not all doom and gloom as the Internet has opened the way for more specialist or obscure genres of music to find a worldwide market. There was an initial bounce back effect on music sales as consumers discovered new artists and went searching for more tracks by the same artist or others in the same genre. This was, of course, the original intention of the P2P services. I know I am back on my soap box again but if the music industry had tried to understand these new services and embrace the thinking behind them rather than attacking them as a threat then possibly the sales losses could have been minimised or changes to the record industry structure introduced sooner. They might also have saved themselves millions of pounds in legal fees. Instead they drove the problem underground, made martyrs of schoolgirls and the average Joe consumer and created an 'us and them' feeling with the music industry as the enemy. Bands like Arctic Monkeys might not have had the success they did (or perhaps had it later) if they hadn't fully embraced the positive aspects of the Internet from the outset.

SO HOW HAS THE MUSIC INDUSTRY SOUGHT TO COPE OR ADAPT TO THESE CHANGES?

CONSOLIDATION
There has been consolidation in the retail and distribution sectors. Many of the major record companies have pulled out of distribution with Universal Music being the latest to do so in 2005. The majors have struck deals either with other majors or with distribution specialists like PIAS, (formerly Vital) and have centralised their operations in one European country.

There has also been consolidation amongst the majors themselves with Sony acquiring BMG's record division and Universal snapping up V2 and Sanctuary Group. On the publishing side Universal has merged with BMG. The on-off merger talks between Warner Music and EMI Group seem to have gone on the back burner since the venture capitalists Terra Firma under Guy Hands took control of EMI Group but no one is betting against it coming back on to the agenda at some point.

COST-CUTTING
The record and publishing companies have also become leaner. They have tried to off-load non-essential personnel through a mixture of voluntary and compulsory redundancies. Accounting and legal/business affairs functions have been cut right back, sometimes on the back of supposed greater transparency in their contracts. They argue that with easier to follow accounts and simplified legal contracts their costs will reduce as will the contributions they often make to the fees of the lawyers advising artists they wish to sign. But there is only so far you can go and still function.

Guy Hands made the newspapers in 2007 with a flurry of stories about how he intended to cut back on what he saw as waste in the record company he was now overseeing. He announced his intention to sell off a Mayfair property worth £6million which had been used infrequently by the company chairman. He challenged the amount of money paid by the major record labels to organisations such as RIAA, BPI and IFPI asking if there wasn't an overlap in their functions, particularly on piracy issues. On this issue there has been some movement in a reduction in the subscriptions paid by the majors, but not, they say, as a result of Hands' intervention. He also questioned the 'flowers and candles' budget and the expensive Christmas gifts sent to the artists. All made for good headlines, but it feels to me like tinkering round the edges when the main problem remains how to monetise music in the digital age. More serious were his plans announced in January 2008 to cut 2,000 staff and reorganise the company to separate the A&R and business functions.

The major record labels remain monolithic structures with physical offices in all major capitals with big corner offices and highly, some might say obscenely, paid executives many of whom are on bonuses linked to share price or sales or both. This remuneration system might militate against pushing the niche artist with low levels of sales, but in reality the majors have really only been there for the commercial artist for some time. Niche artists do still occasionally have a place, but it is rare that an artist with less than 100,000 sales gets to make a second album for a major record company. The executives are fighting for their very existence and there is probably a lot more pain to come before it gets better. They are up against lean operations in the telecoms business that are financially superior and they can choose not to work with record companies who decline to work with them and this threatens to leave them isolated and redundant. The new players can operate at a low level of overhead and from almost anywhere in the world. They can remunerate and motivate their employees differently. They do not have to carry the enormous overheads associated with physical distribution and can, therefore, in theory, move faster and react more swiftly to change. Their challenge remains how to monetise their activities at a level which makes sense for their investors. I think it is fairly certain that advertising will play an ever more important role.

Of course major labels do still have a role to play, and the CD format still constitutes a significant percentage of global legitimate sales of music, but more partnerships and joint ventures are needed. Technology has to be the driver. The record companies seem to some extent to have abdicated their A&R function to production companies and trusted producers and managers, but in so doing their role is changing to just being finders of radio-friendly commercial hits. Where are the mavericks, the Alan McGee's who gave Welsh-speaking Super Furry Animals a start and supported Kevin Rowland in his wish to wear a dress on his album cover? Without risk there is a danger of stagnation. Yes, you can try and expand your income by signing all your artists up to the 360 models that we read about in the chapter on record deals, but they only work for so long as the live sector remains buoyant. If there is a downturn in the economy on the back of the credit crunch that began in the USA and which Britain started to experience at the end of 2007, then will people have the money to pay for expensive concert tickets, and if they pay for the tickets will they still buy the merchandise when they get there? Come to that unless record companies are developing acts who have a chance of a long-term career in the business and aren't just one album wonders, where are the stadium-filling live acts of the future coming from to sustain these 360 models?

LOWER VALUE DEALS

So far, in addition to the cost savings referred to above, and their focus at the moment on the holy grail of the 360 model, the major record companies have tried to minimise their exposure by signing fewer acts and paying less for those they do sign. But despite these good intentions they do still allow themselves to be carried away by hype and bidding wars and lawyers and managers must take some responsibility there too. We are trained to talk up deals and to seek the best deals for our clients and that often means the biggest financial commitment and therefore playing one party off against another. Often these mega signings are done out of a wish by the record companies for a short-term boost to sales to keep the shareholders or the City investors happy. Sometimes it's in order to convince the other labels that here is a label with money and power so they had better watch out: the metaphorical gauntlet is thrown down to rival labels. I do wonder though how many of these deals are done dispassionately with a clear notion of exactly how many records would have to be sold to recoup and how realistic that is.

NEW FORMS OF MARKETING

The record labels are also looking at innovative marketing ideas to drive customers to their product as opposed to that of a rival. These include a number of 'firsts' like Universal's first digital only record signing, followed within the year by signing them up for all physical rights too but they got the initial publicity. Then there were events like the artist Sandi Thom being signed to Sony/BMG on the back of webcasts from her basement flat in Tooting, South London, or the first download-only number one etc.

If I were a gambling woman then my money would not be going into record companies; it would be in technology looking at ways of filtering the vast array of information available online and in companies focusing on marketing to consumers using new technology. One example of attempts which are already being made to filter stuff on the Internet is the service launched by MySpace in December 2007 called Earwig. It is an Internet video channel. The idea is that it will feature short video clips on selected artists in which they will talk about themselves, their musical influences and music. These videos are meant to be self-produced interviews by the artists. It is aimed at unsigned or newly signed artists. MySpace says it will select an artist of the week who will feature on the front page of the website. I know I'm a cynic but what's the betting on that space being available to labels/advertisers for a fee in due course?

PIRACY

But enough of the predictions for now – they have a nasty habit of coming back and biting you. Let's look in more detail at some of these issues. The biggest area of concern remains that of piracy. As I have consistently said the music industry is probably fighting a lost cause with illegal downloading which is after all an invidious form of piracy. Individuals are now pirates as well as the large-scale commercial operations. The genie is already out of the bottle and isn't going to go back in. Whilst there remains a hardcore of law-abiding members of the public who will pay for music, they are joined by a younger generation who are used to free availability and exchange of music. Even those who will pay for it are unwilling to pay at the levels they were in the days of physical only carriers, and they may only be interested in paying for single tracks rather than 'bundled' albums. Making legal downloads easy to get and of a superior quality to the illegal versions may go some way to help but not for those who do not care overmuch about quality and who just want the latest stuff for free. Educating these people may help a bit, but probably not a great deal, so one way to get them may be to get them to pay for something else that they do value, such as a mobile phone service or a favourite website, and include in the price they pay an element for the music content on that phone or website.

Piracy has in fact always been a problem for the music business with CD, tape and video copying a huge business in the Far East and former eastern bloc countries (see Chapter 14). The problem also manifests itself in the leaking of albums via the Internet ahead of their commercial release – albums by artists such as Oasis, Eminem, U2, Beck and PJ Harvey have suffered from this. It is extremely difficult to track how or where the leak occurs: it's not as if someone were smuggling a large tape reel out of the studio. That said, I do have one artist who is so against his music being available online that all pre-release copies of his works were made available in cassette tape versions only on the basis that these are more difficult to copy and put up on the Internet. I suppose with the demise of cassette tapes this will be replaced with lower grade digital copies, but here I wonder if this isn't in fact damaging the artist if the reviewers listen to an inferior copy of the new album and write unflattering reviews as a consequence. There are also examples of almost 'Mission Impossible' style scenes where reviewers are searched before entering dedicated rooms where they listen on a special machine to one numbered copy of the album. The intention being that if the reviewer makes an illegal copy it will be tracked back to him. But even such measures don't stop the determined pirate. The long-awaited Coldplay album was available in full on the Internet days before the official launch. This was despite strenuous efforts by their record company, EMI, to prevent this. EMI made the best of a bad job by bringing forward release plans. Record companies also try and get the websites offering the albums shut down but they do not always get the co-operation of the ISPs and where they do it may already be too late.

SABAM v. *Scarlet*

There are, however, signs that European courts may be prepared to make ISPs responsible for what they carry. The first landmark case to take this line was brought by Belgian collection society SABAM against Scarlet, formerly a branch of the Italian ISP Tiscali in 2007. A court of first instance in Belgium confirmed that an ISP must take responsibility for stopping illegal file-sharing on its network by using file filtering systems. The ruling is the first of its kind in Europe and, as you might imagine, was welcomed by the international record industry, which has been pressing for action by ISPs to curb piracy on their networks. The case seems to have turned on a determination of which of two pieces of European legislation should have precedence. The first to be implemented was the E-Commerce Directive which declared that ISPs as intermediaries were not liable for the content on the websites that they host. However, the later Copyright Directive amending the copyright laws to cover online uses said that in some circumstances copyright owners could get court orders against ISPs if websites using their services were being used for piracy or infringed the rights of copyright owners. In practice up to now once an ISP is notified that a particular website contains illegal material it orders the owner of the website to remove the offending material. This was the first case to decide which of the two conflicting laws should have precedence. The ISPs are reluctant to accept unrestricted responsibility as they feel that this is shifting responsibility for control of piracy to them. However, it is undoubtedly the case that it is much easier for an ISP to take action against users of its websites than it is for rights owners to try and track down and take action against individual illegal file sharers.

The case was decided at the lowest level of the Belgian court system and is therefore likely to be appealed to a higher court. It is also not known at this stage if it will apply to other ISPs within Belgium or if it might have a broader European dimension. That must be a possibility as these two conflicting Directives were to be implemented into the laws of all European Union countries. Belgium does not follow a strict case-law precedent system like we do in the UK so it does not set a binding precedent for similar actions against other ISPs in Belgium. Naturally therefore the telecoms companies and ISPs in Belgium are playing down its significance. However, the existence of such a judgement must be influential on judges trying similar cases there. They certainly cannot be ignored and it is likely that SABAM will try and press home its advantage and try and get the other main Belgian ISPs to come into line without the need for them to bring separate legal actions.

The case also considered various methods of filtering and came down in favour of one particular piece of software called Audible Magic, but the ISPs are doubtful about the effectiveness of this software. The court's expert said that it could identify material on P2P systems which infringed copyright. The ISP was given six months in which to implement the order, with a penalty of €2,500 for every day of delay beyond that date. The ISPs have reservations about the ability of Audible Magic to operate on the necessary scale. They also say that it should not be forced to pay the bill for protecting the assets of other private companies. They feel that they will have to pass on this cost in some way to their users and that this also indirectly penalises those who are entirely law abiding users of their websites. However again that argument could be used in many areas of life: we pay higher insurance premiums because of other dangerous drivers or because our homes happen to be in areas with a high crime rate.

This all feels like the ISPs throwing all their arguments at what is undoubtedly a worrying decision for them.

ANTI-PIRACY MEASURES AND DIGITAL RIGHTS MANAGEMENT

As their well-publicised actions against MP3.com and Napster showed, RIAA and the music industry generally took the view that attack was the better form of defence. Others, including me, believe that in doing so they alienated consumers. Headlines highlighting legal actions against schoolgirls downloading and sharing music with their school friends did the cause no favours. So alongside the legal actions various steps were taken to try and control the making of multiple copies or to track those who did so.

There has been a three-pronged approach. Digital rights management i.e. technological protection measures (e.g. encryption), backed up by end-user agreements spelling out the restrictions on use, education, and legislation, such as the EU Copyright Directive prohibiting circumvention of such protection measures and devices/making illegal devices, including software, whose primary purpose is to enable or facilitate circumvention. There is, however, a growing sense that these digital rights management systems go beyond what is necessary to protect copyright owners or indeed are holding back the development of a legitimate download market. For example, some of the protection measures had the unforeseen side effect of preventing legitimate owners of CDs from playing the CD on their PCs or making a copy for use in their cars.

TECHNOLOGICAL METHODS

Considerable resources were put into anti-piracy devices such as watermarking and ways to track the copying of music to control it or ensure proper payment. In the 1990s, the Secure Digital Media Initiative (SDMI) was hailed as an industry-backed secure system to control illegal copying. In fact, the creators of the SDMI system offered a reward to anyone who could crack it. Predictably, such is the power of the Internet to harness resources and minds, some computer programmers did so within 48 hours. Other ideas included a system of permanent and temporary 'passwords' on computer files, which only allow one copy of a file to be made and played on a legitimate player. Making one copy destroys one of the passwords and if you then try to copy it again, the copy won't play because the player can only find one of the required two passwords.

Considerable resources have also been put into developing systems to track usage of music and to ensure that the legitimate rights owners get paid for the use of their work. These content management systems included ones where there is a kind of pyramid selling at work where a legitimate user who introduces a friend to a piece of music which the friend then pays to download receives points which the first person can use to purchase more music downloads.

Others were just interested in tracking when a piece of music was downloaded and feeding the information back to the rights owner. Efforts were made to make these systems as transparent as possible so that the rights owner and the artist or his advisers could get comfortable with the whole idea that if they grant these rights they will get paid, but there were also privacy concerns as a result of personal information that is embedded in these DRM systems and issues such as devices which monitor what a user does on his computer. The SonyBMG so-called 'Root-kit' fiasco outlined in the chapter on piracy below may have done much to damage the efforts to get the public to accept these tracking systems.

EDUCATION

As a second string to their bow the BPI launched a series of leaflets aimed at educating people, particularly the young, to the illegal nature of much of the copying music off the Internet. There is some evidence that this is helping people to understand that what they are doing is illegal, but less evidence that it is stopping them doing it anyway. One of the recommendations of the Gowers Review, which is considered in more detail below, is that the making of a copy for your own use should not be illegal – yet at the moment it is. The music industry's initial reaction was again one of protectionism. The feeling was that if this were allowed it would be the thin end of the wedge. A Government paper on the topic is expected early in 2008.

LEGISLATION

New laws now confirm beyond doubt that the rights of a copyright owner extend to duplication or broadcast online. In Europe this was confirmed by the European Copyright Directive, which was implemented into UK law in November 2003. After all the fuss that had preceded it the Government finally elected to only do the bare minimum required to incorporate the Directive into UK law. The Government argued that in most cases the UK Copyright Act of 1988 already encompassed online uses. It did make a change to include the somewhat clumsy 'making available right' to extend the right of a copyright owner to control broadcasts of his work to include online usage. The Government did not take up the option to extend the number of exceptions to what is known as 'fair-dealing' i.e. legitimate uses of copyright works for which no permission of the copyright owner is required. In the US the equivalent legislation is the Digital Millennium Copyright Act 1998. Both pieces of legislation were the subject of intense lobbying. ISPs sought, and largely got, protection from liability for illegal material not within their control. In most cases the ISP is only obliged to do something once it is brought to their attention but court orders can be brought against an ISP if it is hosting sites used for illegal file sharing or other pirate activities.

Concern was also voiced as to how you treat 'transient' copying i.e. technical copies or reproductions made as a side effect of, say, sending an email from computer to computer around the world. The EU Directive and the regulations incorporating it into the UK Copyright Act made it clear that transient copying which had no commercial value was not a 'reproduction' and therefore not an infringement of copyright.

In order to support the efforts of the anti-piracy brigade, the legislation made it an offence to circumvent, or make available the means to circumvent, devices intended to protect copyright, but as yet there have been no reported cases of legal actions under this provision.

Finally there were the attempts to bring legislation in granting rights holders greater control over illegal use of their copyrights. In particular they are keen to ensure that the ISPs share data with them which will enable them to target Internet pirates more effectively. The ISPs did not come up with a voluntary code by the end of 2007 and a paper is expected from the government to address this and other cultural issues in February 2008.

DIGITAL RIGHTS MANAGEMENT

The debate over whether or not to place digital rights management protections into music formats rumbled on for most of 2007. Steve Jobs of Apple kicked off the debate in April 2007 by calling for all music to be made available for licensing for services such as Apple iTunes free of DRM. The major label bosses then lined up for or against the idea. Eric Nicoli, then chairman of EMI Group, announced in April 2007 that EMI Music would be licensing DRM-free superior quality downloads across its entire digital repertoire and Apple's online music store iTunes would be the first to make available these new downloads. EMI hoped that by providing superior quality DRM free tracks they would tempt consumers towards legitimate downloads as opposed to the often inferior quality illegal downloads. There was a slight catch in that the audio compression format they use is AAC, not the more widely available MP3 format which is compatible with most portable players. Software 'fixes' are available to decode the AAC format for those whose players don't support it but this may put off the less technically minded music fans.

In contrast, Warner Music initially came out in favour of continued use of DRM. In April 2007 it demanded that the Anywhere CD service for downloading of albums stopped offering DRM free albums from the Warner Music catalogue. In July 2007 Warners tried to get one up on Apple by putting much of its back catalogue online on the Lala.com website for free streamed previews, but not download, with Lala paying a royalty fee to Warners each time a user listened to a track.

The deal with the EMI DRM-free tracks unravelled a little when the tracks went on sale on 30 May 2007 under the iTunes Plus banner and a premium rate of 99p. It was discovered that the tracks downloaded by consumers contained the name, account information and email address of the person who bought the download. This in itself was not new. Apparently such information can be found on all tracks purchased from iTunes. Did you know that? I didn't although I imagine it is contained in the terms and conditions of the website. The objection was that if this was genuinely intended as a DRM-free download then this information should not be present as it enabled Apple to track the subsequent use of that music download. The privacy lobby was also concerned. What else may be embedded in these files and if it were that easily uncovered how might unscrupulous users make use of the information?

Universal Music seems to be playing a waiting game. It has experimented with DRM-free trials and has deals with companies like Amazon and has not as yet committed full scale to iTunes.

In November 2007 the retailers association ERA announced it would be lobbying the record industry to press for the abolition of DRM in download releases and for the use of the MP3 compression format as the universal standard, thereby simplifying the whole process for the consumer buying legal downloads.

Finally, on 27 December 2007 Warners announced that it had dropped its opposition to making available music without DRM systems in place. It confirmed that its entire catalogue was going to be made available DRM-free in the United States off the download website of Amazon.com. It seems that Warners had bowed to the pressure in order to keep pace with its competitors. In contrast to the less common AAC format used by EMI and iTunes, Warners' catalogue will be available through Amazon in the more popular MP3 format. Although at the moment these arrangements apply only to the United States, it is expected that they will extend internationally soon. *The Times* reported on 28 December that Warners was also in talks with Apple to release DRM-free tracks via iTunes. SonyBMG now remains the only major decidedly in favour of DRM.

It is too early to tell if the move to DRM-free music downloads will help to stem the drop in album sales and record company revenues. It does seem as though the battleground has moved from DRM to persuading the ISPs to take more responsibility although that particular debate has, I fear, a long way to run as the ISPs will not give up their non-liable state as an intermediary without a fight.

GOWERS REVIEW

The Andrew Gowers Review of Intellectual Property was published on 6 December 2006. It contained little that was of comfort to the music industry, which had lobbied hard in particular for an extension in the duration of the sound recording copyright and performers' rights beyond fifty years. Performers were looking for parity with songwriters with a copyright protection period of their lives plus seventy years. The recording industry was looking for parity with the period of copyright protection in other countries, in particular the United States at 95 years. Gowers recommended that the period stay as it is, asserting that it represented a fair balance between the right to protection of the intellectual property and the benefits of having work come into the public domain after a period of time. He remained unmoved by the fact that recordings by well-known artists such as Sir Cliff Richard were coming out of copyright. In January 2008 re-issues label Delta Leisure will follow on from its re-releases of 1954, 1955 and 1956 hits with a compilation of 1957 hits including Paul Anka's 'Diana' and Andy Williams' 'Butterfly'.

Despite a brief glimmer of hope when the House of Common's Select Committee for Culture, Media and Sport urged the Government to lobby for an extension across the European Union the Government has accepted Gowers' recommendation that the status quo be maintained.

Other only slightly less controversial recommendations included one that there be a limited 'format-shifting' private copying right without any levy such as the oft touted 'blank tape' levy on the hardware used. Contrary to what many people think, it is illegal to copy a CD to your iPod, even when you own the CD in question. The Government accepted the recommendation that this was confusing and should be rectified. The music industry view this as the thin end of the wedge arguing that if making one copy for a different format is legal it will suggest copying for one's mates is also allright.

The other issue which I have already mentioned and which arises out of this Review is the extent to which the Government will use the law to enforce greater co-operation from ISPs. I await with interest the proposals for this expected in 2008.

NEW BUSINESS MODELS

But I don't want to suggest that the music industry is doing nothing in this area. As new means of delivery of music have begun to establish themselves, so record companies are moving with new business models for payment to artists for these new uses.

It has been difficult to find business models that work financially for both the consumer and the copyright owner. Models that were trialled but which did not survive include micro-billing, where download costs are added to your phone bill. Per-download, pay-per-listen charges, and subscription systems, where a regular payment secures delivery of music to the subscriber online seem to be the ones that are emerging as workable models.

HOW IS THE CONSUMER CHARGED?

Track downloads

First there is the sale of single track downloads such as the system adopted by iTunes, sometimes with a refinement that the customer can buy the right to listen to a piece of music for a limited period of time before he has to buy it in order to keep it permanently. With these systems the customer 'owns' the tracks downloaded and pays about 79p per track or 99p for the premium version. The tracks paid for are then transferable to portable devices and can be burned to disk. 7Digital, an online store which offers to provide shop-fronts for smaller labels, as well as the facility for a label or artist to create its own online store using the 7Digital back room services and its deals with online retailers, also offers tracks at 79p a download. Neither iTunes nor 7Digital offers a subscription service.

Napster offers 79p downloads but also has a subscription service (see below).

MP3.com has a limited selection of music but offers it free for download and streaming.

3 Mobile offers a per-track download rate of £1.29 and T-Mobile one at £1.00 per download. Neither offers a subscription service.

Subscription services
Then there is the subscription model. Subscription services (e.g. Napster) allow subscribers access to all the music they want for a monthly fee, sometimes with an option to purchase selected tracks (from 79p per track). Napster's service has what it calls 'tethered downloads' where the track is transferable to portable players for as long as the consumer remains a subscriber. Once the subscription ends the music is no longer available. Will such a service appeal to the long-term collector? The Napster subscription rate is £9.95 per month to listen to music on a computer; £14.95 per month for Napster To Go membership which allows you to download unlimited music to an MP3 player.

Emusic offers a Basic package of £8.99 per month for up to 30 downloads i.e 30p per song; the Plus package at £11.99 a month allows up to 50 downloads i.e 24p per song and the Premium package at £14,99 per month allows up to 75 downloads i.e. only 20p per song. It is difficult to see how at these low levels a viable percentage can be paid back to the rights owners after all other participants have taken their cut. However, if the take up were high enough that would help to compensate for the low per track average.

Vodafone says it has 1.2 million tracks available and charges £1.99 per week through its MusicStation service.

But the jury is still out on the viability of subscription services. Both HMV and Virgin Retail (as it was known) withdrew their subscription deals in 2007. Napster scaled back its offering and Yahoo and Real decided against launching them in the UK. This may in part have been to do with difficulties in blanket licensing of music as the Copyright Tribunal case was still ongoing in the first part of 2007. Now that that is settled we may see more services venturing into the subscription market. The fact remains though that there is a long way to go in educating music fans to take up these subscription services and the price level has to be right. The £1.99 a week that Vodafone is looking for may prove too rich for the average music fan. In the US subscription models have been around for longer and the model is stronger but it is still in its early days here. It is perhaps significant that the far out market leader Apple with its iTunes service has not embraced the subscription model and none of the subscription model services currently in the market work with Apple technology.

If the pundits are correct that the consumer will pay for access to a service which includes music amongst other content, then the subscription model may be the way forward, but there will be a challenge in getting the percentage share for the music companies and publishers right.

PAYING THE ARTIST
On the other side of the coin the debate continues as to how the copyright owner – usually the record company – will account to the artist for these new types of usage.

Net receipts
When online revenue first became a reality the royalties were generally treated as similar to a flat fee per use charge that you might get from licensing a piece of music for a one-off use e.g. on a compilation. The share of receipts from online was also generally the

same as for flat fee uses at around 50%. This way of calculating shares of income still tends to apply with income that is linked to subscriptions but I have yet to see anyone receive a full and complete royalty accounting from such uses and I would love to see someone carry out an audit as I fear that only a fraction of this income may be being picked up.

Royalty basis

This was the model used in the early days of downloads, before the record labels began to realise that they should think again about how they account to their artist if they weren't going to end up paying out more than they wanted to to their artists. In other words, greed kicked in and the model shifted to a royalty basis. The royalty rate was about the same as applied to a physical CD sale and the price was that which the record label received from the online etailers or aggregators or from the mobile phone companies. This method of calculating shares of income works for downloads or per use payments but is not so effective for subscription revenue.

Deductions

Then the record labels went a little further and decided that if they were going to apply the royalty method then why not calculate the royalties with some of the same sorts of reductions that apply to physical sales, such as a packaging deduction. Don't be ridiculous I here you say. How can there possibly be a packaging deduction when there is no packaging in an online download? You are right, but try telling the record companies that. Of course, it's called something different like 'back end fulfilment charges' i.e. the cost of setting up an online payment system by credit card, or an 'administration' charge, but curiously the percentage charged was almost always the same as that which they used to deduct for packaging on a physical CD sale.

TERRITORIAL ISSUES

I have a feeling that another battleground will be territorial restrictions. At the moment there are deals in place between Apple and individual record companies restricting consumers to only buying music from the iTunes online store in their country of residence. In this way prices can differ from one country to the next. The first chink in this armour came in April 2007 when the European Commission issued a Statement of Objections that such arrangements violated a section of the EU treaty on the free movement of goods. It looks like more pressure will follow on the heels of the launch of the iPhone in November 2007. Apple has struck exclusive deals with one mobile phone operator in each country restricting access to the phone by users of other networks. The German courts initially granted Vodafone a temporary injunction forcing T-Mobile to sell iPhones that were not tied to a single network, despite Apple's exclusive deal with T-Mobile. However, the temporary injunction was subsequently overturned and the exclusive arrangements were reinstated.

Vodafone objected to the exclusivity agreement and said customers should be able to choose between networks. Apple has similar licensing agreements with O2 in the UK and AT&T in the US. In the two weeks since the temporary injunction was granted, the BBC reported that T-Mobile had complied with the injunction and sold the handsets without a network contract for 999 euros (£719). Although strictly complying that price was a hefty premium to the 399 euro cost for a phone with a two year T-Mobile contract. In response to complaints from customers, T-Mobile has now promised that at the end of the two year contracts it will unlock the phones at no charge. However, as always with the Internet and technology, where there is a will there is a way and despite the best efforts of Apple and the phone companies to tie consumers to one provider, programmes have been circulating online that allow users to unlock their iPhone so that it can be used on any network. In an attempt to dissuade people from using these programmes Apple has warned that their use could render the phones 'permanently inoperable' when it releases software updates

This issue is unlikely to go away as in the US alone Apple still faces two lawsuits from people alleging that preventing users unlocking their iPhones is an unreasonable restriction of consumer choice. It would also seem to potentially fall foul of European legislation encouraging free movement of goods but that would have to be balanced against the rights of individuals to make contracts on commercial terms which are acceptable to them.

PHYSICAL CDS

With the proliferation of online download services there is a parallel debate on how to prolong the appeal of physical CDs. The Enhanced CD format was seen by some to be the answer as well as special edition releases, value-added content where extra or bonus tracks are added and fancier packaging or artwork. All major artists now tend to film additional material, whether that be a live concert or backstage interviews to be synchronised with audio material to make a new package. This may be broadcast on television or sold as a package with a DVD being sold bundled together with the audio CD. But the hoped for boost of DVD sales was not sustained. After an initial burst, DVD sales are again falling away as consumers view more material online on their PCs or portable DVD players and new format mobile phones. At the end of December 2007, Apple seemed to be close to a deal with News Corp to offer Fox films through iTunes. At the moment the only films available on the service are from the Disney Company, but if Fox comes on board that might help to open the doors to other film companies.

There remains a feeling in the industry that if you have a good product it will sell and it will sell in physical CD format. The 3 million CD sales of The Eagles' new album in 2007 is often cited as an example. However, whilst I would agree that good music should always find its market, there is I think a case here of physical CDs appealing still to certain sectors of the market. We know that CD singles by pop artists buck the trend and sell a larger percentage in CD form than the usual download sales. It may well also be the case that the fans who are likely to buy The Eagles product some thirty years after they last released an album are likely to be of an older age group more comfortable with the CD format than with the online versions.

MOBILES AND MOBILE MUSIC PLAYERS

Alongside the online download, the other major new carrier format has been the mobile phone. The consumption of music on mobile phones has evolved from ringtones to full audio recordings in ringtones, ring-back tunes, full-track downloads and other media applications. There is still a big issue over how to ensure that everyone gets a fair slice of the cake. The basic issue with the ringtone model is that there are too many people sharing in that cake. Out of a £3.00 download, after the tax man has taken his share a large proportion goes to the mobile phone service provider who gets to charge for the time the call takes to download the material plus a bit extra for the crucial element they provide to the story: without them the whole thing doesn't work. Then there is the middleman aggregator: usually a company that does the deals with the individual rights owners employs the technology that allows the conversion into a form that can be downloaded and administers the collection and payment of the proceeds. These people take the lion's share. Then there are the rights owners: the publishers who own or control the song and in the case of real audio ringtones where the sound recording is also copied, the owners of the sound recording. Out of the amounts that these companies receive the songwriter and artist/performer get their share. That share is usually based on the net receipts that the publisher or record company receives depending on the contract with the artists. In some cases this is a 50:50 split and in the case of the songwriters the share could be even higher, but it still remains that out of every £3.00 download the songwriter may receive less than 30p. Then there are the issues of ensuring proper payment. The whole question of how e-commerce is to be taxed is also fraught with difficulties, which are, thankfully, outside the scope of this book. If you intend to venture into online distribution you should take specialist tax advice.

The challenge for lawyers is to see how we can ensure a fair balance between what the record company or the website company gets to keep and how much is paid through to the artist.

New developments include not only the much promoted iPhone but also services such as Vodafone's MusicStation subscription service whereby the mobile phone owner gets unlimited music for £1.99 per week. All the major record labels and many independents signed up to this service from the outset. Nokia also has a music download store. More profile raising for these mobile services is likely to come with the promise to include music played via the Napster and MusicStation services towards chart placings once the Official Chart Company has resolved the tracking issues. Vodafone claims it is aiming at 10 million subscribers by the end of 2008.

MOVE AWAY FROM ALBUMS

Are we seeing a potential switch away from traditional albums? The CD was liberating in that it permitted over sixty minutes' worth of material far more than the traditional vinyl or tape formats. This was hard on artists who had to maintain consistent quality across twelve or more tracks but not filling the CD felt like the consumer was being short-changed.

Radio and TV and highlights on MySpace-type pages emphasise individual tracks. Traditionally this was as a precursor to persuading you to buy the album but now a consumer is just as likely to be a single track download as he is a bundled album. There is no sign at the moment that the traditional album-based model is being abandoned and certainly all exclusive artist contracts still function round the album model, but lateral thinking may see the rise of commitments based on numbers of individual tracks.

Single sales have risen to their highest yearly level since records began growing by nearly 40% in 2005/6 according to the BPI. Ninety per cent of all single sales are downloads (Source: *Music Week* article by Ben Larder 10/11/07). However, pop artists like Leona Lewis, McFly and Take That continue to score significantly higher on physical CD sales at around 40–50%. In contrast sales of physical album CDs in October 2007 were down 22% on the same month in 2006. But this may have been a particularly bad month as by 17 December 2007, *Music Week* was reporting that sales of albums had bounced back to reach a new high for 2007 but it was still over a million sales down over the same period in 2006 so the trend is still down. We should also bear in mind that although single sales may have increased in volume by 40% that does not mean that the income generated has increased by the same percentage. The average download price is around 79p, not the £1.99 plus the consumer may have paid for a physical CD single.

SOCIAL NETWORKING SITES

One of the interesting effects of the growing influence on the music industry of the Internet is the extent to which the consumer is starting to drive the sort of music he wishes to listen to and purchase. Recommendations from online 'friends' are as influential as hearing a track on the radio. One of the side effects of this is that the majority of single tracks downloaded off the Internet are not, according to a *Music Week* survey, current releases but back catalogue both recent and decades old. Interest in old tracks can be boosted by an appearance in a Hollywood film or on an influential television show like *Gray's Anatomy* or *Ugly Betty*. The latest in the series of back to the future television series *Life on Mars* should see a similar rise in interest in 80s music to that which the original series generated in the music of the 70s.

The phenomenon of the social networking site is a key part of this spread of knowledge of obscure or old releases as well as music by unsigned or new artists.

Market analysts Jupiter Research reports that 40% of users of MySpace and Facebook go on to buy music from artists they discover on these sites. This is a sitting target in marketing terms and so it should come as no surprise that the big boys are investing in these sites as a potentially huge source of advertising revenue.

It is a measure of the popularity of these sites that as part of the campaign surrounding the release of her album *X*, Kylie Minogue's record label, Parlophone, part of the EMI Group, announced she was setting up her own social networking site.

Slightly more controversially, Facebook's owners announced the launch of an advertising model which would enable advertisers to precisely target a particular audience. This is not new, of course – loyalty card schemes such as the Tesco Clubcard have for many years analysed the customers' purchases with the card in order to target special offers at them. Why it is slightly different is that it would appear to use information supplied by users of the sites when they register. On sites like Facebook that can be very personal data indeed. So questions are being asked as to whether Facebook has the right to use this information in this way under privacy and data protection legislation.

On the positive side these sites do act as a new launch pad for artists and as an A&R resource for record label execs. It is invariably the case now that A&R people want you to direct them to a MySpace page as opposed to sending them a CD of a new artist. The problem I come back to is that the sheer popularity of these sites means that it is increasingly difficult to find new music and to sort the good from the bad. Some might argue that having a method to target you with the music you like may not be a bad thing even if it did bring with it some annoying banner ads.

Of course, the next logical step for a site like MySpace would be to facilitate the purchase of music direct from the website when you are viewing an artist's profile online. At the moment it is only possible if you link through to another site like iTunes. This seems to be missing a trick and will, I am sure, be rectified soon. Much smaller site, Bebo, with only 34 million users compared to MySpace's 200 million users and rising, has struck a deal with iTunes to do just that. It also introduced the prospect of an artist or label customising their own page with advertising of their choice. Somewhat surprisingly it does not seem to be taking any share of the advertising revenue. Will that last though, and if so how else is it going to make money?

Advertising revenue is the Holy Grail for most of these sites. In October 2007, Microsoft invested $240 million in Facebook. This sum was said to represent a 1.6% stake in the company which therefore values it at $15 billion. But as yet the company has not broken even and its predicted revenues for 2007 are put at only $150million. So Microsoft and other potential purchasers like Yahoo are clearly betting on an upswing in advertising revenue. Microsoft wishes to become a major player in web advertising to challenge the dominance of Google. Facebook has 50 million plus active users worldwide according to Elizabeth Judge writing in *The Times* on 26 October 2007. Part of the deal is that Microsoft becomes the exclusive third party advertiser for the site. Once again suspicions have been voiced that Microsoft will get access to the personal data of the Facebook users as another part of this deal. Facebook's owners need to take care as there are many who might be turned off by a closer association with Microsoft.

A slightly different variation on this theme is the networking site slicethepie, launched in the first half of 2007. It is aimed at unsigned acts, whether new acts or more established ones without a current deal. The idea is that artists enter genre specific competitions online to generate sufficient votes for them and their music to win a guaranteed £15,000 to use to make and promote their own album. These who don't win can still generate enough offers of support to raise the magic £15,000. The fans or users of the site can speculate on the success of the bands by buying and selling contracts in their chosen artists. It has been described as a 'stock exchange for unsigned acts' by Dan Sabbagh in *The Times* on 17 October 2007. The fans who have invested in bands get special access to the bands and the right to a free download copy of the album when it is finished.

It's meant as a source of funding albums without a traditional label and as a talent source for other labels. The artists have no exclusive tie-in to the website, own the copyright in what they create but pay a distribution fee of £2 per album back to slicethepie. If an artist goes on to be signed by a bigger label the label has the option to buy out the distribution contract. Extra shares contracts are awarded to those who engage in reviewing artists on the site.

COPYRIGHT INFRINGEMENTS

But not all is sweetness and light in the world of social networking. On several occasions music and video rights owners have cried foul with allegations of unlawful use of copyrights on these sites. YouTube and MySpace have faced several lawsuits from aggrieved copyright owners.

YouTube is owned by Google who paid £837million for it in October 2006. As you probably know YouTube's USP is allowing users to upload and download content produced by the user – usually funny videos or still photos and occasionally disturbing images of the 'happy slapping' kind from mobile phones. There have also been examples of online bullying of both pupils and teachers. Not of course to suggest that YouTube condones this but it is all part of the debate over how much control ISPs have or should exercise over the content on their sites.

At the time that it was in talks with Google, YouTube faced a massive lawsuit from Universal Music which alleged the site engaged in copyright infringement on a large scale by making Universal Music videos and music available on the site without the consent of the copyright owners.

The lawsuit did not materialise at that time because for once the major record labels decided not to spend their money on legal cases as they did in the early days of P2P services with Napster, but instead to cut licence deals with the site allowing their videos to be shown.

There are of course potentially huge marketing advantages for the labels and artists – particularly if they can engineer a viral marketing hype on an artist's video. But its acquisition by Google meant it was also potentially worthwhile taking legal action against if infringements continued.

Universal began a legal action against MySpace in 2006 claiming large scale piracy of music and videos on the site, seeking damages of $9million. MySpace, perhaps predictably, argued that they were merely the conduit for the users of the site and did not induce, encourage or condone copyright violation. Universal's response was that music and video formed the key building blocks of the online pages and communities of users and, therefore, added considerably to the value of the MySpace business overall. MySpace says it does remove illegal downloads but it seems to do so only after the infringement has been brought to its attention. It does not act proactively to monitor content which is consistent with the line that ISPs are not liable for content. They also point to their users agreements which protect users from posting offensive, obscene, abusive, defamatory or otherwise illegal materials but again their response is reactive not proactive and critics remain unconvinced as to how effective these agreements are. Many users who click on the relevant box to accept the terms have little or no knowledge of what they are agreeing to and may not be worth suing even if they are tracked down.

MySpace does appear to be willing to use filtering software to check uploaded music against a database of copyright materials and block any that do not have the necessary content to avoid setting any kind of precedent.

YouTube also seems to favour the take down after notice approach which places the onus on the rights holders to monitor the site and notify them of any infringements. Copyright owners argue that the search and privacy facilities of the site make it difficult if not impossible to track down all illegal uses and that it is a simple matter for a user to repost offending material under a different 'tag'. YouTube has taken some steps to legitimise the use of copyright materials on its site as witnessed by a blanket licensing agreement it has reached with the MCPS-PRS Alliance of collection societies. The deal relates to the use of material represented by these societies in the UK. The details of the licence deal have not been revealed other than that it includes a one-stop synchronisation and mechanical licence and that it requires YouTube to report every time a video or music is used or played. There is a sum of money paid by YouTube to the Alliance but they have not revealed how much and the Alliance has played down the sums likely to be generated for individual rights owners. There must, however, be merit in the information gathered and the precedent of the one-stop shop is a good one.

Individuals and big corporations such as Viacom have continued to snipe away at YouTube throughout 2007 alleging varying degrees of copyright infringements. Cases were brought by the football Premier League alleging infringement of copyright. Viacom alleges 100,000 illegal videos were on the site and claims $1 billion plus in damages. Opponents of YouTube allege that its business plan from the outset was to build its business on the back of massive copyright infringement. The YouTube business model depends on advertising revenue and the popularity of its pages generating users who are drawn to the pages by attractive content. YouTube features banner ads on video clips and on a featured video of the day. The argument goes that these sites cannot be interested in clearing out the unlawful videos as it is the presence of this material which makes the site attractive to both users and advertisers. In an attempt to address the argument that the law says the USP is not liable where it is acting purely as a host for content, the Premier League litigation alleges that YouTube made and shared unauthorised copies on its servers for further dissemination and was not therefore just a passive host. That this was more than pure transient copying which is permitted by the copyright directive. It is clear to me that we need a high level court decision on the alleged conflicts between the E-Commerce Directive and the Copyright Directive. It is possible that one of these cases or even the more recent one of *SABAM* v. *Scarlet* that we referred to above will prove that test case.

Google announced in June 2007 that it would test new 'fingerprinting' technology to help trace illegal content by indentifying unique attributes which, if missing, would tend to suggest the copy was illegal. But some commentators see this not as Google taking responsibility for content but rather using it as an after the event technology to make it easier to take down content after an infringement has been notified by identifying other examples of illegal content of the same kind. The debate continues.

MARKETING ONLINE

OFFICIAL WEBSITES

The Internet has proved to be an excellent means of marketing the 'brand'. Brands that are Internet-savvy can link their online marketing efforts with those of their record company and their own efforts in terms of live work. We've seen artists successfully sell out a concert in minutes when tickets are offered for sale on their website and some are saying that they will stop using ticket agents and make all their tickets available in that way thereby cutting out the fees to the middleman. By selling tickets online the artist or his advisers also have the opportunity, with the right permissions, to create a database of committed fans keen to learn more about what the artist has planned. This gives the artist a ready-made mailing list and, in some cases, new customers for the inner sanctum on his website where selected information and exclusive tracks or visuals are made available for a small fee. Many artists now use websites to communicate directly with their fans in the form of online diaries or 'blogs', but of course there is then always the issue of ensuring that the website is regularly updated. Many exclusive artist contracts now insist that the artist commits to writing a blog or giving 'copy' regularly to a staff writer at the record company to write one up for them. Others require the artists to record snippets for sale as mobile phone ringtones and to take part in online chats with fans.

A couple of years ago we were very concerned to ensure that artists retained ownership of their domain names and official websites. Most record companies now don't insist on ownership of all variations of the artist's domain name and, even where they do, they provide links to the artists or fan-club sites. Most will now agree that their ownership and control only lasts during the term of the record deal and will make arrangements for transfer of names at the end of the deal. In some cases they only require ownership of one domain name with the artist's name in it, for example a .net or .org domain name, and are happy for the artist to retain all the other names. There is then usually a requirement for the artist to provide links from his website to that domain name which is used for the 'official' record company website page for that artist. There are however still some record labels who would like to control all aspects of the artist's online presence. Sometimes I have artists as clients who really aren't bothered about this and who are unlikely to ever do a good website themselves so in these cases I usually do not resist the record company having these rights exclusively during the term of the contract. But at the end of the contract the rights should transfer to the artist.

Record companies have in some, but not all, cases shown that they have the resources and skills to create interesting, even dynamic websites. Most of the major record labels now focus heavily on the artist website as a means of cross-selling their product – CDs, DVDs – with whatever other activities that the artist may be doing – such as gigs or personal appearances. Record companies who are insisting on 360 models are keen to ensure they control the websites so that any revenues generated online e.g. from ticket sales or sales of T-shirts also come to them. As with all things that make up an artist's brand, the artist should have creative control of the 'look and feel' of any website dedicated to them and maybe also of the designers/artwork providers or other creative elements.

A well-linked campaign can be very effective. If all promotional material contains a website address and that website is vibrant and informative, you create a receptive audience for the marketing material you want to get to potential consumers.

WEBSITE DESIGN RIGHTS AND COPYRIGHT

If an artist does create his own website he may decide to employ someone to design it. The website is likely to be made up of many different elements, all of which could be the subject of copyright or other legal protection.

The website will have words that, if original, could be a literary work with its own literary copyright. The website will no doubt have visual images or graphics. These could be still photographs, moving images or film. Each of these could have its own copyright. It will be made up of a number of computer programs which are also protected by copyright. The designer will have copyright in the original design drawings; he may also have a design right.

When commissioning someone else to design a website, the artist has to make sure that all rights have been cleared for use in the website design, so that he has all the rights he needs to do what he wants with the website. You also need to find out whether these rights have been 'bought-out' for a one-off payment or if there is an ongoing obligation to pay for the use. It's possible that in order to use the music or a sound recording you'll have to pay a royalty or further fee.

If the person commissioned to design the website is your employee then you'll own the copyright in their original work, but the other rights may still have to be cleared.

If you ask someone who isn't employed by you to design the website, you must make sure that you take an assignment from them of all rights in the work they have done. You could make this a condition of the commission fee, or it could be the subject of a separate fee, or occasionally a royalty. The designer may grant the right to use the work only on the website and not, for example, to print design elements from the website and sell them separately as posters or otherwise as part of a merchandising campaign (see Chapter 8 on branding). These additional uses could be the subject of a separate fee.

Assignments of copyright should be confirmed in writing. A written agreement also establishes what rights you have and on what terms. It should contain a confirmation from the designer that he has all the necessary rights from third parties for the use of any or all elements of the design.

HOSTING AGREEMENT

Once you have the website, you need to find a way to make it available to others via the Internet. You could become your own ISP, set yourself up with the necessary Internet capacity to launch your own site and provide that service to others. This isn't, however, the way that most artists get their website on the Internet. More usually, they arrange to have the website site 'hosted' by another ISP or possibly by their record company. Anyone going down this route should have an agreement with the host ISP setting out the kind of service that will be provided and at what cost. These agreements are called 'hosting' agreements.

If you're trying to establish yourself as having a website to which your fans and potential customers return over and over again, you need to know that the host will supply a reliable service. Reliability is improving but we all know of websites where the hardware on the server 'goes down' on a regular basis. These sites get a reputation as being unreliable and people are less likely to go back to them. Fans, or potential fans, won't bother to go to a website that's never available or which is difficult to use. The first is the fault of the server, the second that of the designer – both are your problem.

The hosting agreement should insist that the server will be functioning properly for at least 97–98% of the time. It should provide compensation if the server is 'down' for more than an agreed percentage of the time or for more than a maximum agreed number of hours a day.

If the website is to be used to sell merchandise online, you'll need to know that any credit card payment facility is 100% secure. The ISP should guarantee this in the hosting agreement.

The ISP should also be able to supply a reasonable amount of 'back office' support. These are the support staff that are there to process orders, keep the databases up to date and provide technical support. These are also sometimes referred to as the 'fulfilment centres'.

The ISP should agree in the hosting agreement to provide regular, detailed information on the number of 'hits', i.e. visits that are being made to the website. This is the information you need to establish who your fans are and who's likely to want to buy records, merchandise, concert tickets and so on.

The website becomes your one-stop shop window on the world. Its design and reliability will say a lot about you. A good website will enable you to target your likely market with greater precision.

If you are considering selling records off your website then you will need to have secure payments systems in place and some form of online 'store' or page dedicated to sales. There are companies like 7Digital who will either custom design an online store for you or will provide a 'skin' or a seamless link between your website and a page on the 7Digital website off which they will sell your records. If you use services like this then don't forget your contract for what they will supply and a hosting agreement specifying the reliability of the service. It is absolutely no good having an online shop if it is never 'open'.

DATA PROTECTION

If you're putting together data on people electronically, you have to register with the Information Commissioner (details are in Useful Addresses). You can't do what you want with the data you collect. You have to get permission to use it for a purpose other than that for which it was collected. You'll have seen this in magazine adverts or on websites for a particular product. If you send off for that product or for details about it you'll invariably be asked to register and to fill in a form with your details. The product owner may want to try to sell you other products that he has in his range, or to sell his list of customers and their product preferences to another company. He can't do this without your permission. There is often a box on the form that you have to tick if you don't want your information to be used in this way. This 'negative' consent technique is lawful, and is being adapted for online use, although the Information Commissioner is in favour of you having to tick a box if you **do** want more information rather than the other way around. You'll often find a box that has to be checked or unchecked to block your information being used in other ways. If you're compiling a database and you don't comply with the rules on passing on information you can be fined.[1]

If, however, these data protection hurdles are overcome, a database of consumer profiles and information is a valuable asset. If you own your domain name then, subject to anything to the contrary in the hosting agreement, you'll own the data collected in relation to that website.

MARKETING

One of the big challenges of marketing online is to make sure that fans come to a particular website and, once they have found it, come back to it over and over again. Phrases are bandied about as to how you get more 'eyeballs' (visitors) and whether the website is 'sticky'. The design of the website is, of course, crucial. It should be eye-catching and user-friendly. The text used in it should be designed so that it features prominently in the first twenty websites that come up when key phrases are used to

---

1   The Data Protection legislation extends to information held in hard-copy form as well as electronically. The Data Protection Act 1998, which came into force on 1 March 2000, also implemented the Database Directive.

search for information using one of the search engines like Google, Yahoo or MSN. This is an art form in itself and specialist web designers should be used.

The website should be regularly updated. The ISP host should be able to provide regular access to a webmaster who can help to put the latest news online.

The website should be easy to view. The key information should be available without having to go through several 'click through' layers. It should all be on the home page – the first page a visitor to the website sees.

The website should be different – it should have something that will raise it above the general 'noise' online. It's all very well if you're David Bowie or Prince making your records available online. Just by saying you're doing it, your name (or brand) is well known enough to guarantee you press interest. If you're Joe Bloggs trying to get noticed, you have to be more innovative.

RISING ABOVE THE NOISE

One of the biggest challenges in the online world is how you make potential fans and purchasers of your music know that you exist. Of course, to some extent this is just an extension of traditional marketing which you should also not ignore. Getting an A, B or even C listing on Radio 1 or 2 is still essential for an artist looking for a commercial hit through single sales driving album sales. Adverts, press interviews, personal appearances are all still relevant, but it is now also necessary to consider your online fans and target them as part of your campaign. We looked at your website above and that is an essential element of your online presence, but you must also now think about your pages on the social networking sites like MySpace, Facebook and Bebo. Just like you have to concern yourself about who owns your domain names you also have to consider who owns the name you are registered under on these networking websites. These web pages have to be regularly updated. Someone has to monitor the sites; accept 'friends' where appropriate; update the music available; decide if you are going to make tracks available for download or just streaming and keep your blog and gig list up to date. Will that be the artist or someone else? If it is to be someone at the record company make sure they have the necessary 'copy' to do their job, otherwise they will be tempted to make things up or might present you in an inappropriate way.

When MySpace first started it was a secret known only to a few and it was exciting to customise your own website and share it with friends. Now anyone who is anyone has a MySpace page. It remains the site of choice for those looking for music but almost everyone on there is an unsigned artist or has just released his or her latest single or album. You have to think about how you raise yourself above the noise.

There has of course been a spate of firsts: the first artist to make number one without a record deal; the first download only number one single or album. Then there were new stories such as the artist who sold a limited edition of his album at £100 a go. He didn't sell that many but he got publicity he might not otherwise get. The band The Crimea gave away download copies of their second album *Secrets of the Witching Hour*. They told the *Guardian* that they had done this in the hope that it would help build their fan base and therefore increase their income from live work, merchandising sales and music publishing royalties.

There has also been some good lateral thinking. The classical cross-over artist Katherine Jenkins' new studio album *Rejoice* was promoted by short videos shown in over

1,000 UK doctors' surgeries three times per hour, aimed at the older consumer who is a captive audience whilst waiting their turn for their flu jab or whatever. To cover all bases, the album was also advertised online and was backed by an online single release and some high-profile TV performances.

Believe it or not, wherever there is a new service very soon afterwards you will find people setting up in business to help you make the most of that new service. There are now specialist marketing people who employ what are called viral marketing techniques – a bit like an old-fashioned whispering campaign where individuals are employed to 'hit' certain websites, to tell their mates about tracks they've heard or videos they've watched on YouTube, to spread the word about 'secret' gigs through SMS text messages. These people can be employed under a contract just like any other marketing person either on a flat fee (with or without a retainer) or by results.

There is also a growing number of services dedicated to filtering material to get you what you have said you want. This has been around for some time for online newspapers where you specify what areas of news are of interest to you. That is now being extended to music services. Similarly the social networking sites themselves realise that they are in danger of collapsing if they do not help users find what they are looking for or what they might like. Hence the launch by MySpace's owners of the online video interview service called Earwig.

What might be seen as a kind of master class in what can be done in marketing in the digital era is the campaign around the 2007 release of Radiohead's new album.

It was the first digital only release where purchasers set the price they would pay. This was an excellent move in raising the profile of the band and the forthcoming release. The story reached far beyond the music press to leading articles in the media and financial sections of the broadsheets. This was only for a limited period of time ending on 10 December 2007. *Music Week* reported on 7 November 2007 that the average price paid was £2.88. Thirty-eight per cent paid no more that the minimum handling fee of 45p but this is still a much better strike rate than the estimated 80% of illegal downloads. *Music Week* reported that the website attracted 1.2 million visitors in the first 29 days following release. In an interview with Thom Yorke of Radiohead on Radio 4 on 2 January 2008, he suggested that these figures were not correct but declined to give his own figures merely saying that the band was pleasantly surprised with the results of this campaign.

The online release was followed by a physical release through XL from 31 December 2007. The packaging for this release contains stickers to allow the purchaser to create his own artwork – which is an idea already used to good effect by Beck and which was designed by graphic designers Big Active. The band is very ecologically aware and therefore the packaging is all recyclable. This release was supported by an innovative television campaign which nevertheless is still the use of a traditional marketing medium.

Alongside the main physical release, a special limited-edition box set was made available containing the CD and vinyl versions of the album as well as extras and sold at £40 through the band's own merchandising operation. Another classic piece of brand marketing.

They supported the physical release with traditional methods such as live radio plays of single releases and plan a two-month tour to support the album beginning in May 2008.

Finally there was an international digital release through their publishers Warner Chappell which combined for the first time recorded music master and publishing rights in the same place.

THE FUTURE

It is always difficult to predict where the music industry is going but I will just suggest a few possibilities. Major record companies will survive, but their role will change to become a worldwide distribution and marketing resource with less emphasis on finding and developing talent

The Government in the UK and the legislators in the EU will pay lip service to the need to protect IP and counteract piracy, but their measures will be under resourced and superficial with the view being in truth that this is a problem a united music industry should solve as part of its commercial survival mechanism. The Government does not believe the industry needs subsidy or tax breaks, such as those offered to the film industry, and has not supported a request from the industry to extend the sound recording and performing copyright.

Music will become just another product to be traded on the Internet or included as part of a service. In an ever more crowded world with an over abundance of choice it will be more important than ever to be 'heard' above the noise. How you do that will result in initiatives that appear novel when first encountered – viral marketing peer sites such as MySpace, guerrilla gigs notified by SMS etc. – but are all just new forms of the age old concept of marketing: find a new angle and work it. The players will not necessarily be traditional music companies; they might be venture capitalists or communications companies.

Major record company A&R people will continue to have a role and part of that role will be the identification of music that can be commercialised. This does not mean that they will be involved necessarily in developing talent. Instead they will utilise a network of connections: producers, managers, studios and lawyers who will bring them projects that are already developed, where the hard work has been done in putting together something which works creatively. The A&R person will then acknowledge this project and assess if it can be made to sell in the kinds of numbers that make it worth a punt on signing up the artist.

The need for a quick return on advances means that the first album has to have been written and recorded, often to almost final mix stage. The idea of an artist being successful on his third album will not survive in the major company world. Longer term careers will come when the artist licences records he has paid for himself or does a much lower key record deal where the initial financial rewards are lower but there is a possibility of earning a living through hard work.

Publishers will to an extent step in to the development of artists, but for both major record and publishing companies advances will drop overall and they will be looking for a greater range of rights including live and merchandising rights.

The album will become less important, individual tracks will be what powers the industry commercially. Online people buy tracks they like which they have heard on the radio or through recommendations or social network sites. Internet links to other artists with similar music will lead to an increase in cross-selling like Amazon's and eBay's 'customer recommendations'. We will have to get used to having our music packaged with other services and with adverts

CONCLUSIONS

- Artists can use the Internet to partner up with investors from outside the music industry, or to distribute their own records.

- Piracy remains a major problem, but one way to make money from music will be to ally yourself to another service like that of a mobile phone company.

- Marketing will become increasingly important in raising your music above the noise.

- Artists should try to own their own domain name.

- If you commission someone to design your website, make sure they give you ownership of all the various elements of it and make good hosting and maintenance arrangements.

Chapter 8
Branding

INTRODUCTION

In this and the following chapter I'm going to look at the whole area of branding: first by looking at merchandising deals, at how you get a trade mark and at the benefits of building up a reputation in your name and how to protect it; and then, in the next chapter, by looking at sponsorship deals.

Branding is the way in which you use your name, logo and reputation to build up a particular image in the public mind. You may think that this isn't relevant for an artist just starting out in the business. It's true that new artists are going to be more concerned at getting that first record deal than in worrying about their 'brand'. However, you only have to look at many of the boy and girl bands, and at the image-making that surrounds TV artists such as Il Divo, All Angels, Girls Aloud, the revival of Take That or The Spice Girls and some of the more successful US artists like Beyonce, to be able to see that putting a bit of thought into branding even at its simplest level can pay big dividends. Not everyone can be or wants to be *The X Factor* winner, but all artists should think about getting some of the basics of branding right from the beginning. It can be as simple as getting a good, memorable name and registering it as a domain name. With those two small and cheap steps you've already started to establish a brand.

Branding is big business and the growth of online activities on the Internet has added to the commercial outlets for the brand. At its most straightforward it's the building up of an artist's name and reputation in order to help to sell more records and concert tickets. At its more sophisticated, a name, reputation and public image can help to sell other things, not necessarily ones that involve music. Artists like The Spice Girls used their names, likenesses and the 'girl power' image originally to sell everything from crisps to soft drinks and sweets and are reviving that with their 2007/08 reunion tour when once again they are being used to sell products and supermarkets in TV advertising. Also bear in mind many successful 'live' artists make as much money from sales of merchandise at the venues or online off artist websites than they do from the ticket sales.

This idea of branding isn't anything new. All successful companies have invested a lot of money in the company name and logo and in establishing name recognition for their products. Think of Heinz, Sainsbury's, Coca-Cola or McDonald's. Companies such as Virgin turned branding into an art form. Sir Richard Branson realised the value in the Virgin name, in the fact that the consumer immediately recognises it and the familiar red and white colours. By putting that recognition together with a reputation for being slightly anti-establishment, he got consumers to buy into almost everything that the name was linked with. A healthy dose of self-publicity from Sir Richard himself kept the name and the brand in the public eye.

With nine out of ten new artists failing to make a significant mark on the record-buying public, the strike rate of the record business is appalling. As we saw in Chapter 6 it is increasingly the case that the record companies rely on excellent marketing to achieve one or more big hits, and some more moderate successes to keep them going. Getting the marketing campaign right is therefore crucial if you're to have a chance.

In the last seven or eight years there has been an explosion in the number of acts that seek fame and fortune not through the traditional route of hard slog on the gig circuit but on a fast track through appearances on reality television shows. These are, if you like, the twenty-first century equivalent of the talent show. This started with *Popstars*, which spawned Hear'Say. The runners-up on that programme were Liberty, who, as a result of an unsuccessful court case, had to change their name to Liberty X but nevertheless went on to international success. Then there was the *Pop Idol* phenomenon, where telephone voting by members of the public spawned a lucrative new source of revenue for the TV broadcaster and maker of the programmes. The final of the first *Pop Idol* contest had an audience of about 8 million voting for Will Young and Gareth Gates. Both achieved No. 1 chart success but only Will Young continues to feature largely both as a recording artist but also as a live performer and a stalwart of events such as the Queen's Jubilee concert at Buckingham Palace and the VE 60th celebration concert in Trafalgar Square.

Pop Idol was followed by *Fame Academy*, which was a cross between the reality TV programme *Big Brother* and a *Pop Idol*-type talent contest which did not live long before the phenomenon which was Simon Cowell and *X Factor* hit our screens, initially as a traditional competition for late teen/early twenties artists but then cleverly widened to appeal to a much wider audience through having categories for older wannabes. In most cases the contestants, or at least the finalists, are required as a condition of their participation to sign up to recording contracts and often also to sponsorship and merchandising contracts. The TV production company takes a piece of all this income. In some cases the TV company is in business with a manager who has an option to manage some or all of the successful artists. The artist is offered these contracts at a time when they have relatively little bargaining power and, although there can be some tinkering around the edges, the basic deal is usually already set and non-negotiable. Of course, once the artist is successful renegotiation becomes a possibility but not a guarantee.

This type of programme also took off in the US with the *American Idol* series being a huge success and making a TV celebrity out of judges such as Simon Cowell.

There are few signs that the British public has lost its appetite for these shows even though record sales of winners have generally been much lower than those achieved by Will Young's first single, and apart from him it is difficult to think of any UK winners or finalists who have gone on to sustain a pop career beyond the first single or in some cases album. The albums are often rush released to capitalise on the winner's fame before the fickle public moves on. These albums rarely do much more than present cover recordings of other people's songs and it is difficult for the artist to really show what he is capable of or to build a longer term career. One UK artist who may buck the trend on this is Leona Lewis who for various reasons waited quite a long time before her album was released after she won *X Factor* in 2006. It went to the top of the download and physical album and singles sales charts and managed to stay the course running up the second highest weekly sales figures of 2007 behind Arctic Monkeys.

One of the main drawbacks for me to these shows is that they create an expectation amongst many people that it's easy to get a break, get on television, get a million pound record deal and be set for life. The expectation is rarely met in reality and yet even the evidence of all the one hit wonder winners or finalists who disappear without trace does not dampen this belief. Many people now fail to realise that there is a huge amount of work, effort and time that goes into making a true career in this business. KT Tunstall worked for about six years around the clubs before she got her big break on *Later With Jools Holland* as a last minute stand-in. Many so-called overnight successes have in fact laboured away for years honing their craft until they are finally spotted. Reality television shows lead many young people to believe that they are somehow entitled to their fifteen minutes of fame, that everyone has a record in them and that it's really rather easy. Why else is almost everyone on MySpace plugging their own records? There isn't that much quality around – most is rubbish – and there is a danger that true talent will get lost in the noise. Hence the need is greater than ever for an angle that will bring you to the foreground.

BRANDING OF ARTISTS

Many artists are now recognising the value in the name, the 'brand', and are actively trying to put themselves into a position where they can make some money out of that brand. They may not have followed exactly in the footsteps of The Spice Girls, but do pick and choose the products they wish to be involved with, for example, clothing shops or ranges.

To a greater or lesser extent, a successful artist is always going to be a brand, in the sense of being a name that people recognise. The more successful the artist is, the more likely it is that the name, likeness and image will be recognised by members of the public. If they like or admire that artist's reputation, they'll want to know more about him and will buy things that tell them more about him like books, magazines and records. They'll buy products that have his name or likeness on it such as calendars, posters, screensavers, T-shirts or other items of clothing. If an artist is associated with a computer game, new phone or fast car then those items become desirable and the manufacturers of those goods pay for the association with a 'cool' brand. Witness also the number of perfumes being endorsed by celebrities – there are his and hers Beckham perfumes, for example. Part of this branding process involves doing merchandising deals for these products. If you have taken steps as early as you could afford to protect your brand then you will have an easy means of stopping others from cashing in on your name without your approval.

Cross-media branding is becoming increasingly important. It has been shown that consumers are spending more time online, reading and researching as well as being entertained. No branding strategy should ignore online uses. At the very least the artist's official website should be dynamic and regularly updated. Some labels are using linkage of a well-known artist brand with a website hosted by the label to cement their relationship with the artist and share revenues from products bought on the website such as mobile ringtones or video clips.

It's usually a good idea to use the same name, tag-line/slogan – which could be the title of the new album or the name of the tour – and imagery and logo across all forms of marketing. This ensures a consistent message and enhances the brand. Make sure that all media carry your name and contact details. Check that any online links between sites work well and link to a website that carries a consistent message.

If you're considering linking up with other sites with a view to drawing traffic to your site and theirs, then you may agree to share revenue with that site. For example, if you link to a site which supplies mobile ringtones and customers come from that site to yours and buy your latest record, you might agree with the mobile ringtone supplier to pay them a percentage of the value of the sale as a kind of referral fee of 3–5% and vice versa.

If the name, likeness or logo is one that can be trademarked, you can apply to register a trade mark or marks. Not all names are registrable. If it's too common a name or it's descriptive of something, the Trade Mark Registry won't let you register it.

Even if you haven't got a trade mark registered, if someone tries to pass themselves off as you in order to cash in on your reputation and this results in loss or damage to you, you have the means to try and stop them. This is called an action for 'passing off'.

If a company wants to use your name to promote their product they will do a sponsorship deal. You lend them the use of your name and may agree to provide some other services, such as recording a single or performing in an advert or turning up at a trade show or event, and they give you money and sometimes goods or services such as airline tickets or cars in return (see Chapter 9).

If your fans are looking for information about you or where to buy your records they will look under your name. They aren't usually going to start looking under the record company name. In fact, many fans may not know or care what label your records come out on as long as they can find copies of them in their record shop or online which is partly why record companies are concerned to own, or at least control, artists' websites and domain names. A fan is going to search for the artist's name. If you wanted to find information on Tim Westwood on the Internet you would search under 'Westwood' rather than under his record company, Mercury/Def Jam. There are record company websites and they are getting better. At first they tended to be corporate affairs where the services and information provided was intended for other companies or businesses; now they're generally more of a magazine format where news on all the major artists on the label is brought together in one place. Some have links to specialised websites, many of which are owned and put together by the artist or his management team. These links open up many new possibilities for marketing an artist. Many now also require the artist to submit regular updates to a blog or diary of what the artist has been up to/is listening to/what films they like etc.

Is branding a good idea? There are some that thought the ubiquity of The Spice Girls was taking the idea too far. While I believe we can never underestimate the public's interest in the inside story and behind-the-scenes glimpses of artists, you do have to be careful to avoid overkill. To some artists the whole idea is anathema. Most artists know that they have to work on building up a name and a reputation in order to sell their records. Some, though, think that they're somehow selling out if they put their name to other products – selling their soul as it were. It's obviously a personal thing.

Some artists, particularly those boy or girl bands with a relatively short shelf life before a new favourite comes along, do embrace branding in order to make as much money as they can as quickly as they can. Others are content to limit their branding activities to tour merchandise or sponsorship deals to help support a tour that would otherwise make a loss. It all comes back to the game plan (see Chapter 2).

I've also worked with artists who take the sponsor's or merchandiser's money and put it into charitable funds rather than spending it on themselves. Some make a point of telling the public they have done this, others keep it quiet.

Is it a sell out? I don't think it is. If it's not right for you, don't do it. However, before you come over all credible and refuse to entertain any form of branding, just remember that you're already doing it to some extent when you use your name to promote sales of your records or tickets to your gigs.

There are many artists and bands whose image doesn't easily lend itself to selling loads of posters, T-shirts and so on or whose image is not going to be user friendly for family-focused adverts – I'm thinking here of some of the Death Metal bands. If that is you then fine, don't waste time or money on it. You also don't have to have your name associated with every product that comes along. Indeed, it's probably not wise to do so, as the public will quickly tire of you. The products you choose to associate with should be selected with the overall game plan in mind.

If you do decide to do merchandising deals for your name, logo or likeness, you also need to decide how far you're prepared to go in protecting that merchandise from the pirates who will inevitably come along and try to steal your market, often with inferior products. Even if *you* don't do merchandising deals, you may find that the pirates do. I know of artists that have decided, for example, not to do a merchandising deal for calendars, only to find that unofficial versions appear in the shops anyway. As an interesting side note on this there is at least one enterprising charity which teams up with artists to use illegal pirate merchandise that has been seized at the artist's concerts to supply to disadvantaged children in Africa. It doesn't cost the artist anything and may do a little bit of good along the way.

MERCHANDISING DEALS

In its simplest form a band is involved in merchandising when they sell tickets to their gigs. The band name attracts the fans that have bought the records and now want to see them perform live. The ticket to the gig is bought on the back of the band name. If the band's core business is performing live then the band name is being used to sell records or other goods like T-shirts and posters. At this time it is live concerts which are making the money, not sales of records – see the chapter on touring. If the concert is well attended then the artist may also sell plenty of merchandise. Even the most credible of artists usually has a T-shirt or poster available for sale at the gigs. If they don't offer something it is likely some of the fans will get them from the pirates outside.

In the entertainment business, merchandising has been big business for years. People can buy the T-shirt, the football strip, the video game and the duvet cover bearing the name and image of their favourite cartoon character, football team or pop group. Disney and Manchester United Football Club are good examples. They know that there's a lot of money to be made from maximising the use of the name and likeness.

HOW DO YOU GO ABOUT GETTING A TRADE MARK?
Before you can begin to use your name to sell merchandise outside your core business of selling records, it's essential that you have a name or logo that's easily marketable and that you have or are starting to get a reputation that people can relate to. If your game plan is to do a fair amount of merchandising, you should think of a distinctive name and logo from the beginning. We all know how difficult it is to find a name that no one else has thought of and we saw in Chapter 1 how to check this out. The same thought must go into making your logo as distinctive as possible.

If you're going to have any chance of holding off the pirates, you need to protect your rights in your name and logo as far as possible. If you want to prevent others jumping on the bandwagon and manufacturing unauthorised merchandise to satisfy market demand, you'll need to have your own house in order.

If you are going to go for trade mark protection you should do so early once your career has started to take off as if you wait too long then it may be too late. It's important to get trade mark protection as early as possible. Elvis Presley's estate was not able to protect the use of the Elvis name for merchandising as a registered trade mark in the UK because it waited until ten years after his death.[1]

The Elvis Presley Case

In 1989, Elvis Presley Enterprises Inc, the successors to the Estate of Elvis Presley, filed UK trade mark applications for 'Elvis', 'Elvis Presley' and the signature 'Elvis A Presley'.

The UK trade mark applications were accepted by the Trade Marks Registry but were then opposed by Sid Shaw, a trader who'd been marketing Elvis memorabilia in the UK since the late 1970s under the name 'Elvisly Yours'. He opposed the registration of the marks by the Elvis Estate on the grounds, among others, that they conflicted with Sid Shaw's own prior trade mark registrations for Elvisly Yours. The Registry upheld the Estate's applications; Mr Shaw appealed to the High Court, which allowed the appeal. In a judgement which was quite critical of character and personality merchandising in general, the court decided that the public didn't care whether Elvis Presley memorabilia was approved by the Estate of Elvis Presley or not. The Estate took the case to the Court of Appeal.

The Court of Appeal refused the Estate's appeal and refused registration of all three trade marks. The court concluded that the trade marks were not in themselves distinctive and, as there was no evidence produced by the Estate of any use of the marks in the UK which might have indicated that the marks had become distinctive of the Estate of Elvis Presley in the minds of the public, there was therefore no reason at all why the marks should be registered.

The Wet Wet Wet Case

The courts have shown that they aren't prepared to interpret the Trade Marks Act too narrowly in favour of someone who has registered a trade mark in a band name. One example is a case involving the band Wet Wet Wet: the Bravado and Mainstream case.[2] Bravado had rights in a trade mark in the name Wet Wet Wet. Bravado asked for the Scottish law equivalent of an injunction to be ordered against Mainstream to prevent it from infringing that trade mark. Mainstream was publishing and marketing a book entitled *A Sweet Little Mystery – Wet Wet Wet – the Inside Story*. Mainstream argued that they were not using 'Wet Wet Wet' in a trade mark sense, but rather that it was used to describe the subject matter of the book. They also said that they weren't suggesting in any way that it was published by Bravado and, as such, somehow 'official'. Bravado argued that if they couldn't prevent this use then it would be meaningless having the trade mark, because they couldn't then stop it being used on other merchandise relating to the band.

The court decided that the words were being used in the course of trade but refused to grant the injunction, because it said that would be interpreting the meaning of the Trade Mark Act too narrowly. If it were so interpreted then any mention of the group name could be an infringement of the trade mark.

---

1 *Elvis Presley Trade Marks [1997] RPC 543.*
2 *Bravado Merchandising Services Ltd v. Mainstream Publishing (Edinburgh) Ltd [1996] F.S.R. 205.*

The Saxon Case

The area of trade marks and band names was also recently reviewed by the High Court in the case of *Byford* v. *Oliver and Dawson* (2003). This case involved the use of the name 'Saxon' by Biff Byford, the original singer with the British heavy metal band. Byford had been a band member since its formation in the late 1970s. Steven Dawson and Graham Oliver left in 1995. Biff Byford continued as a member of the band through numerous new line-ups – always called Saxon. Oliver and Graham continued to perform but used a variety of names, often including their own names with a reference to Saxon. Oliver and Dawson never challenged Byford's right to use the name Saxon but in 1999 they registered 'Saxon' as a trade mark and attempted to prevent Byford using the name.

Byford applied to the Trade Mark Registry to have the trade mark declared invalid on the basis that the registration had been obtained in bad faith (under the Trade Mark Act 1994) and that Dawson and Oliver were guilty of 'passing off' and misrepresenting themselves and their trade mark as 'Saxon' when Byford was the 'real' 'Saxon'. Byford failed to have the trade mark declared invalid with the Registrar deciding that with band members (all of whom may have some claim on a band's name) it was a 'first come first served' rule with regard to registration. Byford then applied to the High Court who overturned the Registrar's decision and declared the Oliver/Dawson registration invalid.

There was no formal agreement between the original band members governing use of the band name. Mr Justice Laddie held that, in the circumstances, the band name must be owned by all of the original band members as 'partners'. What this means is that if a band 'partnership' was split up NO member would own the name unless there was a formal agreement governing its use. However, the judge held that, in the circumstances, both Dawson and Oliver abandoned their rights to the goodwill and ownership of the 'Saxon' name which was now owned by Byford and the new members of the band.

This suggests that bands must have a written agreement governing ownership of the band name – because otherwise, if the band splits, no member of the group or members could use the band name without agreement of any one, or more, original members who may not wish to continue.

HOW TO APPLY FOR A TRADE MARK

You don't have to be already rich and famous to register a trade mark in your name or logo. In fact, as we saw in the Elvis case, there are dangers in waiting too long to apply for a trade mark. As soon as you can afford to, you should think about doing it. You can apply to protect your name or that of your brand worldwide, but this would be expensive. To start with, I usually advise that you apply to register the name in your home market, for example the UK for a British-based band, and then in other places where you have, or hope to gain, a market for your records and other merchandise, for example the US, Europe or Japan.

Each country has its own special rules for registration of a trade mark and, in many cases, an application to register a trade mark in one country can help you with applications in other parts of the world. For example, the rules at present allow you to backdate an application for a trade mark in the US to the date of your UK application provided you apply within six months of the UK application. So, if you apply for a UK trade mark registration on 1 July, you have until 31 December to apply in the US and still backdate it to 1 July. Just making the application itself can trigger trade mark protection. Even if it takes a year or more to get a registration, the trade mark, when and if it's granted, will be backdated to the date of the application. It also gives you priority over anyone else who applies after you to register a trade mark in the same or a similar name or logo. This is, however, a specialised area and you should take advice from a trade mark lawyer or a specialist trade mark agent. Your lawyer can put you in touch with a trade mark agent and a good music lawyer should have a working knowledge of trade mark law. While you may be happy to leave all this to your manager to sort out for you, do remember that the name should be registered in your name and not that of your manager or record company.[3]

Once you've decided the countries where you'd like to apply for a trade mark – finances permitting – you have to decide what types of product or particular goods you want to sell under the trade mark. In most countries, goods and services are split for trade mark registration purposes into classes and it's important to make sure that you cover all relevant classes of goods and as soon as possible. You can add other classes later, but then you run the risk of someone selling goods with your name in a class that you haven't protected. For example, you may have applied to register a trade mark for the class that covers records, but not the class that covers printed material such as posters. In theory, someone else could apply for a trade mark in that area, but then you get into the whole area of passing off. It's also not usually as cost-effective. You get a costs saving by applying for several classes at a time.[4]

A registered trade mark has distinct advantages over an unregistered mark. Actions to stop infringements of registered trade marks are generally quicker and more cost-effective than when you're relying on unregistered rights. A registered trade mark puts the world on notice of your rights. A registered trade mark is attractive to merchandising companies, as it gives them a monopoly over the goods for which the mark is registered and gives the merchandising company more of an incentive to do a deal with you.

PASSING OFF

If you haven't registered a trade mark then, in the UK, you can try and rely on the common law right of 'passing off' in order to protect your name and reputation. Before you can do this you'll have to prove there is goodwill in the name. This may not be the case if you're unknown and haven't yet got a reputation or any goodwill in the name. You have to show that someone else is trading on your reputation by passing themselves off as you, using your reputation to confuse the public that they are you or are authorised by you. As well as having this goodwill or reputation, you also have to show that this has actually caused confusion in the mind of the public resulting in damage or loss to you. For example, a band using the same name as yours, or one confusingly similar, might advertise tickets to a gig in the same town as your planned gigs. Fans might buy those tickets thinking they're coming to see you. This loses you ticket sales and might possibly damage your

3 Some details of the process involved are outlined on the government website www.webdb4.patent.gov.uk.
4 In the UK there are 42 classes for goods and services. Some common ones used in the music business are Class 9 for records, Class 16 for printed material such as programmes and posters and Class 25 for clothing.

reputation if the other band isn't as good as you. You have to have established a reputation in the name in the particular area in question. If your name is associated with records and someone trades under the same or a very similar name in the area of clothing, where you don't have any a reputation, there is less likely to be confusion in the mind of the public.

One famous passing-off case involved the pop group Abba.[5]

The Abba Case

A company called Annabas was selling a range of T-shirts, pillowcases, badges and other goods bearing the name and photographs of the band Abba. The band didn't own the copyright in any of the photographs and Annabas had obtained permission from the copyright owners of the photographs to use them. The band had to rely on a claim for passing off. Abba lost their application for an injunction preventing the sale because they were unable to show they had an existing trade in these goods or any immediate likelihood of one being started. The judge also went on to say that he thought that no one reading adverts for the goods or receiving those goods would reasonably imagine that the band had given their approval to the goods offered. He felt Annabas was only catering for a popular demand among teenagers for effigies of their idols. These words have been often repeated in later cases.

It's clear from this case that you have to establish that you already have a trade in the area in question that could be prejudiced, or that there was a reasonable likelihood of you starting such a trade. If you're seriously thinking about doing merchandising you should do so sooner rather than later, and should be setting yourself up ready for starting such a trade (for example, by commissioning designs, talking to merchandise companies or manufacturers, applying to register your trade mark) well in advance of when you want to start business to get around some of the pitfalls highlighted in the Abba case.

The P Diddy Case

In September 2005 a DJ called Richard Dearlove reached a settlement in his case against Sean Combs, aka Puff Daddy, aka P Diddy, to prevent him from changing his name to just 'Diddy'. Dearlove (a successful record producer) claimed he had been using the name Diddy in the UK for his DJ activities since 1992. His High Court action settled on the basis that Sean Combs agreed not to shorten his name, agreed to pay Dearlove £10,001 in lieu of damages and his legal costs estimated at £100,000. Mr Combs agreed not to advertise, offer or provide or cause/procure others to advertise, offer or provide any goods or services under or with reference to the word 'Diddy'. He also undertook to remove from the UK all materials or articles that were in his custody, power or control, the use of which would contravene this undertaking.

Unfortunately that was not the end of the matter. In 2007 the case came back before the court because Mr Dearlove claimed Sean Combs had breached that settlement agreement. This time he was not successful as the judge rejected his claim for an early judgement and ordered the matter to be tried at a full trial.

Material relating to Sean Combs' album *Press Play* had appeared on MySpace and YouTube and on a website www.badboyonline.com, which featured the name 'Diddy'. Six

---

5 *Lyngstad v. Annabas Productions Limited [1977] FSR 62*

tracks on the album contained references to Sean Combs as 'Diddy'. Dearlove claimed this was promotion under the Diddy name in the UK in contravention of the settlement. Whilst the judge made the important observation that placing a trade mark on the Internet from a location outside the UK could constitute use of that mark in the UK. He also recognised that the fact that the lyric to one of the songs on the album contained the word 'Diddy' could also be an advertisement for goods and services in the UK (which could have breached the settlement), particularly as many artists now use lyrics to associate themselves with various goods and services. This didn't mean that every reference to a product or service in a lyric was a potential breach of someone's trade mark; it would depend on how the lyric was used and whether it was intended to promote a product or service. The reason the judge thought this was a matter for full trial was because he could not tell without hearing all the evidence whether this material/use of lyrics was something that was within Sean Combs' control. If it was then he could well be found in breach of the settlement.

The importance of this case is to emphasise the global nature of the Internet and how care has to be used not to infringe a person's trade mark in another country by making something available on the Internet in one country where it wouldn't be a breach, but where it could be viewed in another country where it is a problem. The test would be if the consumer in the infringing country thought the advertisement or reference to the trade mark was directed at him. It also recognised that lyrics could be used to sell other products as well as help promote the artist and his new recordings and so when deciding if someone is advertising themselves under a particular name we need to think laterally and outside what might normally be thought of as promotion e.g. an ad or poster or celebrity interview.

There have been a run of cases where personalities have taken legal action over adverts that they believe play on their voice/singing style or image.

Tom Waits case

Tom has a very distinctive gravelly voice and he felt that a television advert for Opel cars featured a singing voice and style that was too close to his own to be a coincidence. He claimed that the car company had deliberately used a sound-alike on one of their TV ads to imply that he had participated in the marketing campaign. He sought an injunction to stop the ads and asked for an award of at least $300,000 in damages. Early in 2007 it was reported he had reached an out-of-court settlement, the details of which are not known but Mr Waits has indicated he will donate the money he receives to charity. This settlement came almost exactly a year after Waits won a similar court case in Spain where Volkswagen had used a sound-alike in a TV ad. He has also won a $2 million court judgement in the past against a US company, Frito-Lay, who had used an impersonator to mimic his voice. You'd think these advertisers would learn that he means business. He is famously critical of artists who take sponsorship money off big business and so is particularly galled when his voice is used in these very same types of ads.

David Bedford – 118118 Case

Late in 2003 Dave Bedford brought an action for an injunction against the company which was targeting the UK directory enquiries market with the number 118118 using two runners with 70s style hair and moustaches, singlet and shorts. David Bedford, a successful runner in the 1970s and now race director of the London Marathon claimed this was based on his image. The company behind the campaign initially rejected the claims but agreed to settle the matter by making slight changes to the look of the character.

OTHER REMEDIES

If you can't rely on either a trade mark or the remedy of passing off then you'll have to see if there's been any infringement of copyright, for example in a design, or possibly if there's been a false description of goods that might be unlawful under the Trade Descriptions Act 1968.

CONCLUSIONS ON PROTECTING YOUR NAME

Clearly, getting registered trade mark protection is the best way to go about protecting your brand, but when you're just getting started you probably won't have the money to spend on protecting the band name. A balance has to be struck. If you're ultimately successful and haven't applied for a trade mark you may end up kicking yourself if others cash in on your name and market unauthorised products. If you apply late you may be too late, as in the case of Elvis. On the other hand, it's often not at all certain whether an artist is ultimately going to be successful enough to justify the expense. A sensible thing to do would be to register a trade mark in just one or two classes, including records, of course, and perhaps only in one or two countries at first and then add more countries or classes as things develop.

It's also worth bearing in mind that a record company may advance you the money to make the trade mark applications. If you don't want your record company to own your trade mark, make sure the application for the registration is in your name not theirs, even if they offer to register it on your behalf.

As we've already seen in the area of e-commerce, there's also a great deal of mileage to be had from registering your domain name. Among other things, it gives you control of the doorway to official information on you and what you have to offer. Registration is cheap and quick, but please don't forget that it will need reviewing every couple of years. One record company, who shall remain nameless, arranged for all the reminders for domain-name registrations to go to one email address. The owner of that address left the company and no one seems to have thought to check the mailbox or redirect the mail. At least one domain name registration lapsed at a crucial marketing moment and had to be bought back on the open market.

UNAUTHORISED, UNOFFICIAL MERCHANDISE

The line of arguments that we saw being developed in the Abba case was expanded on in a case involving The Spice Girls.

The Spice Girls
The Spice Girls applied for an injunction against an Italian publisher, Panini, of an unauthorised sticker book and stickers entitled 'The Fab Five'. At this time The Spice Girls had no trade mark registrations and, in fact, it probably wouldn't have helped them if they had, because Panini had been careful not to use the name 'Spice Girls' anywhere in the book or on the stickers. So The Spice Girls were trying to use the law of passing off to

protect the band's image. They argued that even though the words 'Spice Girls' were not used, the book was clearly about them. The book didn't carry a sticker that it was unauthorised so, they argued, this amounted to a misrepresentation that The Spice Girls had authorised or endorsed the book.

The judge was not swayed by arguments that it made a difference whether the book was marked 'authorised' or 'official'. He refused to grant an injunction. As a consequence of this decision, if a company puts out an unauthorised calendar featuring pictures of an artist or band then, provided it is made clear that it's not a calendar that has the official blessing of the band and it doesn't reproduce copyright words/lyrics or photographs without permission, then that wouldn't be a passing off nor a breach of copyright rights. The judge decided that even the use of the words 'official' wouldn't have made this a case of passing off, because the product clearly indicated it was not approved by the artist. In this particular case, The Spice Girls had a trade mark application pending, but it hadn't been registered so they couldn't rely on arguing that there had been an infringement of their trade mark. This is a good example of why it's important to have a registered trade mark if you're going to try to put a stop to the sale of unauthorised goods.

You might be forgiven for thinking that all these cases involve millions of pounds and are only of interest to the megastars that can employ people to do all this for them. Well, it's true that it's usually only the big names that have the inclination or the money to bring cases to court, but protecting your name can start at a very low level – like preventing the pirate merchandisers from selling dodgy T-shirts or posters outside your gigs, or stopping another local band from cashing in on the hard work you've put into starting to make a name for yourself.

HOW DO YOU GO ABOUT GETTING A MERCHANDISE DEAL?

You may start off by producing a small range of T-shirts that you sell at your gigs. You can get these printed up locally, put up a temporary stall in the foyer of the venue and sell them from there. You may also sell some off your website. If it's clear that you can sell enough to make money then you might approach a merchandising company about doing it for you on a larger scale. The merchandising company could be a big multinational company or a small independent company. You can get names of merchandising companies out of directories such as *Music Week*. You can also get recommendations from your mates in other bands, your lawyer, accountant or manager.

If you're starting to sell out the larger venues and are a regular on the gig circuit, merchandising companies may approach you or your booking agent. If they do, you could try them out with your concert or tour merchandise before deciding if they're right to do your retail or mail-order merchandising as well.

THE MERCHANDISING DEAL

If you have a registered trade mark, this will increase your appeal to a merchandiser. However, merchandise companies will still be interested in you even if you haven't got a registered trade mark if you're sufficiently well known for them to run the commercial risk of producing merchandise for sale. The merchandise company will take a view as to whether yours is the sort of image that will sell particular types of merchandise. They will know if your image will sell T-shirts or posters at gigs and if it will also sell either the same merchandise or a different range of products through retail stores.

Even quite small acts can often shift reasonable numbers of T-shirts to fans at the gigs or through mail order off their website. If there's a steady turnover, a merchandiser will be interested in doing a deal. Obviously, if you only sell two T-shirts a month, and then only to your close family, then getting a merchandise deal is going to be a non-starter. In that case you should be looking to do it yourself. Why would you want to do this? Well, obviously, the more that you keep to yourself the more of the profit you get to keep. There is, however, an awful lot of work involved in mailing out the merchandise to fulfil orders and in ensuring that you've enough products to sell at your gigs.

If things start to go only moderately well you'll probably need to employ someone to look after that side of things for you. You'll also need to do a deal with a company to make the clothing or other products for you to your design. You'll have to be responsible for selling it either by mail order online, through selected retail outlets such as local record stores, and at your gigs. You'll need to be able to keep a check on the quality of the product being produced, to be something of a salesman, to be able to market the goods and to distribute them. You'll need to make sure that the orders are fulfilled promptly and that the accounts are properly kept. This is quite a tall order, even if you do get to keep the lion's share of the profits. No wonder, then, that many bands find a specialist merchandising company to do this for them.

WHAT IS IN A TYPICAL MERCHANDISING DEAL?

Obviously, each merchandise deal will be different and, once again, it's important for you to use a lawyer who is used to doing these sorts of deals. There are, however, some points that are an issue in every merchandising deal.

Territory
You can do a one-stop, worldwide deal with one company for all your merchandise needs, or a series of deals with different companies for different types of goods. For example, you could do a deal with one company for merchandise to sell at your gigs like T-shirts, sweatshirts, caps and so on. This deal could be limited to the UK or Europe or if the company was big enough in all the major markets you could do a worldwide deal. If they weren't then you could then do another deal for the US, probably with a company who specialises in the US marketplace. If we are talking about merchandise in the wider sense of marketing your name or likeness on sweet packages, computer games or crisp packets, then you'll do your deal with the company that manufactures those goods. That deal could again be a worldwide one or one for specific countries. If you're going to do a worldwide or multi-territory deal, make sure that your merchandise company has the resources to look after your interests properly in each country. Find out if they sub-contract the work and, if so, who to. Is the sub-contractor reliable?

Term
If you're doing a series of concerts, you could do a merchandise deal that was just linked to those dates. If you were doing a world tour with various legs, it's likely you would do a

deal with one merchandise company that covered the whole tour. However, you could do a deal with one company to cover the period of the UK or European legs, and with another company or companies in other parts of the world. This isn't as common, as it's difficult to administer and police. The term of the contract would be the duration of the tour or of that particular leg of it.

If you're doing merchandise deals to sell goods in shops or by mail order then the term is more likely to be for a fixed period of time, probably a minimum of one year and up to three years or more.

The more money the merchandising company is investing in manufacturing costs and/or up-front advances, the longer the term they're likely to want in return. The longer the term, the better their chances will be of recouping their investment.

Some merchandising deals are linked to recoupment of all or a proportion of the advance. The term of the deal runs until that happens. This can be dangerous if sales don't live up to expectations or if the merchandising company isn't as good as you would like them to be. The best thing to do with these types of deals is to have the right to get out of the deal after, say, a year by paying back the amount of money that is unrecouped. This will give you the flexibility to get out of a deal that isn't working and into one that might.

Rights granted

The deal will usually be a licence of rights in your name and likeness for a particular period, not an assignment of rights. The rights granted will be the right to manufacture, reproduce and sell certain products featuring your name and/or logo. If you have a registered trade mark you'll be required to grant a trade mark licence to the merchandising company to use the trade mark on specific goods.

The rights granted could be for particular products or for all types of merchandise. These days the trend is towards limiting the granting of rights to particular products. You could grant the right to use your name or likeness or your registered logo on T-shirts and keep back rights to all other products such as calendars, posters, caps and so on.

You might grant the right to use your band name and/or logo for some particular types of a particular product and keep rights back to other forms of the same product. For example, you could grant a licence for ordinary toys and keep back the rights to use your name on musical toys. You could then do merchandising deals for all or any of those types of toys with one or more other companies. If your music is going to be used in the musical toys then you or your publisher will license the right to include the music for either a one-off 'buy-out' fee or for a fee and an ongoing royalty (see Chapter 4).

Record companies may do a variation on a merchandising deal with an artist to use his voice/catchphrase for downloads of sounds for mobiles. This may be included in the record deal but if that deal is an older type then it may not be covered and there may need to be a separate deal done. Now that the first flush of enthusiasm for quirky mobile ozone downloads has died down there isn't the clamour there was a few years back. Now it is much more likely in an exclusive licence or recording deal that the record company will require that the artist record specific clips for such uses and will be paid usually a percentage of what the record company earns from selling those clips on to the middleman aggregator, who offers the downloads to the public via a communications company. Because there are several parties who take a 'cut' before the record company, let alone the artist, sees a share these deals are not the lucrative earner everyone hoped they were going to be but they do provide an additional revenue source for the record companies. If instead of your voice an extract from one of your songs is used then the aggregator should also clear the right to use the music and lyrics from the publisher, creating an additional income stream for the publisher too. This is not always done and it is not always easy to track what income has been earned from these new revenue sources. There are, however, companies such as RoyaltyShare who are developing software to track usage down to the last penny so in time it is to be hoped that proper accounting will take place across this new sector.

Quality control

Once you've decided what goods are going to feature your name, likeness or logo, you have to make sure that the goods are of the highest possible quality. If you don't keep a tight hold on quality control, you could do potentially serious and possibly irreversible damage to the reputation of your brand. If a T-shirt featuring your name and logo falls apart, or the colours run on the first wash, then that is going to reflect very badly on you. The fan that bought the T-shirt won't care that it was another company that made it – they'll blame you and give you a reputation for selling shoddy goods.

The contract will usually say that the merchandising company must submit samples of designs for you to approve. If they're making the goods to a design you've given them then they should make up samples to that design. Only once you're satisfied with the quality of the sample should you authorise full production to go ahead. Even then, you should have the right to inspect the product at short notice and to insist upon improvements if the quality has dropped to an unacceptable level. The contract should contain a guarantee that the product will be of at least the same quality as the sample you've approved.

It's also important that the merchandising company makes sure that what it manufactures complies with all local laws. Toys and other children's products in particular have very stringent safety standards. You may want to insist that the manufacturer takes out product liability insurance. Be careful also if the company sub-contracts any of the processes. The sub-contractor must also stick to rigid quality controls and ensure product safety, carrying insurance against any damage caused by the product.

If the design is one created for you, either by the merchandising company or a third party, make sure they assign the rights in that design to you. If you don't, you may find that the designer comes knocking on your door for more money. You may want to use the same design as the artwork for the album sleeve. As we saw in Chapter 6 you should have made sure under your record deal that you can acquire the merchandising rights in that artwork.

Methods of distribution

The rights you grant can not only be limited to certain types of products, but also to certain methods of distribution.

You might grant mail-order rights only or limit the rights to selling merchandise to retail shops or at your gigs. There are specialist companies who are good at doing tour merchandising but aren't as good at selling goods to retail shops, and vice versa. There are also specialist e-tailers who are expert at selling online. It is important that you find the right company for the right method of distribution.

Depending on the means of distribution the basis on which you're paid may also change varying from a straight royalty to a flat fee or a percentage of the net receipts. If in doubt, ask for a breakdown of how the end figure is arrived at. Ask for details of who is taking what cut off the top before you see your share. If it seems high or wrong challenge it or ask for further explanations. This is a developing area and at the moment there is no absolute right or wrong way to account – it's a business decision and can be challenged or negotiated.

Advances and Guaranteed Minimum payments

You may get an advance against what you're going to earn from sales of the goods. This advance is recoupable from those earnings but, as we've already seen with other types of music business deals, the advance isn't usually returnable if you don't sell enough to recoup the advance. One exception is if you're doing a merchandising deal for a live tour and you don't do some or all of the concerts. Then you can expect to be asked to repay some or all of the advance. Some tour agreements also say that advances are repayable in whole or in part if ticket sales at the concerts don't reach a particular level. For example, you may get a fixed sum, sometimes called the Guaranteed Minimum, that isn't repayable unless you cancel the whole tour. Then there are other payments that are made which are dependent either on you doing a particular number of big, stadium-type concerts or on you selling a minimum number of tickets over the whole concert tour. If you don't do those gigs or don't sell enough tickets then you don't get those further payments.

There's also another catch with tour merchandise agreements, which is the one that I touched on above. The contract may say that the term continues until you've earned enough from sales of the tour merchandise to recoup either the whole advance or the Guaranteed Minimum. If you aren't certain that you'll be able to do this within a reasonable time, then you'll want to have the option to get out of this by paying back the unrecouped amount. If you don't have this option and your tour isn't a big success then you could be stuck with the same tour merchandising company for the next tour, without the prospect of any more advances. If you can get out of it, you can try to find someone else to do a deal for the tour merchandise for the next year's tour, and may even get them to pay you another advance.

The advances could be payable in full when you sign the deal, or in a number of instalments linked to concert appearances or sales of product with, say, 25–33% of the total being payable on signature.

Royalties and licence fees

You'll usually receive a percentage of the sale price of the goods as a royalty, which will go first to recoup any advances you've already had. This percentage will either be calculated on the gross income or, more usually, on the net income after certain expenses are deducted. Deductions can include VAT or similar sale taxes, the cost of manufacture and printing of the goods, and all or some costs of their distribution and sale. With online sales there may also be a charge for things like secure credit card systems.

When you're doing a tour merchandising deal, commissions or fees are often payable to the owners of the concert venues for the right to sell merchandise on their premises. It's usual for the merchandise company to deduct this payment from the gross income. Some companies will also try to deduct other expenses, including travel and accommodation costs for their salesmen and other unspecified expenses. I'm not convinced that these should be deducted and it's a good rule with all these deductions to look at them very carefully, and to ask for a justification for the deduction if necessary.

Obviously, if you're being paid a percentage of the gross income it will be a much smaller percentage than if it were a percentage of the net. A fee of 20–30% of gross would be equal to about 60–70% of the net income, depending on what is deducted from the gross. For example, if you had a gross income from sales of T-shirts featuring your name of £10 per T-shirt, a 20% royalty would be £2.00. If you had a net income of £2.00, then a 60% royalty based on the net income would be £1.20.

Accounting

Accounts are usually delivered for retail or mail-order deals every three or six months. Obviously, from your point of view you'll want to be accounted to as quickly and as often as possible. You should have the right to go in and inspect the books of account regularly – at least once a year. You should also be able to go in and do a stock check from time to time.

Merchandising deals for tours are different. There is usually a tour accountant who will check the stock and the sales sheet on a daily basis. He will expect to be paid within a very short period of time, preferably within 24 hours of each gig or, at the very latest, within seven days.

Trade mark and copyright notices

If you have a trade mark registered, the contract should confirm that they will include a trade mark notice on each product and a copyright notice for each design.

Termination rights

As with all contracts, the merchandising contract should say in what circumstances the deal can be brought to an end. These should include a persistent failure of quality standards, failure to put the product into the marketplace by the agreed date, and other material breaches of contract, for example, if they don't account to you when they should. If the company goes bust or just stops acting as a merchandise company, you should also have the right to end the deal.

Enforcement

This could be the subject of a chapter in its own right. The contract should say who's responsible for tracking infringements of your rights. There's usually a requirement that the merchandising company reports to you any infringements of your trade mark or copyright that they come across on each product. It's as much in their interest as yours to keep pirate activities to a minimum.

There are civil and criminal remedies to stopping infringements. You can also enlist the help of Trading Standards Authorities and HM Revenue and Customs. Often, these authorities are prepared to seize unauthorised products bearing a name that is a registered trade mark. Even without a registered trade mark, Trading Standards Authorities are sometimes prepared to rely on the Trade Descriptions Act in order to make seizures and bring prosecutions. In my own experience, the Trading Standards

Authorities are an invaluable help in clearing the streets of counterfeit products. It's possible to provide HM Revenue & Customs with trade mark registration details to assist them in identifying and seizing unauthorised products entering the country at ports and airports.

New models

Merchandising (and indeed sponsorship income as covered by the next chapter) now often forms part of the new deals being offered by record labels: the so-called 360 models. These have been dealt with fully in the chapter on recording deals above, but just to recap, a record company or production company may only offer you a deal if they can get access to additional sources of income. These might be shares of publishing, shares of concert ticket revenue or often shares of merchandising or sponsorship income. For a new artist sponsorship income is likely to be quite small but merchandising income may be significant if the artist has a growing loyal fan base and plans to tour regularly. The record company may only want to be paid a share of the income from these other sources of money. If they do then the percentage they want will vary from somewhere around 10% to as much as 50% – this is all negotiable. The percentage could be of the gross income but this would be dangerous for an artist if after deducting the record company's share and the cost of making and distributing the merchandise there is little or no profit left. Much better would be to base the percentage on the net receipts or profit after these expenses have been repaid. Some companies are insisting that this income is shared for the life of the deal but you may want to try limiting it just until the advances have been recouped or to say the end of the first contract period. In some cases the record company will actually want to take the merchandising rights exclusively and exploit them themselves. This is to be avoided unless there is a significant financial incentive to do this. The record company then controls all the income from this source and the artist will not receive any money until all his advances – including the record advances – have been recouped. Issues like creative controls also have to be dealt with. In some cases these other income sources continue on after the end of the term of the record deal as a reducing percentage over a period of time. Again these deals can work if the financial upside is there, but take care that you do not tie yourself for too long and for too high a percentage or you will come to really resent this years down the line.

CONCLUSIONS

- Merchandising is the use of your name and reputation to sell goods.

- Not everyone will want to do lots of merchandise deals and not everyone will be in a position to. You have to build up a name and reputation.

- Consider registering a trade mark in your name and logo.

- If you haven't got a registered trade mark but you do have a reputation, you may be able to stop people trading on your name through the laws against passing off.

- Make sure you own the copyright in any designs you commission.

- Make sure you have the right to use the design featured in your album artwork.

- Think about limiting the territory and the rights you grant.

Chapter 9
Sponsorship

INTRODUCTION

We saw in the previous chapter how an artist protects his name by registering trade marks or through taking advantage of the laws of passing off and of copyright.

Having protected the name, your brand, you can choose how far to exploit that brand. You can decide to only use it to sell your records and videos and to promote your live performances. Many artists choose to do just that and don't really go outside their core area of activity at all. This is fine. No one is saying that you have to, but you may need to look at some kind of merchandising deal to bolster your income from live work. Many tours would make a loss if they weren't underwritten by merchandising deals and often by sponsorship.

Sponsorship is a kind of extension to a merchandising deal. The sponsor uses the association between you and their product to increase awareness of the product and to encourage more people to buy it. The sponsor provides sponsorship money in return for the right to trade on your importance to a particular sector of the market. For example, a sponsor of a soft drink might look for a sponsorship deal with a pop artist who would appeal to teenagers. An alcoholic drinks manufacturer, on the other hand, would want to sponsor an artist that had an appeal to over-eighteens and, in particular, those in their early twenties.

Pepsi has been a keen sponsor of artists in recent years. The Spice Girls released a track as a Pepsi single and featured that track in a Pepsi ad on television. Robbie Williams has done sponsorship deals with Lloyds Bank, for his Royal Albert Hall concert, and several deals with Smart cars, including the premiere of his film, where a fleet of Smart cars was available to ferry celebrities to the premiere. The Corrs have also been associated with Lloyds Bank in television ads and more recently Destiny's Child with McDonald's. McDonald's also launched Big Mac Meal Tracks where the customer who purchases a Big Mac gets an access code worth one free download at the Connect music store. There is also the whole area where a company features a previously unreleased track which is then released as a single. Car companies are favourites for this, with Ministry of Sound releasing the track 'Jacques Your Body' which featured in the animated robotic Peugeot car advert. Gut Records released the Diet Coke soundtrack as a single in 2007 and Positiva is releasing a vocal version of the Lloyds Bank ad featuring Sarah Cracknell in early 2008. Pepsi Max has featured music written exclusively by The Black Eyed Peas.

Sponsorship deals are often done for concert tours. You'll often see the name of a sponsor on the ticket. For example, 'Band X sponsored by Carling'. When you arrive at the gig, you'll find that there are banners and posters from the sponsors. There may be more than one sponsor. You could have a main sponsor (the title sponsor) for the tour, another for the programme and the tickets, another for the soft drinks on sale at the venue and yet another for the alcoholic drinks. Venues often restrict the extent to which they will allow outside sponsors to plaster their brands all over the venue (see Chapter 10).

Interestingly, at a time when the live scene seems to be so vibrant, Carling has recently confirmed the ending of its nine-year sponsorship of the Reading and Leeds Rock Festivals as the 'Carling Weekend'. Carling will also no longer be the official lager at the festivals. The managing director of the company with rights to the two festivals, Festival Republic, said that this was by mutual agreement with both parties feeling it was time to pursue new opportunities. So we may see a new sponsor on board or the southern half of the event may well revert to its original name of the Reading Festival.

Clothing companies often loan clothes for photo-shoots or live appearances in return for a suitably prominent name-check. If you're lucky, you sometimes get to keep the clothes. Diesel and other similar 'youth' brands have looked at sponsorship in the past, and up-and-coming new designers or those trying to break in to the UK market may be keen to do a deal. These kinds of deal are closer to what I would call endorsements than pure sponsorship. You let it be known that you support or endorse a particular product. For example, you might mention in an interview that you do all your shopping at a particular shop in fashionable Notting Hill. Suddenly all the wannabes are queuing at the door of that shop, partly in the off-chance that you'll be in there, but also to try to copy your look. Retailers or designers may pay in goods or hard cash for these kinds of endorsements.

HOW DO YOU FIND A SPONSOR?

There are a number of ways to get a sponsor. It's possible for a band to approach a designer or company to ask for sponsorship. The shoe company who makes Doc Marten boots has, on at least one occasion that I know of, sponsored an artist following a direct approach from the manager. Companies want to promote themselves as supporting and encouraging youth culture of which, of course, music plays a huge part. Such sponsorships by clothing companies are not common.

SPONSORSHIP AGENTS
Apart from the direct approach, another means of getting a sponsorship deal is to approach a specialist agent who both represents one or two big companies looking for suitable projects to sponsor, or who will act for you and go to potential sponsors on your behalf. There are lists of these agencies in the *Music Week Directory* and magazines like *Audience*. There is also the tried and trusted word-of-mouth recommendation from friends or other contacts in the business. If you're sufficiently successful to have a brand that a sponsor might be interested in, they or their agents are likely to approach you or your manager direct. As with all these things, don't feel you have to grab the first thing that comes along. If you're desperate for some funding to underwrite a shortfall on a tour then by all means do a deal, but keep it short and see how things work out before you get in too deep.

WHAT DO THEY CHARGE?
If you employ an agent to find a sponsorship deal for you then they will usually take a percentage of the deal they do for you. This percentage can vary between 5% and 15% of the gross sponsorship income. For example, if the agent brokers a deal for a drinks company to sponsor your next UK tour and the drinks company is prepared to offer

£100,000 for the privilege, the agent would take between £5,000 and £15,000 of that as their fee. If the sponsorship is made up partly or wholly of goods rather than cash, the agent will expect to get their percentage in the cash equivalent of the value of those goods. So if the drinks company were to offer £80,000 in cash and £20,000 worth of free lager to give away to your fans, then your agent on a commission of 15% would still want their £15,000 in cash.

The money is usually paid to the agent at the same time as you're paid. If you're paid in two instalments, half at the beginning of the deal and the rest when you finish the tour, then your agent would get 50% of their fee upfront and 50% when you get the balance of the money.

The agent may want to be exclusively employed as your agent for a period of time. This is usually for a year but could be longer. During that time you wouldn't be able to use any other sponsorship agents, so you have to make sure that they are good enough first. The advantage you get from an exclusive arrangement is the incentive that the agent has to bring deals to you as opposed to anyone else. The disadvantage is that you can't go to anyone else if they don't get you particularly good deals. If you can get an agent on a non-exclusive basis, that will give you more flexibility.

If the agent gets you a deal for some tour sponsorship and that sponsor comes back to you to sponsor your next tour, then some agents insist that they should also get commission on that repeat work, even if they are no longer your exclusive agent by the time of the second tour. The logic is that they made the initial introduction and so should benefit from any follow-up. I can see this logic, but obviously other factors also play a part in you getting the follow-up offer for the next tour, such as the professional way you dealt with the first deal, the benefits that the sponsor saw that came from your efforts and your increased fame in the meantime. So while it might be acceptable to agree to pay the agent for a short while after the end of your relationship with them, I would try and draw the line at, say, six to twelve months. This is all subject to negotiation when you take them on.

The agent could be your only agent worldwide and be solely responsible for getting you sponsorship deals around the world. As many sponsors are multinational companies, this may not be such a bad thing, but if you think your agent doesn't have the necessary overseas connections you might just agree that they can act for you in the UK and decide to use other agents overseas.

If the agent is representing a company that comes to you with an offer of sponsorship, you wouldn't expect to have to pay him a fee for brokering the deal. In those circumstances he should be paid by the company concerned. If he also looks to you for payment you would be right to resist unless there were good reasons.

ETHICAL CONSIDERATIONS

No, don't worry, I'm not going to go all serious on you and talk about your moral values – well actually, I suppose I am a bit. What I want you to think about is whether you'll accept sponsorship from any company that offers it and the more the merrier, or are you going to select who sponsors you on moral or ethical grounds?

When you decide on your game plan to look for sponsorship deals, you have to think about what effect that will have on your brand and your reputation. There is a narrow line to be drawn between using sponsorship by selected companies to enhance the brand and of being accused by fans of 'selling out'. The products you choose to be associated with must complement the image you've established for yourself. For example, if you're aiming at the teenage market you may alienate them (or perhaps the parents who supply the pocket-money) by being associated with alcohol or tobacco. On the other hand, if you cultivate a bad-boy image you won't want to be associated with cuddly toys. The exception to this would be if your plan is to reposition yourself in the marketplace. For example, if you wanted to move out of the teen or pre-teen market, you might choose sponsors of adult products to show you're growing up. You should also consider the moral sensibilities of your fans. You could alienate a large proportion of them if you had manufacturers of GM foods or a fur company as your sponsor. There was a mixed reaction to the news that U2 were sponsoring a special customised black iPod. Some thought it was an astute 'cool' move whilst others thought it odd that a band which was so averse to sponsorship deals was doing one at this stage of their career.

Don't forget that the companies that you're being sponsored by will also expect things from you. They won't want you to do anything that will bring their brand into disrepute or show them up in a bad way. Bear this in mind when negotiating your sponsorship deal. You need to be careful that you keep an even balance between your and their expectations. If you feel at all uncomfortable about what you're being asked to do then that should give you a signal either to try and change it a little or to pull out of the deal.

Your public is a very fickle thing. It's very difficult to know whether they will accept what you're doing as par for the course and what they expect from you. If your fans think you're selling out then you and your press people are going to have quite a bit to do to redress the balance.

The other issues you need to think about are whether you want to be associated with companies that are involved either directly or indirectly in activities or causes that you disagree with. For example, if you're a committed vegetarian you may not want to be involved with a company that has a subsidiary that is in the business of raising battery hens. If you have a strong aversion to anything to do with cruelty to animals or animal testing, you won't want to do a sponsorship deal with a company that had a French sister company that ran laboratories that used animals to test their products. If these things matter to you then you need to have an ethical check made on the company to make sure that they aren't in any way involved with things that would be unacceptable to you. Remember that, although they are using their association with you to benefit their business, you're being associated with them too, and with the sort of things that they stand for.

SCOPE OF THE SPONSORSHIP DEAL

The sponsorship deal could be for a particular tour or for a series of tours. For example, it could be just for the UK or European leg of your tour or could be for the whole world tour. It could also just be for a particular project. A company could sponsor you for a particular event, for example, a one-off concert, or they could expect some personal endorsements of their product. They may want you to do personal appearances or to give private performances at their company sales conferences to rally the troops. They may want you to write and record a song especially for them that they may want to release as a promotion or as a proper commercial release. I'm sure you'll have seen special offers where you get a single or album by your favourite artist if you collect a given number of ring-pulls, packet tops or special coupons. If you have an exclusive record deal, you can't do these deals unless you first get the record company's agreement to waive their exclusivity. They may agree to this if they think that the publicity will help sell lots more records, or if the sponsoring company has access to markets in parts of the world that your record company can't break into without spending a lot of money. For example, some of the soft drinks companies have a huge market in parts of South East Asia or in South America. By being associated with them in those countries, you're getting a huge amount of exposure that should help to sell lots of your records. This exposure could be much more valuable than any amount of marketing money that your record company may be prepared to put into launching you in those areas. Obviously, it makes sense in these cases for there to be a considerable degree of co-operation between what your record company is planning, what you're doing in terms of live appearances and what the sponsor intends to do. If you can dovetail these plans then your chances of world-domination come a lot closer.

Whether it's a tour sponsorship or an individual event sponsorship, it's a reasonable rule of thumb that the more a sponsor expects from you the more you can expect to be paid.

EXCLUSIVITY

You could only have one sponsor at any given time or you could have a series of sponsors for different products. If you're only going to have one sponsor then, in return for that exclusivity, you should get a lot more money.

If you're going to look for a number of different sponsors for different products then take care that you don't narrow down your options too much. If you're going to have a drinks sponsor, then limit the extent of their sponsorship to alcoholic or non-alcoholic drinks, depending on what you're looking for from another sponsor. For example, if Pepsi or Coca-Cola was looking to sponsor you, you might limit their sponsorship to soft drinks. You couldn't have another soft drinks sponsor, but you could have a sponsor for alcoholic drinks. If you have a food sponsor, try and limit it to their particular product, for example biscuits or crisps or whatever. This would leave you with lots more food products to find sponsors for. Be careful what you agree to do in return for the sponsorship money or you could find yourself in trouble.

The Spice Girls v. *Aprila*

An example of this is a case brought by The Spice Girls against an Italian scooter company.[1] The Spice Girls were suing the company for payment of the balance of the monies they said they were due under a sponsorship deal that they'd done with the scooter manufacturer. The scooter manufacturer had produced a series of scooters, each in the colours that were associated with each member of The Spice Girls. For example, they'd produced a bright orange version as the Geri Spice Scooter, Geri Halliwell being otherwise known as Ginger Spice. Geri Halliwell had, however, left the group shortly after the deal was done. The

---

1 *The Spice Girls Limited v. Aprila World Service BV Chancery Division 24/2/2000.*

scooter company refused to pay and counter-claimed that The Spice Girls had misled them, because at the time they did the deal they knew that Geri Halliwell intended to leave the group. In February 2000 the court decided against The Spice Girls and found that they had misled the scooter company, who didn't have to pay them the balance of their sponsorship money. Furthermore, The Spice Girls were ordered to pay damages to the scooter company for the losses they'd suffered.

WHAT'S IN A TYPICAL SPONSORSHIP DEAL?

The Services

The first thing you have to establish is what they want you to do or what event they expect to be sponsoring. Remember to keep the scope of their sponsorship as narrow as you can, without them reducing the money on offer, to allow you the possibility of getting other sponsors.

If the sponsor expects you to do a series of things, for example, writing a new song, doing a live concert tour, making a television ad or a TV special, then make sure that you aren't over-committing yourself. By taking too much on you may not be able to do it all properly and professionally. If you agree to do too much, you'll end up either not doing it or doing it badly. This will reflect back on you and could do you more harm than good. If you fail to deliver the goods the sponsor could decide to sue you.

Exclusivity

Once you've agreed what they are going to sponsor and what the product is that will be associated with you, you have to decide if you're going to have one exclusive sponsor or whether you are going to give them exclusive rights for a particular product or type of product, and still have the option to take on other sponsors for other products.

Territory

Next you have to decide whether the deal is a worldwide one or if it's to be limited to particular countries. You could do a deal for just the US or the Far East, depending on the type of sponsorship. For example, one company that is 'big' in that area of the world but not so well known in other parts of the world could sponsor the Far Eastern section of your tour. You could then switch to another sponsor for the US or European leg.

Creative control

If the sponsor intends to feature your name and likeness in any way in the campaign, whether on packaging, adverts or otherwise, you'll want to have prior approval of those uses. You may want to insist on or ask for a special photo-shoot with a photographer of your choosing. You could then submit to them a number of examples of photos that you like and agree that they can have final choice.

If you're writing a special song then you ought to have some say in what it sounds like, even if the sponsor does give you a brief to work to. If you are recording a song for them that has been specifically commissioned, you'll want to know whether any particular lyric or theme is to be featured and whether you're comfortable with that. If you're being asked to record a new or special version of an existing song, or to allow a particular track to be used in the campaign, you'll need to know whether they intend to change the lyrics or music. If they do, you'll probably want some control over that and to have final approval. Bear in mind, also, that that approval should extend to any co-writers or composers of the original work, and that your publishers and record company may have to give their permission to you making the recording of the new version. You may also want to check the context in which the song is being used in case you find that offensive.

Term

You have to agree how long the deal is to last. If it's for a specific event or a tour then the sponsorship deal will run from the lead-up to the event, which could be weeks or days before the tour and end shortly after the event or tour has been completed. The sponsor may occasionally have the right to use up printed materials or products they have already manufactured, but this wouldn't normally be for more than three to six months and they shouldn't manufacture more of the product in anticipation that the deal is about to come to an end. Obviously, during the time that they're allowed to sell off the product, any exclusivity they have ends so that you can go off and look for a new sponsor. If it's a general sponsorship deal for a particular product then you might agree that it runs for a year, perhaps with an option to extend it by mutual agreement. You would normally only agree to an extension if you got paid a further sum of money. You'll want to make sure that any remaining stocks are sold off as soon as possible at the end of the deal, as it could interfere with either the sponsorship deal for the next part of the tour or a new sponsorship deal for the same type of product.

You should also bear in mind that the longer your name becomes associated with one company for a particular product, the more difficult it will be to get a deal with another company. For example, if the public has come to associate your name with Pepsi for soft drinks, Coca-Cola is less likely to want to sponsor you. Some of you might be saying, 'I wish I had this problem,' at this point.

Banner advertising at venues

If the sponsorship is for a tour or part of a tour, the sponsors will usually want to have their name on banners in each concert arena. They may agree that these only go up in the foyer or they may want them in the concert hall itself. Most artists insist on no banners over the stage and, if the sponsor's name is being projected on to the stage backdrop, that this stops several minutes before they go on stage. Whether you want to insist on these kinds of restriction will depend on your own views as to how closely you want to be associated with the sponsor, as well as your bargaining power. I don't think it's unreasonable, though, to ask that the banners aren't so intrusive that they detract from your own performance.

If your sponsorship deal involves publicity for the sponsor at the concert venue, you have to be careful that you don't run up against any restrictions within the venue itself. The venue owner may already have given the drinks concession to another company. For example, Coca-Cola may already have the right to have their soft drinks on sale at the venue to the exclusion of all other competing brands. If that is the case, the venue won't take it too well if your sponsor, Pepsi, then drapes their banners and logos about the place. That doesn't mean that you definitely won't be able to do the sponsorship deal, just that you'll have to be aware of any restrictions and make sure you don't agree to do anything in the contract that you can't put into effect on the ground. Any sponsor will want to have the opportunity to put a stand in the foyer. You shouldn't guarantee that they can do this, as there may be venue or local authority restrictions. Any permissions required and fees payable should be the sponsor's responsibility.

Meet and greets

Whatever the type of sponsorship deal you do, it's likely that the sponsor will require you to be involved in some kind of 'meet and greet' sessions. These are where the sponsors, their key customers and possibly competition winners get to meet you. This may be before or after a concert or at specially organised events. Bear in mind that a live performance can be very draining. You may not want to meet a lot of people beforehand, and afterwards you may need time to come down from the adrenaline rush of performing. Don't overcommit yourself. I know of some bands that share the meet and greet sessions out between them. It's the job of your manager to make sure that your sponsors don't get overeager and expect or even demand too much of you.

Freebies and promotional activities

By this I mean things that the sponsor will expect to get for nothing as part of the sponsorship fee. They will usually want a guaranteed number of free tickets to your concerts. They will always want more than you'll want to give. There will need to be a compromise. You may offer more tickets at bigger venues and less or none at all at smaller ones.

The sponsor may want you to attend press conferences for product launches or to make personal appearances. These should always be subject to your availability and to the other professional commitments that you have. If you're on a concert tour in Europe, you don't want to find yourself committed to having to return to London for a press conference. You should also try and limit these appearances to a maximum number of days over the term of the deal.

Take care before you guarantee that you'll do a concert tour in a particular region. You may not be able to deliver this or, if you do, you may lose a lot of money. However, the sponsor may agree to underwrite all or part of such a tour if it's important to them that you perform in those parts of the world.

If the sponsor wants to feature you in adverts, they need to specify how many, whether TV or radio, and the extent to which you have to be involved. You should have rights of approval. It's unlikely that you'll be able to limit the number of times they can repeat the adverts unless you've considerable bargaining power. If you do then you should aim to allow them a reasonable amount of repeats without it getting to the stage that every time you turn on the television there you are. There's nothing more off-putting than that. The sponsor shouldn't want that either, but sometimes they need to have the brakes applied for them.

Trade mark licences and goodwill

I discussed in the last chapter the advantages of registering a trade mark. If you have a trade mark either pending or registered in your name, or a logo, then in your sponsorship deal you'll be expected to grant a licence to your sponsor to use that trade mark. You should limit the licence to the uses covered by the sponsorship deal and the licence should end when the sponsorship deal does.

Payment

I bet you were wondering when I was going to get to this. What are you going to get paid for all of this work? The amounts can vary widely depending on what you're expected to do, the size of the company, your fame and the length of the deal and how exclusive it is. Each will have to be negotiated on a case-by-case basis. The sponsor or the agent will usually come to you with a figure for what the sponsor thinks it's worth and, after due consideration, you may want to accept that or try to push it higher. Figures of a million pounds plus for sponsorship of big name artists are not unusual.

The sponsorship contract won't only spell out how much you'll get paid – it will also say when you will get the money. The sponsorship fee could be money alone, or cash and goods, or occasionally just goods (although in that case it's more of an endorsement deal). It's not usually recoupable or returnable. There are exceptions, though. If you break your side of the bargain, for example by not doing the tour, or if it's a case of misrepresentation as in The Spice Girls scooter case above, then the contract may say that you are required to repay some or all of the money. Or you may get sued for its return. You may also be required to return some of the money or to pay compensation if you bring the sponsor's brand into disrepute.

When you'll be paid will also usually be some kind of compromise. The sponsor will want to hold back as much of the fee as they can until they're sure you're delivering your side of the bargain. On the other hand, you'll be actively promoting the sponsor's product and you'll want to be getting some, if not all, of the sponsorship fee in the bank. At the very least you'll want to be paid as soon as specific things have been achieved, for example some of the money should be paid when you sign the deal, some when you start the concert tour and the balance at the end of the tour.

You should also be clear what is included in the fee. If you're doing a recording of a song, remember that there will be mechanical royalties to be paid to your publisher and any co-writer (see Chapter 4). If you have an exclusive recording deal, your record company may want payment in return for releasing you from that exclusivity. If an advert is going to be put together with visual images for television, for example, a synchronisation fee will be payable to your publisher and to the publisher of any co-writer. These can be significant amounts of money. Who's going to be responsible for these fees? Are they included in the sponsorship fee so that you have to sort it out with the publishers? Or is it the sponsor's responsibility? The answer can make a considerable difference to what you end up with in payment.

You should have the right to end the deal if the sponsor breaches the payment terms or otherwise doesn't fulfil their side of the bargain.

CONCLUSIONS

- Decide on the types of product you want to be associated with.

- Either target those companies that produce those products yourself, or through an agent, or decide that you'll wait until they come to you.

- Decide if you're looking for one exclusive sponsor or a series of deals for particular products.

- Decide if you want to do a worldwide or limited-country deal.

- Make sure that the services you have to provide are manageable and that you have any necessary permissions from your record and publishing companies.

- When setting the level of the fees, agree what is to be included.

- Try to get as much of the fee paid up-front as possible.

Chapter 10
Touring

INTRODUCTION

The last five years have seen a change in the fortunes of the record and publishing business as opposed to that of the promoters and concert venues. Mintel estimates that the live music market will be worth £836 million by 2009. Whether it is because people can get recorded music so easily and cheaply that they devalue it or whether it's because we are rediscovering that we are social animals at heart and being stuck in front of a computer for hours is really rather sad. Whatever the cause we are spending large sums of money on going to see artists perform live. Look at the record-breaking 21 night run that Prince had at the O2 in 2007 and at the enormous amounts of money people will pay for tickets to big name artists. This is all at a time when the record companies are struggling with issues of piracy, illegal free downloads and challenges at the very heart of their business models. So it is probably not surprising that some of the more innovative deals emerging in the last few years have centred on the live sector which is one of the few presently making money. Hence the growth in the ubiquitous 360 models where the record company takes a share of the artist's live earnings. The most talked about deal of 2007 however was that between Madonna and Live Nation.

MADONNA AND LIVE NATION

Madonna has always been brilliant at reinventing herself. She has also always been a very canny business woman. The two traits are combined in this deal.

It seems she had one more album to record under her deal with Warners. They also probably have the right to bring out at least one 'Greatest Hits' or 'Best of' album but after the next studio album, which Madonna is currently finishing recording, she will be free of that contract.

She was apparently in discussions with Warners about a new deal or extension of her existing deal but then in a move which surprised the industry it was announced that her new deal would not be with a traditional record company at all but with her live touring promoters Live Nation. What is more it was to be a 360 model deal.

As details began to emerge, Warners put out a statement wishing her well and confirming plans to release the new studio album (the last under their deal) in spring 2008. This ends a twenty-year relationship between the label and the artist. Speculation was rife over whether there had been a falling out or some other upset. But it may be that Warners did not want to pay the kind of sums that Madonna was looking for. Perhaps also they couldn't offer the full advantages of the 360 model for the artist.

Live Nation is the biggest concert promotion company in the world but it lost $161 million in 2005 and 2006 and made a small $10 million profit from revenues in excess of $1 billion in the first quarter of 2007. So why do this deal? Well, they received considerable publicity for the deal and may hope that this will attract other stadium size artists to look to them for their new deals. They get a chance to earn more from

Madonna's touring, endorsement/sponsorship deals and merchandise over the next ten years and the recording income from up to three studio albums. Madonna's live tours attract huge audiences so for her it seems a clever move to receive a reputed £120 million in return for giving these rights to Live Nation. It is however a bit of a gamble because Madonna is now 49 (admittedly a supremely fit 49) and may not want to be still touring at the same pace for the next 10 years. Will her 'brand' remain important enough to command large endorsements and sponsorship deals and if she tours less will the merchandise sales be there?

The *Wall Street Journal* reported on 11 October 2007 that she will be paid $17.5million as a sign on advance, between $50 million and $60 million for the next three albums plus a $50 million payment in cash and shares for the concert promotion rights. When she does tour she will still reportedly receive 90% of the gross touring revenues. Not a bad day's work.

But do bear in mind that the full financial package is nearly always linked to delivery of product and achievement of certain targets. If those are not met then the deal could well be a lot less attractive financially.

MAMA GROUP

Another company, amongst many, which is aiming to capitalise on the current success of the live music scene is UK AIM listed company, Mama Group. Through a thorough analysis of the live industry – observed at the various, mostly small, Barfly venues managed by the group – the founders, Adam Driscoll and Dean James, set about seeing how they could get a piece of not just the profit from promoting concerts but also the ancillary income like the T-shirts and other merchandising, management and development of upcoming artists. They now manage eighteen UK live venues, including recent acquisition Hammersmith Apollo in West London. Their associated management company Supervision signs up talented acts, including some performing at the Mama Group-managed starter Barfly venues, to management deals. They control big money-spinning brands like G-A-Y and own a collection of media and marketing agencies targeting the student market called Campus Group. They are presently working on digital ordering and delivery of the live concert ticket alongside the music track and the T-shirt. The all-round one-stop shop.

Of course, all of this activity rests on the continuing success of the live sector. This has always been cyclical in nature – just like most areas of the economy – and there are some commentators that say it may have peaked with the Madonna deal. As we don't have a crystal ball we will just have to wait and see but ride the opportunities whilst they are here.

GETTING STARTED

When you are starting out you'll probably get gigs in a very hand-to-mouth way. You or your manager will chase them up, probably starting in your home town with local pub dates. If you live in a town with a large student population, you might get on to the university/college circuit. Local bands are often very popular for 'rag' or summer balls, possibly as support to other better-known acts. Getting to know the local social secretary at the university/college can help but remember, all local bands with a bit of ambition will be doing the same thing.

If you can get the local press and radio behind you this can open up more local gigs. Don't forget college radio. If you make a fan of the station manager or a particular DJ, they'll plug not only your local dates but also those further afield. Take copies of your demo to the station and use your best selling skills to convince them they could be in at the start of a future Coldplay, Killers, KT Tunstall or whoever.

Once you have a local following you can look to venture outside the area to bigger and (hopefully) better-paid gigs. A word of warning – don't even think of inviting A&R people to your gigs unless you're well rehearsed and 'tight' in your playing and command an enthusiastic local following. I've been to many gigs where the band makes the fatal error of treating it as just another session in front of their mates. They act far too casually and are under-rehearsed. If the local record company scout happens to be at that gig he could be put off you for life, or it could set back your campaign for a record deal by several months while the damage is repaired. The same disastrous situation could happen if there's a reporter for the local newspaper at the gig who gives you a bad write-up. Don't get me wrong. I know that every act has its off day when, for whatever reason, it just doesn't come off. Scouts and newspaper reviewers will take an off day into account. What they won't forgive is if you aren't acting in a professional way. You should treat every gig as a professional job and the potential one when you'll be discovered. Pete Doherty and Amy Winehouse are the exceptions that prove the rule.

Try to find out who the local scouts are for the major record companies. It may be someone at the local college or radio station. Local bands that have been around for longer may be able to tell you, otherwise ask the reporter on music events at the local newspaper. It may even be them. Whoever the scout is, they may be looking to move into the business themselves using the discovery of a great local band as a stepping-stone. Some managers now also act as a kind of A&R outpost so don't ignore local managers either.

Doing all this is very hard work and mostly unrewarding. Some bands get to play in venues in larger towns by doing a deal with the venue owner or promoter where, in return for booking the band, they guarantee there will be a minimum number of tickets sold. If you don't sell enough tickets you have to make up the shortfall. It pays to drum up 'rent-a-crowd' from among your local fans, friends and family. I know of bands that sell package tours – they hire a coach and sell tickets to the gig and a coach to get you there and back. This proves especially popular where the band manages to get a gig in a larger town or city. Then the trip to the gig is combined with the chance of a day out in the city at a reasonable price.

As I mentioned in Chapter 1, you might also consider entering one of the many competitions run around the country. These might be billed as 'Battle of the Bands' Vodafone Live. Look out for adverts in the local press or the music papers like *NME* or *Kerrang!*. These contests are often viewed as slightly cheesy, not quite a credible way to break into the business. If it gets you noticed, what's the problem? If nothing happens, then you don't have to mention you were ever involved in it.

There are also some venues that have special showcase evenings for unsigned artists or writers. The ones I know about are in London, but there may well be others in a town near you – ask around. Club promoter Tony Moore has an unsigned acts night at a pub called The Bedford in Balham which, although 'south of the river', still attracts the A&R crowd. The Barfly in Camden and other Barfly operations around the country have similar events and are a recognised source of new band talent so are regularly checked out by the A&R scouts. The PRS occasionally supports events for artists who are either completely unsigned or have only signed a record deal. The American collection society ASCAP also holds unsigned artist events from time to time. Contact details for these venues and organisations are to be found in Useful Addresses at the end of the book.

You can try and get in on the unsigned acts part of the annual UK music conference called In the City. It is usually held in September and its regular home is Manchester. It has for some years been a place for UK music business people to gather and have a drink or five, as well as the venue for a whole series of music events – mostly for unsigned acts. The unsigned gigs are held in local music venues and pubs and are a magnet for A&R scouts and record label honchos. This is because in the past this event has been a fruitful source of new talent, including Suede, Oasis and Muse. The 2008 ones to watch included Elle s'Appelle, The Moths and Sky Larkin. To be part of the unsigned section you have to submit your demo and a brief biography to the unsigned organisers, who then have the unenviable task of wading through a vast pile of material to come up with a shortlist of about 30–40 bands over the 4–5 nights of the event. The best bands from each year usually end up doing a gig in London either immediately after the event or a while later. In 2007 they did a showcase at the Camden Barfly on 20 December which was broadcast live on Xfm, so a great piece of promotion for the acts involved.

Most artists who are already signed see live concerts as an essential marketing tool. People that haven't yet bought one of your records may go to one of your gigs and love what you do so much that the next day they go and buy up your entire recording output. A good review of a live gig can give your latest release very valuable publicity. Also, the current emphasis being placed on radio-friendly artists means that if your records aren't the sort that Radio 1 or 2 or other powerful radio stations are going to play, you have little alternative than to build a fan base through live concerts (see Chapter 6). For some non-mainstream genres such as folk, blues or jazz, sales of the artist's recordings at gigs forms the main part of their sales income alongside mail order or sales off their websites.

GETTING A BOOKING AGENT

The next stage on from you or your manager doing all the legwork yourselves is to get a booking agent. This will probably happen after you sign a record deal (see Chapter 3). It may, however, happen before if you've established a reputation as a good live act and have attracted the attention of local agents because they can see you're a safe bet for venues they regularly book acts for.

Do you need a booking agent? Possibly not. If your horizons are set at only playing local pub venues and you don't mind doing the work yourself, you probably won't need one. It's someone else that you're going to have to pay commission to, so you want to make sure it's going to be worthwhile before you get one. Also, they aren't likely to be interested in you unless you've already established a reputation for live work so you'll probably have to be passed the pure beginners stage.

What you may find is that certain venues are closed to you, because the venue owner only books acts brought to him by selected booking agents. Having a booking agent can also give you credibility to get into more prestigious or bigger venues, and open up the possibility of supporting bigger 'name' acts. As the booking agent is on a percentage of what you get, it's in his interests to drive a hard bargain. If the agent is any good you should end up with a better deal than if you had negotiated it yourself.

You might think that your manager could do the job of a booking agent. Yes, they could and in the early days they probably will, but specialised booking agents are the experts in putting together larger events such as a UK or European tour of the medium to large venues and stadiums. They know all the promoters, they can get the best deals and have a better chance of getting the prime dates than you or your manager, who don't do this on a day-by-day basis. The agents also know about all the main venues you're likely to want to play, and one or two that you'll not have thought of. If the venue is outside the main concert circuit, they have the specialised expertise to negotiate a good deal for you. With everything else that's going on around a tour, you or your manager may not have the time to do this properly. It may pay to find someone who can. 2006/07 saw a consolidation of some of the UK agencies but also the invasion of US-based agents such as William Morris and CAA. This has given agents not only a bit of a shake up but also consolidation has increased their bargaining power, so getting a strong agent on board can greatly increase your chances of getting good gigs at good money.

HOW DO YOU FIND A BOOKING AGENT?

You can ask your mates in the music business. Which agents do they use, which ones do they rate and which have they found to be trustworthy? Word of mouth is often a very reliable method of finding a good booking agent. Be sure that the booking agent works in the same area of music as you; otherwise he won't have the contacts in the right places to be of use to you.

Booking agents are also listed in directories such as the *Music Week Directory*. You could call local ones and try to find out which sort of acts they regularly work with and what venues they book. Another good source of information on agents and who does what is the monthly magazine *Audience*. It also gives you music business news, including details of up-coming festivals and other music industry events.

If you have a record deal it's likely that your A&R man will direct you or your manager to a good booking agent. While obviously you should take on board their suggestions, you shouldn't blindly follow their advice. As with finding a manager, you should also ask around and arrange to meet more than one agent. You should get them to come and see you perform live. This should show you who seems the most enthusiastic. You should also ask around as to which booking agents are seen as having the most 'clout'. Your record company, accountant and lawyer should all have had experience of dealing with booking agents and can give you some guidance. It's also important that your agent has a reputation as being honest. You don't want a booking agent who's going to run off with the ticket takings. If the agent who is interested in you works for a big organisation, find out if you'll be dealing with him in person or if he'll be passing you on to someone else in the organisation.

Booking agents will probably approach you or your manager, either direct or via the record company, if there's a good buzz or hype about you and you're signed to a record deal. If this happens, the same tips apply. Ask who else is on their books. Ask around about their reputation, honesty and reliability. Get them to meet the band and see you perform live. Make sure the agent 'gets the picture' as to what you're trying to achieve.

One thing that you should also be aware of is that some booking agents may also be getting a financial kick-back from the record label to come on board as your agent. I know of record labels that are keen to see their artists perform live and encourage agents to get involved by paying them either a retainer or a small percentage of record sales (usually 0.5–1%). This should be at the record company's expense and not recoupable against you or deducted from your royalty or other record income. It's not necessarily a bad thing, but there could be a conflict of interest between what you want and what your record company thinks is best for you. Also, when you work out your deal with an agent who's being paid in this way, you need to bear in mind what they're also getting from the record company.

WHAT'S IN A BOOKING AGENCY CONTRACT?
Some agents don't have written contracts with the artists they represent. They prefer to work on trust. They tell the artists what commission rate they take; they leave it to the artist's tour manager to sort out things such as the riders (see page 225), security requirements and so on. The risk for an agent in not having a written contract isn't as great as for a manager, because the agent is probably only booking one tour at a time and will have sorted out in advance his commission on that tour. He has no interest in ongoing record or publishing royalties, or in merchandising or sponsorship income. That said, even though some agents don't bother with written contracts, most booking agents like to have a contract to keep things clear and to give them some certainty so that they can plan what's to happen in the future. Indeed since the introduction of new employment agency regulations they may have no alternative in future than to put their terms in writing

EMPLOYMENT AGENCY REGULATIONS
These regulations came into force a couple of years ago[1] and apply to all kinds of employment agencies who charge a fee to the people they get work for and the work seekers include actors, musicians, singers, dancers and other performers as well as songwriters, authors, directors, those involved in the creative aspects of film and theatre productions, models and professional sports people. The rationale behind the regulations is to ensure that the client knows the terms on which he is doing business with the agent and what the fees will be. The regulations seek to ensure that the client cannot be made to suffer a penalty if he terminates the agency contract, nor require the client to take other services provided by the agency. The terms of business have to be given to clients in writing and can't afterwards be changed without the clients' agreement. A separate client account must now be kept and regular statements provided. Most decent agencies will already have adopted these aspects of the regulations as best practice but it may help to weed out some of the charlatans.

Also, in a nod in the direction of health and safety issues, the regulations require the agents to consider the suitability of the client for the job in question, e.g. not putting forward someone as a trapeze artist who suffered from vertigo. On the other hand they also require the client to inform the agent if he becomes aware of any reasons why he is not suitable for the job.

The terms on which the agent is employed by the hirer – the circus owner looking for the trapeze artist – must also be clearly stated and written down in one document. The regulations do place more of an obligation on the agent too, to ensure that the client has all the necessary permits/union membership etc. necessary for the job in question.

1   The Conduct of Employment Agencies and Employment Businesses Regulations 2003.

If the agent wants the right to deduct his fee from the fees for the job he has to have specifically agreed that with the client in the engagement agreement. So this may prompt a review of agents' terms of business. The agents can be sued in a civil court if they breach the regulations.

WHAT IS IN A BOOKING AGENCY CONTRACT?

In many ways the booking agency contract is similar to a management contract (see Chapter 2). There are several parts of the contract that are common to all booking agency contracts.

Exclusivity

The booking agent will be looking for an exclusive arrangement. He won't want to be competing for your work with other agents. The arrangement with the booking agent sits alongside the management agreement. Indeed, the manager may be very involved in the appointment of the booking agent. The management contract will usually give the artist the right to approve the identity of any booking agent. The manager looks after all other aspects of touring other than the actual booking of the concerts. There is danger of an overlap in the commission arrangements. The artist doesn't want to be paying a booking agent and the manager out of his gross income. The management contract will usually say that the manager takes his commission after any commission to a booking agent has been deducted. The management contract will usually give the artist approval over the terms on which the agent is appointed, particularly if he wants to charge more than the industry norm of 10–15%. The booking agent's fee should be deducted from the gross income first, and the manager's commission should be calculated on the net amount that's left after the agency commission and any other deductions agreed in the management contract have been taken off.

Territory

The contract could be a worldwide one or it could be for a specific territory, for example North America. If it's a worldwide deal then it's possible that the booking agent will want to use local sub-agents in some territories. For example, the booking agent may have his own offices in the UK and Europe, but be linked with another company or individual in the US. Until the recent influx of US agencies into the UK market there was a kind of gentleman's agreement that they did not try to poach acts in their respective territories, but the gloves are now off.

The artist may want to have the right to approve the identity of any sub-agents. Any sub-agent's fees should come out of the booking agent's fee and not be payable by the artist.

If it's a worldwide deal, the artist will want to be satisfied that the booking agent has the necessary contacts himself or through established sub-agents to do a good job in all countries where the artist is likely to want to perform live. It's no good appointing a UK booking agent worldwide when he can do a great job in the UK but hasn't a clue how to deal with promoters or venues in other parts of the world.

Term

The length of the term can vary considerably. It could be for a particular tour, for example the 2008 UK Arena tour. In that case the contract will end after the last date of that tour.

The artist is free to do a deal for the next tour or for the US leg of the same tour with another agent, as long as it doesn't interfere with the UK booking agent's rights.

The term could be open-ended, continuing until one party gives the other notice to end the arrangement. The usual notice period is a minimum of three months. There may also be an agreement that notice can't take effect during a tour, or that the agent gets commission on the whole of a tour they have set up, even if the arrangements with them are terminated before the tour is finished. This is only fair, because tour arrangements often have to be set up many months in advance.

Many booking agents are looking for the certainty of a fixed-term contract. This could be as short as a year, but terms of three to five years aren't unusual. Obviously, from your viewpoint, the longer you're committed to one booking agent, the more need there is for a contract that puts definite obligations on the booking agent to try and get work for you. The contract should also contain a get-out if it's not working out, because the booking agent can't get any work or is otherwise falling down on the job.

The booking agent's duties
As we saw with management contracts, the agency contract doesn't often set out in any great detail what the booking agent will do. The agent's duties are usually expressed in very general terms. There should at least be some kind of obligation on the agent to try to get work for you. After all, that's his job. If there's a fixed-term contract and if you're ready to do gigs and your agent can't or won't get you any work, then you should have the option to go to another agent.

On the other hand, if the agent does get you work, you should have the right to decide whether you actually want to do the work. The contract will probably give you the right to turn down offers of work if you do so on reasonable grounds. For example, if the booking agent gets you three dates in the North of England and a fourth a day later in Torquay, it might be reasonable to say that you can't reasonably get yourself and your gear from one end of the country to the other in that time. Or, if you did, it wouldn't be cost-effective once you take into account the travel costs in getting there. If, however, your booking agent has got you work which you turn down for no good reason, you can't then turn around and say that the agent hasn't done his job.

Your duties
You will usually have to agree to refer all offers for live work that come to you to your booking agent. Because of the exclusive arrangements, you mustn't act as your own booking agent. You will also usually agree to keep your booking agent aware of your plans. For example, if the plan is to release the new album in September, you'll be expecting to do live dates to help promote that release. You'll need to tell the agent at the beginning of the year so that they can begin to outline a tour in consultation with you and your manager. Many of the bigger venues are booked up months, if not a year, in advance for key dates, and the earlier the agent is told of the plans the sooner they can start to take options on the key venues and dates. These provisional bookings are confirmed when the details of the tour are firmed up. If you're tying a tour in with the release of your album, the dates won't probably be finally confirmed until the approximate delivery date for the album is known. That said, it doesn't always work to plan. If the recording overruns then the delivery date will shift and could have an impact on the tour dates. However, gigs

at big venues are usually set up for a few months after the album release and as an integral part of the promotion surrounding that release. Tours also have to try and tie in with any plans to release the album overseas.

You'll usually agree to use your best efforts to do the dates that the booking agent has booked and which you have agreed to do. Obviously illnesses do occur, and sometimes tours or particular concert dates are cancelled at short notice due to this. It's usual to take out insurance against having to cancel a tour, or one or more dates, if illness or accident affects one or more band members. These insurance policies aren't cheap, but if the artist gets laryngitis halfway through a world tour or, as happened with Oasis, three band members were involved in a car crash causing the cancellation or postponement of some US dates, it is comforting to know that insurance will cover any losses. Meatloaf had to cancel and reschedule some of the dates in his 2007 tour because of health problems, and Velvet Revolver had to cancel dates because of visa problems. Insurance policies can also be taken out to cover dates that have to be cancelled because not enough tickets have been sold. These are, of course, very expensive and are probably only worth it for big stadium dates. If you've got yourself a decent manager, you shouldn't have to worry about whether the necessary insurance is in place as he, or the tour manager, will do this for you.

Insurance policies can also be taken out to cover things like bad weather on open-air gigs. The owner of the site that hosts the Glastonbury Festival described in the press how he'd been offered insurance cover against bad weather, but hadn't taken it up because the premium was too high. Given the number of years that the site turns into a giant mud bath it probably is too high a cost especially as the mud has now almost become a part of the experience for the stoic British concert-going public.

You can get insurance cover for most things at a price. I remember a situation when a member of a band was spending a year living outside the UK for tax reasons. The rules at the time allowed you to return to the UK for a given number of days in that year. The band was doing a world tour, which included some dates in the UK. The last of these dates fell on the last day that he would have been entitled to be in the UK and not lose the tax advantages. The concert was due to finish at 10.30 p.m., which meant that with a helicopter standing by he should have been out of the country in time. If he wasn't he would lose significant amounts of tax savings, so an insurance policy was taken out to cover him against that happening. Everything was going very well until the band got a little too enthusiastic in the number of encores, and it was getting nearer to 11 p.m. when the band finally left the stage. A very swift dash to the helicopter followed and, luckily, our man was just away in time.

Van Morrison (Exile) v. Marlow

But don't think you can always be protected against cancellation or no-show. Van Morrison's service company, Exile, got into trouble in 2003 when it was ordered by a court to pay Gary Marlow, the owner of the Crown Hotel in Marlborough £40,000 in damages. Mr Marlow had booked Van Morrison to appear at his hotel and was also the promoter of the gig. There was a written contract which, according to Exile, gave them a prior right of approval of all advertising and promotional materials i.e. it would seem Van Morrison wanted to keep it relatively low profile. But, the contract also said Mr Marlow should do his best to promote the show. Mr Marlow mentioned the intended appearance of Van Morrison in answer to some enquiries from the press. As a result Exile decided Van Morrison would not perform, arguing that this interview breached its right of approval over publicity. However, the judge decided that it was the nature of a promoter's contract to promote and if the artist wants to place restrictions on that promotion these have to be clear, unambiguous and not contradictory. This contract was not drafted in this way so Exile was found to have wrongfully prevented Van Morrison from performing and had to pay up.

I have heard of some odd grounds for cancelling tours but the one advanced by opera singer Dame Kiri te Kanawa that she feared being bombarded with underwear certainly takes some beating.

Kiri te Kanawa Case

In an Australian case reported here in April 2007, Dame Kiri te Kanawa was booked to appear as co-headliner on a 2005 tour with Aussie veteran John Farnham. She cancelled after watching DVDs of his shows where he was thrown underwear by fans. The promoter, Leading Edge, sued her for A$ 2 million for the money it says it had lost on publicity costs and ticket sales. The Supreme Court judge rejected the claim ruling that although emails had been sent with details of venues and fees for the proposed concerts there had been no firm commitment by her to do the concerts and no contract had been finalised. So it's a question of the most basis aspect of English contract law – was a contract formed?

The fee

What is the agent paid? His fee is usually a percentage of the gross income from your live appearances. It will include the appearance fee and also any benefits that you receive in kind as opposed to in cash. For example, the payment you get for a particular contract could be made up of a £10,000 appearance fee plus a car provided by the tour or venue promoter, or free travel or hotel accommodation. The agent will usually want to add the value of the car, the travel, the accommodation and so on to the gross income in working out his fee. It's here, of course, that you can see the value of a tour accountant. One of his many jobs will be to see that a proper value has been placed on these non-monetary items.

The fee is usually between 10% and 15% of the gross income. If you're paid £10,000 in appearance fees and a car worth £10,000, then your booking agent will receive 10–15% of £20,000 (i.e. £2–3,000). The agent will negotiate with the promoter or with the venue direct, and will usually agree that the promoter or venue pays them their fee direct, with the balance being paid through to you. There may be a deposit paid which the agent may well hold as security for their fee. Once it's clear that there are sufficient ticket sales to mean that date won't make a loss, the booking agent may well agree to release that deposit to you, less their agency fee. Although as we saw above the new regulations mean that he will have to get your written approval in order to deduct his fee from these monies and he has to keep the fees in a separate client account. Or, the agent may negotiate guaranteed minimum payments from the venue or promoter, which aren't returnable, even if insufficient tickets are sold to make the date viable. The booking agent will usually insist on being paid for any work that has been contracted for or substantially negotiated during the term of the agency contract. For example, you may contract to a forty-date tour through a particular agent and then move on to another agent for the rest of the dates or for the next tour. While you may be free to do this, you will still have to pay the first booking agent for the work they did in putting the original forty-date tour together. Sometimes the agent will limit their commission to concert dates that you do within six months of the end of the term of their contract. This could be a little hard on the agent. If the artist is doing a world tour, it's likely that that could run well beyond six months. If the agent has done the work in setting up the tour, there are strong arguments for saying that they should be paid for that work. As it's unlikely that you will have to pay any other booking agent for that same tour, you aren't going to get a double-hit for fees. If the booking agent has done an all-right job and the contract isn't being disputed, or hasn't been brought to an end because the booking agent is in breach of contract, this position is a reasonable one to take. Sometimes, if your agent leaves one company to go to another one and you move with him he agrees to pay some of his fees to the old agency in return for taking you with him.

Accounting
The booking agent will usually want to collect the money and deduct their commission before paying the balance through to you.

You'll want to make sure that the money is paid into a separate client bank account. You'll need to see detailed statements of what has been received, from where and how the commission is calculated. You'll want the balance to be paid through quickly and will need to have the right to carry out an audit of the booking agent's books and records to make sure you've received amounts properly due.

This is particularly important where some payments may be received up-front in the form of deposits from the venues, or as guaranteed sums regardless of the number of tickets sold. The deposit may be returnable in some circumstances. One of the jobs of the tour accountant is to keep a track of all these arrangements as well as keeping a close eye on any sums paid in cash on the night. These deposits do not automatically have to sit in the separate account under the new agency regulations so you might want to specify in your agreement that they should.

The balance due to you should be paid through at the end of each gig, but that may not be possible, in which case it should be at least weekly. Sometimes payment may come at monthly intervals if the arrangements are particularly complex or involve overseas tax issues. If you aren't going to be paid on the night and payment is to be delayed then a rough outline – called a settlement sheet – should be prepared at the end of each gig and given to the artist or the tour accountant within three days to check.

Assignment and key-man provisions
You need to establish who is going to be your agent – your key contact at the booking agency. The larger the booking agency, the more important it is to get this sorted out. There's nothing worse than signing up to an agency thinking that you're going to be dealt with by one of the hot-shots, only to discover that he has passed it to a junior with no experience or clout.

If you can, you should get a right in the contract to terminate it if that key-man isn't available to you as your agent. Obviously, a good agent is going to be working for more than one artist and is going to be in great demand. You can't therefore expect him to be there for you every minute of the day. But when it comes to putting together a big tour, whether you're the headline or support act, you need to know that the agent is there for you to lend their experience and bargaining skills to sorting out the details. The agency isn't going to be very happy about agreeing to key-man clauses in the contract. If a particularly good agent wants to go off to another agency, or wants to set up on their own account, that puts them in a very good bargaining position. You can terminate the contract if the agent leaves and then move to their new agency if you want to. The agent can use the fact that you could terminate to negotiate better terms for them if they're to stay with the agency or better settlement terms if they still want to leave. If the agency does agree to a key-man clause then it will probably say that the right to terminate only arises when the agent is consistently not around for thirty days or more. They will also usually exclude periods when the agent is genuinely ill or on holiday.

If the agency plans to sell up or sell on the contract to another company, or it wants to buy into a bigger company, you should have the right to refuse to be tied to these arrangements unless the agency first gets your approval.

Finally, the contract should give you the right to terminate the term of the contract if the agent is insolvent or breaches his obligations, for example, if he doesn't pay the balance of the ticket money when he should and he fails to put this right within a reasonable time of you putting him on notice that they should.

PROMOTERS

A promoter is responsible for booking artists to perform live at particular venues. This could be one man promoting a single venue or a multi-million-pound multinational corporation owning the right to promote a whole raft of large and small venues such as Live Nation.

WHAT DO PROMOTERS DO?

Promoters are responsible for securing the venue and for selling the tickets. The promoter may be the venue owner himself, or they may be a separate company who have an arrangement with a particular venue. This arrangement may be exclusive or non-exclusive. The promoter may deal direct with the artist or his manager or he may negotiate through a booking agent. Promoters make their money on their margins. If they own the venue then they want to cover their costs and make a profit. If they just deal with a venue they make their money on the difference between what they have to pay through to the venue and what they have to pay to the artist/booking agent after allowing for their own expenses. The promoter may also control the sales concessions at the venues, for example for selling food, drink or merchandise. The promoter may charge for the rental of these concessions and/or take a percentage of the takings.

A promoter may promote just one venue or perhaps a festival or a series of venues. There are promoters who operate nationwide, but also those who operate only in particular parts of the UK.[2]

Once the dates are pencilled in, the promoter will want an agreement committing the artist to do these dates and laying out the terms on which they will perform.

---

2 The Regional Promoter's Association (UK) is an informal grouping of promoters. Contact Josh Dean, Concorde2, Madeira Drive, Brighton, BN2 1EU. Tel. 01273 207241.

Naturally, these sorts of arrangements are only likely to affect the main artists on the bill – the top billing or headline acts. A supporting artist will have little or no say on the terms of the deal with the promoter. The promoter will usually agree a fee with the headline act and it's up to that act to agree a deal with the supporting act as to the terms on which they will appear on the bill.

As discussed above, some promoters like Mama Group and Live Nation are also branching out into controlling other ancillary income streams not generally within a promoter's remit, such as merchandising.

WHAT'S IN A PROMOTERS CONTRACT?

Your obligations

The contract will set out what concerts you will do, when and where. The contract could spell out the length of time you are required to perform. For example, it may say that you're expected to do one 'set' (performance) of at least forty minutes duration. For smaller venues it may say that you're expected to do two forty-minute sets with a break in between.

Promoter's obligations

The promoter will agree to provide at least the venue, ticket sales facilities and basic door, stage and backstage security arrangements. Thereafter it's down to the individual arrangements agreed in each contract. The promoter may agree to supply certain equipment and personnel, for example, a particular sound desk or sound engineer. If the dates include any overseas gigs, then any personnel they supply should be provided with all necessary permits, including work permits for overseas dates or for overseas personnel working in the UK.

The promoter will also usually be required to provide an agreed level of backstage amenities for you in the form of dressing rooms, toilets and meeting or VIP areas.

It's also usually the responsibility of the promoter to provide insurance cover against injury or death caused to members of the public. This is called public liability insurance. It's vital to ensure that this cover is in place. Obviously, this will be the manager's job once there is a manager on board, but a member of the public can get injured in the early days as well, so you should think about this. Unfortunately accidents do happen at live gigs; people do fall or get caught up in the crush at the front of the stage. If there isn't insurance in place, the person injured could look to you direct for compensation. If anyone is employed to do any construction work, for example for the stage or lighting rig, then those sub-contractors should also carry insurance or, once again, responsibility could fall back on you. There was an unfortunate spate of concert related deaths and serious injuries in recent years, beginning with the deaths of 9 music fans at the Roskilde Festival in Denmark in 2000, followed by the deaths of 21 clubbers in Chicago and hundreds of deaths at the Rhode Island Club where a fireworks display as part of the band Great White's set led to disaster. An accident involving one of the trucks carrying concert equipment for George Michael forced the singer to cancel a show in Prague. In Atlanta opening artist Ray Lavender and Akon band members had completed their sound checks and left the stage when the canopy suddenly caved in. In the UK incidents like these have led to greater insistence on health and safety issues and to the setting up of the Safety Focus Group as an offshoot of the International Live Music Conference in 2001.[3]

The Licensing Act

The Licensing Act which became law in 2003 and began to have an impact in 2005 brought about major changes to how venues are licensed. The focus is on health and safety and public order issues and is a radical overhaul of the UK licensing system. One major change is that venues that put on live music regularly will need a premises licence from the local authority whereas before it did not need an entertainment licence for one or two musicians performing together. The exceptions for occasional events and purely acoustic sets have been maintained but there was initially concern for the impact of the changes on the live music scene and this led to the launch of the government supported Live Music Forum, whose remit includes the evaluation of the impact of the Licensing Act and the promotion of the performance of live music generally. Its report in mid-2007 found that the effect of the Act on live music was broadly 'neutral' but that there had been an impact at grassroots level with increased bureaucracy and regulations. In an attempt to minimise some of these side effects of the legislation, which was after all meant to ease restrictions on live music, the Forum has recommended making exceptions from the need for licensing for acoustic sets or for venues where live music was incidental to the main event. They are also lobbying for an exemption for small venues holding fewer than a hundred people. The report is now being studied by the Licensing Minister who promises to respond fully in due course.

There have been casualties. The Brecon Jazz Festival which relies to a large extent for its special atmosphere on the open air live sessions had to cancel about ten events in 2007 because it was apparently impossible to license the whole of the town centre as a premises.

In a related matter George Michael was fined £130,000 for overrunning the licensing curfew at Wembley Stadium on 9 June 2007. He was fined £10,000 for every minute he overran.

The Private Security Industry (Licences) Regulations 2004

As if this weren't enough additional red tape, new regulations intended to protect against unscrupulous bouncers or doormen were also introduced in 2004. The Private Security Industry (Licences) Regulations 2004 are effective from 1 March 2004 and require all door supervisors and security staff to be licensed and to display an identifying licence at all times. The application requires them to declare any criminal convictions or cautions. There are separate regulations and licences required by those supervising these activities. Private security firms who provide security for pubs, clubs and the like must also be licensed.

Artist riders

Anyone who's seen the spoof film about the music business *Spinal Tap* will know about the occasionally ridiculous artist riders. These are the lists of specific requirements that

---

3 Buckinghamshire Chilterns University College (now Bucks New University), the International Live Music Conference Safety Focus Group and the European Agency for Health and Safety at Work (OSHA) created a website in 2004 dedicated to safety issues called Safety Rocks www.safety-rocks.org. It contains a risk assessment tool for those operating in the live music scene.

the artists have for their comfort and entertainment backstage. Only black jellybeans and sandwiches cut in circles will do! I've seen some very strange riders in my time. One was twelve pages of very detailed menu requirements, including very specific types of cereal and drinks that can only be bought in the US. As this was a European tour that was pretty unreasonable and changes had to be negotiated and substitutes found. Other riders specify only a crate of good whisky and five crates of beer. Well, this is rock 'n' roll. Some artists take their own caterers with them or will only use a caterer that they know is familiar with their particular requirements. Some riders are there for a very good reason. For example, an artist may be a vegan or vegetarian, or allergic to particular food. I've also seen riders that insist that all hotel rooms have hypo-allergenic bedding and pillows.

It's usual to leave the negotiation of the details between the manager or the tour manager and the promoter. It's not usually cost-effective to get your lawyer involved in this. The riders do form part of the contract, so the promoter has to make sure that the requirements are reasonable, affordable and obtainable. If they don't and the omissions are sufficiently serious, this could be a breach of contract. Even if the omissions are more minor in nature, it can cause major grief with the artist, which is the last thing a promoter wants just before the artist goes out on stage.

Fees

You and your booking agent are dependent on the promoter for ticket sales and income. You'll want to be sure that you're guaranteed a certain level of income. If you're already an established artist, you may be able to get a Guaranteed Minimum included in the contract. This guarantees you will be paid this amount, regardless of whether the promoter sells enough tickets. This is where the promoter takes the risk. They have to get the level of the Guaranteed Minimum right, because they'll have to pay it even if they don't sell a single ticket.

Over and above any Guaranteed Minimum sum, you might receive a fixed percentage of the promoter's net receipts. For example, if the Guaranteed Minimum is £10,000 and, after the promoter has paid out certain agreed expenses, you are entitled to 10% of the net receipts, then if the net ticket sales are £100,000 you will only get the Guaranteed Minimum. If the net receipts are £250,000, then 10% is worth £25,000. After deducting the Guaranteed Minimum of £10,000, you are now due another £15,000. The tour accountant will have to check very carefully that the expenses that the promoter can deduct are reasonable and that the percentage you receive of the net monies represents a reasonable return. The alternative is that you receive a further fixed payment dependent on levels of ticket sales. For example, it could be agreed that you get a Guaranteed Minimum of £10,000 plus, if ticket sales exceed £250,000, you receive another £15,000. With this type of payment arrangement, you must assess how realistic it is that ticket sales will be high enough so that you have a reasonable chance of receiving further payments.

Payment and accounting

The contract should set out when any Guaranteed Minimum payment is to be made. Usually at least half of it should be paid up-front and the rest on the night of the first of the concerts.

The balance of any payments should be made on the night of each gig or possibly at the end of a particular leg of a tour or end of each week of a tour.

It's important that the tour accountant has access to the box-office tills and receipts on the night of the concert and that all ticket stubs should be kept for at least three months afterwards in case they need to be checked by the accountant. Further payments under the merchandising deal may be dependent on a given number of people being at each concert (see Chapter 8). The ticket stubs and any head count on the night will prove the number of people at a particular date, so access to this information and proof is very important. Receipts for any expense that the promoter is allowed to deduct should also be scrutinised and kept for later checking. Only those expenses allowed by the tour accountant should be deducted.

Other income

The promoter or the venue owner may have done deals with catering companies or drink suppliers. The contract should set out whether or not you should get any share of the profits from such sources. For example, the venue may have a deal with Coca-Cola that they are the official suppliers of soft drinks to the venue. An artist that commands a very loyal following of fans who will ensure that his concerts are a sell-out can only be of benefit to Coca-Cola in the considerable number of soft drinks it will sell at those concerts. If you have sufficient bargaining power, you can insist on sharing some of the money that Coca-Cola pays to the promoter or venue for the right to be the exclusive supplier.

The sale of merchandise can be an important source of income for you. The promoter/venue may make a charge for the right to set up merchandising stalls at the venue. The merchandising deal will cover whether the merchandising company is allowed to deduct some or all of this charge from the gross income before you receive your percentage.

If you have sufficient bargaining power, you could insist that you alone have the right to sell food or drink and that the promoter gets no income from these or from merchandise sales. You can then do sponsorship deals with food and drink companies as well as merchandising deals. These kinds of arrangements tend only to apply to established, successful artists with a team of people able to give effect to these arrangements.

Restrictions

The contract should insist that the promoter stops anyone from recording the performances, unless of course a live recording or film of the concert is being made. Your record contract will probably say something about you not allowing anyone to make a recording of your performance. While it's very difficult to prevent a bootlegger unofficially and unlawfully recording the performance, you can show the right spirit by putting this requirement in the contract with the promoter. This will demonstrate that you don't condone this sort of activity. If you do intend to make a film of the performance, perhaps to make a video or for a live webcast or television broadcast, the contract should make sure that the promoter will allow access to the venue for the recording at no extra charge. You also need to be sure that the audience knows they will be filmed and for what purpose. Signs at all entrances usually spell this out.

Each venue has its own restrictions on parking and when the stage crew can gain access to load equipment in or out. Any particular stipulations or restrictions should be set out in a rider or schedule to the contract. In residential areas, there may be severe restrictions on how late the artist can play and there may be an early curfew on when the crew can load the equipment back out. They may have to come back the next morning. If so, you need to ensure the equipment is kept securely and that it's insured against loss or damage. If it's a nationwide tour, the tour manager will need to know these restrictions well in advance. It wouldn't be funny if you had a date in Scarborough on the Friday night and your equipment was still in Torquay because the crew couldn't get in to load out the equipment after Thursday's Torquay gig until seven o'clock the next morning.

An important part of protecting your brand is to ensure that there are no sales of unauthorised merchandise inside or outside the venue. It's easier for a promoter to control illegal merchandise inside the venue, but he may say he has no control over what happens outside. In that case you should try to make sure that the venue and the promoter co-operates with Trading Standards Officers or other personnel who are trying to stop unauthorised or pirate merchandise.

GETTING FUNDING FOR LIVE WORK

Funding for a tour can come from a number of different places. At the lowest level, where you're just starting out and doing local gigs, you can expect to be paid little or nothing over and above some petrol money and a few free pints of beer. As you progress, you may get a small percentage of the ticket sales and may make some money from sales of T-shirts or recordings of your performances that you sell at the gigs. There probably won't be much in the way of profits after the cost of hiring a PA, paying for transport and maybe an agent or manager.

It is possible for an unsigned act to get sponsorship for live work. As mentioned in Chapter 9, companies such as Doc Martin or lager companies have sponsored live tours by unsigned acts. More recently Sony Ericsson and Orange have sponsored an interactive talent show called 'MobileAct unsigned'. It is possible to make a decent living from live gigs if you can keep your costs down, play decent-sized venues and have a loyal following of fans, but it's very hard work.

Once you're signed to a record deal, bigger venues may open up to you. A booking agent may come on the scene and get you slots as support bands or lower-down-the-order gigs at summer open-air festivals. Money can be made from merchandise sales or from tour sponsorship. However, it's likely that you won't make a big profit on live work until you've achieved quite a degree of success and fame as a recording artist. Even then you may barely break even if you have an expensive live set with lots of special effects and a cast of thousands. If your live set is kept very simple, without loads of backing singers or a live orchestra, then you stand a better chance of making money. But it's important to balance cutting expenses back to a minimum against the risk that the show is a disappointment to the fans, which would be counter-productive.

TOUR SUPPORT
Most artists need the support of their record company to get them out on the road. The record company will rarely agree to put this in the record contract unless you have a lot

of bargaining power, or you're prepared to hold out for this support at the expense of perhaps a lower advance or royalty. Even if it's not specifically in the contract, it's usually in the record company's interests for you to be out touring and promoting your new album. If you can only do this by making a loss (the shortfall) then the record company has to come to your rescue and underwrite this shortfall. This is usually called tour support.

Tour support is usually 100% recoupable from royalties from record sales. This is, however, negotiable and could be reduced to 50% recoupable, with the remainder being treated as a non-recoupable marketing expense of the record company. Sometimes, if the tour support is for a tour in a particular part of the world, for example Japan, then you could agree that the tour support is only recouped from Japanese record sales.

In addition to making up any shortfall, the record company may pay a 'buy-on' fee. This is the fee payable to the headline artist on a tour or to his record company for the privilege of being allowed to support them. For some new artists, the association with a more established name gives them an opening to a much wider potential audience, as well as the chance to perform in bigger venues. For the headline act this is an additional source of income, reducing the amount of tour support they'll need from their record company. Buy-on fees for large venues and for concerts by big-name artists can run to tens of thousands of pounds. It's one of the reasons why you'll often see a big-name artist being supported by another smaller act who's on the same label. That way the costs are kept in the family.

How much tour support will you need?

Before you can go to your record company to ask for tour support, you need to have an idea how much you'll need.

First, you'll need to get someone to prepare a tour budget. This could be your manager or your regular accountant or bookkeeper. However, when doing a bigger tour, either as headline or support, consider getting a specialist tour accountant on board. The tour accountant could be someone at the regular accountancy firm, or one recommended by them, or by friends. Your A&R contact or manager can suggest people, as can your lawyer. Most importantly, the tour accountant must be honest, must understand how tour promoting works, and be brave enough to tackle unscrupulous promoters about to run off with the cash midway through the gig.

The tour accountant, or any other person doing that job, will put together an outline budget that will make guesstimates of income and expenditure. As details such as any Guaranteed Minimum, any buy-on fees, merchandise advances and so on become known they are factored in. The accountant will work very closely with you or your manager to work out what type of shows you intend to put on. The number of musicians and how elaborate the stage set or lighting effects will be will all affect the tour budget.

Once your tour accountant has a good idea of the likely profit (or perhaps loss) he prepares an outline draft budget which your manager then takes to your record company to negotiate the level of tour support. It's important, therefore, that he doesn't make wild guesses and is as accurate as he can be as to what you're likely to need.

The record company will usually set a maximum amount that they will pay to underwrite the shortfall. For example, the tour accountant may have estimated a tour loss of £18,000. The record company checks his figures and makes its own assessment of how valuable it will be to them in record sales if the tour goes ahead. It may decide that one or two dates should be dropped, or that some of the costs could be saved. It will set a limit on how much it will pay. In this case, after some adjustments it may say that it will pay up to £16,000 in tour support. You and your manager have to then sit down with the tour accountant, and any production manager working on the tour, to see if savings can be made. If the tour then goes ahead and it does better than expected and only loses £15,000, then the record company underwrites a £15,000 shortfall not a £16,000 one. The actual amount they will pay (up to that maximum) is determined by the actual costs supplied by the tour accountant after the end of the tour with supporting invoices. If the tour does worse than expected and makes a £17,000 loss then the record company is only obliged to pay £16,000, and may insist that you pick up the rest of the bill yourself. So it's important to get the figure for the anticipated shortfall as realistic as possible.

The record company will usually agree to pay part of the tour support up-front. This means that the essential personnel can be paid some of what is due to them and essential equipment can be hired. The tour accountant then has to juggle who gets paid along the way, and who has to wait until the final instalment comes in from the record company. Needless to say, the tour accountant is rarely the most popular man on the tour.

Even if there is something in your record contract about tour support, it's unlikely that all the details will be included and it is usual to set out these detailed arrangements in a side agreement to the main record contract. Copies of all side agreements should be kept together with the record contract. If you're reviewing the accounting statements or are considering doing an audit, you need to have details of all the arrangements you've reached about what amounts are or aren't recoupable and from what sales. Unless the side agreement is very simple, a lawyer should review it before it is signed.

OTHER ISSUES

There are some other things that have to be taken into account when planning a tour.

TAX PLANNING

Your accountant should advise whether there are any tax advantages to you in putting your touring services through a limited company and, if so, should that be a UK-based or offshore company (see Chapter 11).

If your accountant does advise use of a limited company, a service agreement should be put in place between you and that company. The contract with any promoter will then be with the limited company.

In some countries, there is an obligation to pay tax in that country on earnings from live work undertaken there. The promoter may have to deduct the tax before he hands the money over. In that case the contract with the promoter must make sure that the promoter has to hand over the sums he has withheld to the relevant tax authorities. In countries where there are reciprocal tax treaties in place, it's possible to claim exemption from some of these taxes or, if they have a tax treaty in place, you may be able to reclaim some or all of the amounts withheld. The promoter should be obliged to do all the necessary paperwork and to supply you with any forms you may need to complete to show the country in which you or your service company is based and pays tax and the local tax authorities should either confirm exemption from tax on the income or provide a certificate of how much tax has been withheld so this can be offset against UK income for tax purposes.

Obviously, everyone's tax circumstances are different and these are only very general comments. Nothing will substitute for proper, professional tax planning and advice. Such planning should be done as far ahead as possible.

PUBLICISING THE TOUR

This is the joint responsibility of you and the promoter. Your record company also has a vested interest and will want to co-ordinate its own marketing efforts with the tour dates. For example, if the label had planned a poster campaign in particular towns in the UK, it may decide to target those towns where you're doing live dates. The tour posters may also give information on when your latest record is to be released. The promoter or the venue will publish adverts in the music and local press listing forthcoming tours. Your press officer and the internal press office at your record company will get to work placing the information in the press, getting interviews and personal appearances for you to promote the tour. You'll be expected to mention it in interviews with the press or on radio or TV.

Your record company has to be careful not to overstep the mark. In 2004, there was a spate of legal actions brought by Camden Council against the senior executives of Sony and BMG in an attempt to curb illegal fly-posting. Camden Council took the unusual step of using anti-social behaviour orders (ASBOs) on the executives after accusing the companies they led of saving money on legitimate poster sites by putting up posters for albums and gigs on any available space, including shop hoardings and pillar boxes. Service of the orders meant that the court had the power to order jail sentences of up to five years (in extreme cases) if the executives did not stop the practice. The ASBOS were seen as a last resort when prosecutions and requests to stop fly-posting had failed. They seem to have had some measure of success as the executives reached compromises with the council to avoid a continuance of the orders and promised not to commission any more illegal fly-posting.

Increasingly the Internet is being used to advertise tours and cult band, The Other, were the first to use SMS text messages to fans to alert them as to the whereabouts of the next 'secret' gig. This is part of the generic form of marketing called viral marketing which uses Internet or other databases to target information at fans. This could be on the record company's website, but more usually it will be on the artist's website, possibly with a link to the promoter's site or that of the venue. Websites are being used to offer the possibility of ordering tickets online and are offering competitions to win tickets or to meet the artist. Artist and record company websites can fulfil an important role in promoting the tour or selling tickets online.

The fan club can also be invaluable in publicising a tour. The regular newsletter sent out to fans can give details of forthcoming live events and where tickets can be bought. Sometimes the fan club does a deal with the promoter and/or a travel company to offer special travel, accommodation and ticket packages at a reduced rate to fan club members. The fan club has to be careful not to offer things that it can't deliver. For example, members of the Boyzone fan club were apparently offered special top-of-the-range seats at Boyzone concerts as part of a special package. It seems that the promoters didn't deliver the expected good seats, leading (apparently) to a demand for the return of monies. Such bad experiences can have a very negative effect on the fan base and their support for the artist. The same things seem to have happened to teen TV star Hannah Montana in 2007. Fans were encouraged to join her fan club not apparently on the promise of tickets but on the promise to help them get tickets on what was expected to be a sell-out tour. The fan club failed to deliver and disgruntled fans began a US class action.

OTHER PERSONNEL

TOUR MANAGER
Depending on the size of the tour and your degree of success, you may appoint a tour manager to work alongside your manager in organising the day-to-day details of the tour. Tour managers go out on the tour and handle all crises as they come up. They are generally paid a weekly fixed fee and receive free travel and accommodation and probably a fixed daily sum for expenses.

SOUND AND LIGHTING ENGINEERS
How your music sounds and how you look on stage is crucial to the success of your live performances. Most bands learn at an early stage the importance of having their own sound engineer and not relying on some stranger in a strange venue. As soon as they can afford it, most bands also like to bring along their own lighting engineer. Both of these will be on a daily or weekly rate with free accommodation and travel and daily expenses.

BACKING BAND AND SESSION MUSICIANS
If you're a solo artist, or only one member of your group is signed to the record label, then any backing musicians and singers have to be engaged for the tour. There are many different types of arrangements that can be reached with regular band members. They can be on an annual retainer or on a small, daily-based retainer for when they aren't needed and a higher fee when they have work to do at rehearsals, at personal appearances, interviews and during the tour. When they aren't needed they could be on a first-call basis, which means they have to drop everything to make themselves available for you. Or, they may be completely free to do other work but on the understanding that if you call for them and they aren't available you'll get someone else. You can only afford to do that if they are replaceable. If they are crucial to your 'sound' then you would be better advised to put them on a retainer on a first-call basis.

Other non-regular members of the band will generally be engaged on a daily or weekly rate plus free accommodation and travel and daily expenses. Additional fees may be payable to regular or non-regular members for other promotional work such as appearing in a video, for a live TV or radio performance or a webcast to promote the tour. The fee that they are paid could include any of these extra activities and fees. It's important that you agree a 'buy-out' of all rights on the musicians' or vocalists' performances, whether they are your regular band members or not. If they are Musicians' Union or Equity members, there will be minimum rates for the work you want them to do and rules on what can be bought out in the way of rights and what will be the subject of further repeat fees (details are in Useful Addresses). If you don't buy out the rights you may get into difficulties if you then go ahead and do a TV or video deal for performances including those of the session musicians or singers. You may believe you've cleared all rights and say as much in the contract. If you haven't then the musician or vocalist or their union can come out of the woodwork at the most unhelpful moment. In the light of the recent successful claims by session musicians years after the event (see chapters on publishing and band arrangements) it would also be advisable to get a written confirmation that they have no interest in the songs they are performing.

All these personnel should be given written agreements specifying their fee, when it will be paid and what you expect to get by way of services and rights in return.

Personnel who aren't regular members of the team should enter into confidentiality agreements. These make it clear that they have to keep confidential anything that they find out about you from being on the road with you. They are intended to head off people selling salacious stories and pictures. If, however, they are regular band members then it could be counter-productive, because they could get upset at what they might see as you not trusting them. For more on the issue of privacy see Chapter 12.

The importance of getting things clear in contracts with musicians is borne out by a case involving Elvis Costello.[4]

The Elvis Costello Case

Elvis Costello employed Mr Thomas as a musician to perform on the European tour with him as part of his band. He was also going to do the US tour, but as a part of a separate contract. Costello employed Mr Thomas through his service company, Elvis Costello Limited. The tour had breaks in it between countries in Europe when Mr Thomas's services were not required. Mr Thomas took a seven-day break between the UK and US tours and put in a claim for payment. When he didn't get paid, he applied to the court to wind up/liquidate Costello's company for insolvency, i.e. being unable to pay its debts when they fell due. The court declined to do that, but did order that Mr Thomas be paid on the basis that the court did think it was part of the European tour.

CONCLUSIONS

- If you are already a successful live and recording artist, consider new partners like promoters for your music industry deals.

- Evaluate so-called 360 degree models carefully – they can work if you do your sums right.

- Get yourself a good agent.

- Get adequate insurance.

- Tie touring in with your record company's marketing plans.

- Use the Internet to advertise forthcoming tours.

4 *Elvis Costello Limited* v. *Thomas*, Chancery Division June 1997.

Chapter 11
Band Arrangements

INTRODUCTION

The solo artists and songwriters among you may want to skip this chapter, but if you co-write or plan any kind of recording collaboration it would be worth you reading it to see some of the potential problems.

It may seem very negative to talk about problems before you've released a record or even got a deal. But that's exactly when you should be looking at the things that cause friction within bands. If you address these things at the beginning when everything is going well, it will be much easier and cause less tension. If you wait to raise these issues until you've been on the road non-stop for six months and can't stand the sight of each other then, believe me, it will seriously strain, if not destroy, the relationship.

WHO OWNS THE BAND NAME?

OWNERSHIP

As we saw in Chapter 1, choosing the right name is vital, but once you've decided on a band name and have done what you can to check that you have the right to use it, you have to decide who owns that name.

The record company won't normally expect to own the band name. There are exceptions, particularly in the field of manufactured bands or ones where the record company thinks up the name and concept and hires in people to perform. In such cases they might have a very good reason to say that they should own the name, but this then forms part of the deal. Some production companies are also insisting on having the right to hire and fire members of a band. Maybe if it is an entirely manufactured band this is acceptable but not, I think, if the band comes to the label already formed. What the record company will expect you to do is to confirm that you have the right to use the name and that they have the exclusive right to use it in connection with the recordings you make under the record contract and a non-exclusive right after the contract ends. Music publishers will also want the exclusive right to use the name in connection with exploitation of your songs during the term of the publishing contract and a non-exclusive right after the end of the term. You don't want to give exclusive rights for all uses of the name to any one company, for example your record company, as that would mean that you couldn't then use your name to sell merchandise or do a sponsorship deal.

WHO WITHIN THE BAND OWNS THE NAME?

It is essential that you sort this out at the beginning. I also firmly believe that you should put what you've agreed in writing. But I realise that I'm probably whistling in the wind. I tell every band about to sign a deal that they should have a band agreement. They usually nod and say that they understand why they should have one, but most of them never do anything about it. But, bear in mind the case we looked at in Chapter 1 that decided that if it isn't spelled out in an agreement no band member can use the name without the agreement of the others. It doesn't have to be a terribly formal document – although I would advise that a proper band agreement drawn up by a lawyer would be best. Even if you don't go for that it would be better than nothing to write down what you've all agreed and sign it and then keep it in a safe place. You may think that this is over the top and a bit unnecessary, but if you can't prove who owns the band name you can get the very unedifying spectacle of two or more band members arguing over who has the right to use the name and possibly ending up with none of them being able to do so.

An example of this in practice is the ongoing legal suit in the US where Mike Love is claiming to have the sole right to use the Beach Boys name. He is suing ex-bandmate Al Jardine for, he claims, illegally using the name.

Holly Johnson, former lead singer with the band Frankie Goes To Hollywood, is another who was trying to claim sole right to use the name. For such a relatively short-lived band this one sure does seem to have generated quite a bit of litigation.

Frankie Goes To Hollywood Trade Mark Case

Holly Johnson tried to register a trade mark in FRANKIE GOES TO HOLLYWOOD for goods and services including music, video and recording goods, entertainment, clothing and other merchandise. He was opposed by the other members of the band, Peter Gill, Mark O'Toole, Paul Rutherford and Brian Nash. The Registrar decided that the goodwill in the name was owned by the band as a whole which had accrued from the point that recording and performance started and no agreement regarding ownership of that goodwill had been made at the outset. If Mr Johnson were allowed to use it alone then this would be a misrepresentation and result in damage to the other members. This was the case even though he was the better known of the former band members. Mr Johnson had acknowledged there was a partnership and it was a fact that he had not established any goodwill in that name before he was a member of that partnership. So as soon as they started recording together as members of the partnership goodwill began to accrue to that partnership. In an echo back to the cases of Liberty X and Blue, the Registrar found that even after sixteen years of inactivity there was still residual goodwill to protect. They still sold records and there was other evidence that they still have goodwill – one example was the fact that an episode of the TV series *Friends* featured a character wearing a 'Frankie Says Relax' T-shirt. It can happen that just one or two members of the band own the band name, for example where they form the core of the band and the others aren't permanent members. A band may be made up of a core of the vocalist and the lead guitarist who do most of the writing, and a rhythm section of bassist and drummer on a wage and not signed to the record contract. The core members may not want to share ownership of the band name with the other two unless and until they become full-time permanent band members. But as the Frankie case highlights it is essential that this fact is recorded at the outset.

It's more common to agree that all members of the band own the band name. More sophisticated band agreements could set out who gets to use the name if the band splits up. You may decide that, in that case, none of you could carry on using the name or that those who carry on performing together as a band can continue to use the band name and that the one who leaves can't. Then you get problems if two or more members leave and set up another band. There is no simple solution and it's something that you should talk over with your lawyer, as they will have some suggestions that you may want to adopt.

That said, you may not in fact get any say in what happens to the band name if the band splits up, because the record contract may well decide the issue for you. The contract might say that the record company has final say over who can continue to use the band name. This may seem unfair but, if you think about it, the record company has invested a lot of time and money in building up your name and the reputation in your name through their marketing efforts. They won't want to risk losing control of that if one or more members of the band were to leave and, as a result, no one could continue to use the name. You may get a chance to say no to this if you already have a band agreement in place or, as usual, if you have a lot of bargaining power. If the record company does decide who gets to use the band name then you have to think about whether the other band members should be paid some kind of compensation for the loss of the right to use the name. As made clear by the *Frankie Goes To Hollywood* case above it's possible that, either under the terms of the partnership/band agreement or by the operation of the Partnership Act 1890, the band name will be treated as an asset of the partnership that forms part of its 'goodwill'. There are formulas that accountants can use to work out how much that goodwill is worth. If, for example, the partnership is dissolved because the band splits up and the vocalist continues as a solo artist, then the others could have the value of their share of the goodwill in the name calculated and paid to them as part of the settlement between the band members. It's quite a difficult and delicate question and needs to be treated carefully. This is another good reason why you should sort it out at the beginning before any tensions (or pretensions) get in the way.

BAND STRUCTURES

You can decide on the ownership of the name and other things, such as how the income is to be divided between you, but before your lawyer can put what you've agreed into a legal document you also need to decide what legal form the arrangements between you are going to take. There is no simple answer as to which is best. Each band's needs are going to be different and you have to look at each on its own merits. It's important that you involve both your lawyer and your accountant on this question, as your lawyer will be looking to protect you from a legal viewpoint and your accountant will be looking at the financial and tax implications for you of the different types of agreement. Your accountant will know your personal circumstances and will be able to advise whether one type of structure works better than another for you.

The two main types of arrangement are a limited company and a partnership. There is also a subspecies called the limited liability partnership which is a kind of hybrid of the two with features of a partnership, such as joint liability for debts, but with an element of limitation on the extent of an individual partner's liability to third parties. This structure has been adopted by at least one label I know of and is common amongst professional partnerships such as larger law firms. Ask your accountant if it could work for your band.

If you decide that the band should be a partnership then the band agreement will usually take the form of a partnership deed. This is like a legal contract that sets out how the partnership is going to operate on a day-by-day basis and puts in writing what has been agreed about the band name, the split of earnings and so on. If you decide to become a limited company then you'll probably be advised to have a shareholders' agreement, which does the same thing essentially as a partnership deed but also deals with what happens to your shares in the company if the band splits up or one or more members leave. At the risk of confusing things even more, it's also possible for the band to take the form of a partnership or a limited company, and for the individual members to decide to set up their own company to provide their services to the band through a company. I'll go into this in more detail below.

LIMITED COMPANY

A few years ago accountants regularly advised bands to set up a limited company for some or all of the band's services in the entertainment business. There were good tax reasons for doing so, especially the tax year out, which was only available to employees and not to self-employed individuals or partners in a partnership. This particular tax loophole has now been closed and so the tax advantages have been considerably reduced. The reasons now for setting up a limited company are more complex and you're going to have to take specialist advice from your accountant and lawyer.

The main advantages are:

• You can spread your income (for example, a large advance) over a number of years and therefore not have it all taxed in the year in which you get it.

• It may be a more tax-efficient way of distributing income to band members.

• It might protect you from legal actions because anyone bringing such an action would have to sue the company in the first instance.

Also, if a lot of the band's income is going to be earned overseas, an offshore company may be used to avoid paying UK tax until you decide you need to have access to the money in the UK.

Among the main disadvantages are that there are more rules governing what companies can and can't do, accounts have to be published so members of the public could find out how much you earn (although there are exemptions that allow small companies to file abbreviated accounts) and there are also higher administration charges with a limited company.

Obviously, the sooner you get advice and decide on the band structure the better. If you leave it too late and try and put the structure in place after you've already entered into contracts, things get much more complicated. If you've already done a record deal as individuals and you then decide you're going to have a limited company, the record deals would have to be 'novated' (i.e. renewed) in the name of the company. Also, if you've already received some money as an individual, this might jeopardise a scheme to take money out of the country or may result in the Inland Revenue deciding you should be taxed as individuals, regardless of the existence of the limited company.

On a more basic level, if you decide halfway through the negotiation of a record or publishing deal to change the structure, the business affairs person at the record or publishing company isn't going to find this very funny, as they'll have to redraft the contract to deal with the new structure. I was recently told an hour before a record contract was about to be signed with a major record company that the deal was to be done through a limited company. The record contract was with the individual. When I rang the record company's lawyer to let him know, he was in despair. Ten people were meeting in an hour to get this contract signed – we had no time to change it. So they had to go through a fiction that the deal was signed, drink the champagne and have the photos taken. Then we lawyers went away to turn it into a deal with the limited company so that it could actually be signed and the company paid the money.

If you do decide on a limited company, bear in mind that you'll have to pay to get the company set up, to have the name that you want (assuming that name is available) and you'll have to pay the annual running costs.

The band members will be the shareholders and you'll have to agree how many shares each member is going to have. This will probably be an equal number but need not be. Day-to-day decisions on the running of a limited company generally require a 50%-plus majority. If it's a two-member band and each has 50% of the shares then each can block a decision by the other. Major decisions of the company generally require a 75%-plus majority. So, if you have a four-member band with equal shareholdings, one member could block major changes but three could gang up on the fourth to push through day-to-day decisions. To get around the problems that this could bring, the band is usually advised to put a shareholders' agreement in place which will govern how day-to-day matters are to be dealt with. Major decisions could require unanimous agreement, otherwise three out of four band members could vote through a major change against the wishes of the fourth. The shareholders' agreement will also deal with what is to happen if a member wants to leave. It will usually require that they resign as an officer of the company and that they first offer their shares to the other band members. If a value for the shares can't be agreed, an accountant is usually brought in as an arbitrator to decide the matter.

PARTNERSHIP

This is the main alternative structure for bands at present without the limited liability option but that may change if limited liability partnerships gain further ground. The band members are in partnership together for the particular venture of being a band. All partners are treated equally and profits and losses are shared by all. You'll usually be advised to put a partnership agreement in writing. That agreement will decide how the venture is going to be run on a day-to-day basis, whether all partners are equal (or whether some are more equal than others) and what is to happen to the band name if the partnership is dissolved. It will record whether anyone has put any money (or goods, such as equipment) into the partnership and, if so, whether the money is intended to be working capital of the business or a loan, and whether the equipment has been gifted to the partnership or is still owned by one member and is on loan to the band. Does each band member own the equipment he uses, for example a drum kit or a guitar? What if it was bought with band advances – does that make it joint property? What about the vocalist who has no equipment other than a microphone or two? Does he share ownership of other equipment with other band members? The partnership deed should also deal with these things.

A partnership agreement can also deal with the question of who is entitled to what shares of the songs, the publishing advances and income. This is a very tricky subject and a very emotive one, which is why I say that it should be dealt with at the beginning of the relationship before money starts to be earned from the songs (see Chapter 4).

Even if you don't have a written agreement, there can still be a partnership. The taxman will look at the reality of how you work together and how things like the band income are dealt with.

SERVICE AGREEMENTS

Regardless of the structure in place for the band, it's possible for an individual band member to have his own company, which we call a service company. This service company is exclusively entitled to some or all of the individual's services in the entertainment business. The service company can then enter into the record or publishing deal, hold shares in the band's company or an interest in the partnership. Record and publishing companies are used to these arrangements and are usually happy to incorporate them into their contractual arrangements, especially if they are told at an early stage. They will usually want the individual to sign an agreement, called an inducement letter, to confirm that the service company is entitled to his services and agreeing that if the service company drops out of the picture for any reason he will abide by the contract personally.

A service company is usually set up for tax reasons but the Inland Revenue looks closely at service companies, as they are often used as a device to add weight to an individual claiming that he is self-employed and not an employee. For example, if a record producer was engaged as an in-house producer/engineer at a recording studio, and he had a service company and claimed he was not an employee of the recording studio, the Inland Revenue have said that they will look behind the service company at what the real relationship is between the producer and the studio. If all the indicators are that the relationship is actually one of an employee, then he will be taxed as if he were an employee.[1]

This issue often comes up when an artist engages musicians for a particular tour or to record an album. The musicians may want to be treated as self-employed. The musicians' contracts have to be very carefully drawn up to establish the existence of a self-employed relationship. This is definitely one for the lawyers.

BAND INCOME

Whatever structure you put in place, you have to decide what is to happen to the income.

Record, video, touring, merchandise and sponsorship income is usually shared between all band members. As we've seen, there are exceptions where a band consists of one or two core members who are signed up to the record or publishing deal and the other members are employed to work alongside these. In such cases these 'employed' members are usually either put on a retainer or a weekly wage, or they're employed as session musicians. Session musicians are only paid when they work but, as they aren't usually signed up exclusively; they are free to work for others (see Chapter 5).

While most disputes usually arise in the area of songwriting income, this doesn't mean that arguments never arise in relation to recording income or indeed sometimes both.

---

[1] The Inland Revenue has issued guidelines with some quite useful examples of what are the main indicators to someone being either employed or self-employed. It is called IR35 and can be obtained from your local Inland Revenue office.

The Cure Case

Laurence Tolhurst, the former drummer and co-founder of the band The Cure, who was asked to leave the band in 1989, sued the lead singer of the band and their record company for damages arising out of deals done in 1986.[2] Tolhurst argued that the record deal done with Fiction Records Limited in 1986 gave Robert Smith the lion's share of the recording income and left him with 'the crumbs'. He asked the court to agree that there was a partnership in place and to order Smith to account to him for 50% of all profits receivable under the 1986 agreement. He also argued that he had been forced to enter into the 1986 agreement by undue influence exerted by the record company and its owner, Chris Parry. He said that Mr Parry and Fiction Records should account to him for all their profit under the 1986 deal after an allowance for their skill and labour.

The case turned into a character attack on Tolhurst as allegations were made that his contribution to the band's success had declined as a result of his drinking problems. Part of Tolhurst's case was that he hadn't been given enough information about the 1986 deal before he signed it and that he hadn't had independent legal advice. Once again we see the familiar theme emerging – Tolhurst argued that the deal should be set aside and that the court should order an account of all record income to determine how much he was actually entitled to.

The court dismissed his claim and said that the question of undue influence didn't arise because, although the record company would have been in a position to exercise undue influence, the terms offered were not obviously bad. In fact, the judge thought that Tolhurst was lucky to have been offered these arrangements at all in the circumstances, and found that he hadn't signed the 1986 agreement under undue influence. The fact that he hadn't had independent legal advice didn't affect the court's decision, because the deal was not a bad one. The judge also decided that there was no partnership in place in respect of the 1986 agreement, as Smith and Tolhurst had, in fact, come to a different arrangement on what was to happen to the income.

Disputes often arise in relation to songwriting income. There's no problem if all members of the band contribute equally to the songwriting process. Then the income from songwriting should be split equally. This is, however, rare. Much more common is the situation where only one or two members of the band write all the songs. This can give rise to two possible sources of resentment. Those who write the songs could come to resent sharing advances or royalties with the non-writing members of the band. Or, if the writers don't share the income, this then gives rise to resentment from the non-writers, who miss out on a potentially lucrative form of income.

Of course, leaving aside these tensions, there may also be arguments about who actually wrote what. As we saw in the *Kemp* case, the other members of Spandau Ballet brought a case against Gary Kemp arguing that they were entitled to a share in the publishing income as co-writers of the music on the songs they recorded. They were unsuccessful, but there will be other arguments as to how much band members actually contribute to the creative process by the way in which they interpret or perform the song. If the contribution is a genuine one then they should be credited as a co-writer, but is their contribution the same as that of the main writers? If not, what is the value of their contribution?

2 *Tolhurst v. Smith and Others* [1994] EMLR 508.

What do you do if not all members of the band write and a publishing advance comes in and the band is broke? Just imagine the tensions that could then occur if the main songwriter takes the publishing advance and doesn't share it with the others. Even if he agrees to share the advance equally with the others, what will happen when the advances are recouped and publishing royalties start to come through? Should the royalties then go to the main songwriters or continue to be divided equally? There isn't one answer to this, as it's so personal to the individuals concerned. You only have to look at the above cases to realise how important it is to try to sort this out.

Here are three examples of ways in which I have seen bands deal with this issue. There are many more possibilities.

One band I know had an arrangement where one member controlled all the songwriting and took all the publishing income. When this began to cause tensions, he volunteered to share percentages of his publishing income from some songs with the other band members.

I've also heard the story, which may be a myth, that the members of rock band Queen had an agreement where they got to be credited as writer of the songs on the singles in turn. If true, this is very democratic, but doesn't really deal with the problem if some of the band members are weaker songwriters and don't write such successful songs as others in the band.

A third way of dealing with it that I've come across is to share the advances and royalties equally until the advances have been recouped. After that, each band member would have his own account with the publisher and the income from each writer's contribution to the songs would then be paid into his own account.

Three very different solutions to a very ticklish issue. Whatever works for you should be written down as soon as possible. If circumstances change, review the arrangements and see if it would be fair to change them.

ACCOUNTING AND TAX

One of the main things that cause problems with a band is tax and VAT. In both cases, bands often don't keep enough money back to pay the bills. HM Revenue & Customs (the VAT man) have very heavy powers to impose penalties on you. They are often one of the main creditors forcing a winding up of a limited company and they can and will make you bankrupt. Even if they give you time to pay, there will be financial penalties and interest to pay. Believe me you won't get away with it.

Your accountant will advise you how much should be kept to one side for tax, and if he's doing your books for you he'll be able to tell you what to expect to have to pay the VAT man. He'll also probably advise you to keep all your receipts. You can then sort out which ones you can legitimately recharge as business expenses against tax. If you haven't kept them there is no proof. So do yourself a favour – get a cardboard box and get into the habit of throwing all your receipts into it. If you were more organised you could have a file divided into the months of the year and put the receipts in the relevant month. This makes life a lot easier for you or your bookkeeper/accountant when it comes to doing the books.

You'll need a band account and, unless your accountant is doing all the books for you, you'll need a basic accounting system. This could be a simple computer spreadsheet. In it you'd keep a record of the income you received, where it was from and what your expenses were for doing that work. So if you did a gig in March you'd record how much you received and how much it cost you to do the gig (and don't forget to keep receipts for all your expenses).

LEAVING MEMBER PROVISIONS

These are the clauses in recording or publishing agreements with bands that deal with what happens if one or more members of a band leave or the band disbands totally before the contract is over. The record or publishing company naturally wants to try to prevent this happening. They've invested a lot of money in supporting the band, making records or videos and in promoting them around the world. The last thing they want is a band falling apart on them. But, of course, no words in a contract are going to keep a band together if one or more of them have decided to call it a day. Individuals develop personally and creatively, and not necessarily in the same direction as other band members. One member of the band may get married and have children and not want to spend as much time on the road. Or they may change their artistic style, which might be more suited to a solo career than as a member of a band. Of course, there are also the possibilities that the band members will grow to hate the sight of each other after years on the road, or that the band just comes to the end of what it can do creatively. It used to be the case that when this happened the deal ended and the companies moved on to the next potential big thing. Nowadays, with so much money resting on building the reputation of an artist, when a split happens the record or publishing company wants to be able to try and salvage what it can of its investment. It will want to have the option to pick up the rights in any new projects that the writers or artists go into without having to compete in the open market.

The record company will also want to try to have the right to continue to use the name of the band that they've invested a lot of money in building up as a brand.

Record and publishing companies will also want to have the option to pick and choose whom they continue the deal with (sometimes called the Remaining Members) and whom they drop.

For example, if the drummer leaves the band the record company will want the right to continue with the remaining members of the band on the basis that they continue to perform and record as a band. They will also want to have a contract with any replacement drummer, who may be put on the same terms as the remaining members or may be on a retainer basis.

If the whole band splits up, the company will want the option to do new contracts with each individual member. A publisher might only do new contracts with those they know are writers who will probably go on to do other things. A record company may decide only to continue their deal with the lead vocalist or other main focus of the band, guessing that they will team up with other artists to form another band or will have a solo career.

There's usually a system built into the contract that gives the record or publishing company a breathing space while they try to work out what they're going to do. The record contract will usually give the company the option to call for a leaving member to deliver to them demo tapes of what he would do as a solo artist or with his new band. They will usually provide studio time for him to make these demos. The contract may also require the remaining members of the band to demo new tracks, with or without a replacement member, to see if the company think there is a future for the band or if they should drop them now. The record or publishing company may know immediately whether they want to continue with a leaving member or any or all of the remaining members and may come to a quick decision. Don't hold your breath, though – they will probably take the maximum time they have under the contract in order to look at their options.

Once demo tapes have been delivered to the record company, they usually have a month or two to decide what to do. In that time, both the leaving member and the remaining members of the band are in limbo. The term of the contract is usually suspended in the meantime.

The record company may decide to take up an option on the leaving member's new project but not that of the remaining members, or vice versa. They may also decide to take up their option on the remaining members. They may decide to abandon both to their fate.

For the leaving member or remaining members who are dropped from the contract, that is the end of their obligations to the record or publishing company. They don't have to repay to the company their share of any unrecouped balance on the account. However, their share of royalties from recordings made or songs written by them up to the time of the decision to drop them will continue to be applied to recoup the unrecouped balance. The dropped artist or songwriter won't see royalties from those recordings or songs until that advance has been fully repaid.

For example, let's assume that there was an unrecouped balance on the record account of £100,000 and that the record company continues with three remaining members and drops a fourth (leaving) member. Let's also assume that the band shared advances and royalties equally. The leaving member's share of the debt and of the royalties will be 25%. The leaving member's 25% share of royalties from recordings made while he was a member of the band will go to recoup £25,000 of the unrecouped £100,000 debt. After that's happened, 25% of any further royalties from those recordings will be paid through to the leaving member.

If the record company continues with the remaining members and pays them further advances, the leaving member's share of royalties doesn't get used to recoup those additional advances as he won't have received any share of them. His debt is fixed at the time he is dropped from the contract by the record company, or at least it should be. This is something your lawyer has to deal with when he negotiates the contract.

The situation with the remaining members whose contracts continue is slightly more complicated. Their 75% of the royalties from those old recordings goes to recoup their 75% share of the unrecouped balance (£75,000 in our example). Their share of anything else that's earned from the old recordings first goes to recoup any new advances they have received and only when both the old account and the new account is recouped will they be paid any royalties. It also works the other way around. The royalties from their new recordings go first to recoup the new advances. Any surplus goes to recoup their 75% share of the old debt. Only when both accounts are recouped will they see royalties from the new recordings.

If the contract continues with any remaining members, or if a new contract is issued to the leaving member, the record or publishing company will want to continue to have the same rights to the leaving member and/or remaining members as it had under the original recording or publishing contracts. There are, however, one or two parts of the contract that they like to try to change. The record company will often try to change the minimum recording commitment from an album to singles, the rationale being that until the record company knows how the new line-up will perform in the marketplace they don't want to risk committing to make an album. With singles being seen as largely a promotional tool for album-based artists, if your music isn't directed to the singles market you should hold out for an album commitment.

The record label will also usually want options to future albums. This could either be for the number of albums left under the original deal, or for that number plus one or two more. This should be agreed at the time the record deal is originally negotiated, when you'll have more bargaining power. There's no guarantee that the record company will want to negotiate this with you in the middle of a leaving member/band split situation.

The record royalties are usually the same as under the old agreement, but may go back to the rate that applied in the first contract period so, if you've received an increase in your royalty based either on record sales or because it's later in the contract, it might go back to the rate before the increase took effect.

The advances are usually a fraction of the advance that you would have got for that contract period. For example, if you were a four-piece band and one of you left and you would have been entitled to £100,000 for the next album, then the remaining three members will expect to be entitled to £75,000. This isn't, however, a foregone conclusion. Your lawyer will have to fight for it on your behalf.

Because an artist walks away from the unrecouped debt and has a chance to start again, many are actually crossing their fingers and hoping they'll be dropped. This is a fairly short-term response though, because it will all depend on whether they can get into a new deal. It's certainly no reason to split up a band in the hope that you'll get dropped.

There are leaving member clauses that have special arrangements. There may be different rules on recoupment, or different levels of new advances, depending on which member of the band leaves and how 'key' he is seen to be to the proceedings. They may feel that the lead vocalist/front man should command a larger advance and more preferential terms if he leaves than, say the bassist. They may even say that they're only interested in leaving member rights for the key people.

As you can imagine, these sorts of provisions can be very disruptive and, if it's the band's first deal, such arrangements ought really to be avoided both from the record company's viewpoint and the band's. At this early stage, no one knows who is going to turn out to be the star. Who'd have thought the Genesis drummer, Phil Collins, would turn out to be an excellent lead vocalist and very successful solo artist?

Different arrangements can also occur with publishing deals. For example, one of the four writer-performers in the band may be a prolific writer for adverts or jingles in addition to his work for the band. In these circumstances, it's possible for all four members to have separate accounts and to initially receive an equal share of the advances. It only really works if each writer earns an equal share of the income, as that goes first to recoup the total band advances. After that, if this writer earns significantly more from his work as a jingles writer, his income from that source is only credited to his account. At the next accounting date he will then receive a correspondingly larger royalty cheque.

One area that will probably have to change in publishing deals after someone leaves is the Minimum Commitment. If one songwriter previously wrote 25% of an album and the others 75% and after a split both are expected to deliver 100% of an album each then there is going to be a problem. So in leaving member clauses in publishing deals, your lawyer will usually try to reduce the commitment to an achievable level.

WHAT HAPPENS TO A BAND'S ASSETS ON A SPLIT?

If there is a partnership or band agreement then that will say what happens to the band's assets if the band splits up or one or more members leave.

If there's no written or verbal agreement that you can prove between the band members and if they're in a partnership, then the rather antiquated Partnership Act 1890 will govern what happens. Essentially the partnership is dissolved unless all partners elect that it can continue. If agreement can't be reached on a fair way of dealing with the assets then the partnership is dissolved and the assets have to be realised (i.e. sold) and the proceeds divided equally between the partners. If agreement can't be reached on whether something such as the goodwill and reputation in the band name should be given a value and, if so, what value, the matter is usually referred to an accountant acting as an arbitrator. The way, if at all, that the record company deals with the name in the recording agreement may help determine if it has a value.

If the band were not a partnership but had shares in a limited company then the shareholders' agreement and/or the Memorandum and Articles of Association will say what is to happen. Usually, the remaining members would want to have the right to require the leaving member to resign from any office as director or company secretary and also to sell his shares. The arrangements would normally give the remaining members the right to buy those shares back at a certain price or in accordance with a fixed formula. Or it may require the shares to be valued by an independent accountant. Tax questions could arise here, so everyone should take advice from an accountant or a tax lawyer if a split occurs. In the absence of written arrangements, there is a danger that the company could become unworkable. If the leaving member is a director or a company secretary and he hasn't been guilty of any wrongdoing, then without a written agreement it won't be easy to remove him from office. If he has service contracts, employment advice should be sought before terminating those arrangements. Without an agreement you can't easily get shareholders to sell their shares and, depending on the size of their shareholding, they could block votes requiring a 75%-plus majority or, indeed, those requiring a simple 50%-plus majority if it's a two-man band or two or more members out of a four-piece band have left.

Once agreement has been reached as to what to do with the band's assets, this should be recorded in a settlement agreement, which should be drawn up by a lawyer. This is particularly important for matters such as rights to band names or copyrights.

If no agreement can be reached, the parties are headed almost inevitably towards litigation and the courts. Even though the reform of the legal system in England and Wales now places considerable emphasis on conciliation and alternative dispute resolution (ADR) we still see the largely unedifying spectacle of bands fighting it out in court.

The partnership or band agreement should be very clear as to who owns what and who has brought what into the deal. For example, if one of the band members has a Transit van that he allows the band to use then that should be noted. A band member could also have put money into the band to keep it going. This is either a loan to the band, with or without interest, or, more practically, it's a gift for the use of the partnership that they may or may not be allowed to get back an equivalent sum if they leave. It's also usual for the leaving band member to take with him any band equipment that he particularly uses. This is fair, unless one person has the use of a lot of expensive equipment, which was paid for out of band advances. In that case you would expect the equipment to be valued and for each remaining band member to either get equipment to that value, or be paid his share of its value by the leaving member who is going to take the equipment away.

If a band name is genuinely closely associated with one individual then it's fair to say that that individual should be allowed to continue to use the name after the band splits. But as it will have been all the band members that will have helped to make the name successful, the person using the name after a band splits up should compensate the others. If a figure can't be agreed it can be referred to an accountant to value it. In many cases, however, the name dies with the end of the band.

Each band member should continue to be responsible for his share of the record or publishing company unrecouped balance. This will usually be covered by the record or publishing deal. Once the old accounts are recouped, the individual band members should be entitled to their agreed share of any royalties.

It's also wise to decide whether the band members have to unanimously agree before something can be done with the material that they created together, or if it's going to be a majority decision. For example, a few years after a band splits the record company wants to put out a Greatest Hits album. The record contract may give the band approval over whether the record company can do this. The band agreement should say whether all the band members have to agree or not. The democratic thing would be to say yes, they should. The practical thing would be to say that it has to be a majority decision, so that one person couldn't hold a gun to the heads of the others or their record company. The same situation arises with approvals of the use of material in adverts or films. My own view is that it should be a decision of all band members where this is practically possible but that, if the band has split up and one or more have gone out of the business and aren't easily contactable, then the decision of the remaining members who are in contact should prevail.

Recently there has been a spate of cases and claims involving the boy band, Busted.

James Bourne v. *Brandon Davis*

Between December 2000 and October 2001 James Bourne, Matthew Sergeant, Kiley Fitzgerald and Owen Doyle composed and performed songs together as an early line-up of the band Busted. There was no written agreement but the judge accepted that there was a partnership at will just as we saw in the Frankie Goes To Hollywood case above. This line-up split in 2001 and James Bourne and Matthew Sergeant joined up with Charlie Simpson to form the new Busted line-up and in March 2002 this line-up signed a record deal with Universal-Island Records. As part of that deal James Bourne assigned all his performing rights in the earlier recordings to Universal-Island. This is quite common. This line-up was very successful and continued until January 2005 when it again split up and James Bourne went on to form a new group called Son of Dork. In August 2005 he did a new record deal with Mercury Records and again assigned his performing rights in performances of his before the date of the contract.

In 2005 Brandon Davis issued a nine-track CD featuring performances of the original line-up made in a hotel in 2001. Immediately James Bourne, Mercury Records and Universal-Island issued proceedings for an immediate injunction alleging infringement of Mr Bourne's performance rights and passing off by using the name Busted in relation to these recordings. The court ordered an immediate injunction in September 2005. In October 2005 Mr Doyle, from the original line-up, purported to sell to Mr Davis all the consents necessary in respect of his performances and assigning to him the copyright and performer's property rights and other rights in connection with those recordings. Mr Davis argued that this agreement had the effect of assigning all the performer's property rights of all four – on the basis that it was partnership property and he as a partner could deal with it and bind all his partners. The judge accepted that all performers' property rights could become partnership property. It would not be necessary for there to be a formal agreement to give effect to this. Where Mr Davis's claim failed was because he had waited too long after they split to do anything. Four years was too long a gap to claim that Mr Doyle was acting in the ordinary course of their partnership to sell the property rights of the partnership. Nor could it be seen as part of the winding up of the partnership. But even if they were partnership property they were still held by the individuals who retained a beneficial interest so the partnership did not have exclusive rights to dispose of the rights. At best they could argue that the rights should be applied for the benefit of the partnership not of the individuals. So James Bourne was within his rights to grant his individual performer's rights to the record companies, Mr Davis did not have the right to the rights because he knew Mr Doyle didn't have Mr Bourne's authority for the assignment and in any event for something like this the consent of all four members would have been required under the Copyright Act (s 191 A(4)).

The main lesson to be learned from this somewhat complex legal case is that to avoid any doubt it is best to deal, in writing, with partnership arrangements and rights such as performer's rights as well as copyright.

But that is not the end of the disputes involving members of Busted. Two of that original line-up – Kiley Fitzgerald and Owen Doyle – have brought an action arguing that Universal-Island released recordings featuring their vocal performances in the 2002 eponymous album *Busted*. They also claim that they were integral in the creation of Busted including coming up with the name and co-writing some of the band's early hits. They claim that there were unfairly cut out of the equation by the manager, Richard Rashman, and that Rashman failed to fulfil his contractual commitments as a manager to protect their interests by making them sign agreements on their departure that greatly favoured Rashman and the remaining band members. They are claiming a share of the royalties from the bands' early songs and trade mark use. Unless it settles the trial is set for February 2008.

CONCLUSIONS

- Decide on a good name for the band and protect it as far as you can.

- Decide on a band structure and put a written agreement in place.

- Decide who is going to be allowed to use the name if you split up.

- Make sure any leaving member clauses in your contracts are fair.

- Decide these things while you're still friends.

Chapter 12
Moral Rights and the Privacy of the Individual

INTRODUCTION

Moral rights have their origins in well-established European principles of law aimed at protecting creative types and ensuring their works are treated with respect. These are also called *droit moral*. In this chapter I'm only going to give an overview of these rights and of where they can be used. There are many books on the subject if you want to read into this further.[1]

Moral rights are separate from copyright. In some circumstances you can keep your moral rights when you've had to assign your copyright to someone else.

In Europe it has long been felt that an artist's rights to receive economic (i.e. financial) reward for the use of his work can be adequately protected by the copyright laws. However, the integrity of the work itself deserves separate protection. Hence the development of a separate *droit moral*. The UK legal tradition makes economic rights more important than those of artistic integrity. Why doesn't the UK value the integrity of creative works, you may well ask? It's not that we don't give them a value. It's a question of emphasis and the answer lies in the cultural differences between the UK and the rest of Europe and in the different legal histories they have.

The European principles of moral rights were included in the major international legal convention on intellectual property, the Berne Convention[2] and, in particular, the 1948 Brussels Revision of the Berne Convention.[3]

The UK lagged a long way behind and, indeed, the fact that we didn't incorporate the two basic moral rights into UK law meant that for many years the UK was unable to fully comply with the Berne Convention.

As the UK became more integrated into Europe it became clear that we were out of step not only in not fully complying with the Berne Convention but also in not giving sufficient weight to these rights. The general principles of harmonisation, which govern the operation of the European Union, meant that the UK had to come in line on these moral rights. As we will see, it did so, but in a peculiarly British fashion.

The 1988 Copyright Designs & Patents Act was the first UK statute that effectively incorporated all the principal moral rights. There had been limited moral rights in the 1956 Copyright Act but the 1988 Act was the one that brought the UK in line with Europe and enabled us to comply with the provisions of the Berne Convention.[4] Since 1 February 2006 performers also have the legal right to be identified as the performer and to object to derogatory treatment of their recorded or broadcast performances[5]

---

1   See Copinger & Skone-James on Copyright, (15th edition Sweet & Maxwell, 2005) for a more detailed legal description of UK moral rights.
2   It first appeared in the 1925 Rome Treaty.
3   Article 6 bis of the 1948 Brussels Revision to the Berne Convention contains two basic moral rights: the right to be identified as an author of a work and the right not to have that work distorted, mutilated or otherwise altered in a manner which would be prejudicial to the author's honour or reputation.
4   The moral rights are found in Chapter 4 of the Act in sections 77–89. The remedies are found in section 103ff.
5   The Performances (Moral Rights,etc.) Regulations 2006.

The moral rights aren't linked to who owns the copyright in the work in question. They may be the same person, but not necessarily. For example, you could assign your rights to the copyright in a musical work to a music publisher, but as the author of the work in question you could retain your moral rights. In fact, in law you can't assign moral rights, they remain with you or your beneficiaries on your death. This is intended to protect you from unscrupulous people who may want you to assign your moral rights alongside your copyright. However, there is more than one means to an end.

If you and your fellow band members write a musical work together then you each have these moral rights independent of each other. Just because one of you has decided to abandon his moral rights doesn't mean that the rest of you have to.

In reality, the 1988 Act merely put into law what had previously been dealt with in contracts. The crucial difference was that in a contract you can only bind your contracting partner, whereas with moral rights you can enforce them against third parties who were not party to the contract. For example, you may have a clause in your contract that says you have to be credited as the composer of the music. If your publishing company forgets to do this, it's a breach of contract and you can sue them. If, however, the works are licensed for inclusion on a compilation album and the compilation company doesn't credit you, then unless you have your moral rights you can't take action because the contract is between the compilation company and your record company and not with you. If you have your moral rights, you can take action against the compilation company for breach of your moral right to be identified as the author, whether or not your publishing company wants to take any action.

WHAT ARE THESE RIGHTS?

There are four moral rights, but only three of them are likely to affect you. These three rights only exist in respect of copyright works.[6] If a work is out of copyright then you don't have moral rights in relation to it.

THE RIGHT OF PATERNITY

The first moral right is the right to be properly identified as the author of the work or the performer when the performer's performance is broadcast or when a recording of his performance is communicated to the public.[7] This is also known as the paternity right.

The right is owned by the author of a copyright literary, dramatic, musical or artistic work, and the performer in relation to his performances. So, as a composer or lyricist of original songs, you would have the right to be identified as having written the words or composed the music and as a performer your name or stage name or the name of your group should also be identified in a manner likely to be noticed by the audience for your performance.

It's also possible that you'll have moral rights in the artwork used for the packaging of your records if you were the person who created that work (see Chapter 5 on artwork). You'll notice, though, that the owners of the sound recording copyright don't have moral rights in that sound recording.

---

6 Sections 178 and 1(2) CDPA.
7 Section 77 CDPA.

The right exists in relation to a musical work and lyrics when that work is exploited in one of five ways:

1. When the work is commercially published; this includes not only sheet music but also in sound recordings or as soundtracks to films.

2. The issue to the public of copies of the work in the form of sound recordings.

3. The showing in public of a film, the soundtrack of which includes the work.

4. The issue to the public of copies of a film, the soundtrack of which includes the work. Remember that the definition of 'film' will include videos and DVD.

5. If a work has been adapted and the adaptation is exploited in one of the above ways then you have the right to be identified as the author of the work that has been adapted. If the arrangement itself is capable of copyright protection then the author of the adaptation may also have a right to be identified as its author.

There is now a moral right to be identified as the performer when that work is broadcast, or a recording of it is communicated to the public but there are exceptions. The requirement that the performer must be identified does not apply when it's not reasonably practicable and it also doesn't apply when the performance is given for reasons relating to advertising or news reporting. What about the poor DJs who'd be in danger of breaching your moral rights every time they irritatingly didn't give you a name check after playing your record on the radio? There is no guidance at present as to whether it would be taken as being 'not reasonably practicable' to name all the performers on a recording. Common sense suggests that a failure to give the group or performers name or stage name would be a breach unless it was inadvertent but it would not be practicable to name every performer, including session players. It may now be necessary in session musicians' agreements to specifically waive the moral rights to be identified.

If you have moral rights in the artistic work (the artwork), that right comes into effect when that work is exploited in one of the following ways:

1. If the work is published commercially.

2. If it is exhibited in public.

3. If a visual image of it is broadcast or otherwise made available to the public.

4. If a film including a visual image of the work is shown in public or copies of the film (which will include videos and DVDs) are issued to the public.

Section 77(7) of the 1988 Act sets out details of how the author is to be identified. One example is that the author of the musical or artistic work must be identified on each copy. This is logical: you wouldn't want a record company to be able to get around the right by identifying you on the first, say, one hundred copies issued and not on any of the rest.

Assertion of the right

There is, however, one very big 'but' here. In order to be able to rely on the paternity right, you have to first have asserted that right. You may have noticed on the inside cover of books published since 1988 that there is a statement along the lines of 'the right of [author's name] to be identified as the author of this work has been asserted in accordance with sections 77 and 78 of the Copyright, Designs and Patents Act 1988'. This is the book publishing world's way of asserting the author's right of paternity. If you write a song and don't want to have the right to be identified as the author then you just don't assert your moral right of paternity and you don't insist of having a credit clause in your contracts. But why wouldn't you want to be identified?

If you do want to be identified then you can assert your right generally – as in the statement above – or in respect of any particular act. For example, you could assert your right to be identified as the author of the musical work in the sound recording but not if that sound recording is then included in a film. Again, you may wonder why anyone would make the distinction. You can choose to assert your rights in the document in which you assign any copyright in the work, for example in an exclusive music publishing deal where you have to assign your rights for a period of time (see Chapter 4), or you can do it by some other written means that brings your assertion to the attention of someone. They are then responsible if they breach your right. The problem with this is that it's only binding on those people to whose attention the assertion of rights is brought. For example, you could put in a written document that you asserted your right of paternity, but if that document was then put away in a drawer you wouldn't have brought it to anyone's attention and so couldn't rely on your moral right later if someone failed to identify you as the author of the work. Putting it in the assignment document is the best way of ensuring that anyone who later takes any interest in the work assigned will have notice of your assertion of your paternity rights.

If the musical work has been jointly written, for example by all members of a band, then each is responsible for asserting his own right of paternity. One band member can't take it upon himself to assert it on behalf of the others.

There are a number of exceptions.[8] The most important one for you is likely to be the fact that, if the copyright is one that you created as an employee, your employer and anyone acquiring rights from him doesn't have to identify you as the author of that work. So, for example, if you wrote a jingle as part of your job as an employee of a jingle company then unless there was anything in your contract that said your employer had to give you a credit, he wouldn't have to do so and you wouldn't be able to rely on any right of paternity.

The integrity right

The second moral right is the right of an author of a work or a performer in a broadcast on a recording which is then communicated to the public not to have that work subjected to derogatory treatment (i.e. to have someone treat your work in a way that reflects badly on the work and, indirectly, on you).[9] This is sometimes called the integrity right. The right

---

8 Section 79 CDPA.
9 Section 80 CDPA.

is owned by the author of a copyright literary, dramatic, musical or artistic work, by the director of a copyright film (which includes a video and DVD) and by a performer in relation to a broadcast of his performance or where a recording of his performance is communicated to the public. Once again, the right only applies in relation to a work that is in copyright and it doesn't apply to sound recordings.

The right has several hurdles to it. First, you have to establish that the work has been subjected to some form of treatment, i.e. that it has been added to, or parts have been deleted, or the work has been altered or adapted in some way. Something has to have been done to it. This can be as little as changing one note or one word of the lyrics. It isn't a treatment of a work if all you do is put it in an unchanged form in a context that reflects badly on its author. For example, if someone uses your song as part of a soundtrack for a porn video, that of itself *isn't* a treatment of the work for the purpose of your moral rights. Nor is it a treatment if someone just changes the key or the register of the music.

In a case involving George Michael, the court was asked to consider the question of what was a treatment.[10]

Someone had put together a megamix of George Michael's tracks using 'snatches' from five songs. They had also slightly altered the lyrics. The court decided that this was definitely a treatment.

Once you've established that there has been some form of treatment, you then have to show that that treatment was derogatory. For these purposes that means a distortion or mutilation or something that is prejudicial to your honour or reputation.

When you've established both these points, you then have to look at whether the treatment has been subjected to a particular type of use. In the case of a literary or musical work the integrity right is infringed by:

1. Publishing it commercially.

2. Performing it in public, broadcasting it or otherwise making it available to the public.

3. Issuing copies to the public of a film or sound recording of, or including, a derogatory treatment of the work.

In the case of an artistic work the treatment has to have been used in one of the following ways:

1. By publishing it commercially.

2. By exhibiting it publicly.

3. By broadcasting or including in a service which makes available to the public a visual image of a derogatory treatment of the work.

4. By showing in public a film including a visual image of a derogatory treatment of a work or issuing to the public copies of such a film.

10 *Morrison Leahy Music v. Lightbond,* 1993 EMLR 144.

In the case of a film (which includes a video or DVD) the integrity right is infringed by a person who shows in public or includes in a cable programme service a derogatory treatment of a film or who issues to the public copies of a derogatory treatment of the film.[11] In the case of a performance it's the broadcast of the work or where a recording of a performance is communicated to the public. These rights also apply to online or digital reproduction via the Internet.

FALSE ATTRIBUTION
The third right is an extension of a right that existed under the previous Copyright Act of 1956. It is the right not to have a work falsely attributed to you. This would happen if someone says that a piece of music is written by you or that you directed a particular film and that isn't in fact the case. This false attribution needn't be in writing – it can be verbal. It also needn't be express – it can be implied. So someone could suggest on a television programme that you were the author of a particular piece of music when you weren't, or could imply that you were without coming straight out and saying so. In many ways, it is the mirror image of the right of paternity.

If there has been a false attribution then it has to be applied to a work that has been used in one of the following ways before it can be said to be an infringement of this moral right:

1. If a person issues to the public copies of a literary, dramatic or artistic work or a film in which there is a false attribution. So, for example, if the credits wrongly identify you as the author of the music, this could be an infringement of your moral right.

2. If a person exhibits in public an artistic work, or a copy of an artistic work, in or on which there is a false attribution.

3. If in the case of a literary, dramatic or musical work, a person performs the work in public, broadcasts it or otherwise makes it available to the public, saying wrongly that it is the work of a particular person or, in the case of a film, shows it in public, broadcasts it or makes it available to the public as being directed by someone who had not in fact directed it.

4. Material issued to the public or displayed in public, which contains a false attribution in relation to any of the above acts, is also an infringement. This could catch publicity posters for films, or adverts in magazines for a book, or the false credit on the packaging for a recording of a piece of music.

There are also rights against those who indirectly infringe this right.[12] The rights extend to making available over the Internet or making digital online copes of the works.

PRIVACY OF PHOTOGRAPHS
The final moral right is the right to privacy in any photographs that you commission.[13] This is intended to protect against unauthorised use by newspapers and such like of private

---

11 See section 83 CDPA for details of other persons who could be liable for infringement of this right and section 81 CDPA for exceptions.
12 Section 84(3) CDPA.
13 Section 85 CDPA.

photographs that you have commissioned. When you're starting out in the business this right may not be of immediate practical interest to you. There's always the motto that there's no such thing as bad publicity. However, later in life, when you're a megastar seeking to protect your privacy at all costs, you may remember this right and use it against unscrupulous photographers keen to sell their soul and your life to the tabloids. This right can be used alongside the privacy and confidentiality rights that are being developed by the courts implementing the Human Rights Act as we will see later in this chapter.

OWNERSHIP OF RIGHTS

As we've already seen, the moral rights belong to authors – to composers of musical works and writers of lyrics intended to be spoken or sung with music and to performers on sound recordings or broadcasts of their performances. A record producer may have moral rights but not as the producer but because he may have also performed on the record or contributed to the writing of the words or music (see Chapter 5).

The real beauty of these rights is that they are rights of the author or performer, who can't be made to assign them. A songwriter may have been required to assign the copyright in his words and music to a publisher as part of a publishing deal (see Chapter 4), but he can't be made to assign his moral rights. If he retains his moral rights then he is in a position to take legal action against someone infringing those rights, even if the publishing company wants to take no action.

There are, of course, difficulties with the moral right of paternity, as you would have to show that you had the right, that it had been infringed and that you had asserted the right in such a way that the person infringing it had notice of the assertion. If your assertion was in an assignment document and was general in nature, you could take action against the assignee of the rights and against anyone else taking an interest in the rights subsequently. This could help you take action for infringement of your paternity right against your publisher or one of his sub-publishers, but not so easily against someone who was acting unlawfully.

The other moral rights do not have to first be asserted.

DURATION OF RIGHTS

The paternity and integrity rights last for as long as copyright exists in the work in question. The same applies to the right of privacy in commissioned photographs and films.[14] After a person's death, the right to take action for infringement passes to whomever he specifically directs. This can be more than one person. The right against false attribution lasts until twenty years after the person's death. If there is an infringement after his death then his personal representatives can take action. It's not a criminal offence to infringe your moral rights but, if proven, you have the right to seek injunctions and/or damages. Most importantly, you can exercise a degree of control over what's being done with your work.

THE CATCH

There is, though, one other big problem with these rights and it has been dealt with in a peculiarly British way. You'll recall that the two main moral rights were first introduced into

---

14 Section 86(1) CDPA.

UK law in 1988 in order to enable the UK to fully comply with the requirements of the Berne Convention. The Convention said that the laws of signatory countries ought to contain the author's moral rights. There was, however, nothing in the Convention that prevented a country incorporating the rights into its laws but then making concessions to other economic interests. This is exactly what happened in the UK. It arose largely as a result of intensive lobbying by the powerful record and publishing interests in this country. It is also a result of the long-standing laissez-faire tradition that we spoke of earlier. In the UK we still favour economic interests over author's rights. So what happened was that, having included the rights in the 1988 Act, the law then went on to say that the author could then elect to waive his rights, to agree not to assert the right of paternity or to enforce any of the other rights. The waiver must be in writing and signed by the person giving up the right. The waiver can be for a specific work, for works within a specific description or works generally. It can apply to existing and future works, can be conditional or unconditional and can be revocable. The same points would now also apply to the moral rights of performers.

What was the consequence of this waiver provision? I'm sure you can guess. As soon as the industry realised these rights could be waived, all contracts were changed to include as standard a waiver of these rights in the widest possible terms. Clauses were included which provided for an absolute, unconditional and irrevocable waiver of any and all moral rights of whatever kind in relation to all existing or future works. They even put them in record contracts where there was little or no chance of the right existing in the first place.

CONCLUSION

So why bother discussing these rights if you're going to have to waive them anyway? Once again, it comes down to bargaining power. If creative controls are important to you then you could try and insist on not having to waive them. If you're forced to waive your moral rights then try and only waive them against uses of your works by properly authorised people. Try and retain the right to enforce your moral rights against unlawful users of your works and infringers of your rights.

If you're made to waive your rights, your lawyer will then usually use that as a lever to try and get some of the benefits of the rights through the back door. It helps us to negotiate more favourable credit clauses for you and to cover what happens if you aren't properly credited. We rely on the integrity right to get you contractual consents as to what can or can't be done with your work. For example, that your words and music can't be changed without your consent.

PRIVACY OF THE INDIVIDUAL

I've been talking in this book (in Chapters 8 and 9 in particular) about how you capitalise on your fame and fortune – but there is another side to the coin. What rights does a famous person have to prevent others from cashing in on his fame and intruding into his private life? Can celebrities protect their privacy? What happens if the press gets too intrusive?

There are two opposing schools of thought at work here. On the one hand, you could argue that personalities have worked hard to create their fame; why shouldn't they be able to benefit from the results of this hard work and control what others do with that celebrity?

On the other hand, some consider that the fame of a personality is created by the public – it is society at large that decides whether or not an individual is famous or not, so their name and image should belong to the public.

The courts of different countries adopt different approaches. In the US it's much easier to protect your personality and the publicity associated with it. In the UK the courts have, for over half a century, adopted the approach that if you choose to go into an arena where you get fame and maybe fortune, then your name and reputation is a matter of public interest and public property.

The cases on the laws of passing off that we discussed earlier clearly show that the courts are not keen on assisting famous personalities to clear the market of 'unofficial' merchandise (see Chapter 8). So, if there is no trade mark or copyright infringement and no breach of the Trade Descriptions Act, what can you do? Well, in most western European countries you'll find that the law gives you a much broader protection, indeed a right of privacy.

The Petula Clark Case

One of the first French cases involved Petula Clark, who had authorised an agency to interview and photograph her for a particular publication. The agency concerned, however, sold the photographs to another agency that used them in a weekly publication. Petula Clark was successfully awarded damages by a French court proportional to the loss of the opportunity to earn revenue from the publication of the photographs. This line of approach has been consistently followed in France but not in the UK.

The Eddie Irvine Case

A very different case, involving the racing driver Eddie Irvine, has given some hope that the courts are starting to acknowledge that there is a commercial value in the named image of a well-known individual, which the individual is entitled to protect.[15]

Talksport produced a limited run advert with a doctored picture of Eddie Irvine showing him seeming to hold a radio, not a mobile phone, in his ear with a 'tag' line that suggested he supported a particular sport radio station.

Irvine brought an action for damages for passing off and argued that he had a substantial reputation and goodwill and that the defendant had created a false message that a not insignificant section of the public would take to mean that Irvine had endorsed the radio station. The radio station argued that there was no freestanding right to character exploitation enjoyable exclusively by a celebrity, and a passing off claim couldn't be based on an allegation of false endorsement.

The court agreed with Irvine and held that an action for passing off could be based on false product endorsement. The judge recognised the fact that it was common for famous people to exploit their names and images by way of endorsement in today's brand-conscious age, not only in their own field of expertise, but a wider field also. It was right, therefore, for valuable reputation to be protected from unauthorised use by other parties. The fact that the brochure had only had a limited distribution was not relevant. Even if the damage done may be negligible in direct money terms, the court accepted that potential long-term damage could be considerable.

15 *Irvine and Anr v. Talksport Limited* Chancery Division 13/03/02.

The 118 case referred to in the chapter on branding also suggests the regulators are beginning to accept in some circumstances that there is value in a person's image which they are entitled to protect.

The implementation of the Human Rights Act into UK law in 2000 attracted much interest among personalities and those advising them as they thought it might afford them more protection.

The Human Rights Act gives an individual the right to respect for his private and family life, home and correspondence. This must, however, according to the Human Rights Act, be balanced against the importance of freedom of expression and of the press. The courts are required to perform this balancing act.

The introduction of the law saw a flood of cases, some juicy ones involving stories of sex and drugs. Others were less tabloid in nature, but both sorts centred on the very serious question of the right to privacy. Here is a selection of some of those cases:

The Michael Douglas Case[16]

This involved a claim by actor Michael Douglas and the publishers of *OK!* magazine that *Hello!* breached his privacy by secretly photographing his wedding to Catherine Zeta-Jones and publishing the photographs ahead of the exclusive that had been given to *OK!*

Three judges reviewed the history of the developing law of confidence, not privacy, and the effect, if any, of the introduction of the Human Rights Act 1998. They considered the acceptance of a right to appropriate protection of one's personal privacy as an extension of the law of confidence – placing a fundamental value on personal autonomy. The court declined to expand on a new right of privacy saying that Mr Douglas and *OK!* had sufficient protection under existing laws of confidence.

The earlier CA case of *Kaye* v. *Robertson* was not followed on the basis that the law had moved on to develop a law of privacy without the need for first establishing the relationship of confidentiality, which sometimes had to be done very artificially.

On balance, they decided Mr Douglas had a right to privacy, even though he had waived that right by agreeing a deal for publication of photographs of the event in question, his wedding.

The legal saga continued with £14,500 damages being later awarded to Mr Douglas and Ms Zeta-Jones and just over £1million to *OK!* for the commercial damage.

Hello! then announced it would appeal the amount of damages awarded and the decision of the House of Lords in May 2005 was that whilst Douglas and Zeta-Jones were entitled to damages for breach of their right of privacy *OK!* was not also entitled to damages. This was both a significant blow to *OK!* which had anticipated £1m in damages and the bulk of its legal costs and one which has created a huge hole in the case law which was thought to protect a magazine from a 'spoiler' story run by a rival. It would seem that protection is not available under the privacy or confidentiality laws in those circumstances. Unless there is an appeal to the European Court this would seem to be the end of this particular saga but we can expect more cases in this area as magazines seek to establish the extent of what they can or cannot protect in terms of exclusives.

16 *Michael Douglas, Catherine Zeta-Jones, Northern & Shell Limited v. Hello! Ltd.* [2001] EMLR 199.

Ms Dynamite Case

In 2003 Ms Dynamite sought to rely on her right to privacy under Article 8 of the Human Rights Act and complained to the Press Complaints Commission that the *Islington Gazette* had published information which made it possible to identify the location of her home, against the PCC Code of Conduct. The PCC upheld her complaint and found that the Code had been breached. But whilst this may have acted as a sharp slap on the wrist to The *Islington Gazette* without stiff financial penalties in the form of compensation it lacks bite.

The courts have shown more of a tendency to grant injunctions in the area of privacy than, for example, libel. This fact, together with the hope of celebrities for an improvement in their right to privacy from intrusive paparazzi and tabloid reporters, has led to several new cases in this area.

The Footballer Case[17]

A footballer wanted to prevent the publication of kiss-and-tell stories by getting an injunction against a newspaper. The court had to balance the interests of the individual against freedom of speech and decide whether there was a public interest to be served in allowing publication. They decided that, on balance, they wouldn't prevent publication.

This case made it clear that nearly all intrusions on privacy will be dealt with in the area of breach of confidence. This seems to be a move away from the Douglas case, which clearly wished to establish a separate law of privacy. By returning to this law of confidence, it will be necessary for celebrities to show that the information was obtained in confidential circumstances. The case also seems to show the court's sympathies tipping in favour of freedom of the press, while stressing the need for a balancing act between privacy of the individual and the public interest. By that, I don't mean that just because it's a piece of juicy news that it's in the public interest, but that public figures have to accept that their activities do, in some circumstances, make it in the public's interest that they be written about, whether they like it or not.

This approach seems to have been followed in other cases brought by celebrities.

The Jamie Theakston Case

Another celebrity caught, as it were, with his trousers down, was the TV presenter and actor Jamie Theakston, who visited a brothel and was photographed by one of the women there, who then threatened to sell her story to the press, apparently because he failed to pay for services rendered.[18] Theakston sought an injunction to stop her. The court applied the rules on confidence and decided that the woman owed him no duty to keep the matter secret and that the public interest was served by a story that he had visited this place. They also ruled, though, that that interest didn't go so far as photographs, and made an order preventing the publication of the photographs.

---

17 *A v. B & C* [2002] EMLR 21.
18 *Theakston v. MGN Ltd* [2002 QBD] EMLR 22.

The Naomi Campbell Case[19]

The first of the privacy cases to come to trial after the implementation of the Human Rights Act was one brought by the supermodel Naomi Campbell against the *Daily Mirror*. The *Mirror* intended to publish details of Ms Campbell's drug addiction. She sought an injunction to prevent them. The court decided that, while there was a public interest in knowing of her addiction (she had, apparently, previously proclaimed an anti-drugs stance), this didn't extend to details of her therapy with Narcotics Anonymous. It granted her an injunction for breach of confidentiality, but awarded the very low sum of £3,500 in damages – a signal that the court didn't think much of her behaviour. The judge went so far as to say, 'I'm satisfied that she lied on oath.' This was a clear case where the damage caused by the publicity surrounding the case and her evidence in court outweighed that caused by the original article. Appeals took the case right to the House of Lords where in May 2004 the original decision stated above was upheld by the Law Courts on a 3 to 2 majority decision.

There is clearly still a legal tightrope to walk between what it is legitimate to publish and what oversteps the mark. The law is still developing and occasional inconsistencies remain.

Sebastian Coe Case[20]

Shortly after the House of Lords decision in the Naomi Campbell case, Sebastian Coe brought a High Court action seeking an injunction against a newspaper publishing details of his mistress's abortion. As this was private medical information which the courts had declared suitable for protection in Ms Campbell's case he might have expected to succeed but he did not.

Sara Cox v. The People newspaper[21]

DJ Sara Cox sued The *People* newspaper after it published nude shots of her and her boyfriend, John Carter, on their honeymoon whilst relaxing on a private beach. The action was settled with an award of £50,000 in damages.

The Elizabeth Jagger Case[22]

In March 2005 Elizabeth Jagger brought a claim for an injunction in the High Court to prevent further publication of CCTV footage of her 'heavy petting' near the doorway of a nightclub with her then boyfriend Callum Best. The judge agreed she had a right to privacy and that when balanced against public interest he thought it came down firmly on the side of privacy in this case.

As in many other areas of English law, much can depend on the individual judge who hears your case. In this country the press is self-regulated by the Press Complaints Commission.

19 *Campbell* v. *MGN Ltd* [2004] UKHL 22.
20 The *Guardian* 7 June 2004.
21 The Guardian 9 June 2003.
22 *The Times* 10 March 2005.

A 2006 case involving a Canadian musician helped to put to rest some of the inconsistencies and set some guidelines for where to draw the line between the need for privacy and the desirability of a free press.

Niema Ash v. Loreena McKennitt[23]

Although perhaps not a household name here Ms McKennitt was a very successful Canadian folk singer who toured internationally. In 2005 a friend (or perhaps more correctly former friend) of hers, Niema Ash, published a book she had written entitled *Travels with Loreena McKennitt: My Life as a Friend*. Ms McKennitt claimed that the book contained a great deal of personal and private information about her life which she was entitled to keep private. Ms McKennitt was someone who took pains to protect her reputation and privacy. She was relying on the duty of confidence to keep private and business affairs private. She succeeded in this claim first time round but Ms Ash appealed.

The Court of Appeal decision is useful to lawyers because it summarises the present state of the law of privacy and confidence. English law does not have a right to sue for invasion of privacy so the cases have to be brought as breaches of confidence. That area of law also encompasses the provisions of the Human Rights Act but in ways that are not always comfortable. A balance has to be drawn between the right of an individual not to have his private information misused as against the right of freedom of expression. In addition the court has to consider whether the individual complaining of misuse of private information had a reasonable expectation of privacy. This latter requirement is behind some of the inconsistent decisions above. The judges sometimes find that the claimant's own behaviour has led to them foregoing this expectation of privacy. An example might be if a film star used his family to promote an image of a happy family man he might then have given up his right to expect to prevent others from publishing pictures of him with his family.

Ms McKennitt passed the first hurdle in that the Court of Appeal judges found that the information was of a personal nature that did fall within the category of private information. Ms Ash had, rather ingeniously, argued that it could not be private to Ms McKennitt because she had shared the same experiences. But the judges rejected this line of argument. They thought that the book wasn't about Ms Ash's experiences but those of Ms McKennitt and so was not being used as an expression of her personal experiences.

The judges also decided that in this case merely because Ms McKennitt sought publicity for herself she hadn't lost all right to protect herself against publicity that she didn't like.

So having decided this was private information that she was entitled to protect the court then had to decide if that right was outweighed by the right of freedom of expression.

The judges found here that the freedom of expression didn't automatically outweigh the right of privacy. Each case had to be looked at in detail. In this case they found that Ms Ash did not have her own story to tell, only that of Ms Mckennitt and just because it had as it were come into the public domain by being told to Ms Ash by Ms McKennitt did not mean Ms McKennitt had lost her expectation that that information would be kept private. It might I think have been different if Ms McKennitt had already given a 'warts and all' interview to a newspaper.

---

23 *Niema Ash v. Loreena McKennitt* [2006] EWCA Civ 1714 (14 December 2006).

Ms Ash thought that she had the right to expose what she saw as Ms McKennitt's hypocrisy in the difference between her public and private life. The judges disagreed that there were any special circumstances that would justify the revealing of that private information. A charge of hypocrisy alone was not enough of a reason. And in any event they found on the facts that Ms McMennitt was not in fact a hypocrite.

On the other hand the court also made clear that there was no automatic right to a private life by a person in the public eye but that in some circumstances there were areas of their lives that they were entitled to keep private. Special circumstances would need in future to be shown if for example the private life of a football player were to be made public without his consent. Special circumstances would be matters that fell within the area of political or public debate and would not therefore normally apply to the private lives of individuals, even politicians and those in the public eye.

Exactly a week later the Court of Appeal handed down its judgement in the appeal by Associated Newspapers to be permitted to publish extracts from the Prince of Wales' private journals.

Associated Newspapers Ltd v. *HRH Prince of Wales*[24]

In some respects this case looks to be obvious but it nevertheless ended up in the Court of Appeal. This is probably a reflection of the amount of money newspapers can make from stories of a revealing nature as well as the fact that this is a still developing area of law where the press perhaps senses a chance to gain some ground in the privacy versus press freedom battle.

Prince Charles kept handwritten journals (eight in total) containing his impressions and views in the course of his overseas visits in the period between 1993 and 1999. An employee of the Prince's provided copies of the journals to the *Mail on Sunday* who published substantial extracts relating to a visit to Hong Kong in 1993, including comments which were disparaging of certain Chinese dignitaries he had met. Her actions were a breach of her employment contract. Prince Charles sued her on two grounds, breach of copyright and breach of confidence. On the breach of confidence case the issues were essentially the same as in Ms McKennitt's case outlined above. Was the press freedom of expression enough justification to override the Prince's right of privacy in his private life?

The court which first heard the case thought it did not and gave judgement to the Prince. The newspaper appealed.

Once again the Court of Appeal judges outlined the state of the current laws of confidence and in this case also discussed the extent to which the employee was in a position of confidence such as to fairly and reasonably recognise that the information was private.

Once again there was the question of the balance of interests to be weighed but also in addition the Court of Appeal felt they had to consider how this weighed up when you also took into account that the information had been obtained as a result of a breach of a confidential relationship based on a contract – here an employment contract

In this case both the fact that the employee had a contract which contained a clause obliging the employee to keep the contents of the journal confidential and the balance in

---

24 *Asoociated Newspapers Limited v. His Royal highness, the Prince of Wales* [2006] EWCA Civ 1776 (21 December 2006).

favour of even the heir to the throne having a right to keep his thoughts private fell in the Prince's favour. No one is so famous that they have lost all right to a private life.

CONFIDENTIALITY AGREEMENTS

What this last case in particular highlights is if a confidential relationship does exist (for example, between a celebrity and his housekeeper, driver or bodyguard), then it's important that there is a confidentiality agreement put in place. This will make the extent of the confidentiality clear and confirm that such matters will remain confidential. This will add a claim for breach of contract to that of confidence.

However, it doesn't always go the way of the celebrity.

The Beckhams v. *Gibson*[25]

In April 2005 David and Victoria Beckham brought an action in the High Court to prevent further disclosures by a former nanny, Abbie Gibson, about their marriage and private life. There was a confidentiality agreement in place which the Beckhams claimed had been breached. The judge refused to grant the injunction but when the matter came before the courts the former nanny voluntarily undertook not to release any further information pending a full hearing. In many cases this is usually the end of the matter.

HARASSMENT ACTIONS

Apart from seeking court orders in the civil courts for injunctions, celebrities can, and do, seek the involvement of the police to prevent the activities of paparazzi and reporters whose activities border on that of stalking. They rely on legislation introduced in the 1990s to prevent private individuals from being hounded or stalked. If the police can be persuaded to get involved, they can be very effective in 'moving on' recalcitrant members of the press. If they won't, then private criminal actions are possible, although such cases rarely come to trial as the celebrity would have to give evidence and many are reluctant to do so. Whether it's a police or private criminal case, the court is going to want to see detailed evidence of the extent of the harassment, so private detectives are often hired to produce photographs of the paparazzi hounding the celebrity, and his private security staff are often called upon to produce detailed statements of the extent of the harassment. Many of these paparazzi are freelance and make their money from selling stories and photos to the highest bidder. 'Exclusives' can net them tens of thousands of pounds in syndication rights worldwide. No wonder they are keen, and no wonder that many celebrities are forced either into almost total isolation in the UK or to move overseas, France and the US being particular favourites, where the privacy laws are stronger.

CONCLUSIONS

• Try to retain your moral rights if you can.

• Assert your right to be identified as an author of a work early and as widely as you can.

25 *The Times*, 17 May 2005.

- If you have to waive your moral rights, use this to get improved creative controls in the contract.

- Put confidentiality agreements in place with those who work closest with you.

- Consider harassment actions if intrusion becomes too much.

- Before embarking on privacy/breach of confidence actions, consider whether the potential bad publicity of a trial could outweigh any advantages gained.

Chapter 13
Sampling And Plagiarism

INTRODUCTION

Sampling and plagiarism are two sides of the same problem. Plagiarism is the taking of someone else's ideas and passing them off as your own. Sampling is essentially the same thing but the subtle difference between them is that to be guilty of plagiarism you need to show that someone had access to your material and that it was not just coincidence that it sounds very similar to your work. Sampling is always only a deliberate act. The person doing the sampling deliberately takes parts of someone's work and then, possibly after manipulating it, includes it in their own work.[1] Both sampling and plagiarism are infringements of copyright.[2] If you sample the actual sound itself by copying the digital recording, this is an infringement of the sound recording copyright.[3] If you don't actually make a copy of the sound recording copyright, you could take the piece of music that you're interested in using and get someone to replay it, to re-perform it in an identical way. This is still sampling, but it would then only be an infringement of the musical copyright in the music and the literary copyright in the words.[4]

Is sampling theft? Many people argue that all cultural evolution is based on taking bits of existing popular culture and adapting and changing them. They argue that all new musical genres 'borrow' or are influenced by earlier ones. R&B from gospel, and rock 'n' roll from R&B and so on. Those that believe this think that clamping down on sampling stifles this growth. They would be in favour of the removal of all restrictions on using parts of someone else's copyright.

This is all very well, but if you were to take this to its logical conclusion then no one would be able to protect their work, music would be devalued and people wouldn't be able to make a living from their work. Surely that's likely to lead to less creativity rather than more? I believe that it's wrong to deliberately take someone else's work without their permission, without paying them anything for it and without giving them proper credit.

HOW MUCH IS A SAMPLE?

Although sampling has been around since the 1960s, there's still an awful lot of confusion about what is a sample. A lot of people think that just because they've only sampled a couple of notes or a few seconds of someone else's work they haven't sampled it at all. That simply isn't true. What the 1988 Copyright Act says is that there has to have been copying of a 'substantial part'.[5] It's a question of the quality of the part sampled and not the quantity.

---

1 For an overview on the state of sampling see also 'Plagiarism and originality in music: a precarious balance' by Reuben Stone published in *Media Law & Practice*, Vol. 14, No. 2, 1993.
2 Sections 16–21 CDPA.
3 Section 5A CDPA.
4 Sections 3 and 4 CDPA.
5 Section 16(3) (a) CDPA.

There are a number of cases where the courts have considered what is a 'substantial part'.

Colonel Bogey Case

In the case of Hawkes & Son,[6] Paramount had included the sound of the 'Colonel Bogey' military march in a newsreel. They used 28 bars of music lasting about 20 seconds. The question was whether twenty seconds out of a four-minute piece was a substantial part. The music performed by the band made up the main theme of the march. The court clearly looked at the quality of what had been copied as well as the quantity and found that an infringement of copyright had taken place. Judge Slesser said, 'Though it may be that it was not very prolonged in its reproduction, it is clearly, in my view, a substantial, a vital, and an essential part which is there reproduced.'

The Beloved Case[7]

So, could something shorter than twenty seconds constitute a sample?

The band The Beloved sampled eight seconds of a recording of a piece called 'O Euchari'. The sample was repeated several times in The Beloved's track, 'The Sun Rising'. The sound recording of a performance by Emily Van Evera of the work had been sampled. Hyperion owned the rights in that sound recording and sued. At a preliminary hearing, the judge gave his opinion that an eight-second sample was not too brief to constitute a substantial part. He wanted the matter to go to a full hearing. However, as happens with so many sampling cases, Hyperion settled out of court and permission to use the sound recording sample was given retrospectively.

The 'Macarena' Case

A claim was brought by Produce Records Limited, that the dance hit 'Macarena', which had been released by BMG Records, infringed the copyright in a sound recording by The Farm called 'Higher and Higher'. The sample consisted of a short sound made by the vocalist Paula David, which Produce alleged had been used or 'looped' throughout 'Macarena'.

Because so few sampling cases get to court, a lot rested on this case. If it went to a full court hearing and the court confirmed that such a short sample could constitute a substantial part, this would be a firm ruling that could be relied on in later disputes. After such a judgement it would be very difficult to rely on the widely held view that three seconds is the minimum amount necessary to constitute a substantial part. It was more important as a potential guideline for samplers than it was for BMG to win this particular case. A decision that the part sampled didn't constitute a substantial part would mean success for the record company, but it wouldn't necessarily have given any guidance on what is a substantial part. Each subsequent sampling case would continue to be decided on a case-by-case basis. On the other hand, if the case had gone against BMG and such a short sample had been said to be a substantial part then BMG would have lost this particular case, but all record companies would also have lost the argument that such a small sample couldn't constitute an infringement of copyright. BMG settled out of court on terms that remain confidential. Possibly the potential downside was too great.

---

6 *Hawkes & Son Ltd* v. *Paramount Film Service Limited* [1934] 1 Ch 593.
7 *Hyperion Records Limited* v. *Warner Music (UK) Limited* 1991.

The question also comes up from time to time as to whether you can sample a rhythm or a drumbeat. I would argue that you can if it can be shown to be original and distinctive and if a substantial part has been copied. There are, of course, only so many rhythms in popular music and many drum and bass lines used currently are, in fact, the same as have been used in earlier works. This is particularly true in the area of reggae music. Inevitably there is going to be duplication. I tend, however, to agree with Aaron Fuchs. He's the man behind an eight-beat drumbeat used in the classic hip-hop track by The Honeytrippers, 'Impeach the President'. In 1992 he brought legal actions against Sony and Def Jam alleging that this particularly drum sound is one of the more distinctive in the hip-hop genre and worthy of the protection of copyright. I can find no report of that case coming to court, so I presume it was settled out of court like so many of these cases.

In the United States the courts are handing down decisions that suggest they are leaning towards giving protection to a distinctive or unique 'sound'.

The rap artist Dr Dré has been both successful and on the receiving end in court proceedings, perhaps reflecting the nature of the rap/hip-hop genre of music.

In 2003 Indian composer Bappi Lahiri won a court injunction halting the sale of the debut album by Truth Hurts – a protégé of Dr Dré and signed to his label, Aftermath Records. Lahiri argued that the hit song 'Addictive' contained a four minute sample of one of Lahiri's songs, 'Thoda Restiam Lagta Hui', which Lahiri had composed for a film in 1987. Lahiri sought proper credit for the use of his work and compensatory damages.

In 2005 a songwriter, Michael Lowe, brought a copyright infringement action arguing that the track 'X' on rap star Xzibit's successful album *Restless* used a beat created by Lowe. Dr Dré was named as a co-defendant because he was one of the co-authors of 'X'. Lowe argued unsuccessfully that he had created and recorded the beat and gave it to a record producer, Scott Storch, in the hope that he would pass it on to Dr Dré. Storch denied this. However, Lowe admitted that he did not expect to be paid anything in return for the beat. The judge decided that on that basis he couldn't then sue for payment and didn't rule on the facts of the use of the beat itself.[8]

HOW DO YOU CLEAR A SAMPLE?

If it's clear that you've sampled someone else's work then this is an infringement of their copyright – unless you get their permission to copy and reproduce their work. If you don't, they could sue you for damages for the copyright infringement and also for an injunction stopping you from continuing to use that sample. As you can imagine, record companies aren't very happy about having an artist who samples material from others and doesn't get their permission. It's very expensive for the record company if there's an injunction and they have to recall all the copies of the single or album and remove the offending sample before re-cutting, re-mastering and re-issuing the record. In fact, if it's too expensive they may not bother redoing it and just kill the single or album. That isn't a very good solution for you, so it's best to get permission to use any samples. This is called 'clearing' samples.

Most record contracts, whether they're exclusive recording agreements or licences, will have a clause in them that says you are guaranteeing that all samples are cleared

8 www.musicjournal.org/lawupdates.

before the recording is delivered to them. This makes it clear that it is your responsibility. This is only fair if you're the one who put the sample in there in the first place. But bear in mind that producers and remixers also have the opportunity to introduce samples into the recording at various stages in the process. Their contract should make them responsible for clearing any samples that they introduce. Sometimes it's the record company that has the idea that including a particular sample will turn a good song into a great monster hit. If the record company is encouraging you to include a sample then they have to take responsibility for clearing it, possibly as an additional recording cost. That cost may or may not be recoupable, depending on the deal.

In a case on this point, the judge (Terence Etherton QC) had sympathy for the defendant.[9]

The Walmsley Case

Walmsley had recorded a track that contained two sound-recording samples. The track was licensed to Acid Jazz and the contract required Acid Jazz to pay royalties to Walmsley. Walmsley gave a warranty that the copyright in the track was free from any third-party claims. Why he signed such an agreement is unknown, but part of the explanation may be that he didn't pay much attention to it, as we will see. Acid Jazz refused to pay any royalties, even though the track was a chart success. Acid Jazz said the track had given rise to a number of disputes and that it had had to pay out monies in settlement. It said that it was relying on its warranty, which it said Walmsley had breached. Walmsley's evidence was that he'd told Acid Jazz at the time of the agreement and subsequently of the samples, and had been told by Acid Jazz that no licences were required and, if any were to be sought, Acid Jazz would do it.

The judge found that Acid Jazz owed the royalties to Walmsley and, although Walmsley was in breach of contract, Acid Jazz was not permitted under equitable principles to rely on it because it had had full knowledge of the true position from the outset.

With some types of music, particularly in the dance, electronic, hip-hop arenas, the record company is fully aware that there will be samples and will often help to clear them. This can be an advantage, as they can use their greater resources and clout to pull favours and get things cleared quickly. This clout can have its downsides. If you're a small, struggling dance label that asks to clear a sample, the person whose work is sampled is less likely to ask for large amounts of money than if you were EMI or a Sony BMG for example.

WHEN SHOULD YOU SEEK PERMISSION?

Ideally, you should try and get clearance before you've recorded the sample. Then if you don't get permission you haven't wasted recording costs and time. In reality, this won't usually be possible. It can take time to track down the owners of the work sampled to find out who you have to ask for permission. Even once you find them they may take their time in getting back to you. You may then have to negotiate terms for the clearance. In the meantime you can't get on with finishing the recording of that track. This could hold up delivery of the record and its eventual release. Also, you're going to need a recording of what the sampled work is going to sound like in your version of it, even if it's only a demo.

9 *Richard Walmsley v. Acid Jazz Records Limited* Chancery Division 2000.

In practice therefore, the clearance process takes place after the recording has been made or during the recording process. Sometimes it's left until the record has been delivered. I think this is too late to start the clearance process. Some feelers should have been put out beforehand, at least to find out who owns it and to get an idea of whether they're likely to give you a problem.

Most record contracts and licences will say that delivery of a recording hasn't taken place until evidence has been produced (usually in the form of clearance letters or agreements) that all samples have been cleared. If you haven't used any samples they will want you to give a warranty (a sort of guarantee) to that effect. Until delivery has taken place, it's unlikely that you'll get any advances due to be paid on delivery (see Chapter 3). Nor will time start to run for your record to be released and the marketing plan won't be put into action. Therefore, the sooner samples are cleared the better.

Some people say that they're willing to take a risk that the use of a sample won't be spotted. They think that if it's sufficiently obscure or hidden in the track, the sample won't be discovered. Well, it's just possible that you could get away with it if it was a limited edition low-key release. For example, if you were only going to press up 1,000–5,000 copies of the record for release on your own small dance label then you might be lucky. Even if it were spotted, the copyright owner of the sample may not bother to take any legal action because the amounts involved and the legal costs and hassle of suing you wouldn't warrant it. But what happens if a bigger record company licenses your track in and gives it a big marketing push? Or if you make it a big success in your own right and find you're licensing it to loads of different compilations? If you haven't cleared it and you're found out you'll end up with a big problem on your hands, because now the copyright owner of the sampled work has an incentive for taking you to court. The bigger record company that has licensed the track from you may get sued by the sample owner. The record company will in turn usually have an indemnity from you. This means that, if they are sued, they can make you responsible for the damages and costs involved because you've breached your warranty that there were no uncleared samples in the recording. By lying to them you may also have irretrievably damaged your relationship with that label for the future. Is it worth the risk? That is for you to judge. It is also much easier with the Internet to find tracks which might once have been obscure, low-key releases. Whilst this has its advantages if you are looking to launch your career online it has significant disadvantages if you were hoping to keep your track low key. Personally I really don't think it's worth the risk and I have seen many deals come unstuck through issues arising from uncleared samples. At the very least tell the record company as early as possible and enlist their help to clear it.

WHERE DO YOU GO TO CLEAR SAMPLES?

If you decide to clear samples, who do you go to for clearance? If you've sampled the actual sound recording, you need to seek permission from the owner of the original sound, although they may have passed it on to someone else by licence or assignment of rights (see Chapter 3). You can start by looking at the recording that you sampled it from. It should have a copyright notice on it that will say who was the copyright owner at that time, for example '© EMI Music 2008'. So your first point of call would be EMI. They should be able to tell you if they still own the rights. If you don't want to show your hand too soon, you might want to do this through your lawyer on a 'no names' basis.

You must allow yourself plenty of time. The first thing you should be trying to achieve is an agreement from them in principle to the use of the sample. Some artists won't allow their works to be sampled under any circumstances, so it's best to know this as early as possible. Once you've got the agreement in principle then you can negotiate the terms. This can also take time, but you should know fairly early on whether they are going to ask for a ludicrous amount for the clearance, which will make it uneconomical for the sample to be used. Remember that, as well as clearing the use of the sound recording sample, you have to clear the use of the underlying music and, if appropriate, words.

The owner of the copyright in the words and music may be the writer credited on the sampled recording.[10] It's quite possible, though, that the writer may have assigned or licensed his rights to a music publisher (see Chapter 4). So you'll have to look at whether a publisher is credited and go to them to see if they still own or control the rights. They may only do so for part of the world or they may have passed the rights on or back to the original writer. The MCPS/PRS database should contain details of who claims to own or control the publishing rights (see Chapter 15). They would be a good starting point if you're a member of either MCPS or PRS. If the title or the writer's name is a common one, for example John Smith, then the database is going to throw up a lot of names. Try and narrow down the search by giving them as much detail as you can.

The importance of clearing samples with the correct party is highlighted in the following case.[11]

The Ludlow Case

Ludlow published the song 'I'm The Way'. Robbie Williams and Guy Chambers co-wrote 'Jesus in A Camper Van', which was published by EMI and BMG.

Because two lines of 'Jesus' resembled 'I'm The Way', Mr Williams approached Ludlow to acknowledge the resemblance and to agree that Ludlow would be a co-publisher. Ludlow wanted 50% – Williams and Chambers offered 10%. Ludlow refused and, just as the album containing the track was to be released, repeated their demand. EMI registered Ludlow as having a 50% share in the lyrics i.e. 25% of the whole song. Ludlow then brought a claim for 100% of the copyright and of the income and sought an injunction.

The judge found there had been an infringement of copyright, but thought it was borderline. He gave his opinion that what the defendants had offered was generous, but left it to another court to determine the amount of damages. He also decided that, on balance, Ludlow's conduct had been oppressive, governed by money and that they had gone along with things and had seemed to have been agreeing to things up to the last minute before release. He refused an injunction at summary judgement. An injunction was granted at the final hearing, so future copies of that Williams album will have to be minus this track.

This is another example of how one party's conduct can prejudice their case when relying on another's bad conduct.

What sometimes happens is that it's possible to clear the underlying words and music but not the sound recording. If you're adamant that you have to use that sample

---

10 See section 9 (1) CDPA and Chapter 4 for a description of who is the first owner of copyright in a musical or literary work.
11 *Ludlow Music Inc. v. (1) Robert P. Williams; (2) Guy Chambers; (3) EMI Music Publishing Limited; (4) BMG Music Publishing Limited* Chancery Division (2000).

then you can try and get it reproduced almost identically by having it replayed or recreated. Then you haven't sampled the sound recording, so you only have to clear the underlying music/words. Of course, if you do a very good job of it and it sounds identical to the original, they may not believe you've replayed it and still sue you. Then you may need independent evidence from, for example, the studio engineer, that you didn't use the sample sound recording.

I have been involved in a case where this happened. The client sampled part of a sound recording, asked for permission, which was denied, so set about replaying the sample to recreate the sound. He even went to the trouble of getting a specialist report from a musicologist to confirm that he hadn't used the original sound recording but had replayed it. Nevertheless, the owner of the original sound recording wasn't convinced and threatened to sue my client's record company, who had released the track. Using a right they had under their record contract with my client, they 'froze' the royalties that would otherwise have been payable to my client on the track in question until there was an outcome to the dispute. The money stayed 'frozen' for over a year and, as it was a substantial amount, my client was understandably very frustrated. Ah, but I hear you say, it serves him right for copying someone else's work. Well, before you get all high and mighty, just make sure that no one can ever accuse you of sampling or plagiarism.

HOW MUCH DOES IT COST?

This is always a question of negotiation. It will depend on how important the track is that you've sampled and how crucial it is to you that you use it.

Record companies will usually clear sound recording copyrights for an up-front sum, with a further sum when you sell a certain number of records. For example, £1,500 up-front and another £1,500 when you've sold 10,000 copies of the record that includes the sample. This usually comes out of the artist's royalty, but may be shared with the record company if it really wants to keep the sample in.

Publishers of sampled works may clear rights for a one-off fee or a fee and a further sum based on numbers of records sold. More likely, however, is that it will want a percentage of the publishing income on the track. In effect, the publisher of the sampled work is saying that their writer should be treated as a co-writer on the work and receive a co-writer's share of the income. That share could be as much as 100% if a substantial use has been made of their work. For example, in a track by All Seeing I called 'The Beat Goes On', substantial use was made of a Sonny and Cher song of the same name, although the band had altered the track and given it a more up-to-date sound. Warner Chappell, who publish the Sonny and Cher song, insisted that the All Seeing I version be treated as a cover version and they retained 100% of the publishing. If the use is less substantial then a lower percentage may be agreed.

As we saw with the Ludlow case above, claims for 50% or more of a song may be claimed even if a relatively small percentage is sampled – it's a copyright infringement that the owner of the sampled works is entitled to be compensated for. If it's a blatant offence, the court will be asked to award additional damages.

If you're going to do a lot of sampling in your work and are going to end up having to give away some or all of your publishing on certain tracks, do bear in mind that this may make it very difficult for you to fulfil your Minimum Commitment to your publisher – make sure you take this into account when setting the original level of that commitment.

WHAT HAPPENS IF YOU DON'T CLEAR SOMETHING?

If a sample isn't cleared and a dispute arises, your record company may suspend payment to you until the dispute is resolved. There may be a limit on how long it can suspend payment, but this could be a year or more. MCPS also has the right to suspend any payments of publishing income and has a disputes procedure that has to be followed. MCPS won't directly intervene to resolve a dispute, but can sometimes be used as an arbitrator.

The Shut Up And Dance Case

In 1992 the MCPS brought an action against dance label Shut Up and Dance (SUAD) on behalf of ten of their publisher members, claiming twelve separate infringements of copyright of works by writers such as Prince and Suzanne Vega. Legal action was taken after the owners of SUAD, PJ and Smiley, told the music press that their policy was never to clear samples. At the time a very macho culture prevailed over the use of samples, with some one-upmanship going on over who could get away with the most in terms of uncleared samples. It's thought their comment reflected this cultural approach to sampling. SUAD didn't defend the case and damages were awarded against the label.

Failure to clear samples in good time could result in an injunction preventing distribution of copies of your record, or an order that they be brought back from the distributors and destroyed. You could also be sued for damages for the copyright infringement.[12]

However, it's not all bad. Not all copyright owners sue or want payment when their work is sampled. The track 'Ride On Time' by Black Box may have attracted a fair amount of litigation in its time, but there was no claim from Don Hartman, whose work 'Love Sensation' was sampled. Apparently Mr Hartman loved the new work so much he wanted neither payment nor a writer credit.

PLAGIARISM

For the purposes of this chapter, when I'm talking about plagiarism as opposed to sampling I'm talking about a situation where someone takes another's work and copies it, passing it off as his own work. There are, of course, overlaps with the situation where you replay a sound sampled from another's work. But what I'm describing here are cases where a writer has claimed that another writer has stolen or copied his work; where the similarities between two pieces of work are so striking that you would have to believe the one was copied from the other. As we will see from the cases below, once you've established similarities between two pieces of work the crucial test is whether the person being accused of plagiarising the work has had access to the other work. It's possible to unconsciously copy something or indeed to arrive at a very similar-sounding piece of work purely by chance.

The John Brett Case

The composer Lord Andrew Lloyd Webber is no stranger to claims of plagiarism. In the late 1980s a songwriter, John Brett, accused him of copying two songs written by him in

---

12 As to remedies for infringement of copyright see sections 96–100 CDPA for civil remedies and sections 107–110 CDPA for criminal sanctions.

Lloyd Webber's musical *Phantom Of The Opera*. Although there were similarities between the pieces, Lloyd Webber was able to show that he had written the song first. He produced evidence that it had been performed in mid-1985, whereas Mr Brett's evidence suggested that he had not sent demo recordings of his songs to his solicitor until a month later. His claim failed.

The Ray Repp Case

In another case involving Lord Lloyd Webber, a songwriter called Ray Repp brought a legal action in New York accusing Lloyd Webber of plagiarism. Mr Repp claimed that Lloyd Webber had stolen a passage from his song 'Till You' and had used it, again, in *Phantom Of The Opera*. Once again Lloyd Webber was cleared, and afterwards made a passionate statement condemning the increase in cases alleging plagiarism. He blamed the lawyers (oh dear, us again) and people with an eye to the main chance. He said there were too many people around who thought it was worth a chance, because record companies would rather settle than fight potentially damaging court cases. I understand that he returns unopened all unsolicited demo tapes sent to him or to his office. The same policy is, I believe, adopted by other well-known songwriters who wish to avoid any such claims.

The Francis Day and Hunter Case

An early case in this area that set out a number of guidelines for what constitutes plagiarism is the case of Francis Day and Hunter.[13]

In this case it was argued that eight bars of the chorus of a song entitled 'In A Little Spanish Town' had been copied in the song 'Why'. The judge found a number of similarities between the two works but decided that copying (i.e. plagiarism) had not been proved. It went to the Court of Appeal. That court also agreed that copying had not been proved, but took the opportunity to consider the subject of copying generally. The Appeal Court judges said that you had to establish that there was a definite connection between the two works, or at the very least to show that the writer accused of copying had had access to the work of the other.

The 'Chariots of Fire' Case[14]

The film *Chariots Of Fire* and the music written for it has also been the subject of a number of court cases.

The writer Logarides had written a piece for television called *City Of Violets*. He claimed that the writer Vangelis had copied four crucial notes from *City Of Violets* when writing his theme tune for the film *Chariots Of Fire*. Logarides said that, consciously or unconsciously, Vangelis had infringed his copyright. The court decided that there was insufficient similarity between the works for there to have been an infringement. This ruled out the argument that Vangelis had unconsciously copied it, because it wasn't similar enough. The evidence that was produced to show that Vangelis had had access to the work was also not very strong, although the court thought that it was possible that Vangelis had heard the song 'City Of Angels'. Logarides was not able to prove that Vangelis had actually had access to his work.

---

13 *Francis Day & Hunter v. Bron* [1963] Ch 587.
14 *[1993] EMLR 306.*

The Beyonce Case

In 2005 a singer-songwriter Jennifer Armour brought a lawsuit against Beyonce Knowles claiming that Beyonce's 2003 hit 'Baby Boy' included lyrics from Armour's song 'Got A Bit Of Love For You'. Armour brought evidence to show that Beyonce's record label had had access to her song as it had been sent to them by her former manager. She also said that representatives of Beyonce's collaborator on the song, Sean Paul, had also been sent a copy. Whether or not Beyonce had ever heard Armour's song did not have to be decided in the end because the case failed at the first hurdle. When the two songs were compared side by side the court came to the conclusion the two songs were 'substantially dissimilar' and therefore there was no copyright infringement to complain about.

But it isn't always deliberate. It seems that it is perfectly possible for an artist to copy another's work unconsciously. I have a client who was unaware that he had copied a snippet from the Don McLean song 'Vincent' until it was pointed out to him and the same thing happened in 2004 to Scottish band, Belle and Sebastian. Apparently a track on a single by the band to be released in June 2004 entitled 'Wrapped Up In Books' was very similar to a hit single by Sir Cliff Richard entitled 'In The Country' written by his backing band, The Shadows. Belle and Sebastian were seemingly oblivious to the similarity until it was pointed out to them by friends. They decided the best thing to do was to come clean before the single was released and approached the publishers of The Shadows' song Carlin Music with an offer of 20% of the publishing on the 'Wrapped Up In Books' song. Luckily for them this was accepted by Carlin.[15] Contrast this with the Robbie Williams Ludlow case above and take care that you approach the correct people for permission.

SOUND-A-LIKES

This is where someone deliberately sets out to imitate a successful piece of music. It's often used by advertising agencies when they don't want to pay the price for the right to use the original of a piece of work. Instead they commission songwriters to write a piece that is a close imitation of the original. This is an art form in itself. We have already seen in Chapter 8 on branding the cases where Tom Waits has successfully sued advertising agencies or their clients for use of sound-a-likes of his distinctive voice. Here are some further cases in this area:

The 'Chariots of Fire' Case (No. 2)[16]

In another *Chariots of Fire* case, Clarks Shoes deliberately set out to gain a financial advantage from using a piece of music that had a very close similarity with the *Chariots Of Fire* theme. This was found to be blatant plagiarism, but because it was so obvious the case didn't really set any guidelines.

The Williamson Music Case

Another case, involving the advertising company Pearson, used a parody of the song 'There Is Nothing Like A Dame' in an advert for a coach service.[17] The lyrics were changed but the layout of the verse and chorus was similar. The manager of the licensing division of the

---

15 www.eveningnews.co.uk/print/news.
16 *Warner Brothers Music Limited and Others v. De Wilde* [1987].
17 *Williamson Music Limited v. The Pearson Partnership and Another* [1987] FSR 97.

MCPS heard the advert and thought it sounded very like the original song 'There Is Nothing Like A Dame'. He told the publishers of the song, Chappell Music Library. Williamson Music Limited was the exclusive licensee of the song in the UK. They and the other plaintiffs complained of infringement of copyright. Williamson Music Limited retained the right of approval to all requests for a synchronisation licence in relation to that song. No such consent had been given. The judge applied the test of whether an ordinary, reasonably experienced listener would think on hearing the track that it had been copied from the other work. He granted an interim injunction on the basis that the plaintiffs had established that there was a case to answer, but it seems he was of the opinion that there had been infringement of the music but not of the words.

It seems that the test for whether something is a parody that is allowable and one that infringes copyright is that, in the case of the former, the parody has to only conjure up the idea of the original – it becomes an infringement if it uses a substantial part of the original.

SESSION MUSICIANS' CLAIMS

The last few years have seen a spate of claims by session musicians, sometimes twenty or thirty years after the original session took place, that they were not properly paid for the work they had done. These cases point out the importance of ensuring that the agreement with the session musician covers not only their performances as musician or vocalist but also their interest, if any, in the underlying song.

It was thought that the Kemp case that we looked at in Chapter 4 represented the legal position in the UK that band or session members did not have any interest in a song if they merely interpreted or played what the songwriter directed them to.

However, this position was challenged in the Bluebells case in 2002.

Valentino v. *Hodgens*

Session player Bobby Valentino was hired to perform a violin part in a song written by Bluebells member, Robert Hodgens and already recorded by the band. The judge accepted Valentino's claim that he had been given a free hand to create the violin part, whereas Hodgens had claimed that he had told him what to play and had even played it to him on the guitar. Now clearly one could argue that this case just turned on the facts that the judge just preferred Valentino's version of events. This alone therefore would not have opened the floodgates and the 50% interest in the song that the judge awarded to Valentino would have been seen as a one-off.

What made this case stand out was the manner in which the judge side-stepped the issue of why it had taken Valentino so long to make his claim – a delay of over fifteen years. Usually that would have been enough to successfully argue that the claim was time barred. In what appears to have been an attempt by the judge to find in favour of Valentino the judge decided that the correct interpretation of the situation was that Valentino had originally granted a licence to use his contribution to the song for free; **that he was entitled to revoke this licence at will,** and that he had done so when the song was re-released fifteen years later and went on to be a big hit. Valentino was awarded his share of royalties from 1993 when he could be said to have revoked his licence. [18]

18 www.leeandthompson.com/articles/the_bluebells.

Now this is quite an extraordinary interpretation of the situation and really stresses the need for clarity in your session agreements but it also gave many others the idea that they could bring claims many years after the event – some more serious than others – including claims to record royalties from the school choir who performed free of charge in the original recording of Pink Floyd's 'Another Brick In the Wall' to a threatened claim against Rod Stewart by Ray Jackson, the mandolin player on Rod's recording of 'Maggie May'. It culminated in an April 2005 decision in a case brought by session singer Clare Terry against the writers and publishers of Pink Floyd of hit song 'The Great Gig in the Sky' off the *Dark Side of the Moon* album.

The Pink Floyd Case[19]

> Ms Terry was a session vocalist paid £30 to perform on the track, 'The Great Gig in the Sky' and was given a credit for her performance. Some thirty years later she brought a claim, in a similar fashion to the Bobby Valentino case (above), for a 50% interest in the song. In an out-of-court settlement she received a cash payment which must have been substantial as the album has sold over 36 million copies since its original release. The catalyst for the publisher, EMI and the writers in Pink Floyd to reach a settlement may have been because the judge had indicated that he was convinced by Ms Terry's claim that she had employed a special wailing technique, recorded in a series of sessions and effectively helped to compose the song. The parallels with the Bluebells case are obvious.

Finally, of course there is the recent case concerning the song 'Whiter Shade Of Pale' which we looked at in detail in Chapter 4 which is under appeal.

CONCLUSIONS

- If you sample someone's work, you'll have to get permission to use both the sound recording copyright and the copyright in the underlying music and/or lyrics.

- Put the process of clearing samples in hand as early as possible.

- If there is any chance of an uncleared sample being found and legal action taken, don't take the risk, clear it or remove it.

- If you can't clear the sound recording copyright then see if you can replay the sounds to sound like the original and clear the rights in the underlying music/lyrics instead.

- If you copy another's work and pass it off as your own then you're guilty of plagiarism, unless you can show that the similarity was completely coincidental and that there was no way that you could have heard the work you're accused of copying.

- There is a very fine line to be drawn between sound-a-likes, parody and plagiarism.

---

19 www.freelanceuk.com/news.

Chapter 14
Piracy

INTRODUCTION

Piracy is a huge, worldwide problem. The worst offenders in the area of physical pirate copies are Eastern European and Far Eastern countries, including Taiwan, Bulgaria, the Ukraine and Pakistan, with weak copyright laws and little or no means of enforcement, although Taiwan is beginning to recognise it has to do something and declared 2005 the Anti-Internet Piracy Year. Countries in which piracy is rife also export these illegal records into the UK. According to the IFPI Anti-Piracy Report for 2006 it is estimated that one in three CDs sold is a pirate copy. DVD piracy is a growing problem as bandwidth and fast Internet access makes reproduction quick and easy. Taiwan remains the biggest producer of blank CDRs which can be acquired very cheaply by small commercial operations to push out pirate copies.

The online world is even worse. The IFPI 2006 Anti-piracy Report estimates that there were 20 billion illegal songs downloaded in 2005. This is a frightening amount but putting a positive spin on it the IFPI reckons that this shows just how large the potential market is for legitimate use of music online. They point to the fact that record company revenues from legal digital sales tripled in 2005 to $1.3 billion. The record companies claim that this does not balance out the revenues that they are losing from traditional physical sales. As we saw in Chapter 7 they are trying more drastic measures to deal with the problem. Record company trade bodies, like the UK's BPI, the IFPI and the US body RIAA, continue to tackle both physical and internet piracy by legal actions against pirates and illegal file-sharers winning the support of the High Court for orders to force ISPs to disclose the identities of individuals distributing multiple music files illegally on peer-to-peer networks. The individuals face claims for compensation for copyright infringement and legal costs. Here are just some extracts from the Anti-piracy Report highlighting key decisions which are helping them in the battle to control online piracy:

In June 2005 the US Supreme Court ruled (in MGM v. Grokster) that file-sharing services that distribute software with the object of promoting its use to infringe copyright can be held liable for the resulting infringements.

In August 2005 Seoul District Court ordered Soribada, a Korean P2P service, to prevent its users to swap copyrighted songs or shut down.

In September 2005 the Federal Court of Australia held that Kazaa was guilty of copyright infringement and ordered it to shut down or implement copyright filters.

Also in September 2005, a Taiwanese court issued a criminal conviction to the directors of the Kuro P2P service which was in breach of intellectual property rules.

November 2005 saw the Grokster P2P network agree to shut down operations in light of the US Supreme Court's ruling.

In February 2006 the Danish Supreme Court ruled that under EU law, ISPs can be obliged to terminate the connections of customers who illegally upload material.

May 2006 saw the American operators of BearShare agree to cease to operate any music or film download services and sell its assets to the legal file-sharing service iMesh.

In June 2006 the Dutch Court of Appeals ruled against zoekmp3.com, effectively declaring that deep linking to infringing mp3 files is illegal in the Netherlands.

The decision of the Australian court against *Kazaa* was the start of sustained pressure on Kazaa to come in line internationally. Under the terms of an out-of-court settlement, which applies to Kazaa's operations worldwide and concludes the ongoing legal proceedings brought by the record companies against the service's operators in Australia and the United States, Kazaa agreed to pay a substantial sum in compensation to the record companies that took the legal action to stop copyright infringement on the Kazaa network. Kazaa also agreed to introduce filtering technologies ensuring that its users could no longer distribute copyright-infringing files.

There are also signs that some political pressure may be brought to bear on the ISPs to join forces with the anti-piracy organisations such as the BPI to battle illegal downloads of music. Whilst the Gowers Review may not have given the industry its hoped for extension of the sound recording copyright it did recommend that ISPs adhere to the industry practice for data sharing to allow illegal downloaders or indeed uploaders to be identified and targeted. This was not done voluntarily by the end of December 2007 and the Government has announced the intention to release a paper on this and other cultural issues in 2008.

And it's not just online that steps have been taken – legal actions continue against pirates of physical copies too.

R v. *Malone*

In March 2007 it was reported that the airdrie Sheriff Court in Scotland had jailed George Malone who had built up a black market operation selling thousands of fake DVDs and CDs. He admitted producing the illegal copies and selling them at industrial estates across west central Scotland. He was sentenced to nine months in prison and his assets were seized.

In 2007 a partnership was set up between a new police unit dedicated to combating movie piracy and the Federation Against Copyright Theft (FACT), and music videos will fall within its remit. Steps taken to introduce copy protection systems on new CDs to prevent multiple copies being made and improved tracking systems to trace online usage of music illegally have met with mixed success. As soon as a digital rights management system (DRM) is developed and rolled out commercially the computer hackers set out to break it and usually succeed in a matter of days, if not quicker. While we are not all so gifted, you can rest assured that as soon as a way is found to get around a DRM then some enterprising soul will make that available to all users. The whole area of DRM was, perhaps, irreversibly tainted by the scandal that surrounded

Sony's attempts to roll out a new DRM system in early November 2005. This is the so-called 'rootkit' debacle.

In an attempt to limit the number of copies that could be made of a CD SonyBMG introduced copy restriction software which was embedded in copies of some new CDs released by the label. This in itself was not a bad thing but it was the type of software used that caused the problem. The Electronic Frontiers Foundation (EFF) said that the software consisted of a programme called a 'rootkit', more commonly used by spyware companies to track what you do online. The EFF feared that if a CD with this rootkit system were played on a computer it would bury a new program within the operating system of the computer enabling SonyBMG to monitor the computer user's computer activity in order, for example, to prevent the user making additional copies of the CD. Online reports about this system caused such an outrage that SonyBMG issued a new program on its website which enabled the computer user to see if his computer had been infected, but to add insult to injury did not enable the user to uninstall it. There were also claims that it slowed down the user's computer, made it more vulnerable to attack and had the indirect effect of stopping users from listening to legal music on their MP3 players online. Because it was designed to be hidden it was not easy to see what was causing the problem. It was argued that it might also be used to mask other more malicious spyware or computer viruses. Legal class actions were begun in the US and within days SonyBMG announced it was not going to produce any more CDs with this protection system and published an uninstall program on its website. As things went from bad to worse for them SonyBMG eventually recalled millions of CDs and exchanged them whilst publishing an apology to its customers.

This publicity disaster increased the innate distrust amongst many in all DRM systems and led to the system being abandoned altogether in late 2007. The battle against illegal downloads will need to be fought in another way.

WHAT IS PIRACY?

Piracy is theft. It is the reproduction of someone's copyright without their approval and generally on a commercial scale.

There are three different types of pirate records.

COUNTERFEIT RECORDINGS

These are copies of CDs, cassettes or vinyl records that also copy the packaging, artwork and graphics. For example, someone gets hold of a master recording; they use it to make copies of it, which they then pass off as the original. They don't usually care what the sound quality is like, or even if the tape or CD will play at all. They just want to make them look as much like the original as possible so that they take your money and you don't find out until you get home that it's a pirated copy. The trade marks and logos of the original copyright owners are also copied to make them look as much as possible like the originals. This is an infringement of the trade mark, which could give rise to a legal action in its own right (see Chapter 8). Of course, if you're buying these CDs or tapes from a market stall at half the usual retail price, you've only yourself to blame if they turn out to be dodgy copies.

PIRATE RECORDINGS

This is the unauthorised duplication of an original sound recording. The pirate takes a master recording and copies it without the permission of the original copyright owner. The sound quality is usually as good as the original on physical copies but not always on online copies. Pirate recordings are usually put out on a different label from the original and in different packaging. The trade marks and logos of the original copyright owners aren't usually on the record or packaging. The aim is to undermine your market for the original by putting out a pirate copy first, or in a different form from the way you were going to present it. For example, you release so-called 'white label' copies of your next single release to the press and to DJs for review in advance of its commercial release. They are called white labels because, in their vinyl form, they have a white label, which says they aren't for commercial use. Unscrupulous characters then copy that recording and put it on their own compilation record without getting permission and without paying anything for it.

Pirate recordings are generally made in countries with little or no copyright protection and then exported to other countries. The practice is, however, spreading to other countries where the agencies in charge of anti-piracy are less effective. Sometimes publishing rights have been cleared and authorisation obtained from a collective body like the MCPS, but no permission has been obtained to reproduce the master sound recording. For example, if you were putting a pirate copy of a master recording on your own dance compilation, you might apply for a mechanical licence from someone like MCPS to get the right to reproduce the song on that master. This lends an air of respectability to the release and means you have one less collective body to worry about. You don't bother to get permission from the owner of the sound recording. You hope that he either doesn't get to hear about the release, or hasn't the money or the inclination to sue you for copyright infringement.

You could, in some cases, take advantage of different laws on copyright. For example, you might get permission to use the song, and the original sound recording might now be out of copyright in your country. You make copies of it without going back to the original copyright owner and you can import it into other countries where the recording is still in copyright, undercutting the legitimate market in that country. This was more of a problem when the sound recording copyright in the EU was different in different countries. For example, the sound recording copyright in Denmark was twenty years after the end of the year in which it was first released, while in the UK it was fifty years. This meant that after twenty years Danish companies could legitimately say that the sound recording was out of copyright, so no permission was required to reproduce it in Denmark. They then used the principles of freedom of movement of goods within the EU to export these recordings into other EU countries. This began to be a real issue when early Beatles and Stones albums started to come out of copyright in Denmark. It has become less of a problem since the Directive on the Harmonisation of Copyright and Related Rights made the duration of the sound recording copyright fifty years throughout the EU.[1]

Sometimes pirates argue that they have a valid licence to release a sound recording because of a chain of contracts going back many years. Often, in the 1960s and 70s, ownership of copyright was not properly recorded and there have been many changes of

---

1 This was implemented into UK law as section 13A CDPA. The term is fifty years from the end of the year in which the sound recording was first made or, if it is released in that time, fifty years from the end of the year in which it was first released.

ownership down the years.[2] In those days it wasn't unusual for deals to be single-page, sketchy outlines, that didn't make it completely clear who owned what and who could do what with the recordings. This confusion has been successfully exploited by later record companies claiming to have the right to put out recordings under some dodgy deal struck twenty years earlier. It's sometimes very difficult to prove them wrong.

BOOTLEGS

A bootleg is a recording of a live performance, whether it's at an actual gig or off a television, satellite, radio or Internet broadcast, which is made without permission of the performers.

You used to see shifty-looking people at gigs with tape recorders under their macs making terribly bad recordings of the performance. With the improvements in technology and the miniaturisation of the devices, it's now easier than ever to make reasonable digital recordings.

The Phil Collins Case

In the early 1990s, Phil Collins, ex-Genesis drummer turned successful solo artist, brought an action against Imrat, a record distributor, in respect of royalties for sales in Germany of a CD recording of one of his US concerts, which was made without his consent. Under German law, German nationals are entitled to stop distribution of performances made without their consent, regardless of where the performance takes place. Foreign nationals couldn't rely on this law where the performance had taken place outside Germany.[3]

The court decided that all European Union countries should provide nationals of other European Union countries with the same degree of protection as they would have had in their own country. This has been a key decision in the tightening up of performers' rights across the EU.

R v. Langley

A man who was described as 'one of Europe's most notorious music pirates' who was also known as 'Mr Toad' pleaded guilty to selling bootlegged recordings of Led Zeppelin gigs. Led Zeppelin guitarist Jimmy Page gave evidence before the Glasgow court that he had not authorised the recordings, which he said were of poor quality. He also drew a distinction between fans who swapped recording and professional bootleggers. Langley pleaded guilty to two copyright and three trade mark infringements. He sold illegal recordings he had made at live gigs on his Silver Rarities and Langley Masters labels. His arrest came after the BPI organised a raid on his stall at a Scottish record fair.

HOW DO YOU SPOT A COUNTERFEIT, PIRATE OR BOOTLEG RECORD?[4]

Counterfeits

These are often on sale in markets, at car-boot sales and are often obtainable from street traders selling goods out of suitcases on street corners. The prices are usually 50% or less than a full-price record in the shops.

---

2 See *Springsteen v. Flute* as discussed on page 122.
3 *Collins* v. *Imrat Handelsgesellschaft mbH* [1994] W.M.L.R 108.
4 Source: 'Protecting the Value of British Music' published by the BPI Anti-Piracy Unit (see below).

The packaging will often be of poor quality, possibly blurred print, especially when it gets to the small print. Sometimes there is a white border on the edges of the inlay card for the cassette or CDs where it's been copied. These inlay cards may look genuine on the outside; it's only when you open it that you see it's a poor representation on the inside. The trade marks may be removed, smudged or partly obscured as the pirates try to get around an allegation of infringement of trade mark. The name and logo of the original record company may also be missing, blurred or obscured. There may not be a Source Identification Code. This was something introduced a few years ago to show the place of manufacture. The sound quality will often be very poor, particularly on cassettes. Copy protection devices will definitely be absent.

Bootlegs

These are often found on sale at music festivals, second-hand or 'underground' record stores and collectors' fairs. They are aiming at the die-hard fans who want to own every available recording by their favourite artist. The price is often the same or higher than the legitimate product to reflect how desirable they are to collectors and fans.

The packaging may leave off company information; there could be no catalogue numbers or proper credits. Bootleg CDs can be very good sound quality, particularly when compared to the very bad quality of bootleg cassettes. The inlay cards will often be simple colour photocopies.

HOW CAN YOU STOP PIRACY?

It is probably not possible to completely prevent illegal uses of music on the Internet. Whilst BPI/RIAA and IFPI actions may deter the casual or opportunist illegal file-sharer they will not deter the hard-line pirates. Copy-protection devices can be circumvented by reasonably competent hackers and can in any event sometimes prove counter-productive if they prevent a legitimate user from transferring music from his CD or PC to the car or worse as SonyBMG found out in 2005 (see above). It is also accepted that regardless of what might happen with DRM systems in future CDs which have been in the market for some time – so-called legacy CDs – will not be copy protected, and that rights owners should accept this and concentrate on putting systems in place to make sure the copyright owners and creators are paid whenever their music is used. There is certainly the view that not much can be done to prevent pirate recordings of sound recordings that are already in the marketplace. What the music industry and the hardware manufacturers are now putting their efforts into is making legitimate downloads easily and cheaply available using desirable music hardware like the iPod (see more in Chapter 7).

However, this doesn't mean that control of illegal manufacturing plants and seizure of illegal copies has been abandoned. The underlying rights being infringed are the same whether the infringement is online or reproduction of physical tapes or CDs.

Copyright

Pirate recordings may infringe the sound recording copyright and the rights in the music and lyrics as well as the artwork. It's an infringement of copyright to reproduce, issue copies to the public, perform in public or include it in a cable programme (including online). These are what we call direct infringements of copyright.

Indirect infringements of copyright include importing, possessing in the course of trade, selling or exhibiting infringing copies in public and/or distributing them in the course of business.[5] These are obviously aimed at the distributor or retailer. They have to know or have reason to believe that they are dealing with an infringing copy.

Moral Rights

If the writer or composer of the lyrics and music isn't identified, or the work has been subjected to derogatory treatment, this may well be an infringement of moral rights if these have not been waived (see Chapter 12).

Trade marks

If the artist's or record company's trade mark name or logo is reproduced without permission of the trade mark owner, this is an infringement of the Trade Marks Act 1994.

Trade Descriptions

If the record has been misdescribed or represented as something that it is not, this may be a breach of the Trade Descriptions Act.

ENFORCEMENT

First, decide who you're going to go after. Who have you got evidence against? You could try to take action against the pirate manufacturer, but this may be difficult if they're based overseas. You could decide to try to stop distributors from starting or continuing to distribute pirate records. You'll have to move fast. If nothing has been distributed you could try to get an injunction to stop distribution taking place. If it's already been distributed you may need court orders against the person retailing the product.

So, when you've decided whom you want to target, what can you do?

Civil Action

You can apply for an injunction, although you have to move quickly. You can ask the court to make an order preventing infringement of your rights. The court can make orders preventing further sale, distribution and/or import of pirated products. You'll probably also make a claim for financial damages and reimbursement of your legal costs.

Criminal Action

You have to show that the defendant had reason to believe he was dealing with an infringing copy of a copyright work. The penalties are imprisonment and/or a fine. For this kind of action you need to involve the police, who will need to have explained to them how copyright exists in the product and how it is being breached. You also have to convince them that it's sufficiently serious for them to put resources into the case. In April 2005 the US Senate passed a bill to make it a criminal offence capable of a sentence of up to ten years' imprisonment for those found to be illegally copying and distributing pre-release music and films in the US. The obvious targets are those who illegally acquire films or albums by important artists before the official release date. It is hoped that this

5   Sections 22–26 CDPA.

law will help to deter all but the hard-core pirates. There is no indication that the UK government has plans to follow suit.

Private Criminal Prosecutions
The CDPA gives you the right to bring a private criminal prosecution.[6] This was first used successfully in a case run by my firm in 1994 to prosecute someone who was using computer bulletin boards to copy computer games illegally.

The CDPA also makes it possible for an officer of a company to be liable to prosecution for an offence committed by the company.[7] This is to avoid companies slipping through the net.

If someone is found guilty of infringement, the court can order that all the offending articles are handed over[8] and can order their destruction. I'm sure you've all have seen pictures of companies like Rolex using a steamroller to crush fake copies of their watches.

Trading Standards Officers
These are local government officials and they can be very helpful if you get them on side. A good friend of mine is an ex-Trading Standards officer and he tells me they like nothing better than a good raid on a pirate. They usually act to enforce breaches of trade mark using powers given to them under the Trade Descriptions Act among others. They can enter premises and seize goods. Their rights also now extend to infringements of copyright. They can prosecute for offences such as fraudulently applying a trade mark[9] and the application of a false description to goods.[10] As part of the implementation of the recommendations of the Gowers Review on Intellectual Property, Trading Standards received an additional £5million to assist in the fight against piracy. This was to help the officers with their new role as also enforcers of copyright infringement. Changes to the CDPA 1988 were implemented in 2007 to give them the right and authority to enter premises, seize goods and documents relating to copyright infringement as well as trade mark infringements. Because these offences are criminal ones there is the possibility of an unlimited fine and up to ten years' imprisonment so it is hoped this may act as a deterrent to some pirates.

Some further piracy cases

In March 2003 following police and Trading Standards raids Yogesh Raizada was sentenced to three years imprisonment and record fines of £160,000 on eleven counts under the Trade Marks Act 1994 following seizure of thousands of pirated CDs, DVDs and video cassettes.

In 2004 the Glasgow Sheriff Court jailed Stephen Reid for five months for selling pirate CDs and computer games. Mr Reid had been filmed in an interview broadcast on the GMTV breakfast show in which he boasted about his illegal business. He had had previous convictions for selling counterfeit videos. Before raiding his premises Trading Standards officers made test purchases from him and the police and Trading Standards put

6   Section 107 CDPA.
7   Section 110 CDPA.
8   Section 108 CDPA.
9   Section 300 CDPA.
10 Section 1 Trade Descriptions Act.

him under surveillance. The raid led to the seizure of over 6,300 CDs believed to contain pirate material.[11]

Also in 2004 Mark Purseglove was jailed by a UK court for three and a half years.[12] It is alleged that Mr Purseglove was one of the biggest bootleggers in the world and had amassed a fortune estimated to be about £6.6 million in the 11 years he had operated as a pirate. He sold his bootlegs around the world including off the Internet and on Internet auction sites. He was arrested after a protracted investigation by the anti-piracy teams from the IFPI and the BPI and charged with conspiracy to defraud the UK recorded music industry. Under the Proceeds of Crime legislation his homes in Chelsea and Brighton were seized after all his assets were ordered to be forfeit. The judge made clear that the severity of the sentence was intended to act as a deterrent to others and to send out a strong message that the courts will provide effective protection for the rights of copyright owners. Purseglove had collected bootleg recordings from household names in the music business, paying people, including the band's sound engineers, to make illegal recordings. Broadcasts were copied and he made counterfeit copies of legitimate recordings. He had previously been arrested and deported from the US and had shown a contempt for previous court proceedings.

Anti-Piracy Unit (APU)

The APU was set up by the BPI and also receives financial support from the Musicians' Union and the British Association of Record Dealers (BARD).

The APU investigates complaints about piracy. They take information from record companies, musicians and members of the public. They also monitor new technology and how that might affect the record industry. The APU runs training courses and seminars for the police and Trading Standards officers.

The APU can assist in both civil and criminal actions and work with a number of other industry bodies. In 2001 they attended or gave evidence in more than 500 criminal cases. They closed down some 400 websites trafficking unauthorised MP3 files and others who threatened to deal illegally with unreleased tracks. They also closed down 2,315 auction websites offering illegal MP3 compilations and bootleg recordings.[13]

The International Federation of the Phonographic Industry (IFPI)

This represents the international recording industry. If you're a member of the BPI you automatically become a member of the IFPI. It has about a hundred members in over seventy countries. It is involved in the international fight against piracy. It lobbies governments for appropriate copyright protection and helps to ensure the laws are enforced.

Other Bodies

Other bodies involved in the fight against piracy include the Federation Against Software Theft (FAST), which was set up in 1984 to represent the software industry (both publishers and end users);[14] the Federation Against Copyright Theft (FACT), which represents film and video producers, manufacturers and distributors as well as TV and

11 *R* v. *Reid* (2004).
12 *R* v. *Purseglove* (2004).
13 Source: BPI Market Information June 2002.
14 For more details of their activities see www.fast.org.uk.

the satellite industries,[15] and the European Leisure Software Publishers' Association (ELSPA), which represents publishers of interactive software such as computer games and has an anti-piracy hotline.

FACT, FAST and the Music Publishers Association (MPA), which looks after the interests of music publishers, also set up a hotline in the autumn of 1999 for people to report suspected cases of film, music or software piracy. You can also get legal advice on copyright and trade mark issues and they will tell you about their education and training initiatives.[16]

Implementation of the Gowers Review

One of the recommendations of the Gowers Review of Intellectual Property was that the ISPs adhere to their protocols for sharing data with rights owners to identify and disbar from their services those who infringe copyright. The report says that if the ISPs cannot demonstrate that these protocols had proved 'operationally successful' by the end of 2007 the Government should consider legislating. The ISPs do not wish to have legislation imposed upon them and it is to be hoped therefore that this will put pressure on them to reach agreements with record companies and publishers which would assist in the battle against illegal use of copyright. The ISPs are in a potentially very strong position as if they agreed to share information with rights owners which enabled those rights owners to show that the use was illegal then the ISPs would be in a position to quickly bar the illegal user from their service. Now obviously it is possible that the illegal users would then just move their activities to another ISP but if all the ISPs in turn also shared information on users who have been banned that might drive the illegal users off the Internet altogether. The ISPs could certainly do more than they are at present where their position almost universally has been – we do not monitor the content, we just provide the means, the pipeline. But there is still a lot of work to do. The government paper expected in February 2008 should help to move the debate forward. Leaked highlights do not seem to suggest there will be a requirement to share data between ISPs but do seem to propose a three strikes and you're barred rule for illegal file sharers.

---

15 For more details of their activities see www.fact-uk.org.uk.
16 The hotline number is 0845 603 4567.

Chapter 15
Collection Societies

INTRODUCTION

As you know by now, copyright is the right of an individual and, in most cases, that right should be exercised as the individual decides and on his own behalf.

However, there comes a time when it makes more sense for these rights to be exercised collectively by an organisation set up to represent the interests of its members. To make doing business as easy as possible requires a one-stop service. For example, it wouldn't be commercially viable for the owners of a radio station to have to go to the copyright owners of the sound recording copyright and of the rights in the songs on each of the records that the station bosses want to play on their programmes. It would be far too time-consuming and costly. Hence the rise of the collection societies which represent the interests of publishers, record companies, authors and performers. There are several of them, brief details of which are outlined below. They all have useful and informative websites which it would pay you to look at.

WHAT ARE COLLECTION SOCIETIES?[1]

They are, in effect, organisations set up by the various categories of rights owners to administer their rights collectively as their sole, or one of their main, purposes.[2]

On the whole, collection societies are private as opposed to state-owned bodies, but they are subject to some form of government or state supervision. In the UK, that supervision is provided for partly by the 1988 Copyright Act, which established a form of compulsory arbitration in the shape of the Copyright Tribunal,[3] and in part by the Competition Commission (formerly the Monopolies and Mergers Commission). Overseeing the whole thing is of course the EU which does intervene or introduce pan-EU legislation when it thinks that national solutions are out-of-step or require updating, review or harmonisation.

The purpose of most collection societies is to provide a practical and economical service to enable its members to enforce and administer certain of their copyrights. These bodies make it easier for others to get licences to use copyright works. There is also certainty in that the payment for these uses will usually be at a fixed rate or one individually negotiated within certain guidelines. The idea is also that, by acting collectively, administration costs are reduced.

---

1 For a more detailed description of collection societies and their history, see Copinger and Skone-James on Copyright.
2 Section 116(2) CDPA defines a licensing body as 'a society or other organisation which has as its main object, or one of its main objects, the negotiation or granting, either as owner or prospective owner of copyright or as agent for him, of copyright licences, and whose objects include the granting of licences covering works of more than one author'.
3 Sections 116–123 CDPA.

There are, of course, possible dangers inherent in that these collection societies are, by their nature, monopolies. It's the job of the Competition Commission to police whether that monopoly position is being abused.[4]

BLANKET LICENCES

One of the features of collection societies is that they grant so-called blanket licences for the right to use certain rights in all the works controlled by the society for a particular purpose, for a particular period of time and at a particular rate. Anyone wishing to take advantage of these blanket licences has to take a licence for the whole catalogue. For example, the Performing Right Society Limited (PRS) can negotiate a blanket licence with radio broadcasters for the right to broadcast to the public all the works controlled by PRS. The licence would be for a given period of time, say a year, and would then be subject to review. PRS would negotiate with individual radio stations or, more likely, with their representative bodies, the rate that would be applied to these licences. It could be a flat fee per annum or it could be linked to the revenue that the radio station earns, for example, a percentage of the advertising revenue earned by commercial radio stations, or it could be a combination of both.

Whilst the collection societies became adept at negotiating and administrating collective licensing schemes in their own countries and for non-digital means of distribution, things became more difficult for them when it came to digital uses and when they came under pressure from the European Commission to make it easier for new commercial ventures to flourish across the European Economic Area (EEA). Whilst this is a laudable aim it takes time to get all members to agree on a course of action and on the rate to be set for centralised licensing particularly when that involves new media and means of distribution where the people setting and negotiating the rate had little knowledge of which of these formats would have staying power and what an appropriate means of setting a rate was. For some time they felt their way forward. The European Union thought they were being too slow in establishing cross-Europe licensing schemes and issued a Report in October 2005 which urged the societies to review and reform their practices and in particular to 'provide for multi territorial licensing in order to create greater legal certainty for commercial uses ... and to foster the development of legitimate online services'. Perhaps fearing that solutions would be imposed on them from above there have in the two years since the publication of this report been committed attempts to reform their practices particularly in the area of digital music online and on mobile phones. The collection societies are trying to put in place schemes which will facilitate one-stop licensing across Europe. This is an attractive proposition for commercial users of music in new applications or services.

As hard evidence of these efforts two major initiatives were announced at the European Trade Conference MIDEM in France in January 2007. The Music Publishers Association announced a one-stop pan-European digital licensing solution in conjunction with the MCPS-PRS Alliance. MCPS is the Mechanical Copyright Protection Society

---

4   In the past there have been two major reviews of individual collection societies. The first, published in 1988 (HMSO Cm. 530), dealt specifically with Public Performance Limited. The second, published in 1996 (HMSO Cm. 3147), dealt with the Performing Right Society Limited. That report contained several criticisms of the Society, which has since altered its rules to try to deal with these concerns.

Limited. The scheme allows music publishers to appoint the Alliance as their agent for management of online and mobile rights across Europe. Costs are to be minimised by the use of a template agreement.

The second announcement was also one by MCPS-PRS Alliance (who have seized the chance to become a strong player across Europe). The Alliance announced a plan to act with the German society GEMA as an exclusive one-stop shop for Anglo-American repertoire for digital rights belonging to EMI Music Publishing through a new organisation owned by the Alliance and GEMA jointly and called the Centralised European Licensing and Administration service (CELAS). The idea is that in time CELAS may be used by other commercial users looking to avoid having to negotiate individual licensing agreements with all national collecting societies.

Still on the international front PPL announced in November 2007 new international deals with collection societies in Russia, Italy and Switzerland, bringing the total number of reciprocal agreements to 41.

Closer to home too there have been rapid advances in the availability of blanket licences for online and digital uses of music. A glance at the MCPS-PRS Alliance website will reveal schemes for everything from DVDs to memory cards

A recent development has been the introduction of blanket licence schemes to use music in podcasts. Whilst commercial radio has had such a scheme in place for some months the BBC did not finally agree a deal for its podcasts until autumn 2007. This was because the BBC Trust had only finally authorised the full roll out of podcasts in April 2007, thus allowing the BBC to start negotiating with Public Performance Limited which controls master rights to sound recordings for the major labels. The broadcasters had to convince the record companies that these podcasts were not a back door means to download music and to some extent the major labels remain somewhat sceptical as they have only granted licences to use thirty-second clips of music in podcasts. In contrast AIM, which represents many independent record labels, has agreed a deal with PPL for whole track downloads.

On the flip side MCPS-PRS agreed a licence for use of music in podcasts in March 2006. Podcasts have really come into their own in the last couple of years as a means of customising your own personal radio station, but also as a new revenue source. Initially podcasts were made available free of *The Ricky Gervais Show*. This was an immediate smash hit with over 2 million downloads worldwide. This opened up the possibility of a commercial market for these things and the episodes of the show were later made available at 99p a time on online etail sites like iTunes. But many of the podcasts remain free and for promotion only or to add value to another service.

MSPs-PRS also recognised that there was a need for a two-tier licensing scheme as there were going to be non-commercial or small commercial set-ups who could not justify or afford the payment of the minimum £400 per year royalty payable under the scheme. If you are podcasting to a low number of people or are unlikely to generate much revenue then you can opt to licence under the Limited Online Exploitation Licence which sets an annual minimum as low as £200.

The biggest challenge that has faced the music publishers and their collection society MCPS-PRS in the last couple of years has to be the arguments over the appropriate rate to apply to online uses of music. MCPS-PRS reached an agreement with the major record companies and with some of the ISPs in 2006 but some ISPs including

Yahoo refused to sign up to the deal and all ISPs and some of the major labels had issues over how to define the revenue on which they would pay the agreed rate. So the matter ended up being referred to the Copyright Tribunal which is the arbitrator set up by the 1988 Copyright Act to oversee disputes over collective licensing schemes.

After a very expensive and drawn-out hearing, the Tribunal ratified the terms of the settlement on rate, proposed some but not definitive guidelines for the definition of revenue and provided for an arbitrator to be called in if final agreement on that subject could not be reached in individual cases. The agreed rate for on-demand music downloads and subscription streaming services is set at 8% of gross revenues. The rate set for interactive webcasting services is 6.6% of revenues and for non-interactive webcasting it is 5.75% of revenues. A minimum royalty 'safety net' has also been set.

ADMINISTRATION

A main role for the collection societies is the administration of the rights, making sure that a member's interests have been properly registered, that people using the rights have the necessary licences and have paid the negotiated rate. They have to collect in the monies, allocate and distribute them. Most societies charge their members a fee of some kind for the administration of the rights, usually a percentage of the gross income they collect.

There is usually one society for each category of rights. A major exception is the US, where three societies doing identical things compete for the right to administer publishing rights, namely ASCAP, BMI and SISAC.

Sometimes a society will administer more than one right. For example, in Europe a number of the collection societies administer not only the performing rights but also the right to copy or reproduce works. In fact, in the UK, the PRS and MCPS have now combined many of their managerial and administration functions and go under the joint name of The Alliance.

RIGHTS GRANTED

The societies either take an assignment of certain rights from their members or they have a licence from their members or act as agents for them. The terms of membership of a collection society will usually dictate what form the rights granted will take. The idea is to establish through these membership rules a clear mandate to grant licences to use certain rights. As we will see in the section on new issues below, there has been less certainty than is desirable in the mandate of some of the collection societies to deal with new technologies.

The collection societies usually have reciprocal arrangements with other societies so that they can protect their members worldwide. These reciprocal arrangements mean that the UK societies can represent the interests of their UK members and of foreign artists, writers and composers within the UK, with both categories of writers receiving the same treatment.

One of the main advantages of collective licensing is, of course, the greater bargaining power that you can get by being part of a big collective effort. The rates and rewards for uses of your works that the collection societies can get for you should be better than what you could get on a one-to-one basis.

OTHER COLLECTIVE BODIES

There are a number of other music business bodies that represent the interests of various parts of the business. These could be collective bargaining or interest groupings such as the Music Managers Forum (MMF) and AIM (The Association of Independent Music). They also include unions like the Musicians' Union (MU) and Equity. British Music Rights[5] is the collective voice for the British Academy of Composers and Songwriters (BASCA), the Music Publishers Association (MPA) the MCPS and the PRS (see below). What all these groupings have in common is that they act as a forum for debate and, to a greater or lesser extent, as a means of using collective bargaining power to get things for their members that as individuals they could find it very hard to achieve. A brief description of the aims of each is set out in the section on useful addresses at the end of the book.

THE SOCIETIES

In the following section I'm going to briefly describe the structure and function of some of the main bodies that exist in the UK at the moment. More details can be obtained from the individual societies, most of whom also publish brochures describing what they do for their members and their websites are, on the whole, very informative.

THE BRITISH PHONOGRAPHIC INSTITUTE (BPI)

Strictly speaking, this isn't a collection society as such, but an organisation that represents the interests of UK record companies. It's a non-profit-making trade association that was set up in 1973.

The BPI is based in central London (see Useful Addresses) and its members are UK record companies. There are currently about 400 members. There is a fee to become a member and these fees mainly fund its activities. The subscriptions for full members are a minimum fee of £75 plus an annual payment of 5% of the member's performance income collected by PPL. This change to the subscription base is intended to open up membership to more companies. However, in December 2007 in the wake of a public statement from Guy Hands of Terra Firma (new owners of the EMI Group) questioning the level of payments to associations like the BPI, RIAA and the IFPI, the BPI announced substantial reductions in the subscriptions to be paid for the four major record companies. The formula will remain as before for independent record labels. The chairman of the BPI insisted that the decision-making process to reduce the subscriptions had begun well before Hands made his statement. BPI members have to be approved and agree to be bound by the membership rules and the Code of Conduct that the BPI maintains. If you're a member of the BPI you automatically also become a member of the IFPI.

The BPI Code of Conduct deals with how the music charts are drawn up and involves the BPI investigating alleged irregularities, for example if there is an attempt to buy up unusually large numbers of copies of a particular record in order to artificially gain a higher chart position. If the BPI finds that a member has been guilty of infringing the Code it can employ sanctions against that member, including expelling them as a member and/or imposing a fine. It is a part owner of the Official Charts Company.

5   www.bmr.org.

Because it's a trade association rather than a rights body, it doesn't take any rights from its members nor does it grant licences or otherwise administer or collect money from exploitation of rights.

The BPI provides a forum for discussion and acts for its members generally on matters in which they have a common interest. It has a lobbying function at Westminster and in Brussels, and also negotiates agreements with other groups such as music publishers, the Musicians' Union or Equity. It also has an important function in protecting members' rights through anti-piracy initiatives and in promoting British music overseas. Its Anti-Piracy Unit is active in trying to reduce the amount of piracy in the UK. Its role includes taking high-profile litigation cases against pirates and giving publicity to successful seizures of pirate goods.

PHONOGRAPHIC PERFORMANCE LIMITED (PPL)

This is the record industry's licensing body. It licences records for broadcasting and public performance, collects the revenue generated and distributes it.

It represents a large number of record companies (about 3,500), some of which, but not all, are members of the BPI and over 40,000 performers.

The PPL is based in London and was incorporated as a company limited by guarantee in 1934. (See Useful Addresses for contact details.)

The PPL negotiates collective agreements with broadcasters. It also protects the rights of its members and takes legal action to protect those rights. It doesn't, however, have its own anti-piracy unit or staff, but relies on its members to bring infringements to its attention.

PPL has a number of different tariffs that apply to the various uses of the music in its repertoire. These are usually payable annually. There are minimum charges and how much is paid out to the members depends on the use. It does take assignments or exclusive agency rights of various rights from its members. These include broadcasting, public performance, dubbing of background music (a role it took over in 1985), multi-media uses and digital diffusion rights.[6]

PPL distributes the income it collects to the owners of the sound recordings and to the performers on the tracks who have registered their performance with PPL. It is a not for profit organisation so there is no fee to join. They cover their costs by charging a fee to administer the rights.

VIDEO PERFORMANCE LIMITED (VPL)

This is a company associated with PPL. It is the record industry's licensing body for music videos.

Its members are the owners of public performance rights in music videos being publicly broadcast or made available to the public in the UK.

VPL licenses music videos for broadcasting and public performance. It applies a number of different tariffs to the different uses of the music videos.

VPL takes an assignment of its members' public performance and dubbing rights in music videos and a non-exclusive licence of the broadcasting rights.

6　Dubbing is the right to 'copy, produce, reproduce or make records embodying a sound recording'. An example would be a television sports programme that has music in the background. The sound recording of that music is dubbed into the television programme.

VPL collects performing income from use of music videos but, unlike PPL, it's not obliged by law to share this income with performers, only with its record company members. There is no fee for joining as like PPL it covers its running costs by charging a fee to administer these rights.

ASSOCIATION OF INDEPENDENT MUSIC LIMITED (AIM)

This is a relatively new association, set up in 1999. Its members are drawn from the independent sector of the music business, mostly the record company side but including publishers, production companies and manufacturers. It's a non-profit-making trade organisation for independent record companies and distributors in the UK

It acts as a forum for debate and also has a lobbying function. Its function as a trade association means that it also has a collective bargaining role.

AIM is based in London, and provides a legal advisory service to its members with a number of checklists of points to look out for in negotiating various types of deals. It has been forward-looking in the licensing deals it has struck with online distributors on behalf of its largely independent membership.

THE PERFORMING RIGHT SOCIETY LIMITED (PRS)

PRS is the UK collection society for composers, songwriters and music publishers and is charged with administering the public performance and broadcasting rights in music and lyrics. It also administers the film synchronisation right.

Both music publishers and songwriters are members. It was set up in 1914 as a company limited by guarantee. It also represents almost a million foreign music copyright owners through its affiliations with overseas collecting societies.

PRS is based in central London. When you become a member of PRS you have to assign your performing right and the film synchronisation right to PRS. Although members assign rights, they can reserve some categories of rights or types of use of rights in all their works and the rules do allow members to request that PRS doesn't license the performing right in a particular work, for example, if it is unlawfully sampled.

The criteria for membership by a composer is that at least one piece of music has had a public performance or broadcast which has been documented (e.g. set list, programme or playlist from a broadcaster's website).

A letter from a broadcaster, promoter or venue owner confirming broadcast or performance of your music will be needed. There is a one-off fee currently £100 including VAT.

THE MECHANICAL COPYRIGHT PROTECTION SOCIETY LIMITED (MCPS)

This company was set up in 1911 in order to collectively license mechanical reproduction of music, i.e. the copying of music and the synchronisation of music with visual images (see Chapter 4). MCPS and PRS jointly share back-end and administration resources under the name The Alliance and are now supporting online, electronic means for record companies to send data for mechanical licensing which will in due course replace the existing paper registration form.[7]

---

7   For more information on Cateo see www.bpi.co.uk/bisinfo or www.cateouk.com.

MCPS has both publishers and songwriters as members. Its main area of activity is the negotiating and administering of collective licence schemes.

MCPS is a subsidiary of the Music Publishers' Association Limited, a company limited by guarantee.

MCPS doesn't take assignments of rights, but its membership agreement provides that the member appoints MCPS as his agent to manage and administer the mechanical copyright in the UK. It has the mandate to grant licences and collect royalties but there are exceptions which you can retain to yourself and not grant to MCPS. There are full details on their website – see Membership section. It's also obliged to use its best efforts to prevent infringement of its members' rights. It can take legal action in their name and often does so.

The types of licence agreements are listed on their website in some detail as are the exclusions.

MCPS charges its members a commission for administering the rights and collecting the royalties. Its website contains details of its rates[8].

8   www.mcps.co.uk.

Chapter 16
Appendix

WORKING IN THE MUSIC BUSINESS

Here is a brief overview of some of the information available on the music business. It's not meant to be a complete list; it's information and sources I've come across when researching this book. All the contact details are in the next section, Useful Addresses, or in the body of the text.

If you're interested in more formal training in the music business then there are a number of courses now available. If you have access to the Internet this is an excellent resource for finding out about courses. The University and College Clearing site at www.ucas.co.uk is a good start point. Or do a general search, using any good search engine, for education/music. For short or evening courses, check Floodlight and local authority publications for courses outside London. Also check out the BPI website as a good general resource for information on careers in the industry (www.bpi.co.uk).

My own researches have turned up the following universities and colleges who run courses either in the media or the music business. Qualifications vary from NVQs, through HNDs, to degrees. Some don't offer a nationally recognised qualification but more of an overview with a certificate when you complete the course. Check the course details to make sure they meet your requirements. The list isn't a complete one by any means, and neither is it a recommendation of any particular course.

HIGHER EDUCATION

LEGAL AND BUSINESS COURSES

Bath Spa University College is running a full-time two-year Commercial Music course leading to an HND/Foundation degree with the option of a third year leading to the BA (Hons). The full three-year BA is also available. It also offers a Creative Music Technology course.

The University of Westminster offers a BA (Hons) degree in Commercial Music involving music production and music business practice at its Harrow campus as well as a one-year diploma in Music Business and an MA in Music Business Management.

Bucks New University offers HND and BA (Hons) full-time courses in Music Industry Management, as well as Audio & Music Technology, Digital Media, Live Production, Studio Production and Marketing.

The Continuing Education Department of City University, London runs a number of part-time introductory courses such as 'Making Music Work: An Introduction to the Music Industry'. They also offer distance learning and weekend courses in Cultural Industries and the Law and An Introduction to the Music Industry as well as Marketing and Event Management.

Greenwich Community College, south London, also offers part-time courses in The Music Business and Musicianship, which covers copyright law and marketing.

Dartington College of Arts in Devon runs a BA (Hons) degree course in Music, which can be performance, professional practice or composition-based with arts and cultural management.

De Montfort University, Leicester, offers BSc (Hons) courses in Music and Media Studies, Technology and Innovation as well as BA (Hons) in Arts Management and Media Studies.

Kingston University offers a full-time or part-time course leading to a Higher Diploma or BA degree in Audio Technology and Music Industry Studies.

Oxford Brookes University offers a number of combined modules involving music, including Law/Music and Business Administration and Management leading to a BA, BSc or LLB (Hons) degree. They may suit those more interested in a general as opposed to a specific legal course.

The University of Paisley also runs a BA course in Commercial Music and it stresses the involvement of industry professionals.

Roehampton Institute, London Southlands College, has a module in Business Studies and Music within its Business Studies Combined Honours courses. These are either full- or part-time courses leading to either a BA (Hons) or BMus (Hons).

The University of Sunderland offers a number of combined BAs, including Business and Music and Business Law and Music. Intriguingly, it also offers a course entitled Gender Studies and Music.

The University of Wales Institute Cardiff has an HNC HND/BSc (Hon) in Music Production and Technology and in Music and Audio Electronic Systems.

The University of Glamorgan runs degree in Music Technology and a degree course in Popular Music.

For those looking for a more technical emphasis, there is a highly regarded Tonmeister course at my old university, the University of Surrey. This is a BMus (Tonmeister) degree course in Music and Sound Recording. It's a four-year sandwich course with time spent out in work placements. The intention is to prepare you for a career in the professional audio industry.

Canterbury Christ Church University College runs a full- or part-time HND course in Popular Music and Technology at its Thanet campus. Canterbury Christ Church University also runs a BA (Hon) in Music Industry Management, Commercial Music and Music: Sonic Arts.

Thames Valley University also offers various two- and three-year full-time courses covering Music Recording and aspects of the music business, for example Advertising with Sound and Music Recording.

University of Salford also offers a BA (Hons) course in Popular Music and Recording. The emphasis is on popular music and music technology, but it also aims to prepare you for a career in the music business or in the recording industry. They say you'll be directed towards modules as a studio performer or producer depending on your aptitude and interests shown in entrance tests, interviews and by your profile. The course is accredited by the Association of Professional Recording Services.

The Nottingham Foundation for Music and Media is offering further and higher education courses, as well as commercial training courses for the music and multi-media industries. Their courses are validated by New College, Nottingham. They offer BND and HND Certificates in Music Technology as well as Music Industry.

The Academy of Contemporary Music, based in Guildford, has link-ups with many industry bodies. Part of each course is a module in business studies.

City College Manchester offers courses in FDA in Popular Music & Production and in FDSc Music & New Media Management. For continuing studies, the courses are validated by the University of Salford.

BIMM offers Certificate in Modern Music, Diploma in Modern Music, Diploma in Songwriting, Diploma in Sound Engineering and Tour Management, BIMM Professional Diploma (Level 5) in Modern Music, BIMM Professional Diploma (Level 5) in Songwriting, Foundation Degree in Professional Musicianship and BA Hons in Professional Musicianship. BIMM also run annual summer schools.

The University of Aberdeen has a new law degree with an option in music. Courses in performance studies are taken in the first and second year of this degree.

COMMERCIAL COURSES

There are also courses run by commercial organisations that aim to give practical overviews of aspects of the music business. One of the more established organisations is the Global Entertainment Group. They are offering a two-day core programme called the Music Industry Overview. Then they have a one- and two-day specialised modules such as A&R, Artist Management, PR, Marketing & Promotions and Running a Record Label. All courses are delivered in central London.

The Music Managers Forum (MMF) offers short courses called Master Classes to its members and AIM members on aspects of music management and the industry. These are either short evening courses or week-long intensive ones.

The British Phonographic Institute (BPI) occasionally offers one-day training workshops.

The Music Publishers Association (MPA) holds induction courses and specialist seminars and also runs courses in conjunction with the MMF (www.mpaonline.org.uk).

BECOMING A SOLICITOR

If you want to become a solicitor, the Law Society can give you information. If you already have a first degree in law, you need to complete a one-year Legal Practice Course and a two-year training contract. A discretionary fast track to qualifying may be available for those who already have relevant business experience.

The Law Society now includes Media Studies or Intellectual Property as optional courses as part of the Legal Practice Course. The Law Society also requires practising lawyers to keep up to date on the law by undertaking further training during their working life.

If your first degree isn't in law, you'll need to do an additional one-year conversion course.

IN-HOUSE OR PRIVATE PRACTICE?

Once you've qualified as a solicitor, you can choose whether to work in a private law firm or in-house as a lawyer in a record or music publishing company. Managers don't usually employ an in-house lawyer, nor do small labels or publishing companies. They usually use lawyers in private law firms.

The competition between specialist music business lawyers is intense. It takes considerable effort, both in and out of normal working hours, to build up a 'practice' – a body of clients who use you regularly for legal advice. Without a practice you are unlikely to be promoted to associate, salaried or full partner sharing in the profits (or losses) of the business. The financial rewards and job satisfaction can, however, be considerable.

Those of you who think you would find it difficult to build up a practice, or who aren't interested in becoming a full profit-sharing partner or owning their own business, may decide to work in-house instead. That isn't to say that this is an easy option. The work in-house can be very intense. There's no job security and you have to follow company policy, the 'corporate line'. The up-side is that the working atmosphere can be more relaxed, you don't have the stresses of building a practice or running your own business and it can be a very good way to move into management positions.

It is possible to move between the two. A partner in a West End music law firm left to go in-house at one of the big music publishing companies and ended up running the whole of their European operation.

BECOMING A BARRISTER

Instead of being a solicitor you could choose to do a law degree, a follow-up course at a recognised Bar School and a minimum of one year's training to become a barrister. Barristers can't be partners in law firms without re-qualifying as a solicitor, but they can, and often do, work as in-house lawyers. For further information on becoming a barrister, contact the Bar Council.

BECOMING A LEGAL EXECUTIVE

You can also get a qualification as a legal executive. For information on legal executive qualifications, contact the Institute of Legal Executives. It doesn't entitle you to become a partner in a law firm but it does give you a legal qualification. It can be done in evening and day-release classes while you're working and it can be a stepping stone to becoming a fully qualified solicitor although this would take many years. You find legal executives in important support roles in media law firms. In the smaller firms, their role isn't that different from that of fully qualified solicitors. Legal executives also work in-house and, to all intents and purposes, they do the same work as qualified solicitors. However, there is often the view in music companies that, unless you're a fully qualified lawyer or have an additional business qualification such as an MBA (a masters degree in business administration), you're unlikely to get promoted to a management role. On the other hand, you may not have any desire to go into management and may be happy with a non-management role.

NON-LEGAL JOBS

For a general overview of types of careers available in the music business, a good place to start would be Sian Pattenden's book How to Make it in the Music Business.

You could also refer to your careers advisory service and government-backed enterprise and job advisory centres.

Chapter 17
Useful Addresses

ACADEMY OF CONTEMPORARY MUSIC
Rodboro Buildings, Bridge Street, Guildford GU1 4SB
Tel: 01483 500800
Fax: 01483 500801
Website: www.acm.ac.uk

ACCA – Association of Chartered and Certified Accounts
29 Lincoln's Inn Fields, London WC2A 3EE
Tel: 020 7059 5000
Fax: 020 7059 5050
Email: info@accaglobal.com
Website: www. uk.accaglobal.com

AIM – Association of Independent Music
Lamb House, Church Street, London W4 2PD
Tel: 020 8994 5599
Fax: 020 8994 5222
Email: info@musicindie.org.uk
Website: www.musicindie.org

AMIA – Association of Music Industry Accountants
Unity House, 205 Euston Road, London NW1 2AY
Tel: 020 7535 1400
Fax: 020 7535 1401

ASCAP – American Society of Composers and Performers
8 Cork Street, London W1S 3LJ
Tel: 020 7439 0909
Fax: 020 7434 0073
Email: info@ascap.com
Website: www.ascap.com

BAR COUNCIL, THE
289–293 High Holborn, London WC1V 7HZ
Tel: 020 7242 0082
Fax: 020 7831 9217
Website: www.barcouncil.org.uk

BATH SPA UNIVERSITY COLLEGE
Newton Park Campus, Newton St Loe, Bath BA2 9BN
Tel: 01225 875875
Fax: 01225 875444
Email: enquiries@bathspa.ac.uk
Website: www.bathspa.ac.uk

BMI – Broadcast Media Inc.
84 Harley House, Marylebone Road, London NW1 5HN
Tel: 020 7486 2036
Website: www.bmi.com

BOURNEMOUTH UNIVERSITY
Fern Barrow, Poole, Dorset, BH12 5BB
Tel: 01202 524111
Fax: 01202 962736
Email: enquiries@bournemouth.ac.uk
Website: www.bournemouth.ac.uk

BPI – British Phonographic Institute
The Riverside Building, County Hall, Westminster Bridge Road, London SE1 7JA
Tel: 020 7803 1300
Fax: 020 7803 1310
Email: general@bpi.co.uk
Website: www.bpi.co.uk

BUCKS NEW UNIVERSITY
Queen Alexandra Road, High Wycombe, Bucks HP11 2JZ
Tel: 01494 522141
Fax: 01494 524392
Email: advice@bucks.ac.uk
Website: www.bcuc.ac.uk

CANTERBURY CHRIST CHURCH UNIVERSITY COLLEGE
North Holmes Road, Canterbury, Kent CT1 1QU
Tel: 01227 767700
Fax: 01227 479442
Email: admissions@canterbury.ac.uk
Website: www.canterbury.ac.uk

CHAMBERS & PARTNERS PUBLISHING
Saville House, 23 Long Lane, London EC1A 9HL
Tel: 020 7606 8844
Fax: 020 7606 0906
Website: www.chambersandpartners.com

CITY UNIVERSITY
Northampton Square, London EC1V 0HB
Tel: 020 7040 8268
Fax: 020 7040 8995
Email: ell@city.ac.uk
Website: www.city.ac.uk

CONCERT PROMOTERS' ASSOCIATION
6 St Mark's Road, Henley-on-Thames, Oxfordshire RG9 1LJ
Tel: 01491 575060
Email: cpn@makingmusic.org.uk

DARTINGTON COLLEGE OF ARTS
Totnes, Devon TQ9 6EJ
Tel: 01803 862224
Fax: 01803 861666
Email: enquiries@dartington.ac.uk
Website: www.dartington.ac.uk

DE MONTFORT UNIVERSITY
The Gateway, Leicester LE1 9BH
Tel: 0116 255 1551
Fax: 0116 2577533
Email: enquiry@dmu.ac.uk
Website: www.dmu.ac.uk

EQUITY (British Actors' Equity Association)
Guild House, Upper St Martin's Lane, London WC2H 9EG
Tel: 020 7379 6000
Fax: 020 7379 7001
E-mail: info@equity.org.uk
Website: www.equity.org.uk

Equity is an independent trade union representing not only actors but also other performers including singers and dancers. Equity negotiates industry agreements with TV and radio broadcasters, theatres and record companies (through the BPI).

GLOBAL ENTERTAINMENT GROUP, THE
Admin. Office: Design Works, William Street, Felling, Gateshead, NE10 0JP
Tel: 020 7583 7900
Email: info@globalmusicbiz.co.uk
Website: www.globalmusicbiz.co.uk

IAEL – International Association of Entertainment Lawyers
Duncan Calow – General Secretary
DLA Piper UK LLP, 3 Noble Street, London EC2V 7EE
Tel: 08700 111 111
Website: www.iael.org

IFPI – International Federation Phonographic Ltd
10 Piccadilly, London W1J 0DD
Tel: 020 7878 7900
Fax: 020 7878 7950
Email: info@ifpi.org
Website: www.ifpi.org

ILEX – Institute of Legal Executives
Kempston Manor, Kempston, Bedford MK42 7AB
Tel: 01234 841000
Fax: 01234 840373
Email: info@ilex.org.uk
Website: www.ilex.org.uk

INFORMATION COMMISSIONER'S OFFICE
Wycliffe House, Water Lane, Wilmslow, Cheshire SK9 5AF
Tel: 01625 545745
Fax: 01625 524510
Email: notification@ico.gov.uk
Website: www.ico.gov.uk

INSTITUTE OF CHARTERED ACCOUNTANTS IN ENGLAND & WALES, THE
Chartered Accountants' Hall, PO Box 433, London, EC2P 2BJ
Tel: 020 7920 8100
Fax: 020 7920 0547
Email: psogen@icaew.com
Website: www.icaew.co.uk

KINGSTON UNIVERSITY
River House, 53–7 High Street, Kingston-upon-Thames, Surrey KT1 1LQ
Tel: 020 8547 2000
Email: admissions-info@kingston.ac.uk
Website: www.kingston.ac.uk

LAW SOCIETY, THE
113 Chancery Lane, London WC2A 1PL
Tel: 020 7242 1222
Fax: 020 7831 0344
Email: contact@lawsociety.org.uk
Website: www.lawsociety.org.uk

MCPS – Mechanical Copyright Protection Society Limited
29–33 Berners Street, London W1T 3AB
Tel: 020 7580 5544
Fax: 020 7306 4455
Email: writerquery@mcps-prs-alliance.co.uk
Website: www.mcps-prs-alliance.co.uk

MIRACLE PUBLISHING LIMITED
1 York Street, London W1U 6PA
Tel: 020 7486 7007
Fax: 020 7486 2002
Email: info@audience.uk.com

MMF – Music Managers Forum
British Music House, 26 Berners Street, London W1T 3LR
Tel: 0870 8507800
Fax: 0870 8507801
Email: website@ukmmf.net
Website: www.musicmanagersforum.co.uk

MMF – Training
14b Turner Street, Manchester M4 1DZ
Tel: 0161 839 7007
Fax: 0161 839 6970
Email: info@mmf-training.com

This is the UK trade association for artist managers. It was set up approximately twelve years ago as the International Managers Forum to act as a representative body for managers, as a forum for debate on matters of interest to its members and as a lobbying body.

MUSIC WEEK
Ludgate House, 245 Blackfriars Road, London SE1 9UY
Tel: 020 7921 8353
Email: feedbackmusicweek@musicweek.com
Website: www.musicweek.com

MUSICIAN'S ATLAS, THE
Music Resource Group. 38 Porter Place, Montclair NJ 07042
Tel: +(973) 509 9898
Fax: +(973) 655 1238
Email: info@musiciansAtlas.com
Website: www.MusiciansAtlas.com

MUSICIANS' UNION
33 Palfrey Place, London SW8 1PE
Tel: 020 7840 5504
Fax: 020 7840 5399
Email: London@musiciansunion.org.uk
Website: www.musiciansunion.org.uk

The MU is the only UK trade union solely representing musicians. It was formed in 1893. It has over 30,000 members and has a regional structure that includes offices in London, Cardiff, Birmingham, Manchester and Glasgow. It acts as a collective body by seeking to improve the status of musicians and the money they earn. The MU makes national agreements with various organisations, including with the BPI (for recording sessions and promotional videos) and with television companies (for broadcasts).

NEW MUSICAL EXPRESS
IPC Music Magazines, The Blue Fin Building, 110 Southwark Street, London SE1 0SU
Tel: 020 7261 5813
Fax: 020 7261 5185
Email: ipcsales@qqs-uk.com
Website: www.nme.com

OXFORD BROOKES UNIVERSITY
Gypsy Lane Campus, Headington Campus, Gypsy Lane, Oxford OX3 0BP
Tel: 01865 741111
Email: query@brookes.ac.uk
Website: www.brookes.ac.uk

PINNACLE ENTERTAINMENT
Heather Court, 6 Maidstone Road, Sidcup, Kent DA14 5KK
Tel: 020 8309 3600
Website: www.pinnacle-entertainment.co.uk

PPL – Phonographic Performance Limited
1 Upper James Street, London W1F 9DE
Tel: 020 7534 1000
Fax: 020 7534 1111
Email: member.info@ppluk.com
Website: www.ppluk.com

PRS – Performing Right Society Limited
29–33 Berners Street, London W1T 3AB
Tel: 020 7580 5544
Fax: 020 7306 4455
Email: info@prs.co.uk
Website: www.prs.co.uk

ROEHAMPTON INSTITUTE LONDON
Roehampton Lane, London SW15 5PU
Tel: 020 8392 3000
Email: enquiries@roehampton.ac.uk
Website: www.roehampton.ac.uk

THAMES VALLEY UNIVERSITY
St Mary's Road, Ealing, London W5 5RF
Tel: 020 8579 5000
Email: info@tvu.ac.uk
Website: www.tvu.ac.uk

UCAS – University Clearing Advisory Service
UCAS PO Box 28, Cheltenham GL52 3LZ
Tel: 0870 112 2211
Email: enquiries@ucas.ac.uk
Website: www.ucas.ac.uk

UNIVERSITY OF GREENWICH
Old Royal Naval College, Park Row, Greenwich SE10 9LS
Tel: 020 8331 8000
Email: courseinfo@greenwich.ac.uk
Website: www.gre.ac.uk

UNIVERSITY OF NEWCASTLE UPON TYNE
Newcastle NE1 7RU
Tel: 0191 222 6000
Website: www.newcastle.ac.uk

UNIVERSITY OF NORTHAMPTON
Park Campus, Boughton Green Road, Northampton NN2 7AL
Tel: 01604 735500
Email: study@northampton.ac.uk
Website: www.nene.ac.uk

UNIVERSITY OF PAISLEY
Paisley PA1 2BE, Scotland
Tel: 0141 843 3000
Email: info@paisley.ac.uk
Website: www.paisley.ac.uk

The University is seeking approval to change the name to University of the West of Scotland.

UNIVERSITY OF SALFORD
Salford, Greater Manchester M5 4WT
Tel: 0161 295 5000
Fax: 0161 295 5999
Email: course-enquiries@salford.ac.uk
Website: www.salford.ac.uk

UNIVERSITY OF SUNDERLAND
St Mary's Building, City Campus, Chester Road, Sunderland SR1 3SD
Tel: 0191 515 2000
Email: student-helpline@sunderland.ac.uk
Website: www.sunderland.ac.uk

UNIVERSITY OF SURREY
The Registry, Guildford, Surrey GU2 7XH
Tel: 01483 300800
Fax: 01483 300803
Email: info@surrey.ac.uk
Website: www.surrey.ac.uk

UNIVERSITY OF WESTMINSTER
309 Regent Street, London W1B 2UW
Tel: 020 7911 5000
Email: admission@wmin.ac.uk
Website: www.wmin.ac.uk

VITAL
338a Ladbroke Grove, London W10 5AH
Tel: 020 8324 2400
Fax: 020 8324 0001
Email: webmaster@vitaluk.com
Website: www.pias.com/vital

WELSH MUSIC FOUNDATION
33—5 West Bute Street, Cardiff Bay, Cardiff CF10 5LH
Tel: 02920 494 110
Fax: 02920 494 210
Email: enquiries@welshmusicfoundation.com
Website: www.welshmusicfoundation.com

INDEX